Resistance in Practice

Resistance in Practice

The Philosophy of Antonio Negri

Edited by

Timothy S. Murphy

and

Abdul-Karim Mustapha

Pluto  Press

LONDON • ANN ARBOR, MI

First published 2005 by Pluto Press
345 Archway Road, London N6 5AA
and 839 Greene Street, Ann Arbor, MI 48106

www.plutobooks.com

British Library Cataloguing in Publication Data
A catalogue record for this book is available from the British Library

ISBN 0 7453 2338 3 hardback
ISBN 0 7453 2337 5 paperback

Library of Congress Cataloging in Publication Data applied for

10 9 8 7 6 5 4 3 2 1

Designed and produced for Pluto Press by
Chase Publishing Services Ltd, Fortescue, Sidmouth, EX10 9QG, England
Typeset from disk by Newgen Imaging Systems (P) Ltd, Chennai, India
Printed and bound in the European Union by
Antony Rowe Ltd, Chippenham and Eastbourne, England

Contents

Editors' Acknowledgements

This volume has taken much longer to appear than any of its participants could have anticipated when they first became involved, and the fact that it has finally appeared will no doubt surprise some of us. The editors owe this surprise to a number of people, and since our collaboration has taken place electronically, our debts only partially overlap.

First of all, I owe an immense debt of gratitude to Steve Wright, who, not content with his role as contributor, willingly took on every other job I could find for him: referee, go-between, confidante, introducer, and others hard to name and harder to do without. Next, I owe it to our translators, Arianna Bove and Ed Emery, who met more precipitate deadlines than any other participants were compelled to do. I owe it as well to the anonymous referees who reviewed the project for Pluto Press, and to Enda Brophy and Ida Dominijanni, all of whom made important suggestions that have improved the resulting volume considerably. I owe perhaps most of all to the patience of the contributors to this volume, some of whom have waited more than four years to see their chapters in print. Finally, I owe my coeditor, Abdul-Karim Mustapha, a great debt for originally conceiving this project, gathering the first contributions and then permitting me to participate in it as a partner. Here at home, I want to acknowledge my love for and reliance upon Julie and Blackie through all the years of this project and so many others.

Timothy S. Murphy

From the beginning of this project, several people are to be thanked for their resourcefulness and support: Michael Taussig, Jim Fleming, Peter Lamborn Wilson, and Brian Massumi. I would also like to thank some members of the *Multitudes* group in Paris, who have shared much information regarding Toni Negri but also incalculable gifts of knowledge and friendship: Yann Moulier-Boutang, Bruno Karsenti, Maurizio Lazzarato, Antonella Corsani, Anne Querrien, Charles Wolfe, François Matheron, Ed Emery, and Guissepe Cocco in Brazil. Furthermore, other people, who do not appear in this volume but who have worked with Negri and his thought for some time, gave their time and wisdom to the project: Gabriel Albiac, Christian Marazzi, Santiago Lopez-Petit, and Fredric Jameson. And without truth and love, scholarship is never what it can be and for that I thank Jill E. Baron, Robin F. Garrell, François Laruelle, José Rabasa and

Catherine Durand. Tim Murphy, my coeditor, deserves much more thanks in an acknowledgement, since we have never had the chance to meet in person. His patience, determination, and belief in Negri are unparalleled.

Abdul-Karim Mustapha

Sergio Bologna's contribution originally appeared in Italian in the journal *Primo Maggio* 7 (1976), and it is translated here by permission of the author.

The interview with Alisa Del Re originally appeared in Italian on the CD-ROM that accompanies the volume *Futuro anteriore. Dai 'Quaderni rossi' ai movimenti globali: ricchezze e limiti dell'operaismo italiano* (Rome: DeriveApprodi, 2002), edited by Guido Borio, Francesca Pozzi, and Gigi Roggero. It is translated here by permission of the editors.

Introduction: The Real Movement and the Present State of Things

Timothy S. Murphy and Abdul-Karim Mustapha

The publication of *Empire* in 2000 first alerted many in the English-speaking world to the work of Italian philosopher and militant Antonio Negri. That book, a synthetic overview of what Marx and Engels would call 'the present state of things' (Marx and Engels 1970: 57), has become a lightning rod for criticism from the right and the left as well as a fundamental point of reference for many activists in the growing struggle over globalization. The magnitude and intensity of the critical polemics over *Empire*'s basic thesis, the claim that centralized, national programs of imperialist expansion and consolidation have given way to a decentered, transnational regime of production and governance, can be measured in a number of recent journal issues and books dedicated to analyzing that thesis and its consequences (*Rethinking Marxism* 2001; *Strategies* 2003; Balakrishnan 2003; Passavant and Dean 2004). However, many of these recent attempts to assess Negri's thought (in both its solo and its collaborative manifestations) are seriously weakened by their failure to situate *Empire* and its claims within the wider contexts of Negri's overall body of work and the Italian cultural milieu out of which he emerged. In their haste to theorize the 'present state of things', many of these critics overlook the 'real movement' of ideas and activism that seeks to abolish that state.

Over the past half-century Negri has authored hundreds of articles and authored, coauthored or edited over 40 books on a staggeringly wide array of subjects, as well as wielding a defining editorial influence over some of the most important periodicals and book series in European intellectual history.[1] For much of that time he was also active in several mass movements of the Italian extraparliamentary left (most notably Workers' Power (Potere operaio) and Workers' Autonomy (Autonomia operaia)) as a militant teacher, strategist and organizer. This unique combination of sophisticated theory and extensive practice, equaled among Western Marxists perhaps only by Antonio Gramsci and Georg Lukács, informs all of Negri's work, but its import is too often overlooked by his critics. The purpose of this volume is to offer critical assessments of Negri's work that are informed by more comprehensive engagements with the range of his writings and his militancy, and not just with the handful of his texts currently in vogue in the English-speaking world. All of the contributors to this volume have been engaged with Negri's radical philosophical and/or militant activity since well before the publication of *Empire*, and although some of them analyze *Empire* with great care and acuity, they grant it no special priority over his other works. Each of their contributions reflects the depth and breadth of engagement that is necessary to understand Negri's work in the full conceptual and historical density of its 'real movement'.

The first part of the volume is focused on Negri's place in the Italian countercultural context, which we have labeled 'the Long '68' to mark the similarity of its origin to that of the events of 1968 in France and elsewhere, as well as its difference in extension and intensity: in Italy, 1968 didn't come to an end until 1977, while in the rest of Europe and the United States, 1968 was effectively over before 1969. Michael Hardt, Negri's chief collaborator for more than a decade, provides a precise account of Negri's complex relationship to Lenin's thought and its application within the burgeoning Italian New Left of the Long 1968, as well as a perceptive comparison of Negri's work with that of important parallel figures in France such as Louis Althusser, Gilles Deleuze and Michel Foucault. Hardt's chapter is followed by contributions from two of Negri's chief allies and interlocutors of the Seventies, Sergio Bologna and Alisa Del Re. Bologna's 1976 review of Negri's pamphlet *Proletarians and the State* exemplifies the originality and intensity of critique that characterized the internal intellectual and organizational dynamics of the Seventies movements, while Del Re's recent interview offers a leading feminist's assessment of the movements' historical strengths and weaknesses and their continuing influence, with particular emphasis on Negri's role as a motivational figure of the era. Concluding this part is Steve Wright's comprehensive analysis of debates over the party form in different sectors of Autonomy, which situates and criticizes Negri's (as well as Bologna's) contributions to these debates by recovering the full range of political positions that emerged throughout the period.

The second part provides a set of critical attempts to take up points in Negri's work that are relevant to radical militancy in the present. Kathi Weeks traces the genealogy of the refusal of work from Paul LaFargue to Negri in order to identify a dissident, antiproductivist legacy within Marxism, a legacy that has become increasingly influential upon today's global forms of workers' resistance. Nick Dyer-Witheford restages the debate over the centrality of immaterial labor (that is, intellectual, symbolic and/or affective labor) to the global regime of production, and on the basis of this displacement he proposes a critical recuperation of the concept of species being as a way to fill in the blind spots in Hardt and Negri's conception of immaterial labor. In what is perhaps the most far-ranging and complex discussion in this volume, José Rabasa meditates on the relevance of Negri's philosophical categories and conceptual tools for programs of local and regional militancy in Latin America; in Negri's work he finds the means to displace the conventional strategies and historical languages of postcolonial critique, and perhaps to begin to escape from the restrictive aporias that postcolonial resistance has inherited from deconstruction. In the concluding essay, Kenneth Surin seeks to expand and intensify Negri's theory of revolution by confronting the most radically immaterial register of globalization, and thus the one seemingly most difficult to contest through militant practice: the regime of international finance capital. His sophisticated extension of and supplement to Negri's ideas, taking 'Negri beyond Negri' as the other contributors also do, helps to bring the mandarin world of global finance within range of contemporary practices of resistance.

The interventions contained in this volume unapologetically attempt to break with the lamentable tradition of internecine squabbling that continues to mark so much left discourse, both theoretical and organizational. In what the editors consider to be genuine communist fashion, these chapters strive to join 'the *real* movement which abolishes the present state of things', not by proclaiming their compliance with or rejection of any immobilizing left orthodoxy, but rather by resonating with the overall movement of Negri's compelling and provocative work—extending it, expanding it, displacing it, reworking it and intensifying it. Only in this way, through processes of differentiation, dissensus, experimentation and alliance, can we and they contribute to the construction of a truly global and democratic left, one that abandons the exclusive and reactionary categories of sectarianism and nationalism in favor of the inclusive logic of the multitude.

NOTE

1. In addition to his well-known writings on Marx, Spinoza, Lenin, the state-form, worker phenomenology, postmodernism and globalization, Negri has also published books or essays on the biblical Book of Job, the Italian Romantic poet Giacomo Leopardi, mathematical catastrophe theory, and soccer, among other things. He has been the editor or a leading member of the editorial collective of periodicals such as *Il Progresso Veneto, Quaderni Rossi, Classe Operaia, Contropiano, Potere Operaio, Rosso, Critica del Diritto, Futur antérieur, Multitudes* and *Posse*, among others.

Part I

The Long '68 in Italy

1

Into the Factory: Negri's Lenin and the Subjective Caesura (1968–73)[1]

Michael Hardt

The intensity of the workers' and students' struggles of 1968 in countries throughout the world took everyone by surprise. Italy, however, was in many ways an anomaly. There was a constant crescendo of revolts throughout 1968 and 1969 in Italy and in several different permutations the struggles persisted for the next ten years. One of the symbolic centers or touchstones of the movements was the conflict on Corso Traiano in September 1969 when demonstrators directly confronted the Turin police in a violent struggle. The gravity of the situation grew consistently at least through 1973; again the FIAT workers represented the symbolic center: 'On 29 and 30 March 1973, at Mirafiori, at Rivalta, in all the FIAT sections of Turin, *the indefinite-term strike turned into an armed occupation*' (Negri 1973a: 189). For Negri, the explosion of the 'red biennial' and the subsequent years may have come as a surprise, but only in its intensity, its urgency. It came as a confirmation of his intuitions and his hopes and raced forward beyond them, forcing a dramatic acceleration of the timetable for social change; it gave new life to his thinking and imposed a rigorous rhythm on it. The 'revolutionary longing' that Negri had tasted in the factories during the 1960s, which seemed to grow within the industrial working class ever since the Piazza Statuto revolt of 1962, now exploded violently throughout the entire society. A myriad of new political organizations uniting workers and students propagated throughout the country: Potere operaio [Workers' Power], Lotta continua [The Struggle Goes On], il Manifesto, etc. The demand for profound social change, the intense desire for utopia pushed forward an immediate agenda. Negri and his colleagues had to scramble to keep up with struggles, to try to read the changing social reality. In their minds, they were not witnessing an Italian version of the Russian 1905, a dress rehearsal of some future event; rather, these were the 'April days', the immediate prelude to revolution. They saw that it was their role as intellectuals to clarify and lend a theoretical coherence to the direction of the mass struggles in order to further their objectives and construct the newly emerging norms of collective behavior; they sought an order in the exuberance of the struggles. Furthermore, they felt the responsibility of bringing to fruition the exceptional possibilities presented by Italy's anomaly: '*everything depends on us, here where the working class is strongest'* (Negri 1973a: 158). At this point, Negri and his intellectual colleagues definitively make the move out of the university and into the factory.

We have to modify our method of reading Negri's work accordingly, then, to account for the new conditions of theorizing during this period. First of all, if we fail to recognize the intense excitement and the urgency that he and his colleagues felt, we will certainly miss what is valuable here. There are principally two aspects of these writings that we have to keep in mind: their aspiration toward a collective voice and their political immediacy. What might from the distance of 20 years seem to us like inflated rhetoric served a real organizing function in the movements. Negri's work is filled with slogans or *'parole d'ordine'*, some of which he invented and others he took from the stream of political discourse; the objective was, on one hand, to present his arguments in a form which would be understood generally in the movements and contribute effectively to the practical struggles and, on the other hand, to give real substance and a solid theoretical foundation to this discourse and its practical agenda. Negri was very conscious of his role as an intellectual within the movement and accordingly he attempted to integrate the principal terms and ideas that were general in the movement into his own discourse, in order to situate and evaluate them within a coherent theoretical framework. In many respects, Negri was merely trying to keep his head above water through the rapid flux of social movements. His works lose their scholarly tone and formalities such as footnotes disappear completely; rather, they aspire toward the collective voice of political programs, continually proposing 'our immediate task'. This type of work should not be credited with the same kind of originality that is accorded to individual theoretical endeavors; the originality here, one might say, is principally in its effort to read the intelligence of the masses and translate it into an effective political form. Negri was trying to absorb some of the power of the struggles within his own voice. However, it would take an extensive historical study of the period, of the theoretical and practical activities of the various organizations, to disentangle the genealogy of the different lines of thought and verify when Negri was forwarding an original proposal and when he was merely repeating the generally held view. The issue of armed struggle is perhaps the most important in this regard (especially for those interested in the question of criminality) but it is also the most intricate: an adequate analysis would certainly require extensive historical study. Such a study, however, is outside our scope and will have to be taken up in future work.[2]

The other aspect of this period of Negri's work that we must take into account is its political immediacy. The horizon of the political movements seemed in a continuous state of flux and each event added a new urgency. The texts are dated not only with the year but also the month in which they were drafted. Negri felt the need to interpret events as they occurred: for example, in September 1971 he prepared his article 'Crisis of the Planner-State' for the 'Third conference on organization' of Potere operaio as an interpretation of the Nixon measures on the incontrovertibility of the dollar passed just a month earlier in August. Timetables were short and Negri was aware that his writing reflected this urgency. 'It is possible that the weaknesses of this essay—the fact that it is too immediately related to problems of organisation, and that it is perhaps too polemical and summary in its attempt to stay close to the contingencies of political discussion—may turn out to be virtues; if it is true that organised revolutionary practice is not only the only way to understand reality scientifically, but also the only way to bring it closer' (Negri 1971: 96). Negri is attempting to subordinate the theoretical discourse to the pressing practical demands, so that while it loses its scholarly rigor, it gains a concrete import in the world.

Negri's new theoretical approach during this period can be read as an attempt to recast the Marxist framework: from critical Marxism to what I call 'projective Marxism'. We claimed in an earlier chapter that within the framework of critical Marxism, the positive proletarian project is always subordinated to the critique of capital.[3] The project may only arise in the future as a result of the critique in the dialectical supersession of capital: to pose the project in the present, outside of this dialectical context, would be viewed by critical theory as simply utopian thinking. If earlier Negri found this critical position problematic, after 1968 it became completely untenable. He experienced the cycle of struggles as the emergence or maturation of a working-class subjectivity that demanded a political project on its own terms, outside of the objective critical framework. Here the objective critique of capital must be subordinated to the subjective needs and desires of the working class. A new approach is needed to make the leap that the critique itself could never accomplish. Lenin seemed to offer Negri the insight necessary to develop a different approach to Marxism, more adequate to the contemporary needs. The explosion of the social struggles and the Leninist reading of Marx give Negri a completely anti-Althusserian approach: if there is an epistemological caesura which marks the divide between Marx's youth and his maturity, it consists of the real appearance (not the disappearance) of the revolutionary subject, it is the moment 'when analysis emancipates itself from existing conditions in order to turn itself into a program' (Negri 1973a: 102). The critical juncture, for Negri, refers not so much to epistemology as to subjectivity. 'Far from ending up in a "process without a subject," the evolution of Marxian thought instead closely follows the organizational reality of the revolutionary subject' (Negri 1973a: 103, n.7). The Leninist perspective and the growing pressure of the workers' movements marks in Negri's thought a subjective caesura.

CRISIS OF THE PLANNER-STATE

Even though we already find sufficient cause in Negri's thought to bring into question the method of critical Marxism, principally because of its inability to give the subjective standpoint of the working class a central role in the critical process, still we find that Negri pursues this analysis through this period of theoretical and political crisis. The crisis of critical Marxism, in Negri's thought, does not mean that it should be negated, but merely that it must be reoriented and its argument must be grounded in a different context: while in the previous period the proletarian project was subordinated to the critique of capital, in this period we will see that the critique is subordinated to the project. We will see the specific form of this inversion later. For the moment, however, within the same framework of the critique of the state and capital developed in the earlier works, Negri attempts to define the new relations of force that have emerged as a result of the new cycle of struggles beginning in 1968. Once again, the task is to define the modifications of the state form and of the capitalist system of control through a critique based on capital's own reading of itself.

The state has shifted, Negri argues, from a planner-state based on Keynesian economic principles to a 'crisis-state'. By crisis-state Negri does not mean that capital is on the verge of collapse—there is nothing catastrophic in this crisis. He merely means that the capitalist state has abandoned the strategy of stability (in production, markets, monetary policy, etc.) that previously had paved the way for the development of mass industry. This restructuration, then, not only poses new problems for mass production, but it also puts an end to the social contract of planning, to capital's attempt to interact with the working class through institutionalized collective bargaining as a means of control and legitimation. The advent of this 'neo-liberal' state, however, does not mean a reduction in economic and social interventionism, but on the contrary a broadening of social labor power and an intensification of the state's control over the social factory. The new element, characteristic of the crisis-state, is that the state adopts a new degree of autonomy as the agent that regulates development, external to any direct relationship between capital and labor. The tendency of these changes points toward the disappearance of any organic relationship of mediation between the working class and the state as the representative of collective capital. 'The separation and unilaterality between labor and command over labor is thus pushed to the furthest limit; the state can only take the form of a crisis-state, in which it enforces and manages its own freedom of command for the survival of the system as a whole' (Negri 1971: 119). Crisis, then, becomes the normal condition of capitalist development and rule to the extent that the bilateral processes of economic and juridical organization that provided an organic relationship between labor and capital are abandoned.

Negri substantiates this proposition that the state form has shifted with an analysis of the function of money and the state's use of monetary policy. This analysis is inspired by a new reading of Marx's 'Chapter on Money' in the *Grundrisse* (Marx 1973: 115–238) that Negri attempts to relate to the contemporary situation in order to investigate the relationship between the production of value and the mechanisms of legitimation (cf. Negri 1973a: 107–22; Negri 1971: passim). Money is presented in the capitalist system as a general equivalent, as a form of mediation in the exchange between labor and capital. The general tendency within capitalist development, though, is to liberate money from its functions of mediation, as the universal representation of exchange value, and allow it to serve as a direct force of production and rule. Negri reads the Nixon measures of 1971 to decouple the dollar from the gold standard as an exemplary point in this passage. The international stability of exchange rates had played an important role in guaranteeing the stable markets necessary for planning mass production; the decision to abandon the policy of standardized exchange signals the decline of the Keynesian planner-state in that it undermines one of the important conditions of its existence—stable exchange markets. The changing role of money is indicative of the changes in the form of value itself. The planner-state is founded on what Negri calls the 'law of value', which poses a general equivalence and parity between productive labor and capital: as we have seen in earlier chapters, labor is posed through the capitalist constitution as the unique source of value and hence the *Grundnorm* of right.[4] Collective bargaining and dialogue through the mediation of the trade unions and the state provide the institutional foundation for the law of value and its stability. The decision to destabilize monetary markets put into question not only the mediating function of money as a general equivalent, but also the mediating function of the state and the trade unions (in the sale of labor power, the establishment of right, etc.) (Negri 1971: 139). The shift in monetary policy, then, is only indicative of the larger crisis of the law of value that destabilizes the production process and brings into question the established legitimacy of relations of command.

In keeping with the tenets of *operaismo* [workerism] which we examined in a previous chapter,[5] Negri argues that these changes in capital and the capitalist state can only be understood when we grasp the workers' movements as the stimulus for development; capital never moves forward of its own accord. In Negri's typically schematic form, we can say that just as 1917 pushed capital to 1929 and forced it to develop the planner-state in the Thirties, so too the pressures of 1968 brought on the monetary shift of 1971 and the development of the crisis-state in the Seventies. Once again, capital attempts to recuperate its structures of control by subsuming the workers' threat within the continuity of a dialectical progression: capitalist structuration → workers' destructuration → capitalist restructuration. Viewed strictly from the financial point of view, 'the workers' wage offensive has shattered' the illusion of social peace and structural stability projected by capitalist planning and bargaining; the wage demands undermined the bases of monetary stability and pushed capital to the limit of its ability to maintain a balance within the boundaries of its control (Negri 1973a: 115). Once again, however, the situation is better understood when posed in broader terms, in terms of value: not only the wage demands against individual employers, but also the demands against collective capital and the state for the control of social production and reproduction serve to destructure the planner-state as the agent of rule. The organized industrial working class posed such a threat with the new cycle of struggles that capital was forced to abandon its project of stability, to destroy its form of rule in order to protect itself. In other words, capital had to abandon its proposition of labor as the unique source of value, it had to 'devalorize' labor in order to combat the effective organization of the working class. The demonetarization of capital, then, was accompanied by a devalorization of labor. In practical terms this means the beginning of a new era of technological innovation, of the further mechanization and computerization of heavy industry and hence the dispersion of the mass labor force which had come to represent a formidable adversary. In order to combat the threat of the working class, in order to destroy the conditions of its organization, capital is forced to shift its focus from living labor to dead labor in mass production and hence to suffer a falling rate of profit.[6] The crisis of the structures of mass production signals the opening of a new capitalist project for restructuration.

We should note that if Negri's thesis that the early Seventies marked a turning point in the conditions of capitalist production and in the role of the state appeared radical or controversial when he first proposed this view, it no longer does today. In fact, Negri's intuitions in these early years of the transformation have been largely confirmed by contemporary economists: it is standard today to interpret the early Seventies as the period when the conditions for mass production were destroyed and capital began searching for a new basis. In *The Second Industrial Divide*, for example, Charles Sabel and Michael Piore (1984) propose this same periodization from a capitalist point of view and, while they do not refer to the contemporary period as that of the crisis-state, their proposal for 'flexible production' does incorporate several of the characteristics in Negri's analysis.[7] This analysis of collective capital and the state, however, is still limited by the objectivist approach of the critical theory; that is, the critique of political economy still cannot account adequately for the actual working class as a concrete subject. If the critical approach of *operaismo* proposes the working class as the stimulus of capitalist development, it only grasps the class in an abstract form; or rather, the critique of political economy recognizes the working class primarily as the object of exploitation, but never fully succeeds in presenting it as the subject of power. The intense political struggles in Italy, however, forced Negri to look beyond the critique to discover an approach which will pose the subjectivity of the working class at the center of theory. Negri proposes this agenda for theory: from the critique of political economy to the theory of organization. Lenin is the obvious guide for this mission, the one who effectively harnessed the power of the proletariat as the agent of revolution.

SPONTANEITY AND SUBJECTIVITY: LENINIST ORGANIZATION 1

To a certain extent, the study of Lenin was imposed on Negri by the political exigencies of the time and by the discourse common among militants. He explains this step in his intellectual trajectory during an interview from prison in late 1979. 'To me, Leninism is the price we paid for the political composition of the Italian proletariat. There was no way to talk politics other than via Leninism. . . . It was the class lingua franca: it could cause trouble, but you could make headway with the class (and with no one else) only by using it' (interview with Giorgio Bocca in Bocca 1980: 166). Leninism was in the air, part of the culture of the movements; but, perhaps because he feels the pressure of criminal accusations, Negri is certainly overstating the case here: even if initially he did feel compelled to engage Lenin, the confrontation proved to be extremely fruitful and served an important role in the development of Negri's thought. In spite of his reservations, his analysis brought to life a Lenin who was already alive in the contemporary struggles and who could speak to their central political problems. Furthermore, and perhaps more importantly, Lenin provided Negri with a new perspective for reading Marx and a new proposition for the Marxist intellectual endeavor. Nonetheless, even in his enthusiastic appropriation of Lenin's thought, Negri maintains reservations that are expressed as indirect polemics against different propositions of 'Leninism' (particularly those of vanguard and military organization) common in the movement. We are clearly on treacherous terrain, but let us try to be sensitive, as much as we can, to the nuances of Negri's position in light of the practical pressures and needs to which he is responding.[8]

The central question which theory must address, as we have noted, is that of subjectivity: the pressures of the class struggle force it onto the top of the agenda. The critical approach never adequately deals with the subjectivity of the actual working class; the critique of capital never succeeds in unifying itself with the standpoint of the working class so as to recognize the proletariat as the effective agent of social transformation. Critical theory, as we have seen it in the Italian context and in Negri's thought, principally poses the class struggle in an objective form and presents social development through a dialectical dynamic. With the explosion of the new cycle of struggles, however, the working class demanded to be recognized as the direct and effective agent of social change. Negri poses the question in specific political terms: *'what is the working class today,* in this specific crisis, *no longer merely as object of exploitation but as subject of power?'* (Negri 1973a: 105). Critical theory is an effective tool for recognizing the working class as the object of exploitation, or rather as the subject constituted through the complex mechanisms or *dispositifs*[9] of capitalist domination. Lenin helps Negri bring the theory of the subject to center stage and grasp the working class as the subject of power—a subject capable of recreating and managing society.

Negri reads Lenin's theory of the subject in his theory of working-class organization; or more precisely, he locates it in the passage from the analysis of the political composition of the working class to the theory of organization. According to Negri, the subjectivity of the workers and their spontaneous behavior constitute the centerpiece of Leninist organization. We can recognize right from the beginning, however, that Negri's Lenin is not the Lenin that is commonly presented. How, for example, can we reconcile this exaltation of workers' subjectivity with the so-called 'Leninist objection'—that the theory of organization is not dictated principally by the composition of the working class, but rather by the definition of the weakest links in capital's system of domination? (Negri 1973a: 105). The traditional Leninist doctrine locates the foundation of revolutionary organization not in the theory of workers' subjectivity but in the critique of political economy. Negri's proposition of a Leninist theory of the subject seems at first sight to be in direct contradiction to the famous 'Leninist objection', but we will find that in the context of Lenin's thought this turns out to be a false opposition. The critique of political economy only makes sense for Lenin when it is put to use (and thus subordinated) within a theory of working-class subjectivity. In fact, according to Negri, we will be faced by endless dilemmas such as this unless we submit Lenin's thought to a Marxist analysis and trace its development through specific historico-political periods; in other words, in order to appreciate Lenin's reading of Marx, we need first to pursue a Marxist reading of Lenin.

Negri proposes three periods of Lenin's theoretical development: (1) the analysis of the political composition of the working class, 1890–1900; (2) the organization of the party, 1900–10; and (3) the destruction of the state, 1910–17. In the first two periods Negri identifies two complementary approaches to the theory of the subject: the first in the subject's spontaneity, the second in its receptivity; the first, then, will be a subjective path to workers' organization and the second an objective path. We will postpone our study of the third period, which in many ways constitutes the payoff of the theory of the subject, until later. The first period, which includes works such as *What are the Friends of the People* and *The Development of Capitalism in Russia*, centers around Lenin's development of the concept of a 'determinate social formation'. This concept, according to Negri, is the essential point of Lenin's theoretical translation of *Capital*. Marxist sociology recognizes the essential structures of a society by 'reducing social relations to relations of production' and thereby discerning the determinate social formation (Negri 1976c: 16). We should not be misled, though, by this naturalistic and objectivistic formulation: the contemporary culture was thoroughly permeated by this terminology (Negri 1976c: 16–17), but in this early period Lenin uses the discussion of the 'determinate social formation' as a framework for investigating the composition of the working class and for discerning the character of the revolutionary subject. According to Negri, Lenin's analysis of the determinate social formation involves the investigation of the real conditions and behavior of the working class that allows us to identify the actual working-class standpoint. He attempts to cast the social analysis so that it will allow us to interpret the working class as a revolutionary subject. This theoretical approach to working-class subjectivity is, in Negri's view, the key to Lenin's Marxism: 'it is appropriate that the originality of the Leninist reading of Marxism is being clarified here, around this concept of the working class (which is being constituted on the concept of the determinate social formation, that is becoming real as the motive force of an unstoppable tendential process)' (Negri 1976c: 19). Lenin brings the working class into theory as a mature subject.

Negri substantiates this interpretation of Lenin through a reading of his principal works of the 1890s. In these works we find the groundwork for

Lenin's theory of the subject (and hence of revolutionary organization) in his analysis of the spontaneous behavior of the working class: 'the first element that catches the eye in reading the Lenin of those years is the glorification of spontaneity, which is not just occasional but rather permanent and systematic' (Negri 1976c: 20). Lenin was witnessing the intense combativeness of the select group of highly skilled Russian workers during these years and he came to recognize the political importance of these spontaneous economic struggles. Lenin read the determinate social formation in the composition and behavior of the working class. The workers' struggles, however immature they may be from an organizational standpoint, always manifest a political intuition, they always allude to political goals: 'every economic struggle is a political struggle' (Negri 1976c: 20). The workers' struggles always manifest a real political content and furthermore economic agitation and worker spontaneity provide the necessary foundation for any proletarian political program. The intense struggle of these highly skilled workers, the developed consciousness of this elite work force, already foreshadows the characteristics of a powerful organization. Economism and spontaneism: the orthodox 'Leninist' tradition would attack these conceptions, yet Negri finds them as the point of departure for Lenin's work in the 1890s. Spontaneity is the emergence of working-class subjectivity and the affirmation of this spontaneity of the masses is the first moment of Leninist organization.

In the following decade, however, particularly with *What Is To Be Done?* (1902, in Lenin 1967), Lenin's theory makes a leap to a directly political level. He proclaims in this second period that we must refuse the 'submission to spontaneity'; he focuses, in other words, on the specificity of political struggle and organization that is beyond the sphere of economic struggle, beyond the spontaneous behavior of the masses. This proposition of political leadership might appear to be in direct contradiction to the spirit of Lenin's work in the 1890s, but Negri reads this new element as a continuation of the earlier position, as its theoretical complement. The specificity of politics characterizes the second moment of Leninist organization. 'Only the complete elaboration of the assertion that economic struggle is political struggle brings about the leap to the second fundamental assertion: political struggle is not *only* economic struggle' (Negri 1976c: 22). If the first moment, the economic struggles of the workers and the spontaneity of the masses, constitutes the intuition of revolutionary organization, the second moment, that of political leadership and autonomous political organization, is its confirmation; or better, if the first moment is the affirmation of working-class subjectivity, the second moment is the affirmation of that affirmation. The vertical form expressed in the workers' economic struggles, the hierarchical relationship among workers, is formalized (or raised to a power) in the institution of the party. How, then, should we interpret Lenin's attack in *What Is To Be Done?* on the 'submission to spontaneity'? Even though it is of first importance always to adhere to the concreteness of the spontaneous movements of the working class, there must at some point be a qualitative leap that poses political direction, a leap from the particular to the general. However, this leap, Negri insists, is a leap within a continuous organizational development. The intuition nascent in the spontaneity of the masses must be organized, it must be raised to the level of consciousness: 'organization is spontaneity that reflects upon itself' (Negri 1976c: 27). The direction imposed by a conscious political leadership is the necessary fulfillment of the project inherent in the behavior of the working class: 'organization is in fact the proof of spontaneity, its refinement' (Negri 1976c: 27). Political leadership raises the mass subjectivity to the level of truth and gives the working class an interior identity.[10] The Leninist party, Negri insists, assumes the model of a factory: it takes the raw material of the workers' spontaneous subjectivity and transforms it into a coherent and subversive weapon (Negri 1976c: 29–30). This Leninist conception of organization is an implicit critique of the two positions which define its borders: on one side it is the critique of anarcho-syndicalism, which recognizes working-class subjectivity in the spontaneity of struggles but refuses its specifically political organization (Negri 1976c: 43); and on the other side it is the critique of any attempt to pose a revolutionary organization which is not firmly based in the spontaneity of the masses.

DETERMINATE CLASS COMPOSITION: LENINIST ORGANIZATION 2

The paradox of Lenin's theory of subjectivity lies in the perfect identity of the two moments of organization. 'Organization must always "reveal," in the Marxian sense, the free activity of the class—in which prefiguration is possible' (Negri 1976c: 60). What is the logic of this prefiguration? What leads Lenin and Negri to believe that the spontaneous expression of the masses will be directly in line with the conscious program of the political leaders? To answer this we have to look back at Lenin's conception of the determinate social formation and the objective conditions that underpin the 'spontaneity' of the subject. There is an objective substratum in Lenin's thought, functioning as a gloss parallel to the spontaneous path to organization, which moves from the critique of political economy via the analysis of class composition to the theory of organization. The seeds for the character of working-class subjectivity are to be found in the specific mode of production, in the organizational form of capitalist command. We have to qualify, then, our usage of 'spontaneity' in the emergence of working-class subjectivity. We should not understand the subjectivity that is expressed in economic struggles as spontaneous in the sense that it derives from the free will of the workers; on the contrary, the struggles are the result of a determinate will formed in the material work relations in the production processes. The spontaneity resides in the fact that the workers' expression receives no external organization but arises directly from material conditions. In other words, even the Leninist affirmation of spontaneous worker expression in economic struggles should not be interpreted as an idealist definition of subjectivity; on the contrary, in Lenin 'the subject is defined by its material composition: materiality of struggles, of the wage, of institutional setting' (Negri 1976c: 39). The subject is defined in the specific conditions and relationships of its labor.

Lenin proposes the objective conditions that underpin the formation of workers' subjectivity when he defines the theoretical passage from the critique of political economy to the analysis of class composition. Lenin refers the question of revolutionary organization back to a phenomenology of the working class. In the specific case of prerevolutionary Russia, Lenin finds an industrial working class that, in its laboring processes, is organized in the factory through a strict hierarchy of relationships that place the highly trained worker in a position of leadership with respect to the other workers. The specialized character of the labor tasks and the rigid divisions within the factory, typical of Russian industrial production in this period, provide the conditions for the 'professional worker' as the paradigm worker subjectivity. The proposal of the highly skilled worker as the paradigm subject is an abstraction, but in Marxist terms it is a determinate abstraction, that is, it is a concept based not on idealist speculation but on the recognition of a real tendency in the concrete and material world, in this case on the composition of the working class. The paradigm worker subjectivity, then, is determined in the specific mode of production and the composition of this subjectivity, in turn, provides the model for revolutionary organization. In this sense, the workers' organization is 'prefigured' in the organization of labor processes. In order to be grounded in the determinate worker subjectivity, the party should trace the hierarchical organization of Russian capitalist production and reproduce the same relationship between vanguard and masses found in the factory. The Leninist party, then, 'is the party that is tied to the recuperation and re-unification of a diverse series of strata, forms of labor, forms of subsistence, forms of income and forms of struggle' (Negri 1976c: 58). The vanguard party should be 'external' and representative of the working class to the extent that the professional worker is detached from the mass of workers in production (Negri 1976c: 29). Both the power and the limitations of Lenin's theory of organization lie in its close tie to a specific mode of production. The Leninist party is effective as a workers' organization in prerevolutionary Russia because it recuperates the specific organizational forms which are immanent to the contemporary industrial production processes; and it is limited for precisely the same reason—the form of the Bolshevik party is effective only as long as the specific mode of productive organization persists.

THE CONTEMPORANEITY OF LENIN: PROJECTIVE MARXISM

One of the most important lessons of Lenin, then, or of Negri's Marxist reading of Lenin, is 'the need to relate discussion and practice on the question of organisation back to the real materiality of class movements today' (Negri 1971: 112). We find that in fact Negri's affirmation of the Leninist theory of organization serves paradoxically to highlight the ways in which the historically specific form of Leninist organization is no longer appropriate to the contemporary manifestations of worker subjectivity and to the present mode of production. In order for Lenin's discourse to correspond to our needs, there would have to be a general homogeneity between the political composition of the working class which he faced and that facing us today; obviously, however, we can recognize enormous points of heterogeneity (Negri 1976c: 33). When we look at the behavior and needs of the masses of workers in Italy during this period, for example, we find that the spontaneous expressions of subjectivity did not take the vertical form of a select and conscious elite, but rather found a general expression across a broad horizon. After decades of militancy, it was common to say in that era, the workers had internalized the strategies of combat and expressed themselves in a myriad of autonomous forms, with disregard to any workers' elites and outside of the 'official' workers' movements. The detailed studies of wildcat strikes by Romano Alquati at the FIAT plants give an excellent description of the mass behavior of the workers (Alquati 1975). The central point, which is perfectly obvious, is that the mass expressions of the Italian workers in the Sixties and Seventies was greatly different from the limited expressions of the elite Russian workers at the beginning of the century: the spontaneous behavior had adopted a horizontal rather than vertical form. The material movements of the working class demanded a different form of subjectivity.

We reach the same conclusion when we pursue Lenin's 'objectivist' path to organization, which analyzes, in the theoretical passage from the critique of political economy to the composition of the working class, the conditions

that underpin the formation of worker subjectivity. The specialized industrial production in Russia, we have noted, provided the conditions for the
rise of the 'professional worker' as the paradigm worker subjectivity. Negri
has already shown in great detail, however, that in the Twenties and
Thirties, after the full impact of the October Revolution, capital reacted by
restructuring production and thus destroying the conditions for the professional worker. In the process of the massification of production and the
deskilling of the labor force, capital destroyed the hierarchy among the
workers and hence it flattened the relationship between the vanguard and
the masses that previously had characterized workers' organization. It
destroyed the foundation on which the vanguard party could be conceived
as external to and representative of the class.

Negri also poses this historical change that separates us from Lenin in
Marxian terms as the passage from the formal subsumption of society
within capital to the real subsumption.[11] In the phase of the formal
subsumption, there is a certain slippage between social production and
capitalism: certain precapitalist and autonomous forms of production and
social cooperation persist external to capital and they are merely formally
subsumed within the global framework of capitalist rule. In the real subsumption, though, labor power and capitalist relations of production are
extended horizontally throughout society; labor and production are purely
social determinations and hence the 'social factory' is absolutely diffuse.
The real subsumption, in short, is defined by the direct rule of capital over
society. Negri claims that while Marx recognized this passage from the
formal to the real subsumption as a tendency of capitalism, today it has
become a reality. In subsequent years, Negri will make a great deal of this
Marxian distinction, but at this point and for our limited purposes the
argument is quite simple: Lenin recognized correctly in the conditions of
the formal subsumption a slippage between the particularity of economic
struggles and the generality of political struggles, which needed to be
addressed or recuperated by party organization. Today, however, the fundamental presumptions of Lenin's recognition have disappeared: 'The passage from the particular to the general, from economic struggle to political
struggle . . . loses the significance it assumed in Lenin's thought.' 'Instead,
in our situation today, economic struggle and political struggle are completely identical' (Negri 1976c: 34–5). The fundamental passage of Leninist
organization, then, from the particular to the general, from the economic
to the political is no longer adequate to our reality. This distinction between
the economic and the political and the specificity of the passage between
them was the basis for Lenin's proposition of the party outside of the
working class. Today, in the conditions of the real subsumption, since

this distinction effectively has dropped out, there is no basis for political organization external to the class.

Why has Negri entered into such extensive and detailed study of Lenin, then, if he is only to conclude that Lenin's specific analyses are completely outdated and inappropriate for the contemporary class situation? In what sense does Negri consider himself Leninist? 'There is no fetish, Lenin also holds, to demand sacrifices' (Negri 1976c: 69). We do not need any Lenin worship, we do not need to advocate fidelity to the set of abstract models he proposed; rather, what we should adopt from Lenin is a project of reading the real and present composition of the working class and interpreting its subjectivity, its needs for organized expression. The most innovative aspect of Lenin's thought is its mass methodology, its theory of mass intelligence, its ability to dissolve theory into the practice of the masses and crystallize it again in a central insight. 'Thus Leninism as a method, but as a mass method, as a mass practice, insofar as Leninism entrusts revolutionary destiny to the masses' capacity to turn themselves immediately into agents. In this new sense, the complexity of the process is recovered and it arrives at this liminal concept of insurrection as art' (Negri 1976c: 68). Leninism is an art insofar as it grasps, in the practice of the masses, the subject of revolution. In Negri's hands, Leninism is a proposition for a reorientation of the Marxist endeavor, a subordination and incorporation of the critique of capital within the revolutionary project of the working class, a dissolution and refoundation of theory within the practice of the masses. This is the contemporaneity of Lenin.

THE MASS VANGUARD AND THE AMBIGUITIES OF WORKER CENTRALITY

On the theoretical plane, as we have seen, Negri attempts to rejuvenate Lenin's concept of the revolutionary subject by updating it with respect to the contemporary sociopolitical conditions. When we turn to examine how these ideas are played out within the Italian political context of this period, however, we find a clear disparity in Negri's thought and the persistence of certain Leninist propositions that he seemed to have rejected earlier. Negri advocates in his political circles, for example, the theoretical centering of the revolutionary subject on the typical factory worker and hence the organization of a vanguard party to lead the movement. We should be very careful, however, in interpreting these positions, because they are so closely tied to the political contingencies specific to the Italian situation in this period. Therefore, with one eye on the turbulent political scene we will try to position these practical propositions in order to clarify this stage of Negri's thought.

Negri was one of the founding members of Potere operaio [Workers' Power] a political organization that existed roughly from 1969 to 1973. The status of the organization was continually in flux, but one of Negri's central and most problematic texts of this period, 'Partito operaio contro il lavoro' [Workers' Party Against Work], which was circulated in various forms among militants in the movement, constituted his proposition of a program to transform Potere operaio into a revolutionary party. As a party, Potere operaio would be the central point of focus or the vanguard for the various struggles and thus lead the path to revolution. The most problematic element of this proposition, given the theoretical framework which we have established, is the conception of the priority of a revolutionary subjectivity centered around the factory workers: the mass worker is presented as the paradigm subjectivity and hence as the vanguard for the entire working class. The concept of a vanguard party persists here in Negri's thought, even though we have seen that the conditions for its existence have been taken away. Negri does have a coherent means of explaining this seemingly paradoxical position, but to be adequately understood these arguments have to be situated in the context of rapid social change and intense political violence. Once we position Negri's argument, in fact, the call for proletarian unity appears designed principally to fulfill a role of moderation, mediating between the extremes active in the workers' movements.

The foundation for the proposition of a vanguard party in Negri's theoretical investigations is a highly problematic one. His periodization of labor relations and production presents this in perhaps the simplest terms. Capitalist production of the late nineteenth century, Negri has argued, tended toward the development of highly skilled factory production as its central factor. Correspondingly, through the conditions of these relations of production, a paradigm workers' subjectivity, the professional worker, progressively matured to the point that it constituted an independent threat to the existence of capital through its organization in the professional vanguard party. The capitalist transformation, then, to mass factory production both destroyed the conditions for the professional worker and created the conditions for a new worker subjectivity, the mass worker. The formal schema is logically completed, then, by the mass vanguard party as the form of organization adequate to the mass worker subject.

dominant capitalist structure of production	paradigm class subjectivity	adequate organization
specialized industrial production	professional worker	professional vanguard party
mass industrial production	mass worker	mass vanguard party

Therefore when Negri says 'a reprise of the theory of the party (within the current class composition) that predictably repeats Leninist theory is unimaginable' (Negri 1976c: 63), he is not rejecting the contemporary validity of a vanguard party *tout court*, but rather he is arguing for a 'mass' rather than a 'professional' class vanguard: 'In reality the concept of the vanguard is modified, it becomes the concept of a "mass vanguard"' (Negri 1976c: 61). The ambiguities here are all contained in the paradoxical concept of a mass vanguard. The first component of the concept, its 'mass' character, attempts to bridge any possible gap or destroy any externality between the political elite and the masses of workers. In his critique of Lenin, we have already seen that Negri believes that the distinction between the particular and the general, between the economic and the political, that Lenin theorized is no longer adequate to the class situation. Therefore, it follows that political organization must construct a unification of the working class not from a position external to the masses (as Lenin imagined it) but rather from an internal standpoint within the masses: 'This process of unification can only set out, *not "from above," but rather from below, from within*' (Negri 1973a: 130). Revolutionary organization, then, should be a 'mass' organization in that it is situated within the class. Through the power of this mass subjectivity, the working class rejects any form of representation through external leadership and presents itself as the unmediated subject of power. '*The class can only delegate power to itself*' (Negri 1973a: 147). However, this first component of the concept seems to be contradicted (or at least problematized) by the second: this internal organization is nonetheless unified and centered around a vanguard, which is in some sense distinguished from the masses. The distinction is made, on a theoretical plane, principally on the basis of productive labor: the mass workers in the large factories are given the political task of a vanguard because they constitute the heart of capitalist production. Through this political priority and relative autonomy, the factory worker vanguard is privileged with a hegemony over the rest of the working class and indeed the entire society. In this sense, Negri reproposes revolutionary centralization and the political need for a party. In a perfectly paradoxical fashion, Negri proposes that the party be both internal and external to the class.

Here, however, we find the reappearance in Negri's thought of the traditional Leninist distinctions between the economic and the political in the concept of a mass vanguard. 'The concept of the party of mass vanguards is a concept of *the unification of the struggle for wages and the revolutionary struggle for power*' (Negri 1973a: 135). The mass economic struggle (for wages, against work) and the vanguard political struggle (for power) must be seen as both separate and united. This analysis of the two struggles corresponds perfectly to organizational strategies. The communist tradition of antifascist resistance (dating back to World War II) proposes organization on 'dual levels': a mass level and an elite (or clandestine) level. The proposition of the mass vanguard is an attempt to maintain the power of this strategy but supersede its duality in a synthetic unity. Negri tries to work his way out of this theoretical dilemma, in other words, on both the analytical and organizational planes, with a dialectical sleight of hand: the two struggles are dialectically united in the mass vanguard party; the passage from the plural subject of the economic struggles to the unified subject of the political struggle is a passage from quantity to quality. 'Only a Marxian use of the materialist dialectic can allow us to deepen and clarify the concept of the mass vanguard, and thus the concept of a workers' party against work' (Negri 1973a: 136). The appeal to the dialectic, however, does not give Negri a convincing solution to this problem. The concept of mass vanguard remains a paradox. Nonetheless, Negri's objective here is quite clear: he wants to discover a social synthesis to produce a coherent revolutionary subject strong enough to meet the contemporary needs of the class struggle.

POLITICAL VIOLENCE AND TERRORISM

We can only really clarify this theoretical morass when we recognize the practical pressures that Negri felt at the time and the mediating role he attempted to fill as an intellectual in the movement. There was a widespread belief among the militants that in the early Seventies they were nearing the final stages of the overthrow of the Italian state, a period of civil war. The time had come for insurrection. Political violence was no longer a matter of question; in Italy such violence was so general that it had become the normal state of political exchange, from both sides of the conflict. Giorgio Bocca, one of the journalists who attempted to investigate Negri's career, tries to situate the discourse of armed struggle in this turbulent period. 'This would be an ahistorical operation, a merely formal inquest, if it isolated the violence and insurrectionalism of Potere operaio from its times, from the national and international situation. . . . It is important for us as historians to admit that during the years between 1969 and 1974, political violence was a given, a fact of life that was broadly tolerated, we might even say almost normal' (Bocca 1980: 70). Violence, then, was a given element of the political scene. From the workers' point of view, the state had been pushed to its limit by the power of the workers' movements and now in desperation the state looked consistently to violence as the only effective weapon through which to maintain its control. The 1969 conflicts in Turin (in Corso Traiano) and in Battipaglia are the most commonly cited examples (cf. Negri et al. 1983: 233). The struggle against capitalist command, then, according to this view, had no choice but to adopt some sort of policy of armed struggle. Therefore, Negri is not expressing a marginal position when he says, '*only the armed struggle today speaks of communism*' (Negri 1973a: 136). We should be careful to keep in mind, since we are now venturing onto some of the most problematic and provocative terrain, that our purpose here is merely to explain Negri's theoretical and practical positions.

Within the context of political violence, then, Negri's position is defined by two polemics: on one side against the 'populists' or 'narodniks' and on the other against the 'subjectivists'. The populists, he argues, do not sufficiently appreciate the need for central organization in the context of civil war. This is true for two reasons. Firstly, when political dialogue has been reduced to violence, the working class must be able to defend itself and wield a force equal to that of the state; the party must be 'the specular and opposite reversal' of capitalist command and state power (Negri 1973a: 142). If the proletariat is to take the offensive in this context (as a paramilitary force), it must have a centralized and coherent leadership. Every act of class violence should be directed in a concerted project to further the goals and organization of the working class (Negri 1973a: 152). This leads to the second reason for centralized leadership: in a situation of widespread violence, lack of organization will result in senseless damage, to the workers and to the society at large. Negri and many other intellectuals associated with the workers' movements saw their roles as moderating filters that could protect against random violence and senseless excesses.

Negri's other polemic, on the other side, is against the 'subjectivists' or 'voluntarists'. This position, Negri argues, should not be critiqued for the use of violence in itself, but rather 'for not knowing how to enter into an *organic relation* between the subjectivity of workers' power and the subjectivism of the use of violence' (Negri 1973a: 139). The 'subjectivists' are those who propose direct action against the state and capital conducted by an armed vanguard which was external to the working class, but acting in the interest of the class. This was obviously a very strong faction in the movement and one that could not be ignored. It was grounded to a large extent in the heritage of the Italian antifascist tradition of the partisan combatants.[12] The theoretical appraisal of the contemporary nature of the capitalist state, therefore, takes on a tactical importance, and the stakes are extremely high. 'There are some in the militant cadres of the movement who maintain, with great force and conviction, the thesis of a process of *"fascistification" of the State'* (Negri 1973a: 154). Since the state has adopted a fascistic form relatively autonomous from capital, these militants argue, the workers' movement needs to combat it in traditional antifascist fashion with armed brigades relatively autonomous from the class. Negri counters, on the basis of his juridical and economic critiques of the capitalist constitution, that the contemporary state is not bent on destroying the power of the working class as the fascists were, but rather on containing the working class and putting it to use in development (Negri 1973a: 150). Therefore, given the nature of the adversary of the working class, the political direction and the use of violence must arise organically from the mass class subjectivity. 'There is no place . . . for the liberatory sacrifice of the vanguards. . . . There is no space in our organization for outdated forms of voluntarism: we are within the mass movement, developing a scientific (and thus practical) understanding of its composition and its desires' (Negri 1971: 141–2, translation modified). In the context of civil war, Negri finds no condemnation for the violence of the masses. The use of violence, however, must never be fetishized; it must always be subordinated to the advancement of the movement (Negri et al. 1983: 233). The abuses come when an armed military movement is detached from the real movements of the masses and the actual political composition of the working class. The 'subjectivists', Negri argues, propose a reductionist reading of state fascism which leads to the minoritarian practice of violence outside of the context of the masses: 'whenever a practice is forced, the outcome is inevitably terroristic' (Negri 1973a: 100).

Once again we should recognize that Negri's discourse on violence is most coherent when we bring it back to his theory of the subject. The mass vanguard is a subject with two faces: one face is the dispersed and plural behavior of the masses grounded in their rejection of the work relationship and in their desire for freedom; the other face is the coherent leadership of the factory worker vanguard which constitutes the specular antagonist of the state. The first face alone, in the context of civil war and confronted by the violence of the state, would represent a 'narodnik', defeatist position; the second face alone, detached from the masses, could only lead to terrorism. The synthesis of the power of the masses and the direction of the vanguard would provide, in Negri's thinking, the adequate revolutionary subject.[13]

REMARK—LENIN AND NIETZSCHE: THE SUBJECTIVE CAESURA AND THE ONTOLOGICAL CAESURA

The intensity of the social struggles in Italy forced the question of subjectivity to the top of the theoretical agenda. In this context, the theory of political organization appears as only a more practical and more volatile form of the theory of the subject. Negri tries to meet the challenge posed by the social movements in its fullest form; he attempts to accept the emerging subject into his theorizing, and grasp it at the summit of its power. We must come to recognize the working class, Negri claims, not only as the object of exploitation, but as the subject of power, not only as a passive subject constructed through *dispositifs* of capitalist domination, but also as the active subject which constitutes itself and projects a new society on the basis of its own needs and desires. The intense impact of the social struggles as a subjective force marks a rupture in the development of Negri's thought. The scholarly approach of critical theory, striving for an 'objective' reading of the social and historical movements, now has a role that is subordinated to the desires, to the project of the working class as subject.

This reorientation of Negri's thought, this inversion of the approach of critical Marxism, does not by any means signify a departure from Marx in Negri's mind: it is rather a deepening of the Marxist problematic and an attempt to recognize the emergence of the working-class subject as central to Marx's mature thought. The approach of *operaismo* is perhaps better suited than other currents of critical Marxism as a point of departure for this reorientation because of its attempts to ground the critique in the actual standpoint of the working class: the favorite Marx of *operaismo* has always been the Marx of 1848 and of the Paris Commune, the Marx who is theorizing with an intense enthusiasm, buoyed by the hope and power of the proletariat. Negri, though, makes his leap to his new approach to Marx with the aid of Lenin. The working class rises up in Negri's thought, through an interpretation and critique of Lenin, as a strong social subject which, at its base, is rooted in the material conditions of labor and the concrete subjective expressions of the masses and which, at its peak, is aspiring toward power and refining its capacities of self-expression and self-organization in society.

Some have suggested that this return to Marx and Lenin in the Italian context is parallel to the theoretical developments of Louis Althusser in France (Piotte 1986: 17). This *prima facie* similarity, 'the return to a revolutionary Marx and Lenin', reveals on closer analysis, in fact, substantial differences that are indicative of the great gap between Negri's thought and the major contemporary currents of Western Marxism, specifically on the question of the subject. Negri's confrontation with Althusser can be seen most clearly in terms of their readings of the evolution of Marx's thought; Negri cannot accept Althusser's proposition that the major turning point in Marx is the progression from a youthful humanist phase to a mature structuralist phase that poses a critique of the classical economists.

If we want to speak of an 'epistemological caesura' in Marx, it can only be from the moment when the definition of a structure shows not only the relationship between the existence of capitalist crisis and working-class movements, but above all when the analysis emancipates itself from existing conditions in order to turn itself into a program, and the given relation of force gives rise to organizational proposals. *The epistemological caesura is the birth of organization . . .* (Negri 1973a: 102)

By trying to frame Marx's thought strictly on a structuralist horizon of the critique of political economy, Negri claims, Althusser empties the power of the analysis by detaching it from the revolutionary, subjective grounding of the organization of the working class. The structural critique of political economy proceeds on a sterile, depopulated horizon. But this is not Marx:

Far from ending up in a 'process without a subject,' the evolution of Marx's thought instead closely follows the organizational reality of the revolutionary subject. The true result of the critique of political economy is always necessarily this subjective rooting. (Negri 1973a: 103n)

The revolutionary subject is both the driving force and theoretical result of Marx's endeavor.

If it is true, as we have claimed, that Negri is forced to recognize the central role of the subject in Marx's theory by the explosive expression of the Italian working class in the period following 1968, it is equally true that Negri could not have grasped the theoretical importance of this subjective emergence without the aid of Lenin's reading of Marx. Lenin discovers the means to bring the revolutionary subject (in its material desires and concrete practices) into the heart of theory. Here, in the theoretical appreciation of Lenin, we can see even more clearly the vast distance between the paths outlined by Althusser and Negri. Althusser's polemical point of departure is his charge against the academics that they have never accepted Lenin and never sufficiently recognized his contribution as a philosopher (Althusser 1971: 22–70). He invites us to appreciate, that is, not Lenin's practice per se, but rather the ways in which Lenin has brought practice into theory and hence renovated the theory of revolution (or rather, the revolution in theory). This is how Althusser reads Lenin's famous motto, 'without theory there is no revolutionary practice': issues of revolutionary practice must be founded on, or subsumed within, the theoretical horizon. The genius of Lenin, according to Althusser, is to bring the class struggle into philosophy; Althusser wants to admit Lenin into the honored halls of the university. Negri, on the contrary, appeals to Lenin to help him move out of the university and into the factory—he does not look to Lenin to bring the class struggle into philosophy but to put it into practice. His favorite Leninist motto shows his distance from Althusser: it is more interesting and more useful to make revolution than to write about it (from the postface to *State and Revolution*, cf. Negri 1976c: 129, 152). In Negri's mind, Lenin can never be extracted from his concrete practice. The study of Lenin, accompanied by the explosion of the social struggles, marks a rupture, a turning point in Negri's work: a subjective caesura. The strong subject appears in his theorizing as the driving force that overturns and reorients the structures that constitute the entire conceptual horizon.

Althusser's work on Lenin, in fact, is a very poor point of comparison for understanding the importance of Lenin in Negri's thought. If we are to look to the French scene, we could gain a much more adequate understanding by comparing Negri's Lenin to the Nietzsche who was 'rediscovered' by French theorists such as Gilles Deleuze and Michel Foucault.[14] When viewed through the interpretations of these thinkers, the similarities between Lenin and Nietzsche are, to my mind, as striking as they are unexpected: (1) the centrality of the philosophy of the will; (2) the material constitution of subjectivity; (3) the terrifying destructive power of the total critique and terrific constructive power of subjective affirmation; (4) and hence the refoundation of ontology in freedom. We have argued that when Deleuze turns to study Nietzsche he transports the positive logical dynamism developed in the study of Bergson onto a new horizon, a material field of forces where all the logical issues are now posed in terms of sense and value.[15] In effect, Deleuze finds in Nietzsche the logic of will and value which animates the field of subjective forces. Nietzsche operates a materialist reduction of philosophical inquiry relating all issues back to questions of power and subjectivity. In Deleuze's terms, he transforms the question 'What?' into the question 'Who?': the question Nietzsche asks, for example, is not 'What is justice?' but 'Who is just?', or better, 'Who wants justice?' The similarity with Negri's Lenin lies in the fact that subjective forces animate all issues; the terrific power of the will is the pillar which supports the theoretical horizon for both Nietzsche and Lenin. We can see this most clearly in terms of the 'total critique' which we described.[16] Nietzsche and Lenin, driven by extraordinary conceptions of antagonism, present a concept of critique that is initiated by a *pars destruens*, a destructive force so violent that it razes the entire present horizon, completely destroying the state of things as they are. The following moment of the critique, the *pars construens*, constructs a new horizon, with no reference to a metaphysical point of support, but strictly on the constructivity of the immanent subjective forces. The terrifying absolute destruction of the Nietzschean negation is followed by the terrific creative power of the Nietzschean affirmation: the art of insurrection and the art of organization. The essential point here is the interdependence of the two moments: the second moment, the power of future construction, frees each author to pose an unlimited destruction of the present; and likewise, after the first moment has cleared the terrain, the second moment is free to construct a new world with unlimited creativity.

This is the radical and terrific vision that comes with the subjective caesura for both Negri and Deleuze: it is a refounding of ontology. In this context, the opposition between necessity and freedom is broken down, as being is continually destroyed and remade, refashioned according to the movements of subjective forces. The conflictual material field of power constitutes the only terrain of ontology, so that being, if it has lost its transcendental fixity, gains a dynamic plasticity. We can herald an unrestricted assault on the world, an absolute destruction of being, because we know that, on the basis of the power of the will, of our material subjective forces, we can construct a new world and re-make being: we will deconstruct the nature presented us to create a second, a third, an nth nature in line with our desires and needs. In fact, in the context of this view of ontology, nature is always already artificial, in that it has been constituted by subjective forces: the being which is presented to us and which constitutes us is already conditioned, and susceptible to our remaking. The theoretical exclusivity of the field of power and subjectivity in Nietzsche and Lenin permits a transformation of the conception of ontology. Rather than any epistemological caesura, this rupture in Negri's and Deleuze's thought constituted by the emergence of subjectivity represents an ontological caesura. As we repeated so often in our study of Deleuze, once again here, in typically Scholastic fashion, *ratio essendi* is given priority over *ratio cognoscendi*.[17] Why should we continue to use the term 'ontology', though, after this rupture, after being has been torn from the realm of the unconditioned? Would it not be more appropriate, after we have posited absolute plasticity, to abandon the discourse of being and admit a pure relativism? Is this a postmodern twist? Not at all! On the contrary, there is a wide and varied tradition, from Leopardi to Lukács, which proposes a materialist reading of being in the realm of the conditioned, of second nature. For Negri and Deleuze alike, the intervention of subjectivity only makes the ontological discourse more important and more adequate to their projects. That the being facing us has been constituted by previous relations of force does not make it any less substantial for us; that we have the power to destroy and recreate being does not make it any less real. As Nietzsche says, 'no longer the humble expression, "everything is merely subjective," but "it is also our work!"—Let us be proud of it!'

(Nietzsche 1967b: 545). In this context, the traditional opposition between necessity and freedom ceases to make sense, but the terms still carry their meaning. In fact, our freedom relates directly to our power to make an incision into being, to destroy and create nature, to constitute necessity! The subject, in Lenin as in Nietzsche, is no longer merely *natura naturata*, but now it is also *natura naturans*.[18]

We see only the sketchy beginnings of Negri's ontological discourse in this period and in the study of Lenin. It will take on a more comprehensive and substantial vision in his later works on Spinoza and Leopardi. It is important to recognize, nonetheless, that the genesis of the ontology is here, in the explosion of social struggles, in the emergence of the strong subject, in the radical power of the total social critique. The power of the working class as subject will always constitute the pillar of Negri's ontology.

THE SUBJECT THAT DESTROYS THE STATE: LENIN AND PASHUKANIS

Earlier we divided Negri's study of Lenin into three phases and subsequently discussed the first two: the spontaneity of the workers (1890–1900) and the organization of the proletariat (1900–10). These two phases constituted two complementary paths to a Leninist theory of the subject. Now we will return to the third phase (1910–17) that constitutes in many respects the practical payoff of the developed theory of the subject. The central theme of this third period is the abolition of the state and the primary text is *State and Revolution*. Negri devotes ample time to this text and treats it in great detail, but we will focus principally on two arguments that are essential for our discussion: (1) What does it mean to destroy the state? (2) How is such radical destruction possible? Here, in Lenin's revolutionary vision, we see the constitutive ontology which links Lenin and Nietzsche put to work on a material, political terrain.

The destruction of the state is the first condition for the real construction of proletarian power, for the constitution of communism (Negri 1976c: 152). Lenin is very clear in this affirmation. However, according to Negri, Lenin's theory of the state has often been misinterpreted because the state has been considered too narrowly, as merely an instrument of repression. Before we can consider the task of the destruction of the state, then, we have to analyze what the state is, or rather we have to delimit the real object of the antagonism of the workers. 'The State is a power external to society, the fruit of the irreconcilability of conflicts . . .' (Negri 1976c: 135). We can start from an Engelsian definition[19] which poses the state as a coercive force transcendent to society, employed to impose capitalist domination and negate the tension of class struggle. It is the overawing power that rules over social conflict. The state, however, does not only function as an organ of capitalist command, it also conducts the organization of social labor through juridical mechanisms: the state is a complex nexus of command and organization. The state, then, involves not only a repressive weapon but also a juridical mechanism, which is what Negri has described as functioning in 'the constitutionalization of labor' and in 'the law of value'. Lenin recognizes very explicitly that the state must be destroyed not only as a transcendent power but also in its material bases (cf. Chapter 5 of *State and Revolution* in Lenin 1967), so that the destruction of the state is above all the destruction of work, or of the capitalist work relation (Negri 1976c: 156). Therefore, Negri complements Lenin's analysis of the destruction of the state with a reading of Marx's argument for the destruction of the law of value in the *Grundrisse* (Negri 1976c: 164–9): in Negri's view the two issues are not only compatible, but they are only coherent when considered together.

Negri treats the same issue, the material bases of the state and its destruction, in greater detail in another work from this same period: 'Rileggendo Pasukanis: note di discussione' [Rereading Pashukanis: Notes for Discussion] (1973c). Pashukanis, one of the leading Soviet jurists during the 1920s, who was subsequently purged by Stalin, is one of the very few who extended Marx's and Lenin's intuitions in legal philosophy, according to Negri.[20] It is worthwhile to take this detour and delve into Pashukanis' theory, then, because in Negri's mind his analysis makes most clear the amplitude involved in the discourse of the abolition of the state. Pashukanis' point of departure is that contemporary law is neither an indifferent rational schema nor merely an abstract imposition of command and violence, but rather law is intimately tied to the organization of the commodity-exchange relationships of capitalist society: 'As the wealth of capitalist society takes on the form of a vast accumulation of goods, so the society itself seems to be an endless chain of juridic relationships' (Pashukanis 1951: 140). Pashukanis, then, attempts to develop a theory of law by following Marx's lead and reading the juridical logic of social relations of exchange. Negri argues that Pashukanis is fundamentally correct in posing law as the combination of two functions, the organization of social production and the authority or command over social relations, but he insists that we should link this concept of law not only to the domain of commodities but also to the law of value (Negri 1973c: 170). Law tends, through the developments of capital, from its organizational function in production toward its command function: through this combination, law is intimately tied to the production of surplus value

(Negri 1973c: 172). Relative surplus value is the Marxian concept which locates the normative capacity of capitalist relations of production, and which qualifies that normativity as exploitation and domination. 'Law and the process of surplus-value. Thus the form of bourgeois law comes to assert itself, in all its complexity, over the dual face of the process of development of relative surplus-value, over the articulation of organization and violence, of production and command' (Negri 1973c: 174). Bourgeois law is the other face of the capitalist production of surplus value. Here we can recognize the enormous scope of Lenin's call to the destruction of the state. The operation does not merely involve the abolition of state authoritative apparatuses of power and violence, but also an abolition of bourgeois law and the social relations of production that constitute it. 'In good Marxian fashion Pashukanis had no doubt that law was not just a form of capital's society, but it was *exclusively* a form of capital's society' (Negri 1973c: 188). The total critique of capital has to go to the root of the problem: the destruction of the state requires the destruction of law and the destruction of law requires the destruction of the law of value, of the work relation itself (Negri 1973c: 191). 'The communist struggle coherently becomes the struggle against work, against the State, against the law that constitutes the specific authoritarian form of the relationship between the State and the organization of labor' (Negri 1973c: 192). The Soviet Union which Pashukanis saw in the 1920s had of course only accomplished the very first steps in this operation: he called contemporary Soviet society 'proletarian State capitalism.' Indeed, the *pars destruens* of the revolution and the transition to communism, which we find in both Lenin and Pashukanis, is much more radical and much wider in scope. With an inversion of Hegelian logic, we can say that the abolition of the state is also the abolition of the civil society that supports it.

The depth and breadth of Lenin's *pars destruens* begs the question that constitutes our second point: how is it possible? Is it not completely utopian to propose that we can destroy in such a profound sense the bourgeois and capitalist mechanisms of social order? Would not such an operation, if it were possible, lead merely to anarchy and random violence, regressing from the civil state to a state of nature? This issue alludes to a profound alternative which has been central to political theory since the seventeenth century and which has often been posed in terms of democracy.[21] The Leninist perspective, the standpoint that argues for the abolition of the state, can only be maintained on the power of a material social subject, capable of constituting and managing society from below. The state does not wither away of its own accord, nor through the functioning of any objective laws of contradiction; there must be a subject which destroys the state after having prepared its destruction. Specifically, in terms of our investigation here, the third phase of Lenin's thought, which culminates in *State and Revolution*, is only possible on the basis of the first two, which have established the power of the working class and its capacity to create a new social order. In other words, the ferocious *pars destruens* can only be unleashed after the power of the *pars construens*, of the autonomous social subject, has been verified. The proposal to destroy the order and social organization provided by the 'rule from above' of the capitalist state is in fact utopian and anarchistic unless it is backed by the foundation of a subjective social capacity to 'rule from below'. Lenin claims that as long as the state exists there will be no freedom and when there is freedom the state will no longer exist. This Leninist freedom is perhaps best defined as a developed anarchy, an anarchy that is ordered and organized by the fully expressed subjectivity of the working class. 'Militant and revolutionary communism is true anarchism' (Negri 1976c: 163). Leninist freedom raises anarchy to the level of truth, or perhaps better, it raises anarchy to the level of democracy.

This analysis has played itself out to an endpoint: we have reached another turning point in Negri's research. He has revived a revolutionary tradition and posed the issue of insurrection in full and potent form, but the completion of this exposition forces him to move on. The questions are all latent in the insurrectional discourse. If we are to destroy capital, its state, its valorization processes, its social organization—in short, the entire state of things as they are—what, then, will fill this void? What are the internal mechanisms of this radical, proletarian democracy? What are the new means of creating value and norms to organize society? What is the internal and autonomous consistency of this new subject and what will it propose as the constitution of social power? In other words, once being is destroyed, in what shape will it be remade? At this point in his work Negri does not have an adequate answer to these questions. All he can say is, 'the first and the last word belong, as always, to the masses' (Negri 1976c: 162). Certainly, it is a good beginning to assert that any answer must arise in a democratic forum, but this does not exhaust the issue by any means. The subject, power and being: these remain the fundamental axes of Negri's thought, but in the next phase of research he has to shift his focus from the *pars destruens* to the *pars construens*, to the issue of their constitution.

NOTES

1. Editor's note: This text constitutes chapter 5 of Michael Hardt's doctoral dissertation, 'The Art of Organization: Foundations of a Political Ontology in Gilles Deleuze and Antonio Negri,' written at the University of Washington under the direction of

Charles Altieri and submitted in 1990. A revised version of the first three chapters of that dissertation was published as *Gilles Deleuze: An Apprenticeship in Philosophy* (Hardt 1993), but none of the Negri material has been published until now. Aside from the insertion of English translations of Italian and French quotations and a few purely cosmetic editorial emendations, no revisions or alterations have been made to bring this text up to date. Despite this, however, it is still a valuable contribution to our understanding of the philosophical and political contexts of Negri's thought, and we would like to thank Michael Hardt for permission to include it in this volume.

2. Editor's note: While Hardt himself has not pursued this line of enquiry in his subsequent work, other scholars have begun the process of identifying and analyzing the patterns of convergence, divergence, influence and borrowing that mark the thought of Negri, his allies and rivals throughout this period; see in particular Steve Wright's contribution to this volume and Borio, Pozzi, and Roggero 2002.

3. Editor's note: Hardt is referring here to the immediately preceding chapter of his dissertation, 'Calm before the Storm: Critical Marxism (1964–1968)', in which he examines the roots of Negri's philosophy and activism in the early days of *operaismo*. This chapter, which has not been published, analyzes Negri's own critique of capital (in the forms of Keynesian state planning and Kelsen's normative juridical formalism) and its accompanying affirmative project as a break with the purely negative approach of other forms of critical Marxism such as the Frankfurt School.

4. Editor's note: Here Hardt is referring to the analysis in his preceding chapter of Negri's critique of the neutralized juridical definition of labor in the Italian constitution, which Negri argues functions as what Kelsen would call a *Grundnorm* (basic norm) from which the entire juridical structure of the state is derived.

5. Editor's note: The tenets to which Hardt refers are as follows: (1) the 'leading role' thesis, which requires the critique of capital to start from the viewpoint of the working-class struggles that drive capitalist development; (2) the 'strongest link' strategy, which insists that revolutionary energy be focused not on the Leninist 'weakest link of the capitalist system' but on the strongest link of the workers' movement; and (3) the tactic of 'refusal of work', which constitutes an immediate rejection of capitalist relations of production through strikes, sabotage and direct appropriation as well as absenteeism and emigration.

6. Here Negri presents the classic Marxist argument. Surplus value, in Marx's view, can only be extracted from living labor. As the living labor of the workers is increasingly replaced with machinery, capital will be faced with a shrinking pool from which to extract surplus value. Capital, then, will be forced either to increase the rate of surplus value produced by this smaller pool of living labor (through higher productivity or lower wages) or to face falling profits. For Negri's explanation, see Negri 1973a: 107–15.

7. I am not suggesting, of course, that Sabel and Piore have read Negri's work, but merely that they have interpreted the same conjunctural conditions in this capitalist restructuration. Sabel and Piore argue that US capital is still mourning the end of mass production and stuck in a crisis of identity. The new model which they find most promising is that of Italy and the recent economic boom brought on through the flexible production of relatively small-scale industries. Following the tenets of *operaismo*, one might argue that Italy developed this new model more quickly than other countries because in the 1970s it faced the most intense pressure from social struggles. However, extensive study would be required to substantiate this thesis.

8. Here, in Negri's study of Lenin, we find all of the historical difficulties of interpretation which we mentioned above: Negri is clearly attempting to appropriate the voice and the analysis of the militants, directing it toward coherent goals. Extricating his personal propositions from those generally diffuse in the movement would require extensive and detailed historical study. We will attempt merely to navigate as best we can by recognizing the focus of Negri's polemics and the direction of his argument.

9. I would like to refer to Foucault's usage of '*dispositif*' here, but an English equivalent is difficult to find. In *Discipline and Punish* (1979) the translator has chosen

'mechanism', in *The History of Sexuality* (1980a) 'deployment' has been used and in *Power/Knowledge* (1980b), 'apparatus' has been chosen. I would define a *'dispositif'* as a mechanism or apparatus which has both material and immaterial components working in concert.

10. We can certainly recognize the Hegelian resonances in Negri's Leninist proposition of working-class subjectivity, of the party as the interior and reflective subject, but let us postpone the analysis of the dialectic of organization until later in the text.

11. This distinction is posed in a text which Marx once intended to include in *Capital* but which long remained unpublished. It was first published in Italian in the early 1970s with the title *Capitolo VI inedito* and in English it was included as an appendix to the 1976 translation of *Capital* (Marx 1976: 949–1084) under the title 'Results of the Immediate Process of Production'. Negri and his Italian colleagues regarded this new text, along with the *Grundrisse*, as a major contribution to Marxist studies. We will see later [Editor's note: in the final chapter of the dissertation, 'The Constitution of Communism (1973–1978)'] how the publications of these texts allow Negri to reorient his study of Marxism.

12. The clearest example of a group with this analysis which was active in this period is the GAP, Gruppi di Azione Partigiano [Partisan Action Groups], named after one of the historical partisan groups from the struggle against fascism during World War II. The group was small but very well known partly because of the active participation of Giacomo Feltrinelli, a wealthy and famous publisher. Feltrinelli died while attempting to plant a bomb.

13. In 'Partito operiao contro il lavoro' [Workers' Party Against Work], Negri does propose *'basi rosse'* [red bases] and *'brigate rosse'* [red brigades] as part of a concerted proletarian action program. One could imagine that this would constitute sufficiently incriminating evidence for the charges of involvement subsequently leveled against him. However, one should keep in mind that this text is written before the real and full formation of the historic 'Brigate rosse' and that during this period the terms were being used within the movement by various authors with diverse connotations.

14. We are told, in passing, by Louis Fischer (1964) that Lenin did in fact read Nietzsche. The question of influence, though, is completely beside the point here. It is not so important to us either that Lenin and Nietzsche are very similar thinkers; what we find interesting, however, is that the two play similar roles in the intellectual evolutions of Negri and Deleuze. It seems to me that the study of Nietzsche constitutes a similar turning point for Foucault, moving him away from the structuralist framework and forcing him to pose questions of power and subjectivity as central. In other words, perhaps we could locate a similar passage from *ratio cognoscendi* to *ratio essendi* in the period between *The Archeology of Knowledge* (1969; trans. 1972) and *Discipline and Punish* (1975; trans. 1979). This hypothesis, however, deserves serious and careful consideration. [Editor's note: See note 17 below.]

15. Editor's note: In chapter 2 of Hardt 1993.

16. Editor's note: Ibid. *Pars destruens* is a destructive step, followed by a constructive or creative step, a *pars construens*; Hardt derives these terms from Scholastic philosophy.

17. Editor's note: These terms, which Deleuze draws from Scholastic philosophy in his study of Nietzsche (see chapter 5 of Deleuze 1983), refer to the intrinsic essence of a thing and its being in the mode of an object of knowledge, respectively.

18. Editor's note: More Scholastic terminology—*natura naturata* is nature in the passive, past-tense mode of prior construction or result, while *natura naturans* is nature in the active, present-tense mode of ongoing construction or process.

19. Negri notes that Lenin treats Engels' analysis of the state, but with a certain distance. Indeed, Engels' work is not very useful, neither for Lenin's nor for our purposes: it sets out from an inappropriate naturalist perspective and relies heavily on highly suspect anthropological arguments. The important aspect that Engels fails to treat is the role of the state in the organization of labor and in the capitalist law of value. A reconstruction of Marx's ideas on the state, if less direct, proves to be much more useful.

20. Negri insists that Pashukanis is one of the first (and unfortunately one of the last) to have grasped a truly Marxian perspective on the field of legal theory: the juridical analyses of Lask and Lukács approach that of Pashukanis in certain respects (Negri 1973c: 164). For information on Pashukanis' role in Soviet philosophy, see John Hazard's excellent introduction to *Soviet Legal Philosophy* (Pashukanis 1951). Pashukanis situates himself by attacking the work of P. Stuchka, a Russian Marxist, and that of Hans Kelsen, an Austrian neo-Kantian.

21. The clearest example of this alternative in the history of political philosophy is given in the opposition between Hobbes' proposition of state authority and Spinoza's conception of democracy. Spinoza tries to formulate his differences with Hobbes in Letter 50 (to Jelles, in Spinoza 1995) when he claims that no one can ever transfer his power of judgment, and thus his power to rule, to another. The central issue, though, is perhaps most clearly stated in Spinoza's *Political Treatise* (2000), II 4, when he insists that any agreement or contract is only valid so long as both parties want it to be. This effective rejection of the social contract as a construction of a transcendental social authority is the basis for Spinoza's rejection of the Hobbesian state; and, of course, this rejection is only possible on the basis of the power of the *multitudo*, as subject, to constitute society democratically. In his study of Spinoza, Negri locates this political and philosophical alternative in the difference between *potestas* and *potentia*. We will return to this below [Editor's note: in the final chapter of the dissertation, 'The Constitution of Communism (1973–1978)']. The relation to Lenin, however, is clear: the ability to destroy the transcendent authority of the state is based on the material capacity of the masses, as subject, to constitute a democratic social order.

2

Negri's *Proletarians and the State*: A Critique

Sergio Bologna

Translated by Ed Emery

Sergio Bologna has been a central figure in Italian *operaismo* since the tendency's inception more than 40 years ago. A specialist in the history of the German left, he collaborated with the editors of *Quaderni Rossi*, a key journal of the early Italian New Left, together with his friend Franco Fortini. After leaving *Quaderni Rossi* in 1964 along with Antonio Negri and Mario Tronti, Bologna wrote a series of important essays for the journal *Classe Operaia* in the years before the Hot Autumn of 1969. From the beginning, his work displayed a keen interest both in reviewing working-class history and in charting developments within contemporary class politics. Bologna's 1967 essay concerning 'Class Composition and the Theory of the Party at the Origin of the Workers' Council Movement' set the terms for early workerist reflections upon historiography, while his own experiences working for Olivetti helped inform a key essay (coauthored with Francesco Ciafaloni) on technicians and class struggle. Together with Giario Daghini, Bologna also provided a thoughtful firsthand account of the French events of May 1968 for the journal *Quaderni Piacentini*. Active in the revitalized workerist circles of the late Sixties, Bologna made significant contributions to the journals *La Classe*, *Linea di Massa* and *Potere Operaio*.

The journal *Primo Maggio*, for which the following review was written, was a crucial reference point for debates within the Italian revolutionary left of the 1970s. Founded by Bologna and other former members of Potere Operaio, it combined a concern to learn from proletarian history with commentary on the shifting terrain of class conflict. A particular novelty in the latter regard was the attention that Bologna and other editors paid to the place of monetary policy within capital's efforts to restructure its class antagonist.

By then a professor in the same university department as Negri, Bologna continued to collaborate with his old comrade on a number of projects, not least of which was the important 'Materiali Marxisti' series of books for the Feltrinelli publishing house. As his 1976 review of *Proletarians and the State* indicates, however, the differences in political judgement that had seen Bologna part ways with Negri and the rest of Potere Operaio after the latter's formal embrace of Bolshevik sensibilities had not lessened by the mid-Seventies. As the new movement of Autonomia Operaia stood poised to assume its (brief) hegemony over the Italian far left as a whole, few of its militants would pay heed to the hard questions that Bologna would pose to their leading theorist.

Steve Wright

The subtitle of *Proletarians and the State* is 'Toward a discussion of workers' autonomy [*autonomia operaia*] and the Historic Compromise'.[1] Since we are invited to discuss, in my view it is worth making the effort to respond. As regards the basic contents of Theses 1 and 2, I am in agreement: despite the fact that, within the present crisis, capital is not in a position to set in motion effective countertendencies in order to restore the rate of profit, it is nonetheless pushing through a series of restructuring operations which impact on the body of the working class and modify its class composition. I agree that this modification is not quantitative with respect to the relation between c and v, but is quite different in nature; it is imposed by the struggles, and presents itself as a negative component of the forces of production—presents itself as a lowering of the value of labor, not so much through the imposition of different forms of technology, but by the fact that the working class has imposed a different quality of work. I also agree with the definition of the functions of money capital, which, among other things, as argued by Negri represents a summing-up of themes that have already been advanced by the comrades of *Primo Maggio*.

However, it needs at least to be said that the Italian situation has always been characterized by a state support for profits, and that the organization of both easier credit and public financing of industry have assumed the 'falling rate of profit' as a constant frame of reference, as a permanent aspect of the forces of production, in periods both of prosperity and of low growth, masking all this as a support for an economy which is making up for its historical backwardnesses. This means that the Italian state is already predisposed to take steps to deal with the falling rate of profit, since it has made the 'countertendency' one of its constitutive elements. But even if we do not accept that the Italian state is thus predisposed, then we at least have to admit that the sedimentation of 30 years of support for profits has created in Italy *a very specific organic composition of capital*. Furthermore, the crisis has not contributed to bringing the situation back within normal parameters—rather it has intensified aspects of political and state support for profits.

The organization of the state has become virtually synonymous with the enactment of the 'countertendency'. Therefore the problem is not to ask whether the countertendency is efficacious or not, but to ask what position the PCI of the Historic Compromise[2] will take in relation to it, once it has become an institutional fact.

If, in addition to state support for profits, we also examine the Layoff Fund's support[3] for the wage as a transitional way of coping with the crisis, we discover that those who are today polemicizing against the 'non-productive areas' of the economy, and who are keen to reestablish a capitalism without subsidies, risk appearing as the only people in favor of a 'rupture of the state machine'. Let us ask what the attitude of the PCI is likely to be, when it finds itself having to choose between either breaking the continuity of the state and eliminating welfare interventions, or preserving that continuity and privileging relations with the DC in its entirety—in other words, with its clientelist nature and with its 'welfare' practices? Furthermore, how is it possible, today, to attack the 'non-productive sectors' without attacking the guaranteed wages that have been imposed by working-class struggles—in other words without taking up a position against working-class interests on this front too? Negri is correct in saying that ideology counts for little, and that what counts is rather 'the political form of capital's overcoming of the crisis'. He also says:

> Already even to refer to the massified behavior of workers' autonomy once again greatly weakens the hypothesis. A behavior which is linked to the overall rigidification of labor-power in its quantitative and qualitative aspects . . . is tendentially inexhaustible within the political form that is socialism. (p. 22)

But all this says nothing about another contradiction—not that of the PCI, but that of workers' autonomy: why, despite the continuing fact of 'autonomous' behaviors, is the working class today, albeit in the short term, still subject to the political hegemony of reformism? Negri says that *tomorrow* this will become a contradiction for the Historic Compromise, but I am interested to know why such a contradiction between the revolutionary left and the class exists *today*. Explanations in terms of structural changes in class composition are not convincing: talk about home-workers, tertiarization, the end of emigration, new kinds of unemployment, etc., often amounts to little more than alibis. Furthermore, as we shall see when we analyze Negri's text more closely, they imply a hunt for a different social subject—constructing and on occasion inventing another social figure to whom can be imputed the process of liberation from exploitation. At the level of theoretical reflection, this translates into total silence on what the working-class left has done during recent years, and in particular that left with which Negri has been involved also in an organizational sense. On its errors and its achievements. Refounding theory at this point becomes simply a masked operation of burying the past.

Thesis 5, 'On the autonomy of the political: The state today', is one of the more lucid sections of the pamphlet, even if sometimes it reads like a polemic against Tronti c.1975 carried out with the arguments of Tronti c.1962. The problem addressed is the relationship between the state and the Historic Compromise. If the state has absorbed into itself all the articulations of society and reorganizes them as command for accumulation, if the state produces, if the state produces crisis, if the state produces income, if the state produces social classes, etc., that obviously leaves no spaces for usages that are mediatory, alternative or socialist. Hence we have to say that either the Historic Compromise is itself an organ of these state functions, or it doesn't actually exist. I agree, and I agree that there are two aspects to this, one archaic and Kautskian and the other more serious and managerial.

But unfortunately the problem does not end here. Even if the 'autonomy of the political', understood as a dialectical relationship between separate spheres (that of accumulation, that of the party-state, that of the bureaucratic-repressive machine, that of civil society) is no longer given in terms of classical social democracy or in Gramscian terms, nevertheless, the fact that the PCI is seeking to reconstitute this dialectical relationship where it does not exist—as it seeks to 'reconstruct a public function as an expression of the general interest' via a decentralization of powers, direct democracy, etc.—is a fact which should make our judgment more cautious. The PCI as 'shadow state' certainly exists, and it may occasionally be a hundred times more efficient than the real state, but at other times it expresses 'popular' contents which the other state, the official state, does not express. And thus not only does the PCI represent itself as something different—as a proposition of a state wherein mediatory functions might regain significance—but it already *is* this. It already exists as such, and in some cases has existed as such for 30 years. If there is a party which has consciously 'constructed' the autonomy of the political, conscious of the fact that it is not given but has to be created if a historical function of reformism is to be legitimated, and if this party still speaks as the voice of the majority of the Italian workers, then one must conclude that the autonomy of the political exists independently of the laws of the world market and independently of the level of maturity of social capital. It exists because it has been 'constructed', first as a means of making up for the shortcomings of the DC state, then as integration, and today as prefiguration. And it is precisely within this perspective—of building a system of government that can represent an 'other' function of the state— that the PCI is today signing up members, particularly among young people and factory workers, for its line of Historic Compromise.

But is this really a prerogative only of the PCI? The autonomy of the political is the concept that legitimates the existence of the parties qua mystified expression of social interests. But precisely because this legitimation is necessary to them—perhaps even more than legitimating the guarantees of the process of accumulation—even if it means encumbering society with outdated institutions, and continuing to represent themselves as being the same parties as a 100 years ago, even if it means *slowing the rate of profit*, the parties 'produce' this autonomy of the political.

So therefore it exists, despite periodic efforts by both capital and the working class to get rid of it.

Abrogating too hastily the autonomy of the political also prevents one from dealing with other present-day problems. To cite just one: what is the relationship between any government of the left and the bureaucratic machinery of the state? Today the PCI's position is as follows: guarantee the continuity of the state and make the apparatus function according to whatever new parameters are laid down by government. In other words, the same attitude that made it possible for the Legge Reale to be passed, the idea being that at a later stage, with the left having a stronger presence, it would not have been able to operate anyway.[4] In this sense the 'preeminence of the political' reveals itself as a dangerous illusion, since it does not even begin to pose the problem of *purging the state system*—in other words a drastic rooting-out of state murderers, state thieves, state managers, etc. At this point I can imagine Negri looking at me wide-eyed: 'But surely you don't really think . . .?' No, I don't really think . . . Don't imagine that I'm suggesting that the likes of Lucio Magri are about to embark on a general purge of Attorneys-General . . . I'm just saying that to focus only on the relationship between the crisis-state and the working class, eliminating all the other stuff that stands in between and which constitutes (for all that it may be an archaic leftover, etc., etc.) the autonomy of the political, can lead to a failure accurately to understand the specificity of the Historic Compromise in relation to the present political class composition.

Theses 7 and 8 are crucial for understanding Negri's position on the Historic Compromise. Here he ventures onto a terrain which is new and fascinating but which, precisely for that reason, is puzzling in the way he chooses to approach it. Anyone reading his comment about the 'obligation to productive labor' (*obbligo al lavoro produttivo*) in the program for workers' autonomy (Thesis 11) might be forgiven for thinking that it's a printer's error. But there is nothing so very surprising about the phrase, because Negri has never been a theoretician of the refusal of work. In fact he has always criticized this concept for its inability to express a program of power. And I would suggest that the explanation of this 'misprint' is to be found in Theses 7 and 8, and particularly in the latter.

The argument picks up on various pages of the *Grundrisse* in which Marx tries to hypothesize what labor might be *against* capital—labor without capital, labor free from capital. He defines it as pure invention, creativity, the predominance of use value over exchange values. Taking this as his starting point, Negri sets out to define what a new political class composition might look like, saying that we are passing from a 'system of needs' to a 'system of struggles', from the phase in which the 'socialized' worker still made use of exchange values, quantifying his own needs and translating them into demands, into a phase in which this happens through re-appropriation, in the first place of one's own work, of the use value of one's own work.

However, I am not sure that I have understood this properly, so basically I am asking for clarification. I can understand that we have passed from a 'trade union' phase to a phase in which one takes the things that one needs—from a phase in which one negotiates to a phase in which one exercises power. If that is how things are, then to take a schematic example, do women who are asking for wages for housework represent a backward stage compared with women interested mainly in organizing the self-management of their own bodies? Are workers who call for a guaranteed wage backward in relation to those who push for local control of Fargas?[5] I imagine that Negri too would agree that the two things are closely interelated, and would, for instance, see the demand for a guaranteed income as a financing of one's capacity for struggle. It seems to me that he is saying that we should be privileging moments of 'constructivity' rather than those of 'refusal', moments of 'power' rather than those of 'demand'.

It is on this terrain that the unity of the social proletariat is built, and it is on this terrain that the Historic Compromise—which, as an accomplice of capitalism's restructuring, divides and disarticulates the class—finds itself defeated. The crisis, and restructuring itself, had already set in motion objective mechanisms of political recomposition, and would have obtained a result that was the opposite of what was expected. This new political unity of the proletariat, which is a reality, has to be organized in a party along the lines outlined previously: reappropriation of use values, exercise of power and not mediations with power—I'm almost tempted to say self-management [*autogestione*].

But while I agree that this is the tendency under way in the movement, we should also add that there are other things which are going in another direction. How many workers, how many factories have found themselves in the past two years having to face up to the fact of plant closures, and how many battles have been fought over the choice between defence of income independent from the exchange value of labor power or produc-tive cooperation! Guaranteed wage or self-management, factory closure or acceptance of reconversion and restructuring. The revolutionary left in these cases has proved unable to offer alternatives, or, in the best of cases, has limited itself to saying that the problem was posed badly and should be rejected in its totality; the best the revolutionary left could manage was to say that the destruction of the factory worker as labor power was a good thing, and that this would make it easier for the vanguard to be selected and recruited. There have been so many small (and large) battles, but battles nonetheless, during which the political class composition within Italian factories has substantially altered—and certainly not in the direction suggested by Negri. In fact, what has happened has been the opposite of what he claims, the opposite of greater unity. The fact is that a deeper split has been created, not between factory and society but within the factory itself—between the working-class left and the working-class right. In short, there has been an operation of extending reformist hegemony over the factories, and it has been brutal, with no holds barred, determined to root out the working-class left and expel it from the factories. The PCI has got its way, even at the expense of the unions. Will this prove to be a short-term development? Probably, but despite its name, the Historic Compromise is a thing of the short-to-medium term, and for as long as workers' autonomy is incapable of providing alternatives, complete with forms of struggle and slogans, to the hundreds of factories that are closing, and to the dozens of revolutionary militants who find themselves in those situations—or for as long as it does not say openly that the terrain of the crisis of production is a losing terrain, to be abandoned to the enemy, presumably taking refuge who knows where . . . in *Re Nudo* festivals, in terrorism, in women's marches, in making hippy shoulder-bags or whatever . . . in other words, for as long as it lacks the courage to make a realistic assessment of the political composition of the factory after two years of crisis, all talk of programs, programs for the majority, mass programs, etc., will remain useless—as useless as this discourse of Negri's. And to bring it back to life, it is not particularly helpful to say that the new party no longer has its motor in front (the vanguard), but at the back—like a Volkswagen.

Theses 9 and 10 do in fact begin to proceed on the terrain of workers' subjectivity and the party—with much circumspection, it has to be said, taking into account every possible form of class behaviour, from the wage struggle to the armed struggle. The party must be within mass unity, but it must also not disdain the function of attack; it must be within the system of needs and must also be the motor of the system of struggles; it has to exist, but also not exist.

Frankly, at this point, I begin to find this kind of way of proceeding unacceptable—for all that I understand that here Negri is striving (a) to express an overall refusal of any conception of preexisting organizational models, whether past or present; (b) to find ways to interpret 'autonomous' behavior which is capable of giving expression to struggles without formalized organization; and (c) to maintain an openness to all possible solutions. This extreme caution—this saying everything but also the opposite of everything—which ends up no longer being caution but confusionism—appears to be in complete contradiction with the way he puts himself forward as a 'collective intellectual', as someone intent on refounding theory. Negri has gone from the theorization of insurrection (1971) to the theorization of the extinction of the party (in 1973), from ultra-Bolshevik positions to positions of pure objectivism of the struggles: a 180-degree turn. His caution of today is not a result of opportunism, but a refusal to superimpose a tendential schema on what the movement is expressing. However, the result to which this leads him is only to clarify in negative terms the problem of the relationship between political class composition and organization. And it is once again the refusal of the terrain of mediation which is here pompously called a *'fundamental re-dimensioning of the thematic of mediation'* (his italics). In other words, the repetition of the same old nonsense, because then those who maintained it in political practice always ended up denying it. Because mediation at this point also means organized (and therefore mediated) expression of subversive drives; the party form as separate from the class composition; autonomy of the political sphere from the struggles; organization to defeat autonomy, etc., etc.

So if it is really the case that we cannot take the problem of the party beyond the repetition of old formulas, and the best that we can manage is a proletarian behaviorism—nor indeed is there any *will* to go further, for fear of becoming alienated from the movement—then I really do not understand why it is necessary to manufacture ideologies, or rather to present as some kind of mystified 'general theory' what is really just a rehashing of old stuff.

Is another approach possible? I think that it is. First, it is possible to represent in precise concrete terms what we mean by the 'area of autonomy', if this is the sector that we are referring to. That would be useful, since it would mean avoiding always talking in the abstract, overconceptualizing everything, and never making clear what, who and where is being referred to. I don't think that this is a matter of preferring a historicist approach to a juridical–philosophical approach. It's probably just a matter of seeing what one says and writes on the subject as an intervention in a given debate in which there are a thousand other participants. These days I would say that to put oneself forward as the organizer of synthesis is an obsolete vocation—unsustainable in fact. Hence I am rather allergic to all proposals about 'beginning from year zero', refounding theory, setting up journals that are going to refound theory, etc. Precisely because what confronts us today is a partiality of struggles, each of which alludes to one section of the revolutionary project, I prefer to conduct my intervention on the sectional, sectoral nature of that terrain. Finally (and today more so than ever), anyone embarking nowadays on a theoretical discourse about the new party is obliged to come to terms with the real balance of power, and with what it is concretely possible to do within the spaces of the revolutionary left. Negri refers to the 'area of autonomy'. I am not familiar with this sector of the movement, and I must say that I really don't like even the term 'area', because as a territorial term it smacks of the ghetto, of the reservation, of *gauchiste* minoritarianism. But from what little I know of it, within it a process of groupuscule aggregation is taking place around more or less new models of organization. To continue attempting to represent this sector as homogeneous is another operation of the factory of ideologies. Particularly because this process of aggregation, as we call it, is positive, is a factor of clarity, because at least the groups are once again beginning to be clear about what they stand for: 'I am an anarchist, and I am in favor of direct action!' Good . . . I understand . . . ; or 'I am an armed workerist and I am in favor of the vanguard working-class fraction'. Good . . . I understand . . .

Is this a step backwards in relation to the hopes for the party that Elvio Fachinelli[6] might have? Fine, he will continue to hope.

And so, in the end, dislike turns into irritation when, in Theses 13 and 14, Negri proposes an inquiry [*inchiesta*] into workers' autonomy. Precisely if this, as he says, involves '*describing in practical terms a possible consciousness of a party process under way*' (his italics). I ask myself how an operation of this kind can be plausible when it begins by excluding an inquiry into the present relations of power between organized institutions of the mass movement—in other words the present relations of the parties, the groups and the non-groupuscule area of the movement. How can it be plausible, if it means shelving the inquiry into what has happened and how things have moved from 1968 to the present day? Which would mean asking why it is that some groups have given more space to 'living a left life' than to the debate within the working class; and have theorized marginalization as the only form of autonomy; and (to give just one example) have in fact handed over the entirety of factory politics to the reformists. And so on. And then comes the suspicion that the abrogation of the autonomy of the political is becoming precisely a shelving of the subjective experiences of the past, forgetting how much the sum of these subjective experiences today constitutes the real political class composition. We are not at some 'year zero'; the present period is not the same as the reawakening of the 'New Left' in the 1960s; we are not even at the point of definition of a social figure that is different from that of the mass worker. And yet, if it is true that the relationship between the 'socialized' worker and the party is different, if it is true that civil society no longer exists, if it is true that the theory of consciousness is different, then why continue to pursue the worn-out trade of the theoretician or ideologue? This form of political discourse is obsolete; this millenarian language is so infuriating; this autonomy of the theoretician should be combated, precisely as a negation of a 'general theory'. I began this article by saying that it was worth taking up the proposed debate suggested in the subtitle of *Proletarians and the State*. I now end by saying that debate on this terrain is not possible. It is pointless. We need to find a new terrain. Certainly *'there is great disorder under the heavens*. The situation is therefore excellent'[7] (my italics).

NOTES

1. Editor's note: This essay is a review of Negri's 1976 pamphlet *Proletari e stato: Per una discussione su autonomia operaia e compromesso storico* (Negri 1976b). An English translation of Negri's pamphlet will appear in Negri, *Books for Burning* (London: Verso, 2005).
2. Editor's note: The PCI is the Italian Communist Party, and the Historic Compromise was a political program of alliance between the PCI and the center-right governing party, the Christian Democrats (DC), that called upon the PCI to establish restraint and order among its constituents so that it could enter the governing coalition. In practice this meant policing movements such as Autonomia operaia, Lotta continua and other non-PCI sectors of the Italian left. The Historic Compromise failed in that the PCI was never formally admitted into a governing coalition, but it succeeded to the extent that it split the Italian left into one camp committed to hierarchical statist reformism (the PCI and its allies) and another committed to decentered cultural revolution (the New Left movements).
3. Editor's note: The Italian term is 'Cassa Integrazione', which refers to a specifically Italian form of unemployment compensation in which the state pays around 90 per cent of laid-off workers' wages for roughly one fiscal year, in order to reduce the financial burden on private enterprise; see Ginsborg 1990: 353, and Wright 2002: 168–9.
4. Editor's note: The Legge Reale was an 'emergency' measure passed in 1975 to facilitate the investigation and prosecution of terrorist activities; it authorized police to make 'provisional' arrests and searches without warrants and to hold suspects accused of terrorism-related crimes in 'preventative detention' without trial for years at a time. These laws (and others like them) were used against Negri and many of his comrades (including Alisa Del Re) during the 'April 7' case.
5. Editor's note: Italian manufacturer of gas appliances; the workers of its Milan factory were among the most militant of the day (see the last page of *La violenza illustrata* in Balestrini 2001).
6. Editor's note: Fachinelli (1928–89) was a leftist psychoanalyst who specialized in the study of mass youth movements and political dissidence in the wake of 1968.
7. Editor's note: A well-known aphorism of Mao Tse-Tung that Negri cites at the conclusion of his pamphlet.

3

Feminism and Autonomy: Itinerary of Struggle

Interview with Alisa Del Re
July 26, 2000

Translated by Arianna Bove

What was the course of your cultural and political development? Have there been important people and points of reference in the course of your development?

During the Sixties I studied political science here in Padua. In 1967 I strongly challenged Toni Negri, who was so enthusiastic about being challenged that in 1968, as soon as I graduated, he took me under his wing first as a funded postgraduate, then as research assistant. My cultural points of reference touched upon a wider range of issues than those of *operaismo* in the strict sense, though my political development took place mainly in Marghera[1] and outside of the students' movement, in the sense that, not knowing anything about the capital–labor relation, I was dragged out of the factories, like many others at the time, and through the method of workers' enquiry that I always appreciated—which is why I like your work too—I managed to understand the exploitative relations I had previously ignored. I think I read certain books only later: to give you an idea of my path, I first read Tronti, then *Capital*, and finally the *Grundrisse*. Thus, I think that the most important point of reference, to be honest, was this environment that made you understand things, this collectivism that moved as one in the whole of Italy, because I immediately started going from meeting to conference with the comrades of Potere operaio, Guido Bianchini, Luciano [Ferrari Bravo], Toni. It was unthinkable not to try to understand, I mean, there was so much intellectual elitism (its most obvious expression was summed up by the sentence 'Frankly comrade I don't understand you' which meant 'You are an idiot') that I spent nights studying just to feel adequate. At the same time there was this way of learning in the field, in the workers' cadres (those of Italo Sbrogiò and others, the Marghera workers' cadres that I think are rather notorious) who taught us the hard reality of social relations that was not that evident after all. Thus I must admit that in my case there were not teachers first and political practice afterwards, I think that everything more or less got into motion at the same time and the origin of it all was a form of boorish antiauthoritarianism that I felt deeply, a form of individual rebellion that found the right place and time to express itself, in the sense that it was later channeled in a more useful and productive direction, toward a serious political activity, rather than toward forms of individual anarchic expression or such things. Then in everyday life there was not just the relationship with Toni—I immediately started working with him in the Institute, even though I graduated in economics, not with him: I cannot say that he was my teacher in my education, even if in fact I depended on him intellectually for very many things—but in everyday life apart from him there were also Guido Bianchini and Sandro Serafini, with whom I joined the Institute and started working not only politically but also on research projects, organizing seminars, etc.[2] I had a daily and uninterrupted contact with these people and it was a very collective way of living that I no longer find today; maybe it is my age, I do not know, but back then we used to live much more together.

So we come to the period of Potere operaio.

The period of Potere operaio was not as homogeneous as people say; there were moments of great expansion and moments of reduction to smaller areas, especially here in Veneto, with the idea, that the other interviewees must have told you about, of opening up to the movement, that is to students and subjects who differed from those of the more traditional factory. This was probably a larger vision than the one we had theorized in the notion of mass worker, maybe it was already a departure from the worker form. However, I remained in the area where the Marxian tradition was purer, and this sometimes meant that we suffered some isolation at the national level. I must say that I was particularly involved with the journal *Potere Operaio*, as an editorial board member, and when the hypothesis of a merging with *Il Manifesto* emerged through political collectives, I made a very autonomous intervention between Pordenone and Conegliano,[3] Rex and Zoppas, and constituted the first political collective with the comrades of il Manifesto. I must say that I was not very sectarian and never liked either labels or overly strict membership. So I had this experience, which I found interesting, and it was the only possibility in that area given that the forces were scarce, but we put together a political committee (or political collective, I cannot remember what it was called) that for a long time operated in these factories and with really good people, some technicians, some extraordinary students, the very workers' intellectuality of the time. This was in the context of the hypothesis of local forms of organization that I liked very much and that perhaps allowed us to foresee (although unconsciously) a reading of the future Northeast, with diffuse factories, small factories, and a possibility of transforming the large factory into a relatively independent microentrepreneurship (let me use the word 'independent' to distinguish them from the small factories dependent on larger ones). Thus, this kind of territorial organization seemed extremely reasonable to me for the place and I think this is the reason it worked and brought together cadres (as they were called at the time) of many villages around Pordenone and Conegliano, cadres that would then remain in the workers' left for a long time.

What direction did you take after Potere operaio?

During the conference of Rosolina, where Potere operaio lost the prerogatives that interested me and the idea proposed by Piperno and the Romans of turning it into a party prevailed, with the emphasis on organization, at that stage I was already going through a crisis. I was already interested in feminism and so I left Potere operaio without joining Autonomia operaia, in the sense that I never formally joined it even though there was still a clear proximity. I started constituting the first feminist groups that then carried on autonomously: I did it through an argument linked to the recovery of time and of an autonomous dimension within the overall life of women. I undertook an argument on social services and reclaiming time that to an extent opposed Mariarosa Dalla Costa's argument on wages, even though in the end there were similarities: the issue of wages was perhaps more 'revolutionary' but from the political practice that Rosa endorsed it was difficult to understand who was demanding these wages and when. It was nonsense, but then maybe my issue was much more reformist even though it is true that we annoyed a few people when we occupied local government meetings, demanding the construction of nursery schools and proposing concrete forms of 'liberation from housework'. I needed these things anyway because I started having babies and felt very justified in demanding things I immediately needed. If you like, this was a translation of the theories of *operaismo* in Marghera: when people demanded 'Five thousand lire now', everyone would say, 'But this is not revolutionary', and the workers used to reply, 'It might not be revolutionary but we wouldn't mind five thousand lire!' Back then money was different, and it was the same when it came to nursery school: maybe it was not revolutionary, but I had to put the babies somewhere! I later theorized these issues in *Oltre il lavoro domestico* [*Beyond Housework*] (Del Re 1979), because for me they made sense. I experienced the 1977 movement from the margins because I realized that the interesting things were the more marginal ones: I helped set up Radio Sherwood here in Padua because the radio seemed to me to be a meaningful, nice, intelligent and needed form of communication and circulation of information, whereas

I did not like at all the more militarized organizational forms set up by the Collettivi politici (political collectives) here in Padua, which were more engaged in heavy militancy, so they certainly were no longer part of my view of how to change the world. Aside from not understanding 'Why me?' one of the things I thought when we got arrested—not in a nasty way— was that I was pleased that we had not won! Because to be honest, some positions really perplexed me. But after the arrest there was a sort of identification because even if I had not been part of it, what could I say the moment I got arrested? Nothing to do with me? I could have said that to the judge to defend myself, but that was it.

At that time I had two children (one born in 1974, the other in 1976), I had gotten married, I lived here in Padua and had not even moved that much around Italy. Actually I had done very little, so I have a very restricted view of the movement and its organizational forms and political expressions, a view that stemmed from here, from the political collectives. I read their papers through the lenses of what Toni and Guido used to tell me: the Institute still continued to function as a center of theoretical production and in that period I published a book on the public enterprise in Italy. I was doing something and was not out of the world, but for several years I ceased to have the direct (and I must say more satisfying) participation I was used to in the Sixties and early Seventies. I must say that I miss this extremely rich period, that was also productive for me, but I think that—in the social field—things were constantly moving and giving the impression that we could seize power and change things; in other words, it seemed that each one of us could somehow influence our own destiny and each other's destiny. Perhaps it's personal, limited and utopian, but this sensation was so evident and palpable, as well as collectively felt, that I have missed it ever since and I know now that the feelings to come were linked to solitude, isolation and the search for some kind of placement in some way or in some corner. I do not know what Oreste [Scalzone] said about this, but after moving to Paris in 1982, even the attempt at reconstituting a common identity of the exiled that could somehow bring us together always failed, due to the differences we had interiorized at the end of the Seventies. Thus, despite the fact that all of us shared an initial common element of great significance, i.e. the fact of being exiled in a foreign land with common problems and issues, we could never do it and there were terrible meetings in Paris in the early Eighties. So if I miss those times it is because I have not witnessed the same feeling and power of a communitarian kind since then, even though subjectively and individually now I have much more power over my life and decisions about it than I used to: but it is a very solitary thing.

Keeping to an analysis of the present, what were for you the possibilities but more importantly the limits expressed in the more or less organized movements and ideas between the end of the Sixties and the Seventies?

I don't know if this was a limit, but my hypothesis is that at least in my experience and recollection of them, they were movements with a strong reformist impact. What was revolutionary was only our will: the only possible outcomes that, retrospectively, were predictable, were really reformist ones. In fact there have been reforms and for me they are ascribable only to this strong social impact of the movements in general: I am referring to a number of things, from the workers' statute, to the national planning of nursery schools, to the 1977 equal opportunity laws, not to mention the laws on abortion, divorce, family rights, and such things. What did not work? The fact that we did not account for this: in my opinion, we assumed that the revolution, radical change, was a rapid and uninterrupted process, without pause, and instead we were probably defeated by the reforms and by what could have been the immediate results of these struggles. I always talk about the mass movements of the Seventies, seeing clandestine armed organizations such as the Red Brigades, Prima Linea, etc. as aberrant moments that were out of sync with the strong forces that were moving the whole of society. Maybe I say these things only with 30 years hindsight, because back then I would probably not have said the same: but I have to say that had I been conscious of this good reformist process, it would have been different. I say 'good reforms' in the sense that the point of departure for Italy was really minimal in comparison to other European countries. Take France for instance, where there was a great movement in 1968 that involved both students and workers: the kind of reforms France accomplished did not turn it into a happy country, but at least a country that more fully met, and still does, the expectations of the proletarian side. Nothing is definite or extraordinary, but if we look to the guaranteed minimum wage that we still can't even dream of (here), or to all the forms of income that somehow can be found, even if they are not called citizenship income, there are forms of *allocation* that in some way support people. Between 70 and 80 per cent of French families do not pay substantial taxes: such things sound miraculous to us. If we think of the immigrant women who have lots of children and receive *allocation* that permits the family more or less to survive until the children are six to seven years old—we refuse to call it citizenship income and it is handed out in a highly controlled way—but at least they have it and if we had it we could start fighting for other things. Had we had the awareness that we were aiming for reforms maybe we would not have done all we did. It's funny, sometimes I think that our lack of awareness of the results of the large movement we were part of in the end made us accomplish good reformism; it forced institutions to come up with better changes than those they would have carried out without our push. In fact, now that, for instance, this apparently irrational push no longer exists and there are no waves of movements in society, I have the impression that in Italy it is impossible to carry out reforms. I assume that the elected officials (whether we call them parliamentarians or political managers) are roughly the same; their names might differ but they have the same intelligence and the same abilities: yet there is not a single meaningful reform in Italy. But I have to look into the educational one more carefully; I realize that it changes many things and I want to understand more about it. The most dramatic problem we are going through now, especially in Italy (because from the little I know something more gets done in other countries), is that without any interlocution with civil society, due to this real deafness, detachment, noncommunication, or perhaps the sense of disgust and refusal on the part of civil society and without any relation to it, this country does not even have a 'modern' character, and I am not referring here to great revolutionary transformations. Moreover, any attitude that looks for dialogue or communication—which could also be struggle, but this is irrelevant—is easily forgotten: take for instance all the young people's interventions in social centers and in general. I have been involved with the Greens for a year now, and I do not know if it was a good idea. I am national adviser and I would like to leave, so maybe it is a mistake: here we all are involved with the social centers and it was not just my decision, or I would have not gotten involved. What the social centers are doing here, with Bionova, Tebio and all the active participation that is capable of imposing itself, is then absorbed into an institutional pseudo-dialogue, like Pecoraro Scanio, which is unable to produce new elements of struggle, or even refusal, of anything. It seems that there are no ideas in circulation and the few that emerge are immediately used to do something, because little can be done since the parameters lie elsewhere and are already determined at the European, international, global or universal level: so much so that nobody can move and little ever gets done.

The possibility for me was this great ability to be in the future, to see changes taking place. Initially, the analysis according to which the mass worker was the center of society seemed futuristic. The events and changes in the mode of production have too rapidly surpassed us. On the other hand, what I have to recognize is that women had this ability to grasp the global elements of the working day and its relational form: maybe they did so with little lucidity of exposition, but linking this to daily experience provided great tools to later understand the changes in labor as a whole. Today, when I hear of the feminization of labor, affective labor or immaterial labor, I laugh: it feels like they are joking because we used to say these things every day in the Seventies, when we imagined that there is a form of labor that is neither accountable nor measured and yet is what makes us reproduce the labor power and allows for material production to take place, something without which material production is impossible. The fact that, when it was emerging, the movement never made these issues its own allowed the capitalist productive structure a great advantage that we are now chasing after, because all current debates on immaterial labor and, I insist, affectivity (Toni calls it precisely that, as well as 'affection') in production, are things that capital has already made operative. In this there is another issue that women have long debated and that in my view could correct from a theoretical standpoint this analysis of immaterial production: this is the issue of the body. This is not to say 'we have a body that we have to take care of because we have to be healthy, we are not happy with our body, and so on'. Capital has already talked about this. Our argument is rather that production is certainly immaterial, but this cannot come into reality independently of bodies. We (the feminists of the Seventies) talked about the impossibility of measuring domestic labor (we call it domestic) because it was impossible to follow a process of valorization of the commodity, because they used to say that the commodity was the worker's body, whereas what could not be measured was the mind, the relational environment, the psychic and affective stability. But from the workers' point of view the aspiration to live well made sense (I recall Lotta continua used to talk of quality of life, which meant living well rather than good or bad quality) and it was the only aspiration of political significance, because I wonder what political discourse could say that one must have a bad life—not even the Protestants. Feminists then turned this issue into a question of our exploitation, in the sense that we were the ones who made sure that people, workers, comrades and whoever, somehow would survive if not live well. Had this issue been the collective aspiration back then, its significance would have been greater and at least have conformed to the transformation effectively undertaken by capital over the following ten years, because things were not moving slowly and it did not take one hundred years for these changes to take place and for what today is synthetically and with little definition called post-Fordism to come about. Thus I believe that we can ascribe to the feminist movement a series of analytical qualities that were not grasped, but feminism itself probably failed to grasp them in their more universal value. I think that one of the problems of feminism in this respect was that when talking about this question it addressed itself to women and failed to put forward a gender perspective on the world, which would have been very different. However, there was a mechanism of general misunderstanding or incorrect exchange and communication of ideas. In fact, there has almost been a divergence, as if back then people were split in half, partly doing political militancy in the world and partly being feminist, and these two worlds never met. There was never the opportunity to have a common language even with different points of view: this common language did not need to be homogeneous, but from different points of view one could have at least raised an issue that for me has only become a real one at the end of the Eighties.

In your opinion, how can we interpret the fact that for some time women who were militants in, let's say, a mixed environment and those who initially were not militant at all began to show an interest and participate in the feminist movement, but then very quickly this changed and only a few feminists of that time still think about these things and continue to follow certain issues? Perhaps the others tried to make use of that experience in their own lives and in the education of their children, but they did so in private and are now seemingly absent from the political scene.

Here you are asking me two questions: one is that of 'double militancy', the relation between parties, political groups and feminism; the other concerns this Karstic trend in feminism. Double militancy is a difficult issue because it splits belonging: for instance, I met women active in extraparliamentary political groups who were also feminist and faced with dramatic decisions, because feminism forced women to make dramatic personal choices. The enemy was often in the home: if a woman was to gain a kind of personal autonomy and have relationships with lovers, friends, husbands, fathers and men who were on the left and thus shared many of the ideas of changing society, she would feel great discomfort. I am thinking of the chauvinism of the workers of Marghera at the time, when they dared to make crude judgments on our physical appearance, not to mention the poor big-breasted women who really felt like dying when they went distributing leaflets at six o'clock in the morning. So it was a very complex issue linked to a very personal identity and to a life choice: one could not always let the husbands off because some of their positions were right, even if some marriages failed. The decisions were so drastic and violent that I can understand why some were hidden feminists and public comrades. With the party things get more complicated because some women always thought of the Communist Party as a kind of benevolent father who somehow would have accepted their little babies' demands, yet there was not one party in Italy that took up the issues of the feminist groups, at least in the Seventies. Militancy in the Communist Party was largely a family question of tradition; I met many families (mothers, grandmothers and daughters) who were members of the PCI, and this was lacerating, because it was a historical affection and one that was difficult to change. The UDI (Italian Women's Union, originally affiliated with the PCI) was ferociously hostile to the feminist movement and the movement for divorce. The UDI disassociated itself from the Communist Party when in 1976 the PCI refused to let its members protest in the streets in favour of abortion rights after the facts of Seveso (the case of dioxin and pregnant women who wanted an abortion for fear of giving birth to monsters). At the time of the separation of the UDI from the PCI, many party militants left the party and joined the feminist movement. Later there was the theory of difference, Luisa Muraro and Lia Cigarini, women who, despite their intelligence and capability, were a tragedy for the feminist movement, in my opinion, not for saying the wrong things, but for inciting to an absurd practice. These women were for the Carta Itinerante, the pact proposed by Livia Turco in 1987, and supported this pact inside and outside of the party. This pact was founded on one of the theories of difference, that of reliance [*affidamento*]: what came under question was the fact that women were always reliant on powerful men. When writing a bibliography, women writers would refer to and cite a male theorist; whilst according to these critics, women had to refer to female theorists because they had to rely on powerful women instead. Thus, transferring this theory to the relation between movement and party, the women in the party received legitimacy from the women of the movement, and vice versa, the women of the movement had a privileged channel for dealing with institutions through this reference to the women of the party. So after a first instance of double militancy of an affective and coercive kind—coercive because difficult to untangle—women then separated themselves from the institution, only later to be thrown back in by the women of difference together with Livia Turco by means of this Carta Itinerante in 1987. What I am trying to say is that this relation between feminism and the structuring of political demands through parties and groups is an unstable one in Italy, as it is abroad, and depends heavily on contingencies and fashions.

As to how the movement followed a Karstic trend, i.e. it was first apparent, then concealed and then apparent again, I do not know the reasons. All I know is that it surely enjoyed a mass expansion on specific objectives both at the European and the Italian level: we had a feminist movement on abortion, something on divorce, but mainly on abortion, contraception and family counselling everywhere. The rest is more linked to individual behaviors and lived experiences, at the price of blood and hard decisions, and had little expression at the mass level and more at the level of forms of behavior rather than taking the form of obvious demands or organizational forms. We always think of the feminism that brought 100,000 people into the street, but we neglect to notice that in the Eighties, for instance, when feminism did not seem to exist, in Italy roughly 300 Case delle Donne [Women's Houses] were set up. These are antiviolence centers set up by women in negotiation with local institutions; in Turin there were many of them. Then there was the Buon Pastore [Good Shepherd] in Rome; we even have a Casa delle Donne here in Padua (which seems impossible). Then we had some women's forms of expression; I am only talking about women, not considering the participation of women in initiatives such as the antiwar movement and the Donne in Nero [Women in Black]. We tend to forget that these initiatives are part of a course of events whereby many people who occupied the streets in the Seventies now find themselves out in the street dressed in black in the Nineties, or managing a center of women's documentation in Bologna in the Eighties. So in my opinion, rather than an unchanging movement (which would be an idiocy), there is a rooting in a gender awareness of society that is always evident and manifest in various factors, not only in feminism as we know it from the Seventies, but also in the fact that in Italy, for instance, women have increasingly gained exposure in social commerce, working and earning, which gives them more autonomy from the rest of society and also from its structure, and in the fact that having joined the labor market at a later stage, women tend to occupy its most atypical structures. In fact, something upon which we need to reflect more is the fact that we find many women wherever there are companies with atypical time schedules (such as the service industries and the like), wherever there are atypical forms of diffuse productivity, microentrepreneurship, etc. I am not saying that women constitute a majority in these places, but there is a trend towards an increased presence of women there, not to mention the general issue of education, which is in all the papers so I won't repeat it.

Who were your mentors, people who had a particular importance in the course of your development?

I will certainly omit many, but let's try. Surely the first one is Marx. Then, Tronti's *Operai e Capitale* was very important to me. I would not mention Toni's early writings because I did not understand anything he wrote, I swear, and I was not too interested in it either, but now I think he writes better; however, his vicinity and ability to convince us that we had to act as if the revolution was taking place was very important to me. It was a way of experiencing events as if they were already happening and it helped to determine them from within: in politics I think the optimism of the will is important in order to be clearer and perhaps more banal. So, it was surely also what he wrote, but the determining factor for me was primarily Toni's political ability and enthusiasm and this crazy lucidity that he displays in making up a reality that we might now call virtual but is actually a reality dictated by the will: things are not as they are because our common sense tells us so, they are what we desire. For me this was the extraordinary thing that makes you do politics, otherwise you would not do it. I miss this. Surely many other people said and wrote things that are still important for me today. But what I miss most and regard as most important is this collective intelligence that we put into operation in the Seventies and that I now no longer find. I try to reconstruct it in the things I do now, but with much effort: I set up research groups at the international level with valuable and intelligent people, but there is not the same atmosphere. I never again found the same intelligence of the Seventies, this force of thought built together in practice, and I miss it very much. This is without disregarding what I owe to Luciano Ferrari Bravo, Guido, [Alberto] Magnaghi and all the extraordinary people I met—like Romano Alquati for instance, at the Institute, who was an intelligence that emerged at the national more than the local level—and it worked in a way that made people in themselves almost interchangeable, even if each person had a particular expressive and educational capacity.

Who are the authors of today who you think are most useful in reading and analyzing reality and its transformations?

Now I find more good books than good people. I would say, since we always speak well of the dead, that Luciano Ferrari Bravo was very important for me and others in Padua because he was able to listen, appreciate and also address forms of thought *in fieri*. Apart from this I really have the impression that many people in the current I belong to are important, for instance in Paris there is Yann Moulier [Boutang] who wrote an extraordinary book on slavery; there is Maurizio Lazzarato, who used to be one of my students and is now becoming an all-around intellectual and his rediscovery of Tarde seems important; not to mention Christian Marazzi and the things he writes, but also Bifo [Franco Berardi] and people who are more distant from me in terms of their development. In this theoretical current I find many people who are still producing interesting work. But I must admit that, due to my more immediate and concrete interests at the moment, I would place myself with those who need to find in reality and research some solutions that I can no longer find in books, so my need now is to work with the people I work with at the international level in order to search the field for certain answers that I find hard to find. This is not to be arrogant, rather it is because I think that many answers are not present today and must be looked for, so it is necessary to go through a moment of active reflection in which all of us should participate, and quickly, because great questions and theories do not seem to be emerging and getting elaborated. I have marked out a more precise and delimited space for myself, since I am involved in a gender perspective that is hard to construct as a theoretical stance, and I am doing so with very competent and capable people at the international level, so I might not have an over-all view of things even though I try and keep myself up to date. So it is not a matter of providing the names, since there are too many to mention right now; rather, I have a need to put on some shoes and start walking and going and seeing how things are in order to understand not only what is going on but also how to face changes that happen so fast that I think they even surpass many analyses, however compelling and critical they may be. For instance, I am not too convinced that Toni's story of empire is so up-to-date. Empire was already over by the time Toni wrote it: Clinton could not make Camp David work and this is obvious since the story of the American policeman in the world might have been true at some point, but is it now? In any case this was not the right perspective because it is a matter of seeing what China, Japan and Korea will do. So it seems to me that in order to understand changes effectively at the moment, we have to go and see them rather than write theories that quickly become not exactly obsolete, but at least the few I read and know of through my readings fail to establish significant tendencies.

Regarding the capitalist process of development and change, beyond macrotheories, what are the peculiarities and fields to which research and analysis must be addressed, in your opinion?

At the moment I am very attentive to what is going on at the micro-territorial level. I believe that understanding and creating forms of interrelations, presences, critiques, questions, etc. on the territory is a way to understand what is happening not only at the national but also at the global level. This is also because I have the impression that what is happening is not too different at different levels, at the micro and the global level; I also think that without this outlook, one runs the risk of having no interlocutors. What is of particular importance to me at the moment (probably due to my age) is understanding to whom the critique must be addressed, who must be opposed and with whom a series of processes can be shared. This is not more important but I would say that understanding whom I am with is as important as understanding whom I oppose and what the possibilities of materializing and channeling precise demands are, as well as having an influence on concrete changes. Whilst I look with surprise at phenomena like Seattle or Tebio in Genoa, I ask myself whether real forms of aggregation and movement lie behind them: surely the Bové trial in France that brought 100,000 people to his village is linked to processes like Seattle, Tebio, etc. But we should also bear in mind that Bové is a farmer there, who had his trial there, and who smashed a McDonald's there. So, the territorial concreteness of a political attitude perhaps also produces less sporadic forms of aggregation than Seattle or Tebio. For instance, what interests me is that here in this quarter of the city there are committees against antennas: in this semibourgeois quarter, inhabited by university professors and people like that, there are so many determined people that one day they will march on the council unless it removes the antenna it is building! The same happens in Larcella: there is a nearby committee against an underground car park for 70 cars that would ruin the area. These are extraordinary and spurious forms of aggregation (there is even a countess, a general's wife, surely right wing, probably a royalist, in the group against the car park), but I look at them and they are made up of people with whom I can talk concretely about things that have to do with their lives and mine, people who create precise and substantial forms of groupings with a clear objective, with a clear interlocutor and eventually really modify the political composition of the territory or of this city. On the other hand, I see little of the rest. Bionova for instance, and what happened here, had a significance I cannot deny, yet it never produced anything beyond four newspaper articles; when I take my mother to the hospital the doctor comes to me and says: 'Ah, Madame, I saw you in the committee against antennas, I have one in my own area because they built one there too.' This is fine but what does it lead to? I do not know. Now antennas are in fashion so it is easy to find these things, but it is also true that there have been a series of committees. For instance there is a problem at the general hospital in the children's unit—this is something I had never thought about before, but where there are sick children there are also parents who have to go there and nobody knows where to put them, how they could sleep there, what money they need, so a series of groups was created to turn this children's unit we have (which is also linked to the university) into a welcoming place for parents. So, perhaps this is not the revolution, but I think that starting from these things some real aggregation is created; with a civic movement that is capable of breaking institutional balances and party alliances and that could change our view of how to live in our territories. If I manage to engage in discussion on an aim that I deem correct, just and meaningful with all those who live in the same area, then it is fine for me because I live here, I don't live somewhere else. So I don't know if this is the new form of politics, but I pay attention to this because this is what moves civil society (at the local, territorial level). I must say I am not impressed when I see factory workers every year on the first of May: they hold banners saying 'I want a wage increase because I have a family', as if people today still had a family. It is not true: there are people who would like a wage, an income, but having a family cannot be a justification for it. They look like antediluvian monsters to me, whereas all the university professors, small-time lawyers and what have you, all the people who live around here, seem to make more sense. On the one hand there has been a process of proletarianization of all these professions, so that there certainly is still a wage difference between them and factory workers, but the difference in status is minimal. The fact that these classes feel obliged to participate in making life better in the area they inhabit, even if for personal interest—well, this seems to be very important. I say this because I live in Larcella for instance, which is a working-class area, but you find these committees here too. Committees have been an element in the shift of the electoral trend in the last elections: the list called 'Together for Padua' (which won) had promised them that all the antennas would be removed, so the committees voted Destro (who is right wing, from Forza Italia) the new mayor, whilst Zenonato, who was a DS mayor, lost by 500 votes. This is to show that from the institutional point of view these issues count quite a bit in the end.

A debate on the issue of class has recently emerged: that is, on whether one can still talk about class, the way it has changed (earlier for instance you briefly mentioned this process of long-term proletarianization), and on whether within this class (or something that is no longer called that) there can be a tendency toward a central subject (for instance Bifo has recently come up with the neologism 'cognitariat'). How do you analyze this complex situation at the macrolevel?

This is the issue of class composition: from a strictly Marxist point of view, I think that it must be revisited, as the analysis of commodity production and the creation of value must probably be rewritten. However, if we meant by class the supposedly physical participation in the production of commodities, whatever they are, and if we could include in this production all the present changes of laboring, we would say that the concept of class must be much more inclusive. According to Tronti, class was not only the driving engine in so far as it was linked to productive structures of a certain kind—obviously reduced in comparison to the rest of society—but it also became the element capable of constituting the general social interest and the satisfactions of its demands became the satisfaction of the general social interest. Today this works the opposite way: given that the production of commodities (any kind of commodity, even communicative commodities and the most immaterial ones) invests the whole of the relational structure of society, class is identified with citizenship or, even worse, with citizens and then legal and illegal immigrants, with all those individuals capable of understanding and willing and maybe even others. This is to say that if any social and relational behavior has now become a productive one, then the definition of class ought to be more extended, which it probably is not, I do not know; so, undoubtedly if it is so extended it has to be central. In that case then one would only have financial capital, which is to say absolute immateriality. On this I will digress: in Marghera there are incredible places where you can dance right in the middle of an industrial area, in former factories, like in the periphery of Padua where there used to be factories and now another commodity is produced: entertainment. What is produced is leisure time and its satisfaction. But the factory is there; the weirdest thing is that the shift occurred so fast that what contains these two things has not changed and what is produced is still a commodity. So I was asking myself: the managers of these places (half dance classes, half nightclubs), the dance teachers, what are they? Are they the working class of today? I don't know—maybe they belong to the working class but have an extraordinary character; they must keep training in order to produce this commodity and pay attention to fashions. Is this the new working class? Is this class? What class-consciousness the manager of a dance school in the middle of the industrial area in Marghera has I honestly don't know, but it must be this way. The change in the physical space is so limited that something must be happening, you see: this is a very immaterial commodity, yet it allows an extraordinary circulation of general equivalents because none of these commodities is free; there are people who make a living out of them and these commodities are bought and sold. What is extraordinary is this physical contiguity.

This expansion of the notion of class creates some difficulties with respect to the individuation of subjects who can be leading, for instance, according to an old Seventies model: back then the factory worker used to lead the process of capitalist development along with the revolutionary process. Today it is difficult to individuate a subject of such import. Guido Bianchini, who is unfortunately dead too, would have said that this kind of individuation could only bring about a model of the revolution resembling an upside-down pyramid, in the sense of the Winter Palace, some rather old attempt at proposing once again the dictatorship of the proletariat and Leninist models. Perhaps he might have been right in some way, yet the inability to identify a subject probably carries with it clear organizational deficiencies, an organizational poverty and an unproductive discontinuity of initiatives. My tendency would be to identify leading subjects amongst women and in their behavior; but thank God women do not present homogeneous behaviors. There are reformist women, revolutionary women and conservative women, so I never speak of women as a subject in itself. However, the appreciation of gender issues in political practice is surely a source of transformation of a 'revolutionary' kind, because it rules out and provides an alternative to productivist views of social relations. In relation to the issues of progress, productivity, production, etc., seen in a socialist and good light, as the distribution of wealth that allows for freedom, a gender perspective on the other hand puts forward a problematic linked more to the use of productivity, the use of production, the use of wealth and issues thus connected to relational and personal development, well-being, etc. Here we can find a source of great transformation.

Something has always worried me: I think that all the elements we have analyzed, seen and developed in the Seventies (the mass worker, the rupture of the capitalist plan, etc.) were essentially right; however, capital anticipated us so these elements would have been right only if we had won, to use extremely modest words. Now the same thing seems to be happening; we try and understand these changes, to grasp this need. For instance, women made an issue of the question of time, flexibility, the need to live as elements of production and reproduction at the same time without the two conflicting and creating forms of double labor and things like that. Once we face forms of production that are framed exactly on this basis, the only difference is that the winners were those who are now organizing these forms of labor, rather than us. So I do not really understand why—given that we had the ideas—this is true: what happened? How come we always come second or always lose? I cannot answer this, but I can respond to this analysis. I evaluate European research projects and often travel to Brussels to look at them. I know people in the European Commission who tell me what they do: they put in practice things that my girlfriends and I had thought of two to three years earlier, but they do so for themselves. We say: 'Look at the poor women who must go to work in the morning, take their children to school, and there is the problem that school schedules conflict with work schedules, and when do they go shopping?' These are banal things, but we do enquiries on these issues and two years later the European Commission comes up with a great project to make labor in the family compatible with wage labor. This is a great defeat, because we were not asking for these to be made compatible, because that simply entails that you do one thing first and the other second, and life is not made easier this way! So there is a reason we asked certain things and they were understood differently: is it a kind of misunderstanding? Is it a form of nastiness towards us? I do not know: it is possible that we conceived of the issue in one way, we expressed the issue and they translated it in their own way. What is certain is that we lost, because I then find all the women in institutions, those who make up what I call institutional feminism, who immediately and diligently put these things into practice with the result that things never work for us. And I cannot understand the reason for this.

The feminism of the Seventies carried forward a program of liberation rather than emancipation, and did so with force and some violence; later, what seems to have survived time is exclusively the discourse on processes of emancipation, which has effectively been defended at the institutional level (as you were saying earlier) because many women choose autonomous labor and achieve a status, and some of them also take up positions of leadership in cooperatives where they make use of their feminist past. However, in the end, even if these roles are not taken up by men in the same way, they are equally functional to the same system: thus the issue of liberation seems to have been completely eliminated from the practices of these women.

I have my doubts about this, because what someone subjectively says of herself is one thing, and what objectively occurs when competences linked to a different body are inserted in a system where only male competences of a certain kind were previously allowed is another. I absolutely do not think that there is a biological destiny whereby women do different things from men, but I recognize their different historical and social development and experience: Roman slaves had a different experience than that of free people, a different attitude and sociocultural and relational background. So when a different body with a different experience is inserted, it does not do the same things and is not always functional to the demand of the productive or social structure. No studies have been done on this issue, but I am currently working on a research project, funded for three years by the European Commission, on gender and local management of change, in order to see if the few elected women bring with them practices and experiences that change the structuring of local policies, their form and substance. This is a project carried out in seven European states; in many cases this has already been confirmed by previous enquiries and I must say that here in Italy, at least judging from the three interviews we did (we work on the regions of Veneto, Emilia Romagna and Calabria), we began to realize that even if unconsciously women insert practices that will absolutely not be revolutionary, nevertheless they are different, even if they don't realize the differences in their behaviors. For instance, in local politics there is a greater awareness of civic duty, a more rational use of time, the reduction of meeting time, etc.; if they are local councillors they show a greater interest in relations with citizens, making sure that the relation between citizens and institutions is as smooth as possible, and rationalizing their offices, etc.; greater attention is given to the reproductive life of the city, old and disabled people, cyclists, nursery schools, etc. These are indications of a change that we could notice, which has nothing to do with the changes for instance of the party alliances of the local council or of the mayor, but has to do with a change of gender—they occur when a woman replaces a man. This is often due to the subjective awareness of women mayors who choose women councillors to lead departments of education or social services because they are more sensitive; but the change occurred whether this awareness was present or not.

To go back to your question, I would like to see enquiries made into this process of feminization, whether it is so painless and neutral, because I believe (and so does Drude Dalerup, a Dutch sociologist, and Ann Philips, a British political scientist) that by increasing the number of women in predefined social fields, not randomly—Drude Dalerup talks of a threshold of 40 per cent—if we reach this gender percentage we surely obtain individual and subjective forms of behavior that are more spontaneous and natural than those linked to a gender presence of 10 per cent. This is to say that so far this 10 per cent of women entrepreneurs or mayors has manifested behavior that is not too different, as you were saying, from that of men (even though I would always go and see what they do rather than just listen to what they say about themselves); however, the reason no perceivable change has occurred is that women as a minority group in this case tend towards homologation and thus identification with predefined forms of behavior: this is the easiest thing to do. Any individual, when entering a group, behaves like the elements of the group because the group has survived with this set of behaviors. This is an ethnological and Lorenzian analysis if you like. But if we were to exceed the 40 per cent threshold, individuals would start acting with greater freedom and would no longer need to conform to the dominant group, so only then could we see whether women can really do something different. Given that the tendency is to have more women in various social strata, in productive sectors, etc., maybe we will be able on the one hand to verify whether this is true, but in my opinion we will probably also see changes in the social and behavioral structure, especially in the relational one. I am absolutely certain of this, because to think otherwise would be like saying that if we put 40 per cent of immigrant workers in a factory they would all produce the same way because that's how capital forces them to produce: this can only be true if only 10 per cent of the workers were immigrants, but with 40 per cent of them I think something would happen, especially if they were culturally homogeneous, if they could represent themselves as a group. I think women can introduce, not revolutionary, but innovative elements that are not always and necessarily functional to the productive model. Then there is also the ability of capital to adapt, which seems infinite I must say, and always moves faster; but women are certainly neither directly nor simply functional—someone must give something up and I do not think women will do so from this point of view. Up until now they have manifested an attitude of assimilation to male behavior, but I think that when they have an option they will no longer do so. For instance, if we look at the analysis of choices to work part-time or in short-term contracts, everyone says: 'Yes, it is because women have babies so they prefer to work part-time so they can stay at home with the children.' But women who have children work full-time because they need money to raise them—they do not choose to earn less! Those who opt for part-time are young women who want to do shiatsu or go dancing. So there is this attitude of lack of respect for social rules, aside from the constraint to earn, I insist (when you have children you work to maintain them and cannot do otherwise); this attitude of disrespect for social rules is more manifest in women than in men, especially in young women, in the few investigations I have seen. This is also a wager, similar to the one we made when we said that the working class, when in power, would have accomplished extraordinary things.

In your opinion, would the change in behavior introduced by women once the 40 per cent threshold is reached in itself go in a direction that is incompatible with the system?

I think so, unless, I insist, the system goes through processes of adaptation that are as fast as those it has gone through recently; but generally I think this is not too compatible with the kind of productivity required today, though I do not know about the future. I think we are faced with such rapid processes of transformation that frankly I sometimes feel unable to grasp them. I am deeply involved in them, when I think that in 15 years' I have gone from one writing system to another with incredible rapidity: it took us cultures and centuries to move from one writing system to another in the past, whilst now the world has done it in 15 years. I say 15, but maybe it took longer. I started using a computer in 1984 or 1985 and I was one of the first ones: now I cannot live without it nor without the peripherals that I carry with me and attach to the computer. I now live in this system of communication (when I say 'writing system' in fact I am referring more to a communication system). It was 1986, perhaps 1987 (and I am old, but I'm not that old after all): I remember that the first time I saw a fax being sent, I had tears in my eyes looking at this piece of paper that was sending an article to Toni in Paris (I had just got back here), and I said: 'They will immediately see it there, on paper': I swear I was in tears when they installed a fax machine here in the university department and that was one of the first ones I sent. Things change incredibly fast and it is difficult to say 'Women will surely come and change everything': women can come to do exactly what they want in the labor market, but capital has already changed its needs. I do not even know whether women will be privileged subjects of change: all I can think of is that women are subjects truly capable of rapidly shifting from production to reproduction (also of themselves, though I hardly ever talk about children), and especially that they are capable of being extraneous to and not necessarily identifying themselves with the world of production (and in this women are the privileged subject). I have a notion similar to the exile, who lives away from her country and has somehow to invent how to live and what to do and who has no roots: in this sense I see women as well as immigrants as the subject. In other words, it must be a subject that has no memories, no history, and thus nothing to lose. If you asked me whether the unions will be the new organizational forms of class, I would answer no because they have already lost, not because they have something to lose. The subject cannot be that, though what remains is perhaps also to construct a subject. I think that young people embody well the idea of a new subject that I have in mind and I say it is women, but not necessarily: it is a subject that is gender-conscious and is thus aware that the world is made up of two genders that have a different social history that somehow we must entangle and turn into one, or maybe keep two of them and make them interchangeable, but this is not important. At the same time women represent for me the subject that moves easily, traverses borders and even though it has a place, it is a well-defined place that is not the ideal place; it has no homeland or anything like that and is more or less at home anywhere: this is the idea of the exile who has nothing to lose but can also insert herself everywhere, at ease when communicating and critically adaptable. This is normally the condition of the exile, and it is what I see in women when they assume working roles, even traditional ones. They are less participative than men and this perhaps is not linked to investigations I carried out but more to a personal and probably bodily knowledge, which I can see. I do not know to what extent these forms of behavior can produce organizational forms because I also have great perplexities regarding all organizational forms hitherto used in politics, parties as well as the party form itself, the party to build from groups to movements: beyond ephemeral forms that register a strong involvement and participation with very clear objectives (as I mentioned, the committees, and there can be many different objectives), the rest seem really bound to fail to create the stronger collective interest and participation that I witnessed in this area (people are always the same, so we cannot say that maybe it was better in Milan, but I speak of Padua). I regard the Internet and virtual organizations with great curiosity, but they do not convince me; rather than being inside them, I am passively involved with mailing lists and virtual communication. I am on the editorial board of the journal *Multitudes* so I am in Multitudes-info, but I do not even open some of the e-mails. I do not have the time and given that some things really don't interest me, I don't read them. So I don't really know if these are the new forms; Bifo believes so, but I don't as much, also because I do not believe in virtual participative forms, in the sense that at some point if the bodies don't come out I am distrustful, as I can observe from the way I relate to these structures.

On this topic, how much is left of the feminist militant practices of the movement, for instance the forms of self-consciousness or the criticisms leveled against organizational models?

The problem is that when you talk about this you are referring to a feminism that—in Italy for instance—lasted a very short time, no longer than two or three years; as far as forms of self-consciousness are concerned, in feminism this was an essentially elitist event, and there have been few consciousness-raising sessions. What is left of the critique of organizational forms is the fact that the organizational forms of that time have disappeared. If there was a relation of cause and effect it was a very effective critique, so it was the right one; it seems normal to me that the movement would not produce permanent alternative organizational forms. Some of the movement has been institutionalized and created relations with local institutions: all these women's houses that exist—maybe we do not realize it because we do not often go there, but they do exist. It is also true that the movement had a greater variety of organizational forms because it is false to say that it did not have it. We only have to think of the groups, journals, document centers, forms of political expression of the movement, such as the antiwar movement, etc. An interesting issue that seems more modern and recent is women's strong participation in movements linked to volunteering and in this sense I must say that there is a discourse of political practice very closely linked to women's behaviors, such as a political practice that has a more concrete aspect and can have some self-exposure: when one becomes a volunteer and cares for immigrants for instance, she knows that by the evening she fed 50 bowls of soup to 50 immigrants, or if one cares for prostitutes she knows that she is part of a team that goes around at night to distribute condoms or to ask prostitutes if they need help, advice or things like that. So it is a political practice, but maybe not strictly feminist in the traditional meaning of the term, yet it is practiced by a great majority of women: I ascribe it to one of these new practices of women that are not called feminist because when we interview these people, it is obvious that they are charity ladies, women with the awareness of being so and of caring for other women, and there is also an object that identifies their labor which seems very interesting. This new political practice is a mixture: it often relies on institutions because it has projects and asks for funding, but it creates an absolutely autonomous space for itself, often substitutive of what the institutions are supposed to do or do badly. Thus all this is done with a very reasonable attitude with regard to the policies of the institutions, and it is linked to a very feminine practice of relations that allows any mother of a family to organize the different timings, characters and bad feelings of a family, and to put together a social group that, despite living together, somehow does not kill itself in the majority of cases. This relational practice becomes the new way of doing politics and also registers innovative changes. I have been following for some time an association called Mimosa (now renamed Welcome; it had internal problems but this is not important). This association was practically set up by women, and then there is one priest and two boys. These women are medical students, nurses, who form a night team and go around to talk to prostitutes, do health projects and distribute condoms and do other things, so they often manage to get underage women out of the circle, they cooperate with the police to charge their exploiters so the police leave them alone for six months, they get placed in houses, etc. So these are problems I would not know how to deal with, yet they manage to find solutions that are extremely original and proper to civic living. We know of citizens' groups (you must have some terrible things in mind in Turin) who demonstrate against transvestites and prostitutes in their area: for instance, in a nearby area they managed to convince these so-called good citizens to enter forms of mediation by dividing up a street and getting the prostitutes to work somewhere further up the road but granting them a space, whilst pacifying a situation that was exploding into a civil war. In another area, prostitutes used to work near a supermarket and a school, because as we know the buildings that are full during the day are empty at night; they used to go there with their clients and there were condoms everywhere. So this group asked the municipal police to place some trash bins with lids there so that, when taking their children to school, mothers could find a clean road; then they went to the prostitutes and taught them to put everything in the bins, so they managed to create some kind of balance and nobody got killed or lynched in this area. These are trifles in comparison to the big issues, but this is a practice that institutions cannot create (imagine doing it here, where there are people who demand sheriffs!) and citizens cannot create, for they can only imagine forms of rebellion; so that these structures set up by women make relations in society and the territory more fluid. We might say that they are functional (to the system) in this way, that nobody rebels anymore, but the other form of rebellion against prostitutes scares me. Rebellion is not good in itself: this is why I think this kind of political practice constitutes a margin of good sense. They are not feminists, but they are feminists subjectively, even if they are in associations that are not necessarily feminine, since they do work with women. Another encouraging result (and this is why I would like to study these behaviors) is the fact that these people, unlike the local institutions, have a direct knowledge of the territory, of the subjects. For instance, I talk to them about how Nigerian, Albanian, Romanian women behave, and I would never dare to say prostitutes because each culture (not to say ethnicity because there are not that many of them) has a different attitude toward clients, toward condoms, hygiene, abortion even, toward whether or not to have a protector, toward criminality and drug dealing: so they have an impressive knowledge. Who is doing politics in this case? The head of the security department or these groups of women? Who is doing the real politics? Who is making the changes? Who manages to do something different on the territory? Let's not dwell on whether this is functional or not (to the system). I don't know. I ask myself this series of questions because this interests me more than understanding who the feminist groups are. I am part of the Casa delle Donne; we practically put it in the hands of a group of immigrants who manage it, organize lots of parties, and enjoy themselves a lot, and then there is a group of old women who have a library. We no longer go there; we like our own houses, so why should we go there? It is good for them to manage it and I prefer seeing what these people do with it. We invited them to tell us about their experiences, this is how I met them, and then they did not become a feminist group, but their issues for me are gender issues, in this case regarding prostitution for instance.

In relation to the university in general and to what the production of knowledge and science is (which is something you have worked on), what changes do you see taking place?

This is a complex issue: first of all there is a huge change in the university, with this three-plus-one scheme, this adaptation to European standards of diplomas. We still don't know what it will entail at the level of education. I have taught and continue to teach both here and in France, and the obvious rigidity in the structures of education in Italy scares me; I hope that this reform can shake that up at least. With respect to educational processes in general, for me it is the same thing: for our own happiness as well we have to get used to the fact that life is a process of continuous training. In the Nineties for instance there was a law proposed on the politics of time, that rather than dividing time into work, rest and free time, it divided time into work, rest, free time and time for oneself, which was the reproductive time, when one could also get education, study a different language, enrich oneself, go to the hairdresser, in other words enrich oneself by changing oneself. Well, this seemed a modern, intelligent and meaningful thing to do, because we have to learn to think in these terms. It is obvious that capital already does it, and it does it much better than the state, because capital rightly imagines educational processes as investment processes: this is what private schools are for, and they are surely better than state schools because they are regarded, I insist, as education for investment. On the contrary, for the state the school is often regarded as expense, as an expense item. If we do not manage, at the state, regional, local level, in any case at the public level, to create this attitude of investment for education, I think that everything will end up in the hands of capital and private schools—not necessarily Catholic ones, even though many Catholic schools are moving in this direction. In any case, these schools will be functional to capitalist needs rather than functional to what I like about education, which is the fact that one never finishes learning, but since it is not functional, learning is necessarily continuous and linked to the pleasure of understanding things and enriching oneself with knowledge. Clearly knowledge can be, historically and necessarily, socially productive; if it is only done by him who makes it functional to his own interests, then it will be productive for capital, but these are political choices that states have to make. Now in France 80 per cent of the population reaches secondary school, and I think they will get up to 100 per cent because the French state is following the idea that to educate and train people means to create wealth in the country. I don't know if it will be functional to capitalism but creating wealth also entails giving people the opportunity to enrich themselves. Today capital certainly needs educated individuals, but individuals also need education, and this would not scare me. I think that the important thing is the possibility to choose how, where and in what subject to get it. If one is forced to study marketing or go to one of the schools that now function to sell commodities (since producing them is no longer that useful), then the decision makers will have to take responsibility for having left education in the hands of those who necessarily will make it partial rather than a terrain for the achievement of freedom. On the other hand I am absolutely opposed to anyone who says that schools are places of indoctrination, that it is useless to attend them (here in Veneto we are familiar with this debate) and that one can produce, earn and live without going to school, which is often done.

NOTES

1. Editor's note: Porto Marghera, adjacent to Venice, was the largest petrochemical complex in Italy and a key site of early New Left organizing and agitation; in 1963 Negri and Massimo Cacciari organized a *Capital* reading group among workers there, many of whom subsequently joined Potere operaio. See Wright 2002: 110–14.
2. Editor's note: The Institute of Political Science at the University of Padua, which Negri directed. Among its members were most of the people Del Re mentions: Ferrari Bravo, Bianchini, Serafini, Marazzi, and Dalla Costa, as well as Sergio Bologna and Ferrucio Gambino. Most of them were arrested along with Negri on April 7, 1979. Negri reminisces about the Institute in his 2003 preface to *Trentatre lezioni su Lenin* (Negri 2004: 9–12).
3. Editor's note: Villages in the Veneto northeast of Padua and Venice.

4

A Party of Autonomy?[1]

Steve Wright

In loving memory of Ivan Conabere (1963–2002)—'Uno di noi'

Autonomia operaia is a party, from the phenomenal,
organizational and structural point of view.
—Judge Pietro Calogero (*La Repubblica* 1979: 120)

If only!
—Mario Dalmaviva, Luciano Ferrari Bravo, Toni Negri,
Oreste Scalzone, Emilio Vesce, Lauso Zagato (1979: 23)

This chapter seeks to explore, in a preliminary if critical manner, the debate over the party form played out within and around the groups of Autonomia Operaia during the late 1970s, when that area of revolutionary politics was briefly the dominant force within the Italian far left. Having assumed a leading role during the initial stages of 1977's 'strange movement of strange students' (Lerner, Manconi and Sinibaldi 1978), Italian autonomists finally found a mass audience for their debate around the meaning and purpose of political organization. This was to be a many-sided discussion while it lasted, conducted not only between the various 'microfractions' (Scalzone 1978a) that together claimed the label of Autonomia organizzata, but also with a range of critics 'outside and on its borders' (Martignoni and Morandini 1977).

Such arguments of a generation ago remain significant for a number of reasons. To begin with, they throw light on the work of Antonio Negri, surely the best known of those who then debated out the merits or otherwise of a 'party of autonomy'. Secondly, and without minimizing the differences that separate us from that time, the Italian experience of the late 1970s resonates in important ways for those seeking today to challenge the 'present state of things'. Did Autonomia's project fail despite its ambition to build a new kind of revolutionary party, or because of it? Can some new reading of Lenin and Leninism lend coherence to the multitude of struggles that circulate today, or should we rather 'let the dead bury their dead' (Marx 1852: 106), and seek instead forms of anticapitalist organization particular to the contours of contemporary class composition?

It is my contention in what follows that the Italy of the 1970s put paid once and for all to vanguardist pretensions, whether Leninist or otherwise.[2] With its roots planted firmly in a range of sectors—students (many of whom were also engaged in wage labor), workers in small firms, public employees from hospital staff to clerks—the so-called 'Movement of '77' brought together a rich tapestry of mass anticapitalist practices. Infused with an iconoclasm previously confined to feminist and left libertarian circles, the movement challenged not only the Communist Party's project of the Historic Compromise, but also the common sense of the New Left groups (Bologna 1977a; Cuninghame 2002a; Lumley 1990; Wright 2002). As Sergio Bologna (1980: 28–9) recognized at the end of that decade,

> the movement of 1977 was not only a totally different way of conceiving of the relation between life and politics, but a series of contents and values that had never been placed on the agenda of the political project. Despite having apparently left a void in its wake, despite having apparently only laid bare the crisis of political forms, including the crisis of the party-form, 1977 has to be considered one of the greatest anticipations of the forms and contents of political and social life seen in recent years. After 1977 there is no turning back, despite all the errors committed, and for which many are still paying in an atrocious manner. 1977 was a year in which the wealth and complexity of problems was such that the political form able to contain and organize them all adequately could not be found.

Before going further, however, it is worth asking what exactly is meant when talking of 'Autonomia'. The difficulties involved in this exercise have again been set out by Bologna, this time in a 1995 interview:

> there is always this danger of misunderstanding Autonomia as a political elite (*ceto politico*), Autonomia as a new type of political thought, Autonomia as the definition of a mass movement, or what? So, it's very difficult. Where can we begin? I believe the first thing to say is exactly to specify, to articulate these differences, basically between the different levels. As a result, from time to time, we have called Autonomia all three or four of these things together. So, we have to premise that this word, 'autonomy', is at the same time a very complex word but also highly ambiguous. What is important is not to create through this ambiguity some major contradictions. Keeping in mind that in fact the thought of Organized Autonomy, in particular the thought of Toni Negri, is a system of thought which in a certain sense has theorized ambiguity. Exactly on this point: the relationship between political elites, ideology and movement. This attempt to refuse

Leninism, to say essentially that the political forms of today are dynamic political forms which open (and) close, which are not permanent. Obviously, it was a way of hiding, shall we say, the dialectic between political elite and movement. (Cuninghame 2001: 97–8)

Let's briefly address each of these facets—'political elites, ideology and movement'—in turn. Like all political ensembles, whatever their creed, Autonomia possessed its own *ceto politico*: a multilayered stratum of activists committed to the movement's continuity through the ups and downs of its daily routine.[3] Such layers were constituted around different, yet often interpenetrating axes: class location, ideology, shared experience, personal and group loyalty.[4] As the movement waxed and waned across the decade, so too would the various fortunes of different layers and aggregations within this stratum. While the ultimate fate of its *ceto politico* was tied to Autonomia's self-defined 'organized' components, it cannot simply be reduced to the latter, given the important networks of militants to be found in other sections of the 'area'.

Then there is the question of ideology. The constellation of forces within Autonomia drew their ways of seeing from a broad array of traditions: not only the homegrown Marxist tendency of 'workerism' (*operaismo*) (Wright 2002), but also a host of other, often competing threads. For all that, there remained an identifiable core of shared beliefs within the movement, which Luciano Castellano (1980c: 8–15) would sum up as follows: the refusal of work (itself open to a variety of interpretations); the defence and extension of working-class needs against the logic of the market; the reading of capital as a social relation of power; and finally, as a consequence of the latter, a notion of capital's state form at odds with the mindset of orthodox Marxism. Regarding the state, as Negri (1979b: 190) was to put it in one of his early interrogations of 1979,

For 'Autonomia', take-over [of the state] is a meaningless term at least on two accounts: that no State power exists outside the material organisation of production; that there is no revolution except as a transitional process in the making and partly realized. It is therefore clear that 'Autonomia' rejects any idea of a State 'coup' through actions directed against the institutions. For the B.[rigate] R.[osse], proletarian liberation and any other effort and any moment of struggle in this sense are impossible if the State power structure is not attacked and destroyed.

Finally, there is Autonomia as a movement. As Cuninghame (2002a, 2002b) has carefully documented, there were in fact a number of

'Autonomies' (Borio, Pozzi and Roggero 2002) in the 1970s, even if here too each would at some point intersect with the others.[5] These were, in a rough chronological order of appearance:

1. the network of workplace militants that had inspired the movement's initial foundation;
2. an uneasy alliance of regionally based 'microfractions' striving for hegemony within the broader 'area of Autonomia' and beyond;
3. a 'diffuse' galaxy of independent local collectives, often courted by the 'organized' autonomists;
4. a 'creative' wing preoccupied with the politics of subversive communication;
5. last but not least, a myriad of tiny clandestine groups that had emerged from Autonomia organizzata or Autonomia diffusa—most commonly, from the stewards' organizations formed (as elsewhere in the Italian left) to protect members at demonstrations from police and fascists.[6]

This chapter concentrates on the second of these 'Autonomies', while casting an eye over the others to the extent that they engaged in the movement's debate around the party form. Then again, if a party project is by definition inseparable from the organization of *ceti politici* in pursuit of state power,[7] it is hardly surprising that the loudest calls for a 'party of autonomy' would emanate precisely from the ranks of Autonomia organizzata.

UNDERSTANDINGS OF THE PARTY IN THE EARLY AUTONOMIST MOVEMENT

> It is as the cutting edge [*punta offensiva*] of social class unification that the workers of the large factories reveal themselves to be an *absolutely hegemonic political and theoretical figure* within the current class composition.
> —Antonio Negri (1973a: 128)

We can begin the discussion by examining the notions of the party raised back in the very first days of Autonomia. What Cuninghame (2002a, 2002b) calls the 'autonomous workers' movement' began in part as a rejection of the party-building exercises of the New Left groups formed after 1968.[8] Increasingly preoccupied with their own organizational development, by the early 1970s such groups had shifted their focus from the workplace militants they had recruited in and around the Hot Autumn of 1969, towards projects of a rather different kind. For Lotta Continua, this entailed a reorientation from factory-oriented meetings wherein only workers were allowed to speak, to an emphasis by 1972 on campaigning in the streets against what it saw as the increasingly authoritarian involution of the ruling Christian Democrat party (Cazzullo 1998). Or take the case of the group founded by Negri and many other prominent workerist intellectuals: by 1971–72, as Bologna (1979: 11) once recalled, 'Potere Operaio chose instead as its reference point the *ceto politico* of the extra-parliamentary formations, to which it continued to pose the problem of militarisation.'

In the same period, a significant minority of radical workplace militants had come to agree with the Assemblea Autonoma di Porto Marghera (1972: 24)—long the mainstay of Potere Operaio in the petrochemical industry—that 'neither the groups of the revolutionary left, nor the [factory] councils weighed down by union control', were adequate vehicles for the mounting working-class struggle. A new party was sorely needed to 'direct the opening of a revolutionary process', argued a Roman circle of service-sector workers who chose to abandon the Manifesto group in 1972.[9] But this was to be an organization built first and foremost in the factory and office, and within which workplace militants could finally realize the earlier promise made by Potere Operaio and other groups of a 'working-class direction' to revolutionary politics. A weighty anthology of autonomist texts compiled in the mid 1970s by the Romans provides ample documentation of the prevalence of such views during the movement's early years. For militants at Milan's Alfa Romeo plant, writing in 1973, the 'party of the working class' had to be the direct expression of 'the various autonomous movements', rather than of 'intellectuals who provide the line, and then descend to the factory in search of vanguards to carry it out'. According to the introductory report tabled at the first national gathering of autonomist circles in 1973, the revolutionary party could not be established through the existing New Left groups, but only through 'the centralisation from below of the mass vanguards' (now in Comitati Autonomi Operai (CAO) 1976a: 23, 25, 42).

Given this equation between revolutionary leadership and the workers of the large factories—popularized by Negri (1973b) with the phrase 'party of Mirafiori'—nonworker activists were always going to have a particular role within the early Autonomia. To be sure, there were many struggles in which workers and others could act side by side: for example, in local neighborhood campaigns supporting housing occupations and the 'self-reduction' of rising public utility and transport bills (Ramirez 1975). There were also arenas—such as the schools—in which nonworkers were encouraged 'to start from their own needs' so as to then feed the latter into the wider class struggle against capital (Collettivo Politico del Berchet 1974: 23). Even here, however, autonomy meant 'being with the factory organisms, uniting on the basis of the program rather than dividing over lines, affirming the centrality and leadership of the factory organisms rather than of professional politicians' (Collettivo Politico del Berchet 1974: 23). As for political activities around the large factories, nonworker members of Autonomia were commonly assigned the kind of support role that 'external' activists had provided at FIAT and elsewhere in the late 1960s. Indeed, those who argued, like Negri and his close associates, that 'the working class becomes party through the centralisation of its own movements' (Potere Operaio 1973: 211), soon abandoned the ranks of Potere Operaio in favor of collaboration with such 'factory organisms'. But such a division of labor also held the potential to breed considerable resentment, as is evident in the following account from the Veneto:

> . . . in this donkey-work argument, one side was loaded with work and then found it counted for nothing, treated like shit. They used you, but if someone had a problem they sent you home. People didn't eat, they were there every morning to hand out leaflets, do pickets, they really bust themselves, but the organisation was done by the Workers' Autonomous Assembly. (Quoted in Cuninghame 2002a: 72)[10]

Working in a region where the 'mass worker' of Fordist production was far from the most typical component of the local class composition, many of the Veneto activists soon came to rethink this role:

> the argument we made was that the organisation had to be inclusive, that beyond the strategic argument the complexity was in the fact that we were all in this organisation [. . .] made up of students, workers, [that] it would be better if it called itself an inclusive organisation and not one calling itself workers, even if autonomous. (Quoted in Cuninghame 2002a: 72)

At first predominant within Autonomia, militants from the large factories had largely lost their earlier influence by 1977. The reasons for this are myriad, from the political disaffection of some of the original workplace activists to the savage impact of industrial restructuring, which saw many revolutionaries expelled from the immediate process of production after 1974. Equally important was the growing interest in the movement's ideologies and practices amongst a new generation based in schools, the service sector, or smaller firms, locales from whence the 'diffuse' collectives of Autonomia would draw much of their sustenance. Last but not least, there was the strategic realignment of many within the *ceto politico* that increasingly described itself as Autonomia organizzata. Conscious of the movement's shifting social base, many of the latter chose with the Veneto collectives to reconfigure themselves as miniature political organizations (Wright 2002: 158–62).

In these changed circumstances, the autonomist debate over the party would assume connotations that were both new, and yet somehow strangely old.

THE PARTY BUILDERS OF ORGANIZED AUTONOMY

> There still exists the concrete risk of 'groupuscule' [*gruppiste*] temptations, a risk that Autonomia Operaia Organizzata absolutely must not run.
>
> (CAO 1974: 242–3)

If nothing else, the debate within Autonomia organizzata over the party form was often fierce, closely entwined both with ideological disagreements and the practical realities of shifting realignments amongst the various 'microfractions'. A cursory glance at the joint statements issued across 1977 by most of the major groups within 'organized autonomy' (the notable absence being the Romans of the Comitati Autonomi Operai)[11] might suggest the beginnings of national cohesion. But this is a false impression, as even a preliminary survey of the groups' various perspectives throws light on the reasons why a 'party of autonomy' was never a serious likelihood in the Italy of the 1970s.

A Party for the Soviets?—the Comitati Autonomi Operai

> Not the party of Autonomia Operaia . . . but the party-instrument . . . that from the beginning must contain the premises of its own extinction.
>
> (CAO 1978c)

With its own trajectory and traditions, grounded in a class composition very different from that found in Lombardy or the Veneto, it is little surprise to discover that the major Roman autonomist grouping held distinctive views on the party. In a first attempt to clarify its politics, the Manifesto group (1971: 433–4) had spoken briefly of those 'councils' through which the mass movement must organize itself in the contemporary struggle 'for communism'.[12] For the Comitati Autonomi Operai (CAO),[13] by contrast, the championing of councils was from the beginning at the heart of their understanding of political organization and social change. Indeed, by the end of the decade this advocacy of working-class 'direct democracy' against the 'delegated democracy' of capital would join the aggressive assertion of working class needs as the defining features of the Volsci's political ideology (CAO 1978c).

More than most sections of 'organized autonomy', throughout their existence the Comitati Autonomi Operai retained some of the distinctive characteristics of the early autonomist movement. Its basic unit was a collective constituted in a specific suburb or workplace (most famously, the Policlinico teaching hospital—Stame and Pisarri 1977): in some cases these were also open to militants from outside 'organized autonomy'.[14] Coupled with this was a broader 'city-wide assembly', also open to participation by circles outside the CAO (Del Bello 1997). Not surprisingly, then, the group's initial efforts to make sense of the party form would echo these structures, through an original interpretation of the meaning of revolutionary organization.

Writing in 1974, the CAO reflected upon the failure of the Russian revolution, and in particular upon the process by which the power of workers organized in councils (soviets) 'was transformed into the dictatorship of the party over the proletariat'.[15] Against this, the Volsci expressed considerable interest in recent Chilean events, which before the military coup had seen the emergence of councils (*cordones*) seeking to group together all sections of the class, including the unemployed. Rejecting the traditional models bequeathed by the communist movement, the Romans proposed a form of organization that would maintain for a 'long' period to come the dual characteristic of ends and means, the anticipation, that is, of soviet and party. Accomplishing this, however, requires from the start those characteristics of direct democracy and autonomy that characterize the anticipation of the soviet, and the subjectivity, the starter motor (*motorino*), the cadre schools, that characterize the anticipation of the party (in CAO 1976a: 68, 68–9). Another document from May of the following year indicates that, at least in the period before 1977, a number of more conventional Leninist precepts continued to inform the Romans' outlook. Arguing that as a means rather than the end of revolution, 'the party must develop working-class autonomy and not substitute itself for it', a case was made nonetheless for the view that the 'full expression' of working-class consciousness could only be brought 'from without' (in CAO 1976a: 376). At the same time, there were already hints of a shift towards some alternative framework. The CAO's 1976 anthology closes by interviewing a prominent Volsci member at the Policlinico hospital. According to Daniele Pifano, Italian workers were now obliged to make a 'qualitative leap', carrying them from the defence of working-class needs to a political strategy of imposing such needs upon society as a whole. This, he stressed, was a task that could not be left to the party alone. Citing the Chilean case, Pifano noted with disappointment the absence there of

any revolutionary party or force that didn't limit itself to providing the maximum impulse to these structures [the *cordones*—SW], but promoted their city-wide, regional, national centralisation, that restored to the masses their own capacity to elaborate directly a political–military strategy, to take charge of and practice this directly beyond the restricted professional cadre of the party. (In CAO 1976a: 384)

The CAO would be very prominent in the upheavals of 1977. Like many other components of Autonomia organizzata, it was often accused by its political rivals of attempting to impose its hegemony both within movement assemblies and through a confrontational approach to street demonstrations (Bernocchi et al. 1979: 38–42). At first, the group was hopeful that the new cycle of struggles would reinvigorate the various 'organized autonomist' circles as part of a wider project of 'mass counterpower' (CAO 1977: 166). As it became clear by early 1978 that more and more of the initiative within the Italian far left was passing to the Brigate Rosse and its program of clandestine politics, the CAO would lay much of the blame at the feet of its northern counterparts. Building upon criticisms first voiced with Potere Operaio's collapse (CAO 1979b), the Volsci accused that group's former members not only of seeing the construction of a revolutionary vanguard as necessarily separate from mass organization, but worse still of privileging the former over the latter (CAO 1978d: 13). While the CAO placed its emphasis upon establishing 'stable institutions of the proletariat' (CAO 1978e: 1), many of the ex-members of Potere Operaio were accused of holding to 'a rigidly Leninist conception of the party' (CAO 1978f: 13). Compounding the problem, the Volsci continued, was the failure of the 'organized autonomists' to maintain any serious and sustained work around the large factories, despite this being the original rationale of the movement (CAO 1978b: 19). As for particular tendencies within Autonomia, Negri's circle— already criticized in 1976 for the abstractness of their notion of the 'socialized worker' (Wright 2002: 171)—was now dressed down for the voluntarism of its program of linked 'campaigns' (CAO 1979a: 6). Once dismissed for the overly reductionist nature of their analyses (CAO 1976b), many of Oreste Scalzone's longtime associates received a similar drubbing, this time for writing off the whole of Autonomia organizzata as a political failure (CAO 1979d).

After the Bologna conference of September made clear the growing isolation of Autonomia organizzata within the broader Movement of 1977, the CAO proposed its own project of national unification. This was to be a 'Movement of Workers' Autonomy'—MAO, to use its Italian acronym— pitched above all at 'autonomia diffusa' (CAO 1978c). Insisting that the Movement of 1977 had proved incapable of converting its 'antagonistic force' into 'programmatic terms', the document reiterated the Volsci's longstanding commitment to the development of mass forms of dual power. Since the primary concern of the proletariat was 'to win as a class, rather than lose as a party', the purpose of political activity was to work towards the creation of soviets as 'the representative expression of class unity' within a project of counterpower. Here a party organization—'as the self-management of revolutionaries, as the prefiguring of a new form of cooperation between communists'—had a key role to play. This time round, however, its function was not to bring consciousness to the class from outside, but rather to help clear away those obstacles to the latter's own struggle for self-emancipation, since 'an awareness of capitalist laws is not immediately given in the proletariat's class behaviors'. In a period when no single sector of the class had emerged as a pole of recomposition, the MAO was intended to encompass both party and soviet functions. Within it there was no space for either full-time militants or professional revolutionaries: instead, 'each of us is the party and together we will all form the political line', while wielding an equal political weight in decision making. Nor was the formation of authentic soviets the project of one organization or ideology, but could only be achieved in cooperation with 'other social political forces'.

In the end, the MAO initiative would prove stillborn, unable to break the Volsci's isolation within the broader movement. On the other hand, the project hinted at the degree to which some sections of Autonomia organizzata were prepared to rethink their role. In this regard, perhaps the most intriguing aspect of the CAO's reflections upon the party was the explicit connection made between organizational structure and function on the one hand, and *ceto politico* on the other. Noting that the goals of the latter often entailed 'its own self-preservation' and/or the consolidation and extension of influence, an anonymous writer in *I Volsci* suggested a link between pretensions to the status of 'external vanguard' and theoretical rigidity in social analysis. Indeed, they insisted, 'The more external a *ceto politico* is to social subjects, the more centralized, hierarchical and separate its form of organization' (CAO 1979c: 15).

'From "extremists" to revolutionaries'—the tendency around Oreste Scalzone

> If strategy is *implicit* in the class, in its processes of recomposition, it can be actualized by the subjective action of the party . . . articulating and determining this strategy concretely, through decisive passages of *grand tactics* . . .
>
> (Comitati Comunisti Rivoluzionari (Cocori) 1977: 46)

Despite the Leninist ardor of its leading members, the Comitati Comunisti per il potere operaio (CC) and its successor Cocori were amorphous entities, prone to splits and realignments, with many cadre ultimately being lost to the armed groups, Prima Linea above all (Stajano 1982; Progetto Memoria 1994). Initially, however, the Comitati Comunisti were able to regroup a range of circles in Lombardy around the journal *Senza Tregua* from 1975 onwards. These included not only associates of Oreste Scalzone from Potere Operaio, who had once opposed Negri's proposal to liquidate their organization into the early autonomist movement, but also a significant exodus from the local Lotta Continua. The latter came above all from Sesto San Giovanni, a 'Stalingrad' of older industrial complexes soon to face significant job losses through workplace restructuring (Cazzullo 1998: 238–9). The former members of Lotta Continua included a number of prominent militants from the Magneti Marelli factory, and the Comitati Comunisti's intervention there would pioneer a distinctive approach to organizing, around what it called 'the workers' decree'. Years later, Scalzone and Lucia Martini (Martini and Scalzone 1997: 555) would recall this 'social, cultural, political' experience as follows:

> the discourse on 'the workers' decrees' [concerned] the capacity of a network of revolutionary class vanguards to express their counterpower over the territory, over the entire social organization. The reduction of working hours and the social wage, a guaranteed income for all as the right to life: given these two axes of demands, what was needed was to approximate them in forms of struggle. The struggle against enterprise command, factory discipline, productivity increases; the struggle against prices, tariffs, rents. It was something different, harder and more bitter than the 'We Want Everything' of '69: it entailed affirming a sort of new *citoyenneté*, introducing irreversible modifications into the social state of things.

Stated in less grandiose terms, the 'decree' entailed the imposition of demands upon management in the workplace, theorized as workers 'organizing their own force to exercise power'. Such actions were seen as crucial steps in the consolidation of that 'communist working class fraction' (in CAO 1976a: 108) which had made the workplace department (*reparto*) '*the privileged place of debate, of political decisions, of initiative, of struggle*' (CC 1976: 120). As a consequence, the Comitati Comunisti concluded, party responsibilities 'in the current conditions of conflict' fell upon this stratum, which was obliged to challenge within the factories the 'working-class right' and its project of damping down class conflict (in CAO 1976a: 109, 108).

By early 1977 the CC had begun to echo Negri's thesis of the 'socialized worker'. Even then, the group continued to assign a strategic role to factory militants. Only this cadre, *Senza Tregua* suggested, was capable of bridging the divide between emerging militant sectors such as hospital workers and those parts of the 'old' class composition hit hardest by restructuring (CC 1977c: 73). In a giant broadsheet distributed in March of that year, the Comitati Comunisti (1977a: 4) insisted upon 'the stabilization of new levels of formal organization *for* the revolutionary party of the proletariat as communist organization of combat and program'. This was to be achieved through the immersion and renovation of the existing structures of Autonomia in the new Movement of 1977, itself centered on 'the network of factory communist vanguards who in recent months have promoted (as a minimal but decisive terrain) autonomous struggle, resistance to restructuring and the first forms of opposition to the "social pact"' (CC 1977b: 1).

The hegemony within *Senza Tregua* of the militarist faction soon to be known as Prima Linea[16] would lead Scalzone and others to establish the Comitati Comunisti Rivoluzionari (Cocori). In a pamphlet produced for the 1977 Bologna conference, Cocori spelt out its own distinctive views on the party's role. The problem facing revolutionaries, it stated bluntly, was the conquest of 'a majority discourse' within the working class. For this to succeed, the 'organized autonomists' were obliged to engage in '*a process of radical rectification*' (Cocori 1977: 1). Cocori conceded that 'today we live in a "post-Bolshevik" epoch' characterized by the presence of the 'material bases' for communism. While this excluded the need for any distinct 'socialist' stage under the guidance of a party-state (Cocori 1977: 46), it did not minimize the need for a 'neo-Leninist' approach to organization premised upon 'a subjectivity external to the class'. Unlike the Volsci, Cocori saw nothing inherently revolutionary in the pursuit of working class needs, which in any case risked collapse into 'a paralysing Babel'; only the party could ensure an appropriate 'selection and synthesis . . . within the universe of needs' (Cocori 1977: 45, 44–5). Not that the class was 'backward'; rather, the agility of capital's command demanded the creation of a party instrument possessed of that 'offensive technique for [the state's] destruction' absent from the proletariat's struggles within and against the capital relation (Cocori 1977: 44, 45). At the same time, Cocori did not itself claim to be a pole of regroupment, let alone what it disparagingly termed a 'microparty'. Instead, it aimed to be a 'communist center of initiative' within a broader process of revitalization on the path to 'the party of the revolution' (Cocori 1977: 1).

A year later, Scalzone would reiterate many of these arguments, albeit in a more difficult context and a far gloomier frame of mind. With Cocori now repeating the earlier trajectory of *Senza Tregua* (Progetto Memoria 1994: 89), his attention shifted to a new editorial project encompassing both the *Pre-print* pamphlet series and the journal *Metropoli*. Agreeing with Galvano Vignale (1978a: 29) that 'except as a legacy and wealth of political personnel, *Autonomia is finished*, period', Scalzone (1978a: 34, 35) accused the 'organized autonomists' of placing their continued function as competing components of a *ceto politico* ahead of the strategic rethinking demanded by recent events. Isolating itself from the national metalworkers' demonstration of December 1977, Autonomia organizzata had fallen back upon 'tried and true' formulae from the mid Seventies, such as physical force campaigns of 'militant' antifascism.[17] Faced with the Moro kidnapping and murder, Autonomia had refused to address the social roots of the terrorist phenomenon, let alone engage in political debate with the Brigate Rosse, as Cocori (1978) had counseled at the time. Instead, most of its components had simply wrung their hands, or like the Volsci and Negri's group had demonized those advocating the militarization of class struggle.

As for the party form, Scalzone (1978a: 49) repeated Cocori's argument about the consequences that stemmed from the present ' "post-Bolshevik" epoch'. Since 'the general movement tends to posit itself as a modern "mass Leninist subject"', the specific functions of the party would ultimately decline. Until that tendency reached its full fruition, however, 'a residual necessity' for Bolshevism remained (Scalzone 1978b: xxxiii). Here the party was conceived not as a 'demiurge', but rather as a force able (a) 'to interdict' capital's effort to obstruct the proletariat's constitution as a revolutionary subject; (b) '*to enervate* the organizational processes of class subjectivity'; and finally (c) to develop a critique of politics that challenged the existing 'social common sense' (Scalzone 1978a: 59). Given the woeful state of Autonomia, only modest steps were possible in the here and now. Rejecting the proposal of a 'party of autonomy' as at best a lashing together of the existing microfractions, Scalzone argued instead for a 'center of initiative' able to promote 'elements of partial synthesis' within the class struggle, while conceding '*the long purgatory*' (Scalzone 1978a: 62) facing those committed to revolutionary organization. A few short months later, Judge Calogero and his associates would make of these words a grim irony, as the state crackdown against Autonomia began with a vengeance.

'The reasoned use of force?'—the Collettivi Politici Veneti

> The combination of all forms of struggle, legal and illegal,
> mass action and the reasoned used of force, the capacity

> of political leadership, enabled [*costruirono*] the effective
> hegemony of this experience throughout the Veneto.
>
> (Arsenale Sherwood 1997)

While Negri's presence at the University of Padova was an important intellectual reference point within the Italian far left, the dominant autonomist group in the Veneto region would take a path quite different from his own. According to one reconstruction by former participants, the origins of the Collettivi Politici Veneti per il potere operaio (CPV) lay with a younger generation of activists keen to maintain the structures developed within the local Potere Operaio (M.U. 1980: 11). Perplexed by the divisions that had torn apart their organization at the national level, they felt little sympathy for the orientation of Negri and his ilk towards the existing workplace collectives:

> We couldn't understand—they said—what the choice of the factory autonomous assemblies would mean for us. We were nearly all students, and we didn't see any sense in reducing ourselves to the role of 'supporters' of workers' struggles. (Quoted in Fondazione Bruno Piciacchia e Libreria Calusca di Padova 1997: 465)

Instead, the Veneto group chose to build upon the networks established through earlier projects around public transport, the cost of living and militant antifascism, slowly reaching out from Padova to other centers in the region (Fondazione Bruno Piciacchia e Libreria Calusca di Padova 1997: 465–7; Zagato 2001: 8). While their decision to maintain the local structure of Potere Operaio for some time after 1973, along with the 'classically Leninist' nature of their organizational culture (Benvegnù 2001: 2), indicated certain affinities with Scalzone's circle, the CPV seem to have kept their distance from the Comitati Comunisti (Ferrari Bravo 1984: 194–5). Indeed, for a time in the late 1970s they would align themselves with Rosso, before once again striking out on their own, although continuing to collaborate with some of Negri's associates in the journal *Autonomia* and the movement station Radio Sherwood.

The CPV would also become renowned for the practice of what has euphemistically been termed 'the reasoned use of force', from the sabotage of property (Anonymous 1978a, 1978b) to the physical intimidation (and sometimes wounding) of those deemed the movement's ideological enemies (Petter 1993). If some such acts engendered only revulsion outside its ranks, the wave of 'mass illegality' of which they were part has also been justified by some of the CPV's former exponents as 'the best antidote' to the influence within the region of the likes of the Brigate Rosse and Prima Linea (Fondazione Bruno Piciacchia e Libreria Calusca di Padova 1997: 468).

The views of the Collettivi Politici Veneti on organization would be spelt out at greatest length in a draft document published in the May 1979 issue of the journal *Autonomia*. Following an editorial that lamented the 'insufficient and artisanal' efforts to construct a centralized autonomist movement at the national level (Collettivo editoriale di *Autonomia* 1979: 3), the CPV (1979: 18) argued that while the project of the party must be grounded in class composition, current struggles had seen a dramatic and growing divide between possibilities and their practical realization. Unlike other champions of the socialized worker, they saw the latter as above all a latent political project, one that could never emerge without 'party organization' (Collettivi Politici Veneti 1979: 18). Unlike so many other fractions of Autonomia organizzata, the Veneto group believed it possible and desirable even at this stage to engage in dialogue over political perspectives with what it termed 'the communist comrades of the "armed party" ' (Collettivi Politici Veneti 1979: 20). Criticizing the latter's fixation upon the leadership of the PCI as a central stumbling block for the revolutionary process,[18] the CPV argued for a rethinking of the proper relation between clandestine and 'nonclandestine' practices, since 'The movement needs to enrich itself with the complexity of the problems . . . to arm and strengthen itself and accept the capitalist challenge on all fronts of the class conflict' (Collettivi Politici Veneti 1979: 21). Alongside this, the Veneto group sought to affirm, against what it saw as confusion elsewhere within Autonomia, the necessity of 'separateness between communist subject and spontaneous movements':

> Separateness not in the sense that one is on the Moon and the others here on Earth, but in the capacity to organize with continuity the proletarian initiative within spontaneous submovements, with the autonomy precisely of political struggle and critique within them. (Collettivi Politici Veneti 1979: 21)

Such continuity, it went on, was the responsibility of an 'Organized Communist Movement' (MCO), a network of proletarian activists which differentiated itself from the various mass movements (themselves commonly articulated on a territorial basis) through its 'political line'. Finally, at the head of the MCO stood a *'central structure*, of direction, of political and organizational synthesis', capable of embodying 'the concept and the materiality of the party'. And if there was any doubt on the matter, readers were reminded that the success of such a project demanded *'the maximum possible unity and discipline'* (Collettivi Politici Veneti 1979: 22).

In the final section of the document, the CPV further delineated their views through a critique of other autonomist 'microfractions'. Negri's group, for example, was condemned for addressing the party question in 'wholly ideological and general political terms', as well as for developing an ambitious program that it was ill-equipped to put into practice. The Comitati Autonomi Operai of Rome, on the other hand, were accused of holding an 'instrumental and nonstrategic' understanding of organization, while steadfastly dodging all efforts to be drawn into a centralized, national structure. In the end, the CPV concluded, the Roman's MAO project represented an obstacle not only to the further development of its primary audience of 'autonomia diffusa', but also a step back 'for *all* the forces of Aut. Op. Org' (Collettivi Politici Veneti 1979: 24).

'A party of autonomy'—Antonio Negri and the Collettivi Politici Operai

> The worst and oldest error is the constitution or reconstruction of the 'group' . . . [with its] . . . paleo-Leninist schemas of organization (democratic centralism, professionalization of leaders, organized division of labor).
>
> (Rosso 1975: 235, 236)

Those in the English-speaking world who have heard of Autonomia are likely to have heard also of Antonio Negri. For much of the 1970s, Negri would be a member of the Collettivi Politici Operai (sometimes known as Rosso, after their newspaper), an autonomist group based primarily in and around Milan, and drawing its early cadre from former members of both Potere Operaio and the Gruppo Gramsci (Wright 2002: 153). With a certain initial presence in the local car industry, the group's orientation would slowly shift over the decade, as it looked with increasing interest to the 'proletarian youth circles' of Milan's hinterland.[19] Able to draw upon the prestige both of Negri as an intellectual, and of *Rosso* as a paper (around which an alliance of sorts was formed in the mid Seventies both with the Volsci and some of Franco Berardi's circle in Bologna), the CPO was long the leading component of Autonomia organizzata within the Milan radical left. On the other hand, in the face of competition from *Senza Tregua* and a number of other 'organized autonomist' groupings (Moroni 1994), the CPO was never able to attain the sort of local hegemony secured by the CAO in Rome or the CPV in the Veneto.

How did Negri assess other approaches to political organization within Autonomia? Some pointers lie in his assessment of the Volsci's views on the matter. Dismissing the latter's *leitmotif* of 'direct democracy' as dominated by 'the logic of individual needs and of the scarcity of resources' (Negri 1976a: 134), Negri would offer a more detailed critique of the

Romans' perspectives as part of the Collettivi Politici Operai's contribution to a debate within Autonomia on organization. Here it was suggested that the preconditions that made a 'soviet' model of revolution conceivable— a 'molecular' system of production wherein each enterprise constituted 'a moment of power'; a socially homogenous working-class community; a state form whose functions were 'immediately transferable to the direct management of the masses' (Collettivi Politici Operai (CPO) 1976a: 10)— were all absent in the Italian case. On the other hand, it was argued, the allusion of the soviet model to the '*direct, inalienable* character' of working-class power was both praiseworthy and actual. Rather than offer any detailed alternative of their own at this point, however, Negri's group suggested that the discourse on organization could only arise 'from within the organization of the concrete behaviors of the masses'. The key thing to remember, it concluded, was that 'the problem of organization and that of the program arise together' (CPO 1976a: 10). What this meant in practical terms was spelt out in another article from the same issue of *Rosso*, which identified the primacy of a series of 'current objectives' (*obiettivo di fase*), ranging from struggles in the factory to those against rising costs and repression (CPO 1976b: 2).

If this emphasis upon specific campaigns able to embody an anticapitalist program failed to resonate with many others amongst the 'organized autonomists', it did strike a chord with one of the minor Marxist–Leninist organizations of Italy's north. Already back in 1975, in his pamphlet *Proletari e Stato*, Negri (1976a: 70) had praised 'the party process in the Marxist–Leninist sense' as the path to be followed. These efforts at courtship began to pay off by 1976, with an increasing attention to Autonomia in general, and the work of Negri in particular, evident in the pages of *Voce Operaia* (Leonetti 1976), published by the Partito Comunista (marxista-leninista) Italiano. Indeed, by December of that year, the PC(m-l)I had joined with Rosso to draft a 'platform' with four central points: struggle over the wage; struggle against work; struggle against command; and struggle against the state (Recupero 1978: 34–5).[20] A year later the PC(m-l)I had, to all intents and purposes, become another 'microfraction' within Autonomia organizzata, before ultimately dissolving sometime before the end of the decade.

The question of the party was clearly a central preoccupation for Negri throughout 1977. Alongside some essays in *Rosso* that year, his views are set out in two key texts: the pamphlet *Dominio e sabotaggio* (Negri 1977b), and the closing chapter of the book *La forma stato* (Negri 1977a). Already in the opening chapter of the latter, written in January, Negri (1977a: 24) had posed what he held to be 'the fundamental problem', namely 'that of organization, of *What Is To Be Done?*' Significantly, the title of *The State Form*'s last chapter ('From *Left Wing Communism* (*Estremismo*) to *What Is To Be Done?*') would directly invoke another of Lenin's most strident calls for vanguard organization. For all its talk of self-valorization, or the passing dismissals of the 'autonomy of the political', the notion of the party advanced by Negri here was strongly reminiscent of Mario Tronti's views from a decade earlier. Having posed 'the problem of the *State* as the problem of *capital's party*', Negri turned to 'the problem of the *party* as the problem of the *State of the working class*: better, of the anti-State, of workers' power' (Negri 1977a: 334). Since the process of working-class self-valorization—'the possibility of not working hard, of living better, of guaranteeing the wage'—remained both 'inside and outside capital', it was not in itself able to break free of class society. What was needed, therefore, was the class' 'organized political force' able 'to accelerate and lead towards a definitive rupture of the capital relation' (Negri 1977a: 339). Just as Tronti (1971: 236) had argued in 1965 that 'the *society of capital* and the *workers' party* find themselves [to be] two opposing forms with the same content', so Negri held in early 1977 that

> *The work of the party is therefore the exact opposite of that which constitutes capital's modification of the material constitution.* The party is the anti-State, through and through [*fino in fondo*]. Opposite points of view are exercised upon the dual nature [*duplicità*] of this class composition: the capitalist will to legitimate again the processes of administration and exploitation, and the working-class will to administer proletarian independence, to the point of attacking the State and destroying the wage system. Parallel and opposite, two equal and contrary forces act upon the class composition. (Negri 1977a: 339)

Viewed through these lenses, the meaning of the party was less about structure than function. This was not a party that claimed to represent the class: rather, its purpose was to manage the disarticulation of capitalist domination. It was a vanguard in a literal sense, the minesweeper that cleared a passage for the workers' advance. But it was more than this, too: it was also a general staff. Thus, while Negri (1977a: 342) paid formal homage in this text to the autonomist slogan of 'the refusal of delegation', there was no question but that the process of proletarian unity was the responsibility of a specialized layer within the class. In his words, 'This work of recomposition through the destruction [of capital's command] must be completely in the hands of the collective brain of workers' struggle' (Negri 1977a: 342).

Reviewing the development of the Movement of 1977, a June article in *Rosso* highlighted what the CPO saw as a dangerous polarization between those pushing an 'insurrectionalist' perspective and those who saw the development of struggle in gradualist terms. Since every advance in 'proletarian power' was now matched by 'greater force' and repression, it fell to 'the communist organization' to break this vicious circle from within a strategic approach based upon 'the mass line' (Rosso 1977a: 169). Against those who declared themselves the 'combatant party' and saw class struggle as a battle between 'different and counterposed "state apparatuses"', *Rosso* spoke of the need for 'the party as organizer of civil war and direction of the proletarian army' (Rosso 1977a: 170). The rejection of both insurrectionalist and gradualist sensibilities was continued in a *Rosso* article prepared for the Bologna conference. Here the outlook of the Brigate Rosse was singled out for its militarism, which failed to understand the strategic significance of 'the great masses' process of liberation' (Rosso 1977b: 176). All the same, if 'the bad infinity' between class recomposition and repression was to be broken, the question of 'vanguard organization' could not be avoided. While the crisis of the state form had engendered a crisis of the party form, it was nonetheless the case that 'the constitution of a political instrument that we insist on calling party is as plausible on the scientific level as it is absolutely necessary on the practical level' (Rosso 1977b: 177). Holding that 'a stable organization' could not be established 'in bureaucratic–formal terms', Rosso concluded by reiterating its often stated view that only a series of related campaigns was able to provide the basis through which a new national formation—'the collective organizer of social subversion' (Rosso 1977b: 176, 177)—might aggregate through struggle.

The precise relation between this 'collective organizer' and the broader process of 'social subversion' was made clear in Negri's pamphlet *Dominio e sabotaggio*, written in early September 1977. Significantly, in this piece Negri would requalify his views in a number of important ways. To begin with, in testimony to the Movement of 1977's vitality, the fundamental dialectic in class society was stated in new terms, with self-valorization now coming to supplant the party as the state's chief antagonist, 'the opposite of the concept of the "State-form"' (Negri 1977b: 15).[21] In contrast to his position of eight months previously, Negri here asserted that self-valorization did indeed embody the capacity to break the capital relation, since it was itself 'the strength [*forza*] to withdraw from exchange value and the capacity to base itself on use values' (Negri 1977b: 22; see also 38). As for the party, *Dominio e sabotaggio* bluntly asked whether such an entity still had any useful role to play in the revolutionary project. Echoing concerns long voiced by the Volsci, Negri (Negri 1977b: 67) identified the birthplace of the Gulag in 'the party's monopoly on violence, the fact of its being the obverse rather than the determinate antithesis of the State-form'. And yet, he went on, '*I do not feel able to jettison the problem of the party*' (Negri 1977b: 61). Here Negri returned to arguments made in *Rosso* 18 months previously, where it had been argued that the contradiction between those who privileged 'the movement' and the champions of 'a "Leninist" conception of organization' was 'not a Leninist contradiction', since centralization and an expansive organizational network were not mutually exclusive (CPO 1976c: 229). Writing in *Dominio e sabotaggio*, Negri stressed that the contradictory problem of organization could only be lived out by the movement's militants, who found themselves 'rooted on the one hand in the practice of self-valorisation, and tied, on the other, to the functions of offense' (Negri 1977b: 63). Given this, he concluded, the party could indeed find a role to play in the process of class recomposition, as 'the army that defends the frontiers of proletarian independence. And naturally it must not, cannot get mixed up in the internal management of self-valorisation' (Negri 1977b: 62).

The months between the writing of *Dominio e sabotaggio* and Negri's arrest in April 1979 would see little opportunity to put such notions to the test. Always extremely fragmented, the Autonomia of Milan and its environs would fracture further and further in the wake of the Moro affair (Gaj 1980). And while Negri would soon abandon the agitational *Rosso* in favor of the more reflective environment of *Magazzino*, in the months before his arrest he would continue to insist that

> [t]he most rigorous critique of the Third International cannot negate that essential urgency that we find in our experience of struggle, and which consists in the construction of an adequate form of party organisation, of organisation for the class in this phase. (Negri 1979a: 131)

CRITICS ON THE BORDERS

> But it's the 'Party of organized autonomy' that has demonstrated [*realizza*]—through Leninist idiocy—the failure of a year of manipulation, wild repression and political games against the movement.
>
> (Collegamenti 1979: 7)

Within Autonomia itself, the circle most critical of the party form was grouped around Franco Berardi ('Bifo') in Bologna, where it inspired both the journal *A/traverso* and the movement station Radio Alice. Emphasizing the creativity of contemporary movements against capital and the state, *A/traverso* would insist that proletarian autonomy be recognized 'as a majoritarian social tendency', in which the 'revolutionary line' could not be 'reduced to a party project' (A/traverso 1977a: 149). More than most sections of Autonomia, this 'creative' tendency was also prepared to take to heart, even before 1977, arguments concerning 'the refusal of militancy and the party' (A/traverso 1977b). Instead, it would experiment on two fronts. The first would be the development of a new language of revolution ('conspiring' through 'mao-dada');[22] the second—all too relevant to debates within today's movements against global capital—attempted to develop a participatory media able to facilitate (in real time!) the horizontal organization of struggle (Bifo and Gomma 2002). It is hardly surprising, then, that by late 1975, Berardi and his comrades would formally break with *Rosso*, after its other editors failed to criticize those members of the Volsci who had joined Lotta Continua stewards in disrupting a national feminist demonstration. A year later *A/traverso* could be heard warning that similar problems might well face the Movement of 1977, from

> those who believe in resolving problems with stewards' organizations [*servizi d'ordine*] or through the exhibition of their own virile force . . . The attitude of sectors of Autonomia operaia organizzata (with a capital A), a military behavior of violence and aggression towards comrades, towards youth and women, drawing themselves up in military formation [*schieramento*], signals a profound incomprehension of the new elements that this movement expresses. But what is worse is that today the imposition of a minoritarian logic of organizational patriotism [*una logica minoritaria ed organizzativistica*], whether of a militarist or workerist stamp, risks forcing onto centrist positions sectors of the movement that are certainly not centrist. (A/traverso 1977c: 1)

Nor were critics hard to find on Autonomia's margins. According to one article in the small journal *Neg/azione* (1976: 138),

> These comrades (Aut. Op.) start from a revolutionary reality, namely the need for the autonomous development of proletarian needs, whilst yet again proposing (professional) 'revolutionary militancy' and the party. This has the effect of channelling such revolutionary needs into capitalist schemas of 'politics' and 'ideology'. While starting from anti-revisionist premises (the refusal of the party as 'consciousness' and detonator of the autonomous movement), Autonomia Operaia Organizzata smuggles the party back in through the window, bureaucratising the very concept of 'autonomy' in the process.

Even harsher sentiments were voiced in the pages of *Provocazione* (Puzz 1976: 142, 143), where Autonomia was described as 'a parking bay' for 'malcontents' from the New Left groups intent on domesticating working-class self-activity. A somewhat more discerning picture was painted in Insurrezione's pamphlet *Proletari, se voi sapeste* . . ., which sought to discriminate between the Volsci as the expression of 'the direct organization of consistent numbers of proletarians and a great quantity of neighborhood committees and collectives', and the autonomist groups of the North, whose function in the late 1970s was deemed largely ephemeral and 'spectacular' (n.d.: 9, 11). On the other hand, little affection for 'organized Autonomy' could be found in the pages of the anarchist journal *A*, where a writer poked fun at Scalzone's alleged insistence during one 'encounter' between autonomists and supporters of Lotta Continua at the 1977 Bologna conference that 'militants of the Comitati Comunisti Rivoluzionari who continue fighting will be subject to disciplinary sanctions' (A 1977: 4).

Perhaps the most sustained critiques of Autonomia from those on its borders would come from the circles grouped around the journals *Collegamenti* and *Primo Maggio*. The first had been established in the early 1970s as a small network of workplace militants and their supporters based primarily in Milan, and viewing the world through an original blend of class struggle anarchism, council communism and the *operaista* notion of class composition. For its part, *Primo Maggio* began life in 1973 as a review of working-class history, albeit one increasingly concerned with accounts of contemporary struggles as the decade wore on. Its editors were largely former members of Potere Operaio and Lotta Continua who, in rejecting those groups' 'will to power', were keen to rethink the political roles and divisions of labor that then characterized the Italian radical left.

A common theme across the reflections of both journals (between which there was some convergence of discussion and even membership) was a consideration of the *ceto politico* generated within Italy's far left in the years since 1968. In an early article on Autonomia, *Collegamenti* (1974: 258, 263) identified three components within that movement. The first of these was a 'more or less consistent working-class fringe' organized above all in workplace committees, the second a slice of the 'political personnel' whose previous efforts to lead the class in 'neo-Leninist' groups such as Potere Operaio had proved a failure. Finally, there were a number of 'small traditional Stalinist–Maoist bureaucracies' such as Avanguardia Comunista in Rome and the Comitato Comunista (marxista-leninista) di unità e di lotta in Milan, of which it was said 'only an incurable opportunism can consider them class forces'.[23] All things to all people, according to *Collegamenti*, Autonomia already ran the risk of repeating the trajectory of Lotta Continua in attempting to 'expropriate proletarians of the comprehension of their struggle' by carving out a privileged role for itself within the process of class recomposition.

The first issue of a new series of *Collegamenti* (1977: 5) expanded these criticisms. Here it was argued that the early 'autonomous workers' movement' of factory militants had been hijacked by 'old wolves in new skins', whose antics in 'imposing analyses and divining the most "correct" and "revolutionary" objective' had alienated the movement's original workplace and neighborhood collectives 'one by one'. That this had occurred was not simply due to the perfidy of Autonomia's 'microfractions', however. Rather, its basis lay in the failure of the original workplace committees' premise that the federation of similar bodies 'factory by factory' would eventually lead to 'total control over production' on the path to a 'reborn republic of councils' (Collegamenti 1977: 6). With such hopes dashed by the massive restructuring and layoffs that characterized much of Italian industry after 1973, space was opened within Autonomia for the rise of the 'organized autonomists' and their growing stress upon the overarching dimension of 'political' struggle. While the likes of Negri turned their back upon the large factories, Scalzone's group had made little progress within them by touting their simplistic schemas of a counterposed working-class 'right' and 'left' (Collegamenti 1978: 81). A similar pattern would be repeated with the Movement of 1977 which, isolated from much of the traditional working class and under growing pressure from the state to reduce its dynamic to one of physical confrontation, increasingly lost the social dimension to its struggle. In such circumstances, this vicious circle was exacerbated by the preparedness of many in Autonomia organizzata to accept the state's challenge, while extolling 'the thematic of the party, voluntarism and the separateness of militancy' to rationalize their right to a specialized leadership role within the broader movement (Collegamenti 1978: 85).

A central figure in *Primo Maggio*, former leader of Potere Operaio, and work colleague of Negri at the University of Padua, Sergio Bologna paid considerable attention to the debate on organization within Autonomia. One of his first writings on the matter (1976a, included in translation as chapter 2 of the present volume) was a review of Negri's pamphlet *Proletari e Stato*, which Bologna criticized at length for what he saw as its abandonment of any political project centered upon the workers of the large factories (Wright 2002: 170–1). Along the way, Bologna (1976a: 27; see also p. 44 above) also gave a thumbs down to the model of political organization set out in *Proletari e Stato*, dismissing as 'useless' the idea that 'the new party no longer has its motor in front (the vanguard), but at the back, like a Volkswagen'.[24]

On the other hand, Bologna's reaction to Autonomia's role in the initial stages of the Movement of 1977 was a broadly positive one. Writing in March to Lotta Continua's daily newspaper, he chided the latter for failing to engage in political debate with the autonomists. A crucial difference from 1968, he continued, was that, unlike the political activists of that time, 'today some sectors of the organized autonomy tendency are actual and concrete elements of class composition—i.e., they are inside it' (Bologna 1977c: 99). This point was reiterated in 'The Tribe of Moles', Bologna's classic analysis of the Movement of 1977, where it was suggested that the autonomist groups had early won a hegemonic role because of their ability to anticipate political themes profoundly different from those of the late 1960s. Yet hardly had 'the echoes of the [February] clashes in Bologna' died down 'when everyone whipped out their Lenin masks from behind their backs—in particular the Workers' Autonomy [Autonomia Operaia] tendency in the North' (Bologna 1977a: 56). The very failure of Autonomia to force the pace of struggle, however, made it clear that now, against previous vanguardist notions of class politics,

> organisation is obliged to measure itself day by day against the new composition of the class; and must find its political programme only in the behavior of the class and not in some set of statutes; and thus must practice, not political clandestinity, but its opposite. (Bologna 1977a: 58)

In a long reflective piece published on the eve of the September conference, Bologna devoted some space to rejecting the notion that forcing the pace of street confrontations would inherently promote the process of social self-organization. Citing an episode in Milan four months previously, where a policeman had been shot dead in what was widely seen as a revenge killing by a fringe of the autonomist movement, Bologna argued that 'the critique of the party as an organizational form must *not* end up in a situation where the individual person becomes the Party, and where juvenile behavior can create situations that have a disastrous effect on the whole movement' (Bologna 1977b: 121).

If anything, Bologna's views of Autonomia had become harsher by 1978. While expressing interest in the Volsci's call for engagement with the remaining instances of 'autonomia diffusa' within the large factories, he showed nothing but scorn for the 'organized autonomists' of Italy's so-called 'industrial triangle' (bordered by Milan, Turin and Genoa).[25] The 'workerist *ceto politico*', he argued in February, was responsible for 'having reproduced leadership elites that are elites of revolutionary bourgeois, having suffocated—like their illustrious predecessors—*the working-class direction* of organisation and the movement' (Bologna 1978a: 155). The key to this problem, he continued in a *Primo Maggio* editorial, lay in dissolving the coupling 'crisis of party-form—need of organization'. Little could be expected on this front from the 'old whores' of Autonomia, however, at least in places like Milan, while the Bologna conference had only confirmed that tendency's propensity to reproduce the worst behaviors of the New Left *ceto politico* formed after 1968 (Bologna 1978b: 4).

AFTER THE DELUGE

> How many times we pretended not to be a party! We weren't but we would have liked to have been one. It was very ambiguous.
> —Alisa Del Re (quoted in Cuninghame 2002a: 135)

> In practical terms, the movement died over the problem of the party.
> —Antonio Negri (2000: 10)

The cycle of struggles that opened in 1977 would end badly. Retrenchment, addiction, imprisonment, exile, and suicide were not uncommon. Indeed, even before their decapitation through the mass arrests of 1979–80, many of the 'microfractions' of Autonomia would lose members to burnout or to 'sergeants' coups' that fed the movement's fringe of 'diffuse terrorism' (Progetto Memoria 1994). In the aftermath of its defeat came the 1980s, 'the years of cynicism, opportunism, and fear' (Balestrini and Moroni 1997: 387). On the other hand, the emergence of today's movement against global capital in Italy has prompted a certain interest in the struggles of earlier generations, including those of Autonomia. In particular, recent years have seen the appearance of a number of important studies of the period which draw heavily upon oral sources (Borio, Pozzi and Roggero 2002; Del Bello 1997; Cuninghame 2002a). Amongst other things, these projects have provided space for veterans of those years to offer their own reflections concerning the autonomist movement's successes, as well as its ultimate failure. What light do these accounts throw upon our understanding of the attempt to establish a 'party of autonomy'?

On many scores, serious differences of interpretation remain. Take the question of the organizational structures developed in some sections of Autonomia organizzata. Carlo Formenti (1999: 6), who left the area at an early point in its development, notes 'the paradox of Autonomia' as the product

> of the dissolution of the [post-1968 groups], but then maintaining the logic of the party within itself, that is the logic of leading cadres who had to lead, dominate, direct, coordinate and encompass within a common strategy and tactics everything that moved, every aspect and contradiction.

In the case of many northern autonomist formations, this paradox was inseparable from the establishment, out of their stewards' organizations, of clandestine structures parallel to their public face. More than this, he argues, 'once created . . . there was inevitably a transversal attraction between the various separate organisms . . . rapidly leading to the separation of this level from that of class autonomy and from political direction by the movement . . .' (Formenti 1999: 2–3). Faced with such a contradiction, some in the Autonomia of southern Italy had instead 'chose[n] the self-dissolution of these "parallel structures" ' (Lanfranco Caminiti, quoted in Cuninghame 2002a: 130). Against this, a former member of the Veneto collectives would continue to insist that the answer lay elsewhere, in 'the reasoned use of force': 'there didn't have to be separation between those who did politics and those who did politics and the armed struggle or only the armed struggle . . . practicing politics was to do everything at the same time' (quoted in Cuninghame 2002a: 133).

In what ways did the 'organized autonomist' groups seek to develop their own membership in preparation for the creation of a vanguard party? Speaking as a former member of Rosso, Ferruccio Dendena holds that this question was treated with little seriousness in that organization:

> I put the blame for this on the leaders who did not want to run proper 'cadre schools' and the bureaucratic relationship they had with the activists—'do this leaflet today, go to that march tomorrow' etc.—which pushed them towards the armed groups. (Quoted in Cuninghame 2002a: 145)[26]

Beyond this, Dendena (2000: 8) has identified a broader range of problems within the Autonomia organizzata of the late 1970s. First there were the rivalries between the various 'microfractions'. While some of these rivalries were programmatic in basis, little serious effort was made to thrash out a unified national perspective. Others were no more than the product of petty jealousies and past unpleasantries, leading some to shun the CPO 'simply because Negri was there' as altogether too daunting a figure for theoretical and political debate.[27] Again within Rosso, Dendena recalls a tension between those who saw the vanguard as responsible for developing mass organization, and others who thought it sufficient to lead others into street clashes on the basis of sloganeering. On this score, Negri himself (2000: 10) regrets that the early Autonomia's efforts to challenge the mass/vanguard distinction failed, forcing it back onto a traditional political terrain. According to Bologna (2001: 14), however, a problem with Negri's political perspective, then and now, has been to mistake the intensification of conflict for the broader process of class recomposition. Borio (2001: 9) makes a similar point:

> throughout the seventies Negri emphasized pushing forward, reaching and forcing along the discourse on struggles. He said: the struggle, power, the strength of the class, its organized segments and parts, have reached a level that is irreversible. This focus on the contingent might even be considered a necessary tactic for carrying the struggle forward, for leading the conflict to more advanced dimensions. But in reality, from a theoretical point of view, if you look not only at the immediate situation, but in terms of a broader project, it was a great political error, even a catastrophe.

For his part, Sergio Bianchi (2001: 7) has spoken of the periodic efforts by the 'organized autonomists' of Milan to colonize other parts of Lombardy, which only increased the wariness towards them of many in the 'diffuse' collectives (see also Farnetti and Moroni 1984). Alisa Del Re (2000: 2)—never part of Autonomia organizzata, despite the fantasies of Calogero and his ilk—contrasts the gains around social services made by early feminist collectives in the Veneto with the militaristic model of activism developed by many in the CPV. Finally, for Vincenzo Miliucci, once a prominent member of the Volsci, Negri's group was also guilty 'of incorrect relations, as a *ceto politico*, with the authentic and decisive structures of autonomia operaia in Milan: the Assemblea autonoma dell'Alfa Romeo, the Comitato della Pirelli, the Collettivo operaio della Sit-Simiens' (in Del Bello 1997: 15).[28]

To be fair, their critics hardly remember the efforts of the Comitati Autonomi Operai any less harshly. Piero Bernocchi (1997: 68–9)—a one-time rival of the CAO who now works with many of its ex-members in the Confederazione Cobas—argues that during 1977, the main autonomist formation in Rome lost that 'popular spirit that had characterized it' previously. He further accuses the CAO of abdicating any leadership role, in the process failing to conduct 'a clear and open political battle' with the armed groups, whose culture was quite distant from 'the movementist and libertarian attitudes of the Volsci'. Consciously or not, the CAO had instead allowed free rein to the most militarist tendencies within the Roman far left, leading to a cycle of street battles that only the state could ultimately win. Benedetto Vecchi (2001: 5) recalls things somewhat differently. He holds that, for all their profound differences in ideology and practice, the CAO and Brigate Rosse were ('a little ironically') locked in a competition to win the leadership of the movement in Rome. Dendena (2000: 8) goes further, claiming that the Volsci's network of territorial committees was held together by the charisma of leading militants rather than a political program. As the level of physical confrontation grew after 1977, this left elements within such local units vulnerable to infiltration by, or defection towards, armed groups such as the Brigate Rosse. The former *brigatista* Franscesco Piccioni agrees: the CAO were 'sorcerers' apprentices' who were simply living 'day by day' in the absence of a longer-term political project. Their model of leadership, he continues, consisted of 'being within' the movement, and of saying 'everyone can do what they like, so long as they don't break their ties with us' (in Del Bello 1997: 125, 124). Not surprisingly, Miliucci (2000: 15) disagrees, arguing that the Volsci were right to dissolve into the broader movement for the duration of 1977; if he has regrets, it is that the group did not then seek explicitly to be an 'anti-party, to be movementists'. Pifano, by contrast, is rather more self-critical, looking back with regret upon his organization's 'often instrumental' approach in practice to direct democracy, along with its inability to work with those currents it deemed to be on the moderate wing of the movement (Pifano 1995: 287). Above all, he argues, Autonomia's failure 'to represent a general political force' opened a programmatic void that the armed groups on its fringes and beyond were more than willing to exploit (Pifano 1997: 366).[29]

IN CONCLUSION

> Do I believe that knowledge can still be of assistance to practice? I think so, at least for a limited period, as long as we start from trying to recover that knowledge which capital (in the process of reducing socially necessary labor) is daily expropriating from the working class.
>
> We've had enough of ideology-merchants! Let's set to work again as 'technicians', inside the theoretical framework of class composition. This job is not one for a small group of intellectuals, but for thousands of comrades—the doctors, the technicians, the psychiatrists, the economists, the physicists, the teachers etc.
>
> —Sergio Bologna (1977b: 122)

As has been seen, the project of a 'party of Autonomy'—the formal unification of the movement's *ceto politico* as a revolutionary leadership—remained stillborn for a variety of reasons. Perhaps the most fundamental of these was the inability of the great majority of Autonomia organizzata to rethink its role as a *ceto politico* in the face of the rich and complex class composition thrown up in the late 1970s. Having experimented with and then largely abandoned the role of 'external militant' serving the *ceto operaio* of workplace militants, the 'organized autonomist' groupings commonly fell back upon more traditional notions of a political cadre. Yet even here, the more innovative approaches proffered then—for example, Negri's idea of the party as a specialized army protecting class self-organization, a sort of *servizio d'ordine* writ large—were still very much out of step with the 'good sense' found elsewhere in the Movement of 1977:

> Pacifists such as Lama enlist policemen, while those 'further left' seek the legitimation of 'mass violence', of the 'armed proletariat'. The actual movement was more realistic and less bellicose, more human and less heroic: it put peace up for debate because it criticized war and it shattered the criterion of delegation and legitimization because it rejected the army . . . (Castellano 1980a: 232, translation modified)

And for some, it would seem, little of importance has changed, apart from the language utilized. Negri (2000: 14) has recently wondered out loud whether 'Luxemburgism' might not be 'the Leninism of this epoch', and has dismissed the notion that 'the party has in hand the whole complexity of elements involved in a process of radical transformation' as 'worthy of paranoiacs'. All the same, *Empire* (Hardt and Negri 2000) continues to assign a privileged role within the process of radical social change to the *ceto politico*, this time round presented in the guise of 'the militant' (Sabrina and Chris 2002; Holloway 2002a).

The events of 1977 would not be the first occasion on which those seeking radical social change have failed to take up Marx's (1852: 106) challenge to learn from the past, while seeking inspiration from the poetry of the future.[30] In the specific case of Autonomia, a heavy price would be paid for the privileging of a discourse around the party as the crucial ingredient necessary for overturning 'the present state of things'—particularly when this sought to occlude what Bologna has called 'the dialectic between political elite and movement' (Cuninghame 2001: 98). Reflecting on this problem 25 years ago, one editor of *Collegamenti* suggested that the term *movement* can be thought of as an 'ensemble of behaviors and objectives that, whatever their specificity, refer to common and interconnected needs'. But beyond this, it carried a second connotation:

> in considering the movement, we can't forget that it is also a specific social layer, a *ceto politico* (to use that horrible term) that poses itself as the relatively stable expression of social antagonism, as its memory, as

the bearer of social values expressed by class behaviors. Although the movement, in this second sense, is something different from the class movement proper, one can't understand the latter by overlooking the former. The political practices, the analytical and organizational instruments of the movement's *ceto politico* play a notable role in the general evolution of struggles. (Giovannetti 1980: 7)

The movement's *ceto politico* oscillates between its various roles, therefore, in a manner that is hard to unravel. It can pose itself simultaneously or alternatively as a minority agent for class self-organization, or as a simple appendage to traditional organizations and rules; as a movement of self-awareness, or as the bureaucratic and authoritarian direction of struggles (ibid.).

The irony of Autonomia organizzata's discourses on the party form is that, having developed an understanding of the capital relation that suggested that the latter's abolition presupposed something other than the storming of the Winter Palace, most of its components nonetheless looked to marshalling the movement's *ceto politico* in pursuit of a general clash. That they were unable to do so does not detract from the tragedy of their course. Are other paths possible? For example, might we accept that the generation of *ceti politici* is a necessary consequence of class relations in a capitalist society, without asserting that the dissolution of the latter is premised upon welding such layers of activists into a single political unit designed to monopolize the broader movement's 'strategic reason'?[31] With hindsight, Bologna (2001: 8) has argued that the failure to explore such approaches created serious problems in the aftermath of the Hot Autumn:

we were mistaken to found Potere Operaio, we were mistaken to found an extraparliamentary group. We should have continued working in the social sphere, constructing alternatives there, workers' centers all over the place, social centers already back then: alternative spaces, liberated spaces. We were mistaken, we were mesmerized by the old idea, the old ambition of conquering power. We fell once again into the 'communist syndrome', and we tried to set up an abortion of a Bolshevik party that had in mind the dictatorship of the proletariat, and so inevitably got burned by those with more decisive options, such as armed struggle . . .

In an interview held the previous year, Berardi (2000: 8) offered a similar assessment of Autonomia's failure in the late 1970s:

Think about what happened after '77, after the September conference. There was a movement that in social terms was quite vast, and that contained a quantity of social, scientific, technological, communicative competencies that we've since seen at work over the following twenty years. . . . When this movement reached its pinnacle, in '77, and particularly with the conference of September '77, there was absolutely no capacity (this was the greatest stupidity we committed) or idea of giving a directly social form to those potentialities. That is, of saying, 'from now on we'll establish centers of social self-organization, radio, television, information agencies, this and that'. Instead, everything was reproposed within the classical form of organization.

One of the more interesting debates of the past decade has seen some anticapitalists in Britain and elsewhere make a call to 'Give Up Activism' (Andrew X 1999).[32] Not through inactivity (although much of what passes for organized political action today may well be only busywork), but instead by challenging the divisions of labor currently existing in the various movements against global capital, as well as the latter's relationship with the class composition with which they seek to engage. To be successful, such a course will require the continual rethinking of organizational forms, in pursuit of what Cuninghame (2002b) has called 'the search for an organisational model that is both participatively democratic and structurally transparent'. But more than this, it may require further exploration of what Bologna (2001: 13) has termed the role of 'technicians'. That is, of comrades prepared to share their particular expertise and judgement as part of the necessary movement-wide, collective development of 'strategic reason', without claiming any privileged leadership function as a consequence.[33] If this is so, we may yet see some interesting new answers to the problem posed 30 years ago by the editors of the North American journal *Zerowork* (1977: 6), of how 'to develop and circulate organizational strategies that do not contradict the autonomy of the working class'.

NOTES

1. I would like to thank the following for their constructive criticism of an earlier version of this chapter: Tim Murphy, Chris Wright, Nik, Enda Brophy, Patrick Cuninghame, Arianna Bove.
2. Wright (2002) seeks to explore the *operaista* tendency as the limit case of this failure.
3. I have chosen to retain the Italian term *ceto politico*, as this evokes the notion both of a stratum within a movement and/or class, as well as the vocation (whether realized or not) to provide leadership to the latter. Moss (1989: ch. 2) has some interesting insights into the stratification of Autonomia's *ceto politico* in much of northern Italy, even if his focus upon the question of politically motivated violence tends to filter out other aspects of the stratum's internal dynamics.
4. One of the hardest aspects of any discussion of the role of militants/activists entails unraveling the relationship between the *ceto politico* proper, whose members

commonly define themselves through individual identification with a formal organizational project and its associated ideology, and that broader *ceto operaio* within a given class composition, whose members may promote working-class struggles without necessarily belonging to any organized 'movement'. Some passing reference to this problem can be found in Borio, Pozzi and Roggero (2002). Danilo Montaldi (1971: xii) offers some very thought-provoking reflections upon this latter layer, even if he is adamant that it is 'not a social stratum'. For a discussion of one example of disjuncture between political activists and workplace militants, see Mason (1979).

5. This intersection is vividly portrayed in Balestrini (1989). The history of Autonomia in Italy's south remains the least known of the various 'Autonomies'. There are some sources available—from anthologies of the period (Recupero 1978 above all), to a passage in the new edition of *L'orda d'oro* (Caminiti 1997), and sections of Patrick Cuninghame's dissertation (2002a)—but nothing like the range of materials concerning the Romans or many of the northern collectives.

6. Many such circles would contribute to the phenomenon then known as 'diffuse terrorism', itself sometimes a way station on the path to entry into the larger armed groups. A useful guide to the origins of, and relationships between, the many armed organizations of the 1970s and early 1980s can be found in Progetto Memoria (1994).

7. In the words of John Holloway (2002b: 157), 'The form of the party, whether vanguardist or parliamentary, presupposes an orientation towards the state and makes little sense without it. The party is in fact the form of disciplining class struggle, of subordinating the myriad forms of class struggle to the over-riding aim of gaining control of the state. The state illusion penetrates deep into the experience of struggle, privileging those struggles which appear to contribute to the winning of state power and allocating a secondary role or worse to those forms of struggle which do not.'

8. Some acute insights into the early autonomist milieu can be found in the work of Ellen Cantarow (1972, 1973).

9. The Manifesto circle was for many years probably the best known component of the Italian far left in the English-speaking world, with works by its most prominent members past and present (Magri, Rossanda, Castellina) often appearing in translation over the past three decades. Driven out of the PCI at the end of the 1960s, it remained torn between efforts to push the Communist Party 'further left', and engagement with the party-building exercises of the main New Left groups. Its most enduring legacy is the daily newspaper of the same name (<http://www.ilmanifesto.it>).

10. It is interesting to compare this with the criticisms of so-called 'outside' militants in the New Left groups made by some factory activists at the beginnings of the 'autonomous workers movement'. For example, there is the following from a Turin meeting of 1971: 'Up to now it has always been the former [the "outside" militants—SW] who decided the political line and have imposed it in the assemblies, thanks to their greater preparation and the greater amount of time at their disposal. The workers have been merely the "shit-workers" of the revolution' (quoted in Wildcat n.d.: 2).

11. Many of these statements can be found in Recupero (1978).

12. Enzo Modugno (1981: 242) has recalled the bemusement of Paul Mattick when confronted in 1977 with the 'councillist' views of some leading Manifesto exponents.

13. The CAO were known popularly as the Volsci—the 'volscevichi' to opponents—since their headquarters were in Via dei Volsci, a street named after an Etruscan tribe that had warred with the Romans.

14. 'We, as the Policlinico committee, made reference to the committees of Autonomia Operaia as a political structure. The majority of our comrades adhered to this political structure, not all however' (Ciaccio 1982).

15. Such concerns make it hard to understand the accusations, circulated around 1978 by some circles in the Roman revolutionary left, that the CAO were 'pro-Soviet' in the sense of supporting the USSR of Brezhnev. To date, I have only been able to find second-hand accounts of such charges (Bocca 1980: 96; or see CAO 1980a, where an excerpt from a newspaper article repeating the charges is reprinted without comment). That the CAO's work with certain Palestinian organizations (for which some of the Volsci's leading members would pay dearly—CAO 1980a) may have brought them (like many Italian leftists) into contact with 'pro-Soviet' circles is quite possible. Beyond this, however, a pro-Soviet orientation sits at odds both with the organization's broad practice, as well as its numerous pronouncements concerning 'twenty years of Cold War, with its Budapests, Pragues, Warsaws, and the latest aggression exhibited by Soviet imperialism' (CAO 1980b; see also CAO 1978a).

16. This 'sergeants' coup' is recounted by one of its masterminds in Bocca (1985: 189).

17. Similar arguments about the 'obtuse self-satisfaction' of Autonomia organizzata were offered at this time by the Centro di Iniziativa Comunista Padovana (n.d.: 121, 122), a small split from the Veneto collectives which, as its name suggests, may well have had ties to Scalzone's network, as Progetto Memoria (1994: 90) likewise implies.

18. Such an assessment of the PCI would seem more typical of the Brigate rosse, rather than of other prominent armed groups of the late 1970s (for example, Prima Linea).

19. Early exponents of occupied social centers and of a politics lived 'in the first person', the youth circles fed a growing network of 'diffuse autonomist' collectives outside Autonomia organizzata, in the process anticipating many of the themes later found in the Movement of 1977—see P. Farnetti and P. Moroni (1984).

20. Some passing references to relations between the CPO and the PC(m-l)I can be found in Leonetti 2001. In turn, the alliance with Negri's group prompted opposition from more orthodox members of the PC(m-l)I (Acerenza et al. 1977).

21. In this part I have drawn upon the translation of *Dominio e sabotaggio* by Ed Emery as revised by Timothy S. Murphy.

22. An inherently contradictory notion, mao-dada attempted to fuse dadaism's assault upon the division between art and life with a 'soft Maoist' reading of revolutionary organization that privileged mass needs and self-organization. One consequence of the experience was an intriguing debate with Umberto Eco on language and revolution. A useful discussion of mao-dada's strengths and limitations can be found in Balestrini and Moroni (1997: 602ff).

23. While there is no question about the involvement of the Comitato Comunista (marxista-leninista) di unità e di lotta within Autonomia organizzata (Mangano et al. 1998: 67), it is harder to ascertain the accuracy or otherwise of the assertion concerning Avanguardia Comunista. Bernocchi (1997: 68), a former member of the latter, mentions collaboration with the Volsci before 1977, while another account of Avanguardia Comunista (Mangano et al. 1998: 87) portrays it only as an unconventional Marxist–Leninist formation.

24. Bologna also noted the dramatic shift in Negri's views on the party across the first half of the 1970s: 'Negri has passed from the theorisation of insurrection in '71 to the extinction of the party in '73, from ultra-Bolshevik positions to the pure objectivism of struggles: a 180-degree turn' (Bologna 1976a: 27). A similar observation was voiced by Marcello Pergola during the early stages of the 7 April case, in a passage that also suggests the disparate nature of *Rosso*'s early efforts to establish a national network within Autonomia: 'I remember taking part, in late Spring 1974, in a meeting at Berardi's house in Bologna . . . dedicated to the illustration of the contents of the new series of *Rosso* by Antonio Negri. I remember being struck by the change compared to Negri's earlier discourses on the formalization, on the necessity of the party: now instead he seemed to be paying particular attention to emerging subjects, the youth proletariat, women etc. Berardi was preparing his journal *A/traverso*, with a strongly anarchist content, we of Modena did not want to renounce our links with various union sectors, Bianchini underlined the necessity

of links with factory cadre . . . In conclusion, the meeting ended without any concrete, operative result; and it demonstrated once again the contrasts between the different positions' (quoted in Palombarini 1982: 122).

25. To be fair, the experience of Autonomia was quite different in Genoa from elsewhere in the north—see the recollections of Mezzarda (2001) and Moroni (2001).

26. Dendena's views are echoed by Guido Borio (2001: 9), himself a past militant in Rosso.

27. A less flattering explanation for the hostility towards Negri from within the Volsci can be found in an interview with Graziella Bastelli (in Del Bello 1997: 158).

28. Ironically, Precari Nati (n.d.) have since made similar charges concerning the Volsci's relations with these early instances of the autonomous workers' movement.

29. A similar argument is set out in Mezzarda (2001: 13).

30. Elsewhere I have sought to explore the legacy of the Resistance for the postwar Italian far left (Wright 1998).

31. An examination of the non-Leninist case for 'vanguards' advanced in Bihr (1995), alongside the views set out in Antagonism (2001), would be timely in the light of this question.

32. Amongst other things, this recent debate over activism has alluded to earlier critiques of 'the militant' developed within the ambit of the Situationist International. Commenting on an earlier draft of this chapter, Chris Wright has rightly suggested that many of the perspectives on revolutionary organization surveyed here could be usefully viewed through an engagement with such critiques. As part of that process, it would also be fruitful to examine the efforts during the seventies of the likes of Riccardo D'Este—see for example 'Un'esperienza oltre la politica' in Cevro-Vukovic (1976).

33. Tim Murphy has drawn my attention to the affinities between Bologna's notion of 'technicians' and Foucault's (1980c) discussion of 'specific intellectuals', outlined in his 1977 interview 'Truth and Power'. An important contribution to such strategic reasoning is Thoburn (2003), which directly addresses the questions of militancy and activism.

Part II

How to Resist the Present

5

The Refusal of Work as Demand and Perspective

Kathi Weeks

The refusal of work is a central concept both in Antonio Negri's writings and in the larger autonomist theoretical tradition within which his work can be situated.[1] The significance of the concept, however, extends beyond the concerns of intellectual history. The refusal of work is ultimately important, I want to assert, because of its relevance for political theory and practice today. Work (and this includes the lack of it) is at once one of the most important elements of modern life and among those that we seem least able to subject to critical analysis. Work values, those that celebrate the essential moral value and dignity of waged work, continue to flourish in the contemporary United States and elsewhere; yet their assumptions, not only about the virtues of hard work and long hours but also about their inevitability, are rarely examined, let alone contested by political theorists. '[J]ust what is the reason for public and private silencing around discussions of the work ethic? What is the "secret" that has the force of a social "fact"— that paid work is a condition of human nature and that "one must work till one drops"?' (Aronowitz et al. 1998: 72) Work is not just imposed as an economic activity that most of us need to pursue; it is posed as an ethical practice, and as such, something it is assumed we should want to pursue, something we should want more of rather than less. Why do these work values persist and to what effect? How can they be opened up to critical assessment? The refusal of work, as a practice that rejects the work ethic, as a doctrine that raises questions about the necessity and value of waged work, can serve today, I want to suggest, as an important means by which we can begin to assess critically and confront practically the present organization of work and the dominant discourses that support it.

The refusal of work is best understood as both a demand and a perspective. As a *demand* it names a variety of practices, from calls for shorter hours to slacking, the strike being perhaps the paradigmatic example. But it is also something more; it is at the same time a theoretical and political *perspective*, an intellectual rubric within which distinctive kinds of critical analyses of work and utopian speculations about the potential alternatives

109

to a society organized around it are generated. It is a practice, or rather a set of practices, which both give rise to and are informed by a broader conceptual analysis and political standpoint. In this way the refusal of work is comparable to other propositions of refusal in the tradition of political theory and practice. The tradition of civil disobedience, for example, like the refusal of work, takes as its starting point the refusal of authority. But such refusals of political authority remain inadequate if they are confined to a merely negative project—if, for example, the theory and practice of civil disobedience did not simultaneously gesture towards an alternative configuration of political power and authority. As we shall see, the refusal of work as theorized here is at once *negative* and *positive*; it encompasses both a rejection of the present regime of work and the project of imagining and constructing alternatives.

The explication of the theory and practice of the refusal of work that follows begins by taking up its disavowal of the productivist assumptions and commitments that animate some other Marxist discourses. I shall focus here on classical and humanist Marxisms, each of which provides some instructive points of contrast to the refusal-of-work perspective particularly as it is developed in Negri's writings.[2] The refusal of work points us towards, on the one hand, striking contrasts to these more familiar kinds of Marxism—to their celebrations of labor as human essence or social *raison d'être*—and, on the other hand, some interesting parallels to poststructuralist commitments, specifically, to their critiques of productivist values and Hegelian dialectical logics. So I will proceed by situating the concept of the refusal of work with reference to classical and humanist Marxisms on the one hand and some of their poststructuralist critics on the other, using the latter to flesh out critiques of the former and then turning to Negri's work in particular and the autonomist tradition in general to suggest alternatives.

Implicit in this method of procedure is another thesis, one that I prefer only to suggest rather than to argue here. That is, by situating Negri's autonomist Marxism between these more traditional Marxisms on the one hand and poststructuralism on the other, I am rejecting two closely related assumptions about the place of Marxism in the lexicon of contemporary theory, namely, that Marxism is one, a unitary discourse, and that it is united in its opposition to poststructuralism.[3] Negri's work, my method of exposition is intended to imply, reveals the inaccuracy and ineffectiveness of this commonly posited opposition between Marxism and poststructuralism.

A CRITIQUE OF PRODUCTIVISM

The critique of productivism in Marxism was put forth most succinctly, and certainly most provocatively, by Jean Baudrillard in *The Mirror of*

Production. The term productivism is multivalent, designating several related but nonetheless distinct ideas. My focus here will be rather narrow. I will not, for example, address the issue of Marxism's supposed methodological commitment to the primacy of production. Instead, confining my comments to one aspect of Baudrillard's multifaceted critique, I am interested in exploring the role of productivism understood as a normative ideal based on a valorization of labor. First published in 1973, *The Mirror of Production* was inspired by the activity of new social actors beyond the industrial working class and infused with the antiauthoritarian ethic and utopian spirit of May 1968. According to Baudrillard's formulation, '[a] specter haunts the revolutionary imagination: the phantom of production. Everywhere it sustains an unbridled romanticism of productivity' (1975: 17). Historical materialism reproduces political economy's fetishism of labor and production; the evidence of its complicity can be found in Marxism's naturalized ontology of humans' laboring essence and in its utopian vision of a future in which this essence is fully realized in the form of an unhindered productivity. This is not, by Baudrillard's estimation, a tendency that is confined to one or another brand of Marxism; instead he insists that the 'sanctification of work has been the secret vice of Marxist political and economic strategy from the beginning' (1975: 36). Baudrillard finds within this productivist ideal an allegiance to the values of worldly asceticism in which the richness, spontaneity, and plurality of social interactions and relations are subordinated to the instrumental and rationalist logic of productivity, with its exaltation of activities centered around controlling nature in the service of strictly utilitarian ends. By this account, Marxism's continued commitment to productivism, this inability to break from the work values that have developed alongside and in support of Western capitalist social formations, represents a failure of both critical analysis and utopian imagination.

Baudrillard's critique provides an important opportunity to expose and reconsider the productivist assumptions and values that remain embedded within certain Marxist discourses. Marxism's commitment to these traditional work values is nowhere more clearly evident than when we examine its utopian speculations about an alternative to capitalism.[4] The utopian visions I refer to are not blueprints for a perfect future, but rather, in keeping with a more modest and I think more serviceable conception of utopian thinking, attempts to imagine different possibilities, to anticipate alternative modes of life. As inspiring visions, they both advance the critique of daily life under capital and stimulate desire for, imagination of, and hope in the possibility of a better future. I want to review two versions of utopia within the Marxist tradition, each of which is familiar to students of the dominant models of Marxist thinking and both of which are informed by productivist assumptions and values. These are classical Marxism's utopia of modernization and the romantic–humanist utopia, for which I will enlist V. I. Lenin and Erich Fromm as representatives. As we shall see, although they are associated with very different tendencies within Marxism, they share a central commitment to the essential value of work.[5]

THE UTOPIA OF MODERNIZATION

The utopia of modernization constitutes the most pervasive characterization of communism ascribed to Marxism. In this vision communism is equated with the full realization of the productive potential of forces of production developed under capital. The critique of capital, in this version of Marxism, centers on the problematic of exploitation and the contradiction between the forces and relations of production. Exploitation proceeds from the private ownership of productive forces and consists of the private appropriation of the fruits of surplus labor. According to this well-rehearsed story of capitalist development, these bourgeois property relations eventually become fetters on the full development of modern productive forces: 'the conditions of bourgeois society are too narrow to comprise the wealth created by them' (Marx and Engels 1948: 15). Communism, by contrast, would democratize the economic relations of ownership and control. The relations of production, class relations, would be thus radically transfigured, while the means of production and the labor process itself would be merely 'unfettered'.

This approach is perhaps most clearly articulated by some of the architects of actually existing state socialism. Lenin, in an analysis consistent with the classical theory of revolution, distinguished between two phases after the overthrow of capitalism: the first socialist phase, in which 'factory discipline' is extended over the whole of society, and the final stage of true communism. The first stage, a lengthy period of transition between capitalism and communism, the precise duration of which is unknown, requires from workers 'self-sacrifice', 'perseverance', and a commitment to 'the proper path of steady and disciplined labour' (Lenin 1989: 223, 226). To ensure that communism is achieved in the future, the offensive against capital must be partially suspended during the transition. Socialism thus involves a (still at this point temporary) intensification of capitalism, whereas communism is imagined abstractly as its pure transcendence. In the meantime, '[t]he task that the Soviet government must set the people in all its scope is—learn to work' (Lenin 1989: 240). This includes the use of piece-rates, competition among firms, and time–motion analyses. Nowhere is this utopia of modernization more clearly prefigured than in Lenin's fascination with and admiration for Taylorism and his insistence on the need for an iron work discipline to combat petty-bourgeois laziness, selfishness, and anarchy (see Lenin 1989: 240–1, 257). But what Lenin considered to be only a means to deal with the difficult conditions of the immediate postrevolutionary period became, in the hands of others, as the utopia was either deferred into the ever more distant future or declared achieved, an end in itself. It is perhaps in later Soviet policies and rhetoric that we can find the purest examples of this ideal of modernization. With its affirmation of the heroic, world-building capacities of disciplined, proletarian labor, it is a vision that depends upon and revolves around a valorization of the creative force of human labor conceived narrowly as social production.

The problem with this version of the productivist vision from a different Marxist perspective is that because it is founded upon an insufficient critique of capital, its vision of an alternative preserves too many of capital's structures and values. This valorization of proletarian labor and of the progressive development of productive forces replicates the fundamental attributes of capitalist society; by this account, the working class inherits and carries on the historical role of the bourgeoisie who first revealed to us the 'productive forces [that] slumbered in the lap of social labor' (Marx and Engels 1948: 14). Here we find an endorsement of economic 'growth', industrial 'progress', and 'the work ethic' similar to that which can be found in bourgeois political economy with its naturalization and celebration of the processes of economic modernization. In this form, the critique of capitalist production does not extend, for example, to the labor process itself, and thus does not account adequately for Marx's many pointed critiques of the mind-numbing and repetitive qualities of factory labor or his insistence that freedom requires a reduction of the working day. Communism by this narrative is confined to a transformation of property relations, leaving the basic form of industrial production, and even the mode of capitalist command over production, intact. The future alternative to capitalism is reduced, according to Moishe Postone's critical reading of this logic, to 'a new mode of politically administering and economically regulating the *same* industrial mode of producing to which capitalism gave rise' (1996: 9). By this account communism could be understood as an enhanced capitalism.

THE ROMANTIC–HUMANIST UTOPIA

An alternative to the utopia of modernization gained popularity among many Anglo-American Marxists in the 1960s. What I am calling the romantic–humanist utopia is critical of the utopia of modernization and the classical discourse with which it is aligned. Whereas the classical discourse originated in the context of late nineteenth century and early twentieth century revolutionary movements in Europe, the development and popularization of humanist Marxism coincided with the rise of the New Left. Erich Fromm's *Marx's Concept of Man*, conceived and published in 1961 as an accompaniment to the first US publication of Marx's *Economic and Philosophic Manuscripts*, presents a classic statement of the romantic–humanist reading of Marx. Humanist Marxism is presented as an attempt to rescue Marxism, not only from its association with actually existing state-socialist regimes, but also from its more economistic and determinist tendencies. Drawing on the *Manuscripts* (which, it is important to remember, were not published before the 1920s and were first translated into English only in 1959), Fromm reconstructs a counter-Marx: a philosophical Marx grounded in a humanist tradition and centered around a commitment to the creative individual as unit of analysis and motor of history. Whereas classical Marxism gravitates towards *Capital* and the *Manifesto* as privileged texts, humanist Marxism traces its lineage to Marx's early writings, to the *Manuscripts* and the *German Ideology*. Whereas the utopia of modernization is conceived as a response to the critique of bourgeois property relations and the problematic of exploitation, the humanist utopia grows out of the critique of alienated labor. Whereas the utopia of modernization centers on notions of social progress, social justice and social harmony, the humanist utopia privileges the individual as a crucial category and fundamental value. Indeed, by Fromm's account, Marx's philosophy 'was aimed at the full realization of individualism' (1961: 3). The romantic dimension of this approach, which will be discussed in more detail below, is common to humanist Marxism and is evident in Fromm's description of Marx's philosophy as 'a movement against the dehumanization and automatization of man inherent in the development of Western industrialism' (1961: v), a 'spiritual–humanistic' alternative to the 'mechanistic–materialistic spirit of successful industrialism' (1961: 72). Together, the utopia of modernization and the humanist utopia present us with a Marxist gloss on the two faces of modernity: an ideal of social and economic progress grounded in the continual development of science and industry and the romantic revolt against the forces of rationalization which accompany that ideal.

Both of these visions of the future, the classical and the romantic–humanist, although in some ways opposed to one another, are based on a similar commitment to labor as a fundamental human value. In the first version labor is conceived as social production and valorized as the primary means to social cohesion and achievement. In the second model labor is understood as an individual creative capacity, a human essence, from which we are now estranged and to which we should be restored. Drawing on Marx's *Manuscripts*, Fromm insists that the self-realization of man, which he understands to be Marx's central concern, is inextricably linked to the activity of work: 'In this process of genuine activity man develops himself, becomes himself; work is not only a means to an end—the product—but an end in itself, the meaningful expression of human energy; hence work is enjoyable' (1961: 41–2). The problem with capitalism is that we are estranged from our essential nature, our authentic selves. Alienation is the negation of productivity (1961: 43). 'For Marx,' by this account, 'socialism meant the social order which permits the return of man to himself, the identity between existence and essence . . .' (1961: 69). Unalienated labor, as the reigning ideal around which a future utopian society is to be organized, is conceived as the primary means of individual self-realization and self-fulfillment. Fromm presents a long quote from the third volume of *Capital*—a famous passage in which Marx envisions a realm of freedom above and beyond a realm of necessity—and insists that all the essential elements of socialism can be found therein (1961: 59–60). In Fromm's reading of this passage we find the key to the romantic–humanist vision of unalienated labor: a transformation of the world of work into a cooperative process that is controlled by the individual producers. It is not the planned economy that produces freedom, but participation in the activity of organizing and planning that enables one to be free: freedom is a matter of individual independence, 'which is based on man's [i.e. the individual's] standing on his own feet, using his own powers and relating himself to the world productively' (1961: 61).

Fromm's cure for capitalism is not more work, as Lenin prescribed, but better work. 'The central theme of Marx,' Fromm insists, 'is the transformation of alienated, meaningless labor into productive, free labor' (1961: 43); this is the means by which we can finally realize our true humanity. It is interesting to note that in Fromm's discussion of that famous passage from the third volume of *Capital*—the passage that he characterized as expressing all the essential elements of socialism—he quotes the passage at length up through the part where Marx states that the realm of freedom can only flourish with the realm of necessity as its basis, but omits the next and concluding sentence of the paragraph in which Marx adds that '[t]he reduction of the working day is the basic prerequisite' (Marx 1981: 959).[6] Why work less if work, in its unalienated form, as socialized production, is the expression of and means to self-creation? The goal is to restore work's dignity and worth, not to contest its favored status as the pillar of social value.

Unlike the modernization model, which rejected private property and the market while accepting and adapting the basic contours of capitalist discipline, the humanist paradigm incorporates a more extensive critique of work. One of the problems with this project, however, is that there is a tendency towards nostalgia for an earlier time, a romanticization of craft production that informs its visions of an alternative. Fromm notes, again following Marx's early writings, that alienation is greater now than it was in an earlier stage of capitalism when handicraft production and manufacturing prevailed (1961: 51). Concrete labor in the production of use values is sometimes suggested in these analyses as the alternative to the abstract labor that produces exchange values. Thus, for example, in an essay that fits solidly within this romantic–humanist rubric, David McLellan presents another reconstruction, drawn largely from Marx's early writings, of communism as the unalienated society. In an unalienated society we would have a direct and personal connection to the products of our labor (McLellan 1969: 464); as objectifications of our laboring essence, the objects we create would serve as confirmations of our being. Instead of producing superfluous things to sell on the market in order to produce surplus value, we would produce useful things for immediate consumption. As opposed to abstract labor as both a conceptual abstraction that reduces different kinds of concrete labor to labor in general and a practical process that transforms the concrete laboring activities of individuals according to the exigencies of large-scale social production, this romantic–humanist perspective tends to valorize concrete labor as an alternative. By this reading a nonalienated relationship to the product requires that we engage in useful labor, that we produce use values that can serve as objectifications of our laboring essence.

This tendency to pose concrete labor as the utopian alternative to abstract labor and the production of use values to replace the production of exchange value is, however, based on a rather problematic reading of Marx—problematic both in the sense that it is less consistent with the broader corpus of Marx's writings and, more importantly, in the sense that it is less relevant to the contemporary context. The problem is that Marx's pairings of concepts like use value and exchange value, concrete labor and abstract labor, should not, I argue, be reduced to the judgments of good versus bad, where the first term, use value or concrete labor, is posed as a standpoint outside of capital from which it can be critiqued. A comparison to Nietzsche's use of the conceptual pair of noble morality and slave morality is instructive: although he makes use of the distinction by measuring slave morality against the standard of noble morality, he does not present a return to noble morality as an option that is either possible or desirable; the category of noble morality serves as a tool by which to advance the critique of slave morality rather than as a vision of a better future. In a similar way, Marx's distinctions do not provide us with a utopian solution. A true alternative to capitalist society would require that we move beyond both abstract labor under capitalism and the modes of concrete labor that are also shaped by it.[7]

It is worth noting here that, if we focus on his later writings, Marx does not suggest that we return to an artisanal model for an alternative to capitalism. On the contrary, he argues explicitly in favor of the virtues of cooperation on a mass scale, a form of social labor that he distinguishes qualitatively from handicraft production.[8] The power of social production 'arises from co-operation itself. When the worker co-operates in a planned way with others, he strips off the fetters of his individuality, and develops the capabilities of his species' (Marx 1976: 447). The romantic–humanist notion of the individual laborer is no longer the proper unit of analysis beginning with this stage of cooperation; the vision of an individual laborer producing a specific useful product is inconsistent with this process that comes to incorporate general technical and scientific knowledges that cannot be attributed to specific individuals. According to Marx,

> [i]n earlier stages of development the single individual seems to be developed more fully, because he has not yet worked out his relationships in their fullness, or erected them as independent social powers and relations opposite himself. It is as ridiculous to yearn for a return to that original fullness as it is to believe that with this complete emptiness history has come to a standstill. The bourgeois viewpoint has never advanced beyond this antithesis between itself and this romantic viewpoint, and therefore the latter will accompany it as legitimate antithesis up to its blessed end. (1973: 162)

This development should point us not back to an older mode of organization centered around independent individuals, but rather forward to the possibilities of new ways of organizing work and production and new models of subjectivity.[9]

AUTONOMIST MARXISM AND THE
REFUSAL OF WORK

The attraction of work as a model behavior and human value exerts a powerful hold on both the liberal and the Marxist imaginations. Thus, it is not only capital that moralizes, normalizes, and mythologizes work; as Negri notes, the 'official Socialist movement' also treats the imposition of work as if it were a 'title of nobility' and continually attempts to suppress its refusal (1979c: 119, 124). Despite, however, Baudrillard's categorical indictment of Marxism in general, there are alternative approaches within the Marxist tradition. Specifically, we can find in Negri's writings as well as in the larger autonomist tradition a refutation of and alternative to productivist values in the notion of the refusal of work. In the pages that follow I will try to flesh out the refusal of work, first as theory and practice, and second as a logic of imagination. In the final section I will say something more about the category's relevance to contemporary developments.

Whereas *Capital* is the principal text of classical Marxism and the *Manuscripts* the key text for the humanists, the *Grundrisse* is the privileged text of the autonomists. In *Marx Beyond Marx*, a study of the *Grundrisse*, Negri finds the outlines of an alternative to many existing Marxisms, including both the classical and humanist traditions. Rather than a simple precursor to or early draft of *Capital*, Negri finds in the *Grundrisse* a very different kind of analysis. Unlike *Capital*, the *Grundrisse* was written in light of a specific crisis in 1857 and is best understood as an attempt to theorize its revolutionary possibilities. Thus, in this case, 'there is no possibility . . . of destroying the dynamism of this process by hypostatizing it, by rigidifying it into a totality with its own laws of development that one might be able to possess, or dominate, or reverse' (Negri 1991a: 9). Like Marx and the crisis of 1857, the autonomist theorists took their lead from the revolutionary agitation of a loose coalition of workers, students, feminists, and unemployed people that roiled Italy in the 1960s and 1970s. 'We find ourselves,' Negri writes in 1979, 'in a phase where the revolutionary movement is seeking new foundations, and in a way that will not be that of a minority.' In this situation, Negri explains, '[w]e have nothing to do with orthodoxy' (Negri 1991a: 17). The *Grundrisse*, by this reading, restores Marx as a theorist of crisis rather than equilibrium, of antagonism and separation rather than opposition and synthesis, of subjective agency rather than objective tendencies. Rejecting determinism in all its forms, Negri's brand of autonomist Marxism attempts to restore the methodological and political primacy of subjectivity; thus workers are to be conceived not primarily as capital's victims, but rather as its potential antagonists. In this way autonomist Marxism is part of a longstanding subtradition within Marxism that seeks to theorize not from the 'one-sided' perspective of capital and its reproduction, but also from the perspective of the workers and their potential to subvert that power.[10] This insistence on the power of active subjects requires a dismantling within Marxist theory and practice of all the analytical and organizational apparatuses that held these subjective forces in check, from the Leninist party and traditional labor union to the concept of economic laws of development and the identical subject–object of history. It involves a rejection of determinism, teleology, and, as we shall see, a refusal of the recuperative logic of the Dialectic.[11]

But in refusing determinism autonomists do not embrace humanism. Negri, for one, is adamant about the inadequacies of humanist models of the subject.[12] He expresses no interest in the problematic of alienation with its discourse of interiority, of the loss and restoration of an essential human nature. By Negri's account the 'so-called humanism of Marx', in which actual historical tendencies are corralled into a predictable narrative of 'the organic unfolding of human nature (even if it is defined histori-cally)', is the product of an 'impatience with theory, a usage of positive utopia destined to homogenize transition and communism . . .' (Negri 1991a: 154).[13] From the perspective of the refusal of work, the notion of 'man-the-producer' is part and parcel of the practical and ideological imposition of waged labor; the metaphysics of labor is a mythology internal to and ultimately supportive of capital.

The refusal of work, an important slogan in the Italian social movements of the 1960s and 1970s, is a fundamental ground of autonomist Marxism's critical analysis and political strategy. At one level a clear expression of the immediate desire experienced by working people around the world, the refusal of work was developed by autonomists into a more variegated concept, one that encompasses several distinct critical approaches and strategic agendas. In order to grasp its potential as both a demand and a perspective, however, one must first understand the place of work in the critical analysis of capitalist social formations. That is, fundamental to the refusal of work as analysis and strategy is a definition of capitalism that highlights not the institution of private property, but rather the imposi-tion and organization of work. After all, from a worker's perspective, earning wages, not accumulating capital, is the primary concern. From the perspective of the worker, the wage system is central to capitalism insofar as it is the dominant mechanism by which individuals are integrated, either directly or indirectly, into its mode of cooperation. The autonomist theorist Harry Cleaver thus defines capital as '*a social system based on the imposition of work through the commodity-form*' (2000a: 82); it is a system in which life is arranged around and subordinated to work. Diane Elson's reading of Marx is also helpful in fleshing out this approach. Elson argues that Marx's theory of value is best understood not as a labor theory of value but as a value theory of labor. That is to say, the purpose of the analysis is not to prove the existence of exploitation or to explain prices; the point is not so much to grasp the process by which value is constituted by labor, but rather to fathom how laboring practices are organized, shaped, and directed by the capitalist pursuit of value. 'My argument,' Elson writes, 'is that the *object* of Marx's theory of value was labour' (1979: 123). Whereas Marxist modernization theory and humanist Marxism each conceive the possibility of a postcapitalist society in terms of our ability to appreciate and realize the constitutive power of labor, to grasp the centrality of labor to social life, by this alternative reading of Marx, 'labor's constitutive centrality to social life characterizes *capitalism* and forms the ultimate ground of its abstract mode of domination' (Postone 1996: 361, emphasis added).[14]

Given this point of focus, autonomists tend to highlight two potential points of antagonism. The first is attributed to the growing tension between the persistence of capitalist command over labor on the one hand and the ever-expanding capacities of both general intellect and social cooperation on the other. The second involves the emerging conflict between a society that requires labor to secure the means of consumption and the possibility—created by certain scientific, technological, and sociocultural developments—of a social form in which labor does not serve this function, in which, for example, working time is drastically reduced, what work remains is improved, and the link between work and income is broken.[15] The crucial point and the essential link to the refusal of work is that work—not private property, the market, the factory, or the alienation of our creative capacities—is understood to be the primary basis of capitalist relations, the glue that holds the system together. Hence, any meaningful transformation of capitalism requires substantial change in the organization and value of work.

So, unlike the modernization model, the autonomist tradition focuses on the critique of work under capitalism (which includes but cannot be reduced to the critique of its exploitation). In contrast to the humanists, who also launch a critique of work, they call not for a liberation *of* work but for a liberation *from* work.[16] In their insistence on replacing one slogan of worker militancy, 'the right to work', with a new one, 'the refusal of work', the autonomists follow in the footsteps certainly of Marx, the Marx who, for example, insisted that freedom depended on the shortening of the working day, but perhaps a more appropriate point of origin would be Marx's son-in-law, Paul LaFargue. Leszek Kolakowski's description of him as the proponent of 'a hedonist Marxism' only makes this genealogy more appropriate (1978: 141–8). Of course Kolakowski intended it as an insult, meant to signal LaFargue's naiveté and lack of seriousness, but I find it a fitting classification for a Marxist tradition committed to the refusal of work and open to the possibilities of a postwork future. In his critique of the 1848 right-to-work rhetoric of the French proletariat, LaFargue complained that the proletariat had 'allowed itself to be seduced by the dogma of work. Its chastisement is hard and terrible. All individual and society [sic] misery takes its origin in the passion of the proletariat for work' (1898: 8). In a ploy reminiscent of Marx's insistence that alienated labor is the cause of private property, that the proletarians themselves recreate the system through their continued participation, LaFargue admonishes the French workers rather than the bourgeoisie for the short-comings of capitalist production. So, for example, when the manufactur-ers consume luxuries in excess or when they attempt to build obsolescence into their products, they should not be blamed: they are only trying to satisfy their workers' strange mania for work (1898: 29–31). 'The proletar-ians have got it into their heads to hold the capitalists to ten hours of factory work—that is the great mistake. . . . Work must be forbidden, not imposed' (1898: 37). Once the working day is reduced to three hours, we can begin 'to practice the virtues of laziness' (1898: 41, 32).

Despite LaFargue's provocative tribute to the merits of laziness, the refusal of work should not be understood as a rejection of activity and creativity. It is not a renunciation of labor *tout court*, but rather comprises a refusal of the ideology of work as highest calling and moral duty, a refusal of work as the necessary center of social life and means of access to the rights and claims of citizenship, and, finally, a refusal of the necessity and value of capitalist command over production. Its immediate goals are presented in terms of a reduction in work, both in hours and social importance, and a replacement of capitalist command by new forms of cooperation. 'Communism,' Negri argues, 'appears as the concept of the overthrow of work, of its subtraction from command' (1991a: 162). In this sense, '[w]ork which is liberated is liberation from work' (1991a: 165). Rather than conceiving it narrowly in terms of a specific set of actions— whether they be strikes or slowdowns, demands for shorter hours or expanded opportunities for participation, or movements for improved support for or altered conditions of reproductive work—the phrase is best understood, I think, in very broad terms as designating a general political and cultural movement, or better yet, as a potential mode of life that challenges the mode of life now defined by work.

The refusal of work can be broken down, analytically if not practically, into two processes, one that is essentially negative in its aims and another that is more fundamentally positive in its objectives. The first of these, the negative moment, is what is most readily conveyed by the term refusal, and includes the critique of and rebellion against the present system of work and work values. Negri argues that, given the centrality of wage labor, the refusal of work poses a potentially radical threat to the system as a whole. 'Thus,' Negri insists, 'the refusal of work does not negate *one* nexus of capitalist society, *one* aspect of capital's process of production or reproduction. Rather, with all its radicality, it *negates the whole of capitalist society*' (1979c: 124). If the system of waged labor is the primary cultural and institutional mechanism by which we are linked to the mode of production, then the refusal of work could constitute a substantial challenge to this larger apparatus.

But the refusal of work, as both a demand and a perspective, as both activism and analysis, does not only pose itself against the present organization of work; it should also be understood as a creative practice, one that seeks to reappropriate and to reconfigure existing forms of production and reproduction (see Vercellone 1996: 84). This is the special twofold nature of the refusal of work upon which Negri insists (1979c: 124–8). The term refusal is perhaps unfortunate in the sense that it does not immediately convey the constructive element that is so central to autonomist thought.[17] Rather than being a goal in itself, '[t]he refusal of work and authority, or really the refusal of voluntary servitude, is the *beginning* of liberatory politics' (Hardt and Negri 2000: 204, emphasis added).

The refusal of work thus comprises at once a movement of exit and a process of invention. The refusal in effect makes time and opens up spaces (whether they be physical or intellectual) within which to construct alternatives. We remove ourselves from the immediate relationship of domination, 'and through our exodus [subvert] the sovereign power that lords over us' (Hardt and Negri 2000: 204). But rather than a simple act of disengagement that we complete, this refusal is best conceived as a process, a theoretical and practical movement that aims to effect a separation by creating spaces and times in which we can pursue alternative practices and relationships, that can in turn give rise to collective subjects with different needs and desires, new capacities and powers. 'Beyond the simple refusal, or as part of that refusal,' Hardt and Negri argue, 'we need also to construct a new mode of life and above all a new community' (2000: 204). Paolo Virno develops this same idea through the concepts of exodus and exit:

> The 'exit' modifies the conditions within which the conflict takes place, rather than presupposes it as an irremovable horizon; it changes the context within which a problem arises, rather than deals with the problem by choosing one or another of the alternative solutions already on offer. In short, the 'exit' can be seen as a free-thinking inventiveness that changes the rules of the game and disorients the enemy. (1996a: 199)

In this sense, refusal, like exodus or exit, is an *'engaged withdrawal* (or founding leave-taking)' (Virno 1996a: 197). It should be understood then as a creative practice as opposed to a merely defensive stance. The passage from the negative moment of refusal to its constructive moment of exit and invention traces the path from a reactive gesture of retreat to an active affirmation of social innovation. By this reading, the refusal of work serves not as a goal precisely, but as a path, a path of separation that creates the conditions for the construction of subjects whose needs and desires are no longer consistent with the social mechanisms within which they are supposed to be mediated and contained. This refusal must be understood not as an alternative in itself so much as a process of gestation. This is why, in contrast to both classical and humanist Marxists, Negri locates in the refusal of work not just the symptoms of our exploitation and alienation, but the measure of our freedom (1979c: 126–7).

The defection that is enacted through the refusal of work is premised not on the idea that 'we have nothing to lose but our chains' but on the very different (and far less ascetic) basis of our 'latent wealth, on an abundance of possibilities—in short, on the principle of the *tertium datur*' (Virno 1996a: 199). The separation, exit, or exodus is not predicated upon what we lack or cannot do, but rather upon a wealth of potential powers and capacities, on what we have and what we can do. The refusal of work as both a practical demand and theoretical perspective presupposes an appreciation of the potentially immense productive power of the accumulated knowledges of social labor. 'What we want,' recounts another Italian autonomist,

> is to apply, totally and coherently, the energies and the potential that exist for a socialized intelligence, for a general intellect. We want to make possible a general reduction in working time and we want to transform the organization of work in such a way that an autonomous organization of sectors of productive experimental organization may become possible. (Bifo 1980: 157–8)

This affirmation of the creative powers of social labor notwithstanding, the refusal of work does not simply replicate the productivist glorification of (socialist or unalienated) work: the productive powers of cooperation and the general intellect are celebrated because they carry the potential not only to contest the necessity of capitalist command, but to reduce the time of work, thereby challenging us to pursue other opportunities for pleasure and creativity outside the economic realm of production—for example, in the forging of networks of sociality and the provision of care, in the creation of art or the practice of politics.

OPPOSITIONAL LOGICS AND REACTIVE REVERSALS:
COMMUNISM AND THE TRANSITION

I want to take another pass at what Negri describes as the twofold nature of the refusal of work, that is, its status as both critical force and constructive project. This time we will come at it from another direction, by way of some of Negri's comments on the potential for and possible configuration of a postcapitalist society, or rather, more specifically, on the logic of imagination that governs such speculation. The shape of and prospects for the emergence of an alternative social order and, with it, certain questions about means and ends and the relationship between them was addressed within the Marxist tradition under the rubric of the transition. Since in Negri's account the refusal of work is posed as a fundamental mechanism of social change (or in a Marxist parlance, a key to the transition) and the alternative to capitalism (which Negri continues to call communism) is conceived primarily as nonwork, our explication of the refusal of work leads us to these famous Marxist problematics, of communism and the transition.

In this section we shall proceed as we did previously, beginning with two examples from the classical and humanist perspectives, in this case, of traditional two-stage models of the transition, followed by a critique of each of these accounts, one drawn from Baudrillard's critique of Marxism and the other from Deleuze's reading of Nietzsche. As we shall see, in one case the problem is simply that the vision of communism is separated from the process of transition; in the other case the problem is that because the Dialectical logic that informs the exercise in utopian speculation is oppositional rather than differential, the vision of communism is fundamentally reactive. From the perspective of Negri's work, the problem with these formulations is that they separate or conflate the deconstructive and constructive aspects of the refusal: 'beware of dividing the basic nucleus that produces them,' Negri warns, 'and beware of building homologies between them in their two-fold development: the history of the socialist perversions of the revolutionary process has always been based on the stressing of one of these to the detriment of the other' (1979c: 126). These two problems, that of dividing the twofold process of destructuration and innovation and that of positing homologies between them, correspond to the central shortcomings of our two examples.

Let us consider the classical approach first. According to that model, the first stage, the transition, involves preparing the ground for the second stage marked by communism's arrival. To recall Lenin's account (which he based on Marx's *Critique of the Gotha Programme*), the transition stage involves an intensification of capitalist elements up until some point where, as in the Dialectical movement from quantity to quality, the system will be transformed finally into communism, represented as a complete transcendence of capitalism (see Lenin 1932: 83–5). The problem is that by positing communism in terms of such a dramatic break with the period of transition, and in the absence of a more detailed account of the specific mechanisms by which it can be reached, the vision remains abstract in the sense that, rather than the product of praxis, it is imagined in advance as the necessary outcome of objective developments; the actors work towards one goal, primarily the intensification of factory discipline, presumably leaving something like the 'laws of historical development' to produce quite another. Thus the development of objective conditions takes precedence over all the immediate desires and antagonisms that may erupt in the meantime. Baudrillard (attacking a rather dogmatic version that leaves out the nuances of Lenin's analysis) claims that once Marxism 'enters into the game of the objectivity of history, when it resigns itself to the *laws* of history and the dialectic' (1975: 162), communism then assumes the form of some distant other. This he describes as an effectively ascetic vision, 'a communism of sublimation and hope' that 'demands more and more the sacrifice of the immediate and permanent revolution'—of the rebellious desires and practices of the here and now (1975: 161). This faraway vision of communism, this product of structural forces not yet in place, 'has the effect of stifling the current situation, of exorcizing immediate subversion, of diluting (in the chemical sense of the term) explosive reactions in a long term solution' (1975: 162).

This tendency to ignore, suspend, or control the role of human agency in the period of the transition is typical of what I am calling classical Marxism. Yet this inattention to or underestimation of the creative powers of human collectivities is also a problem found in at least some examples of humanist Marxism—a discourse explicitly committed to affirming the role of subjective factors in history. As an example, let us consider another two-stage model of communism, one that can be situated in a broadly humanist tradition, presented in 1977 by Bertell Ollman. Ollman's reconstruction of Marx's vision, while taking into account the broad corpus of Marx's writings, draws most heavily on the early writings and does so in a way that is consistent with humanist interpretations.[18] The description of the first transition stage is drawn from Marx and Engels' list of ten preliminary measures outlined in the *Manifesto*. But it is Ollman's description of the second stage of full communism, which he contrasts very sharply to the first stage of proletarian dictatorship, that is of particular interest.[19] According to his interpretation of Marx's statements, in a communist society 'all material goods have become as abundant as water is today' (Ollman 1977: 27). In this society, everyone, 'without exception', wants to do factory work (1977: 23), so that '"[f]rom each according to his ability," is a promise that no one at this time would think of breaking' (1977: 30). Such a society, Ollman claims, 'knows no clash of basic interests' (1977: 31), in large part because we think about and treat the needs of others as our own, 'experiencing happiness when they are happy and sadness when they are sad' (1977: 25).[20] By Ollman's reading, Marx imagines

> that much of what people today want to do but cannot will be done under the ideal conditions of communism, that what remains are things which the extraordinary people of this time will not want to do, and, most important, that what they will want to do which we do not . . . they will easily accomplish. (Ollman 1977: 28)

In short, '[l]ife in communism is at the opposite extreme from what exists in capitalism' (1977: 22). It is the status of Ollman's vision of communism posed as an 'opposite extreme'—more specifically, his claim that '[a]s opposites, alienation and communism serve as necessary points of reference for each other' (1977: 40)—that I want to consider below.[21]

My critique centers on the nature of this posed linkage between alienation and communism. As opposites, Ollman claims, alienation and communism are necessary to one another, we cannot understand one independently of the other. The problem is that to the extent that they are conceived as opposites, the vision of communism remains dependent on what it opposes; more specifically, it is reduced to a reaction against the present, a merely reactive reversal. There is a tradition of poststructuralist thought, grounded in Nietzsche and developed most clearly by Deleuze, that can help to elucidate some of the limitations of what Deleuze identifies as a Hegelian Dialectical logic of opposition. Deleuze argues that contradiction, absolute opposition, is a weak or even false notion of difference in that empirical differences (in contrast to logical ones) do not exist as pure oppositions, as absolute differences. As Deleuze explains it,

> it is the profession and mission of the dialectician to establish *antitheses* everywhere where there are more delicate evaluations to be made, *coordinations* to be interpreted. That the flower is the antithesis of the leaf, that it 'refutes' the leaf—this is a celebrated discovery dear to the dialectic. (1983: 15)

Just as the differences between the flower and the leaf cannot be captured in terms of an opposition in this Hegelian example, neither, I would suggest, can the differences between capitalism and communism, the latter of which grows in the soil of the former, be grasped with an opposi-tional logic.

If absolute oppositions have a tendency to eclipse coordinations or continuities between pairs, they can also serve to pose commonalties as if they were differences—and this inability to imagine difference is, from the perspective of the refusal of work, an even more important problem with Ollman's reconstruction of Marx's vision of communism. Work is manda-tory, work is freely desired; in either case, work remains the point of refer-ence, the subject. Nietzsche makes a similar point when he suggests that atheism is not, as it imagines itself to be, the antithesis of the Christian ascetic ideal but only one of its latest phases of evolution (1967a: 160). Christians define themselves in terms of their belief in God, atheists define themselves in terms of their denial of that belief; in both cases the same belief system is central to the sense of self. The problem is that when oppo-sition is substituted for difference, our ability to think creatively is limited. As Deleuze explains it (and here he is following Nietzsche very closely), this oppositional logic moves within the boundaries of reactive forces (1983: 159): 'For the affirmation of difference as such it substitutes the negation of that which differs; for the affirmation of self it substitutes the negation of the other, and for the affirmation of affirmation it substitutes the famous negation of the negation' (Deleuze 1983: 196). To recall Ollman's reading of Marx, '[l]ife in communism is at the opposite extreme from what exists in capitalism' (1977: 22). Communism is conceived as the absolute negation of capitalism and is affirmed insofar as it can be opposed to life under capitalism. As a reactive reversal, the utopian vision remains locked within the orbit of what it opposes and hence, not surpris-ingly, hides a secret identity—in this case, the valorization of work. Thus we find the utopian imagination fails just when it appears to be most successful, that it is unable to imagine true difference because it imagines the difference to be absolute.

THE REFUSAL OF WORK AS A DIFFERENTIAL LOGIC OF IMAGINATION

'Communism is for us,' Marx and Engels wrote,

> not a *state of affairs* which is to be established, an *ideal* to which reality [will] have to adjust itself. We call communism the real movement which abolishes the present state of things. The conditions of this movement result from the premises now in existence. (1970: 56–7)

Ernst Bloch, among others, recovered and developed some parts of this insight: the future conceived as a dynamic rather than static state; the privileged role of historical agents over idealistic blueprints; the importance of grounding one's vision in the 'premises now in existence' rather than in purely abstract fantasies. I want to focus instead on a relatively more neglected aspect of Marx and Engels' statement: the identification of communism with a 'real' movement of refusal and subversion. The refusal of work leads us to an alternative approach to the famous problem of transition, one that I think comes closer to the characterization cited above. Negri offers two methodological principles that may enable us to overcome the problems we found in some of the other approaches: first, communism is inseparable from the transition; second, the logic of antagonism should replace Dialectical logic.

From Negri's perspective, one of the problems with both the classical and humanist accounts of the communist utopia sketched above can be traced back to their adherence to the classic two-stage model of communism. According to that model, the first stage, the transition, involves preparing the ground for the second stage, which is to be marked by communism's arrival. To recall Lenin's account, the transition stage involves an intensification of capitalist elements up until some point where, as in the Dialectical movement from quantity to quality, the system will be transformed finally into communism, represented as a complete transcendence of capitalism. This two-stage model with its separation between the transition and communism, the means and the end, tends to conceive communism in advance, according to some plan or model. 'Now, what interests us,' Negri explains, 'is *the process of liberation*' that lies between the two stages (1991a: 152). Rather than define the transition in terms of an ideal of communism, the challenge is '*to define communism by the transition*' (Negri 1991a: 154). Instead of a period in which capitalism is overturned followed by a separate period when communism is constructed, the transition is conceived as simultaneously negative and positive; utopia is thus not deferred to some far off future, but rather, is constructed in and through this process: '*communism is a constituting praxis*' (Negri 1991a: 163).[22] By these means, Negri hopes to restore the leading role of subjectivity in processes of change. To recall Marx and Engels' formulation, '[w]e call communism the real movement which abolishes the present state of things'. In other words, communism must be conceived in terms of a movement of refusal; communism should be conceived in terms of its coordinations—to recall Deleuze's term—with the movement of refusal. Rather than 'hypostatizing them [transition and communism] in some dialectic of stages and hierarchy' (Negri 1991a: 152), communism must be conceived simultaneously as a process rather than a result, a movement rather than a plan; it is prefigured in the desires that fuel refusal and is enabled—constituted—in the spaces opened up by the separation that this rejection enacts; it is thus by this account inextricably linked to the process of refusal.

By this account the negative and positive moments of refusal can be distinguished analytically, but not isolated from one another practically. Rather than the traditional two-stage model that posits a radical break between the transition conceived as a negative process of dismantling and communism conceived as the positive construction of an alternative, Negri suggests that we consider the value of a more substantial break between the present logic of capital and the transition—conceived in this case as a process by which a different future can be constructed. That is, this formulation of the relationship between means and ends indicates the importance of pursuing more radical strategies that break more dramatically with the present. By this reading, the militancy of the strategy, the call to refuse the present system of work rather than simply reconsider or rene-gotiate a few of its terms and conditions, can perhaps be better appreci-ated. Although the immoderate character of the slogan may strike us today as naive or impractical, if we consider such strategies as laboratories—both conceptual and practical—in which different subjectivities can be consti-tuted and paths to alternative futures opened, the utopian aspect of the refusal of work as demand and perspective, its insistence that we struggle towards and imagine the possibilities of substantial social change, is essential.

The second methodological principle Negri proposes is that we replace Dialectical logic with a logic of antagonism. We must, Negri argues, liberate Marxism from the remainders of these Dialectical habits. Capitalism should thus be conceived not in terms of a smooth systematicity or as the product of a functional fit among its elements, but rather as a relation of antagonistic elements. Whereas Dialectical contradiction is an objective category, the product of a system of structures, antagonism is posed as a subjective category that arises from the expressed needs and desires of historical subjects. Negri wants a Marxist method that is 'completely sub-jectivized, totally open toward the future, and creative', one that 'cannot be enclosed within any dialectical totality or logical unity' (Negri 1991a: 12). The Dialectic, by Negri's account, is the logic of capital that seeks to reduce the wealth of differences to a simple binary, an opposition, which can then be recuperated within a new kind of unity or synthesis. It is the logic by which capital seeks to reimpose functionality within the social factory. We can see the same logic at work among those who, claiming that the proletariat is the purest and thus the true opponent of capital, aim to subordinate all other antagonists to its direction. We should recognize this as another example of what Negri describes as a 'continuist' logic (1991a: 168), one 'which authorizes levels of homogeneity in the development of oppositions' (1991a: 166).

Negri develops his account of working-class activism in terms of an antagonistic logic of separation rather than a Dialectical logic of opposition. Separation is the path of difference, the construction of alternative subjectivities. The logic of antagonism is a plural logic, one that attempts to avoid conceiving difference in terms of binary oppositions that preserve hidden identities, one that respects the potential for autonomous creativity on the part of social subjects, their potential to be different rather than merely reactive. 'We must immediately underline,' Negri argues, 'that in this light the antagonistic logic ceases to have a binary rhythm, ceases to accept the fantastical reality of the adversary on its horizon. *It refuses the dialectic* even as a simple horizon. *It refuses all binary formulae*' (1991a: 189). We must, Negri suggests, liberate the political imaginary from the reactive logic of oppositional modes of thinking, those that reduce the potential wealth of real differences to difference posed absolutely and reactively. Thus, for example, rather than a unified movement or a single category of action, the refusal of work in fact assumes a myriad of forms:

> The refusal of work shows—with the totality of the project which characterizes it, and in a way that is happily contradictory with this project—a great *multiplicity* of aspects, a great wealth and liberty of movements of a complex autonomy. Each step toward communism is a moment of extension and of expansion of the whole wealth of differences. (Negri 1991a: 167)

Antagonism, refusal, separation, autonomy, difference—these are the terms by which Negri conceives how to be *against* rather than *opposed* to capital.[23]

Again, the refusal that is posed here is at once critical and utopian, a deconstructive process and a constructive project. The theory and practices of refusal of work should help in the critical assessment of the present organization of work and work values, but also assist us in imagining and moving towards an alternative, a society in which life is no longer secondary to work. The passage I have traced from an oppositional to a differential logic of imagination points to a rich vein of utopian thinking. The refusal of work is a refusal of the mode of life centered around the capitalist organization of work and, at the same time, a theory and practice that seeks to secure the time and open the spaces within which to create new needs, desires, and practices, new ways of living. There is no homology, as Negri explains it, between work as it is experienced in the present and as it is imagined in the future: 'To mark this transformation in the most rigorous way possible, Marx insists on the abolition of work' (Negri 1991a: 165). Communism, as Negri conceives it, is nonwork, and as such, the destruction of capital in every sense (1991a: 169). Posed in this way the notion of nonwork serves not as blueprint, not as content, but rather as a marker of radical difference or rupture. The notion of a nonwork or postwork future is not, then, the same as an antiwork vision: a society of nonwork is not defined by its opposition to a society organized around work; rather than the opposite of a work society, it names a social order that is substantially different. The refusal of work gives rise to new modes of subjectivity, and this is the key to the transition conceived as the construction of a different future: *'Turning from the liberation-from-work toward the going-beyond-of-work forms the center, the heart of the definition of communism'* (Negri 1991a: 160). Affirming the creative possibilities inherent in the subversive practice of refusal, the future should be imagined not as the simple negation of the present social order, but as something different, something new.

POSTWORK UTOPIAS: BEYOND ASCETIC VALUES AND REACTIVE LOGICS

I do not mean to suggest that classical and humanist Marxisms are inaccurate in their reading of Marx—theirs are selective readings of Marx as are the autonomists' interpretations. My argument is rather that productivist discourses, Marxist or not, are not at this point capable of generating the most timely critiques or the most compelling visions. The refusal of work in its broadest sense has the potential, I want to suggest, to generate a powerful critical perspective on and practical agendas in relation to contemporary developments in the United States. Work values today play an ever more important role in securing consent to the current system. Work is glorified and idealized, praised by the dominant elements on both the political left and right as a civilizing influence, a training ground for that rational, self-reliant, and independent subject of liberal discourse, and posed as a moral duty. The contemporary force of this moralization of work should not be underestimated; it has played a prominent role in pathologizing the poor through cultural deficiency discourses, as well as in the dismantling of welfare and the rise of workfare. Current trends suggest that our attitudes toward work are of increasing importance to the continued viability of present configurations of work. Today, work processes, especially in service-related enterprises, pose new challenges for techniques of control. When workers are given more responsibility and more discretion, particularly when the job involves providing services and instilling in clients and customers certain kinds of emotional states, their performance is more difficult to monitor. Strong work values are increasingly highlighted in management discourses as a significant remedy to the new problems of surveillance simply because they render it less necessary. Thus we see a growing trend in the United States and elsewhere to select and evaluate workers on the basis of their attitudes, motivation, and behavior (Townley 1989: 92). Indeed, now more than ever, 'workers are expected to be the architects of their own better exploitation' (Henwood 1997b: 22). Where attitudes are productive, the refusal of work—understood as a rejection of the notion of work as the necessary center of social existence, moral duty, ontological essence, and primary focus of time and energy, understood as a practice of 'insubordination to the work ethic' (Bifo 1980: 169)—can, I believe, speak forcefully and incisively to our current situation.

This is not to suggest that we should abandon the struggles for better work, for the liberation from mindless and repetitive tasks, dangerous environments, numbing isolation, and petty hierarchies. It is important to recognize, however, that the language and to a certain degree the practices of work humanization have been co-opted. Calls for more challenging jobs with more responsibility, more flextime, more varied work, and more workplace democracy are reproduced in current management literature, but here as strategies for maximizing workers' productivity and management's control.[24] This brings us back to one of the basic assumptions of the refusal of work: the demand for more unalienated work rather than for less work ultimately reaffirms productivist mandates and ideals. The glorification of work as a prototypically human endeavor, as the key both to one's humanity and one's individuality, constitutes the fundamental ideological foundations of contemporary capitalism—it was built on the basis of this work ethic and it continues to serve the system's interests and rationalize its outcomes. The ideology of human resource management, with its various programs for humanizing work to make it a place where employees can be expected to dedicate their hearts as well as their hands and brains, with its techniques for producing more productive models of worker subjectivity, should be recognized as an attempt to prevent and recuperate various expressions of dissatisfaction with work. In this context, the refusal of work, with its insistence on a more thorough critique of and more radical break with existing work values and its support for a politics of work reduction, strikes me as a more compelling demand and promising perspective. My argument is that the valorization of (unalienated) labor is no longer, if it ever was, an adequate strategy by which to contest contemporary modes of capitalist command, that it is too readily co-opted in a context in which the metaphysics of labor and the moralization of work carry so much cultural authority.[25]

The refusal of work includes within its demands and perspectives an important model of utopian thought and practice—something that is ever more necessary in an age in which the dominant view is that there is no alternative. Negri, it should be noted, expresses only disdain for utopianism. Following the example of Marx and Engels' critique of utopian socialism in the *Manifesto*, Negri assumes that utopias, whether posed in an idealist mode as mere wishfulness or in a scientist mode as the necessary culmination of objective laws, are blueprints that are disconnected from concrete trends and collective agents. Despite Negri's disavowal of this very narrow conception of the tradition of utopia, we can, I want to suggest, find compelling examples of utopian strategies and thinking in his approach to the refusal of work. The utopian element does not in this case reside in an expectation that the system of work and the discourse of work values will be easily confronted or in a detailed image of a future of nonwork; it lies instead in a general hope that far-reaching change is ultimately possible and in a logic of thinking that can guide us in imagining its potential contours.

As I have tried to suggest, part of what this analysis of the refusal of work can offer us are some conceptual and methodological tools that help us move beyond the ascetic values and reactive logics that too often shape our thinking about work and nonwork. First, true to the appellation of hedonist Marxism that I appropriated earlier, the refusal of work respects our propensity to want more—more time, freedom, and pleasure—and aspires to a vision of life no longer organized primarily around work. By raising questions about the nature and value of work, it challenges us to consider the rich possibilities of living in the times and spaces of nonwork. It rejects the usual prescription that we should work harder and want less. Rather than a political strategy that pins our hopes on demanding only what is now deemed reasonable, it seeks instead to alter the standards by which we judge proposed transformations in our relationships to work to be possible and desirable. Second, insofar as the refusal of work is conceived in conjunction with a differential logic of imagination, it can suggest some methods by which we can think about a different future, one that is not merely a continuation or reversal of the present. By this reading, the refusal of work as demand and perspective, by urging us to want more and to think differently, can serve as a resource for our all too impoverished social and political imagination.

NOTES

1. On the category of autonomist Marxism see Cleaver (2000a: 17–18).
2. I use the category of classical Marxism to refer to a tradition of Marxist interpretation and scholarship that privileges a vision of modernization and relies on a notion of objective laws of development.
3. I have argued this in more explicit terms elsewhere (Weeks 1998: 48–69).
4. Despite Marx's principled reticence to engage in this kind of utopian reflection, he did present, in brief statements scattered through several texts, glimpses of a noncapitalist society. Later Marxists, despite a widespread hostility to utopian thinking, do affirm the possibility of a future alternative to capitalist society and do, in many cases, speculate about some of its contours.
5. Some may be impatient with my discussions of these two brands of Marxism because their representatives, Lenin and Fromm, are thought to be no longer relevant to contemporary Marxism, their historical moments having passed. Although these representatives of the classical and humanist paradigms may be out of favor, the paradigms themselves, however, live on, regularly turning up in the values and assumptions of a variety of Marxist theories. This is particularly true when it comes to the strategic and utopian tasks of suggesting what is to be done and speculating about possible futures. Their legacies, I would argue, have yet to be adequately assessed and confronted.
6. Later in the text Fromm quotes a shorter section of the same passage and this time includes the final sentence about the need to reduce the working day. Yet his lack of interest in the ideal of work reduction is still made clear: he adds emphasis with italics to every part of the quote except the final sentence, upon which he again neglects to comment (1961: 76).
7. 'Overcoming capitalism,' Moishe Postone argues, 'also involves overcoming the concrete labor done by the proletariat' (1996: 28). As Harry Cleaver describes it, '[t]o speak of postcapitalist "useful labour" is as problematic as to speak of the postcapitalist state' (2000a: 129).
8. Jean-Marie Vincent develops a similar analysis (1991: 80–2).
9. See also Moishe Postone's analysis of this aspect of Marx's argument (1996: 336–9).
10. On the one-sided perspective Marx presents in *Capital* and alternatives to it, see Lebowitz (1992). On Autonomist Marxism as part of a broader tradition of Marxist interpretation and scholarship, see Dyer-Witheford (1999: 62–4).
11. I capitalize 'Dialectic' to signal that the target here is an essentially Hegelian version of the Dialectic and not necessarily other conceptions of dialectics. For a notable alternative to the Hegelian Dialectic, an approach to dialectics that does not necessarily rely on an oppositional and recuperative logic, see Bertell Ollman's model of internal relations developed in *Alienation: Marx's Conception of Man in Capitalist Society* (1971).
12. It should also be noted that Negri rejects structural Marxism as well. That is, Negri concurs with Althusser's antihumanism, but is only willing to follow so far: 'In avoiding humanism, some would also seek to avoid the theoretical areas of subjectivity. They are wrong. The path of materialism passes precisely through subjectivity. The path of subjectivity is the one that gives materiality to communism' (Negri 1991a: 154).
13. In response to the humanist position, which posits some essence or nature from which we are now estranged and to which we should be restored—an ideal or trope that appears frequently in Marx's early writings—Baudrillard declares, '[w]hat an absurdity it is to pretend that men are "other", to try to convince them that their deepest desire is to become "themselves" again!' (1975: 166). How can we be empowered to act on the basis of what are now presumed to be corrupted and inauthentic desires?
14. Although developed independently of the autonomist tradition, Postone's analysis in his excellent book, *Time, Labor, and Social Domination* (1996), is compatible with

that general approach, from his privileging of the *Grundrisse*, to his critique of productivism and the metaphysics of labor, to his insistence that what is distinctive about capitalism is that it is constituted by abstract labor, and finally, to his tentative speculations about the possibilities of a postwork society.

15. On the first potential point of antagonism see, for example, Negri (1996a); on the second see, for example, Postone (1996: 361, 365) and Vincent (1991: 19–20).

16. See the definition of refusal of work in the glossary of concepts in *Radical Thought in Italy* (Virno and Hardt 1996a: 263).

17. In *Capitalist Domination and Working Class Sabotage* Negri describes the refusal of work as both a struggle against the capitalist organization of work and a form of 'invention-power' (1979c: 127). The term self-valorization is also used as a separate category by Negri to characterize that second creative element of the movement of refusal.

18. One reason for classifying Ollman's text as an example of humanist Marxism, despite its many substantial differences from a perspective like Fromm's, has to do with his privileging of the concept of alienation, with its notion of a human nature or essence from which we are now estranged and to which we should be restored (Ollman 1977: 40; see also 1971).

19. It is important to recognize the particular context in which the essay was written. In an introduction, the editors of the journal in which it was published endorse the piece as part of a larger effort to refute the usual identification of Marx's vision of socialism with actually existing state-socialist regimes (see Ollman 1977: 6). The description Ollman presents of human behavior radically transformed offers a sharp contrast to both actually existing capitalist and state-socialist societies.

20. One of the reasons why Ollman's reading of Marx—even of the early texts—is problematic can be traced back to a tendency within humanist Marxism to privilege the individual as the unit of analysis, whereas I would argue that Marx more typically presumes the collective as unit of analysis. Thus, for example, Marx's claims about the importance of gaining control of the social environment is interpreted to mean that each individual must have this kind of control, and Marx's statements regarding our need to recognize ourselves as social beings is read as a claim about individual feelings—that each individual should care for others as for themselves (Ollman 1977: 25)—rather than a claim about the necessarily collective bases of human achievements.

21. There are several potential limitations of this utopian vision. Ernst Bloch's (1986) concept of the concrete, anticipatory utopia—one that is firmly rooted in existing trends and possibilities—can help to reveal the shortcomings of such a comparatively more abstract, compensatory scenario; Tom Moylan's (1986) notion of the critical utopia can help to expose the limits of this vision of a state of static perfection; and there are a number of invaluable analyses that can point out the inadequacies of the relative absence of politics in this imagined future (see, for example, Nordahl 1987). But I think that there is a further problem with this exercise in utopian speculation, or perhaps an additional aspect of the problems identified above, and it is related to the oppositional logic through which the vision in Ollman's interpretation is articulated.

22. See Bifo for a similar critique of the traditional concept of transition (1980: 169).

23. The term 'overturning' (*rovesciamento*) is often translated in the English version of *Marx Beyond Marx* as 'inversion' in a way that fails to capture this aspect of Negri's project of moving away from Dialectical logic.

24. On this point see, for example, Aronowitz (1985: 21) and McArdle et al. (1995).

25. This is not to say that the valorization of proletarian labor was not at one time a more viable strategy. As Postone suggests, perhaps it was more appropriate for the early stages of working-class development and organization (1996: 70–1).

6

Cyber-Negri: General Intellect and Immaterial Labor

Nick Dyer-Witheford

Over the last three decades Antonio Negri has insistently spoken of a prospect other intellectuals, left and right, would prefer to leave unmentioned—that of a world beyond capital. But while faithful to this possibility, he has frequently changed his theories about the agency of such a transformation. If the 1970s saw the 'workerist' Negri of the shop-floor industrial struggles, and the 1980s the 'autonomist' Negri of new social movements, the last decade has witnessed a Negri whose ideas find their most compelling examples in the turbulence of the Internet. In what follows, I trace the emergence of this 'cyber-Negri', from his writings on the 'socialized worker' to his participation in the *Futur Antérieur* group's analysis of 'immaterial labor' and 'general intellect'. These concepts have resonated strongly with net-theorists such as Tiziana Terranova and Richard Barbrook, but simultaneously provoked spirited attack from within the autonomist Marxist tradition by such critics as George Caffentzis. Consequently, a major thrust of *Empire*, the widely discussed coproduction of Negri and Michael Hardt, is a response to the controversies ignited by its authors' earlier emphasis on the importance of 'cyborg' or 'immaterial' labor. This attempt is, I feel, only partially successful, and in some ways raises more difficulties than it resolves. So I conclude by suggesting a revision of Negri's digital insights that preserves his concept of 'general intellect' but reconfigures it in relation to two other categories that could be critical to a twenty-first-century Marxism, 'universal labor' and 'species being'.

CYCLE OF STRUGGLES: FROM THE MASS WORKER
TO THE SOCIALIZED WORKER

If Negri's account of counterpowers against capital has been in constant flux this is surely because one of his key theoretical tenets is the dynamism of subversive subjectivity. The protean nature of struggle against capital was crucial to the *operaismo* ('workerism') that connected Marxist intellectuals such as Negri to industrial shop-floor militancy of northern Italy in the late 1960s and 1970s, a movement whose central conceptual innovation was the theory of 'cycle of struggles'.

Reviving Marx's own emphasis, theorists such as Mario Tronti, Raniero Panzieri and Sergio Bologna took as their premise not the power and dominion of capital, but the creativity and autonomy of labor.[1] This inversion broke sharply with the orthodoxies of Soviet-style Marxism. Scientific–socialist accounts of linear, mechanical progression through capitalism's different levels or stages on the way to a final crisis caused by the inevitable declining rate of profit were discarded. Instead, *operaismo* told a story of escalating cut and thrust, spiral attack and counterattack. Capital attempts to expropriate the inventive, cooperative capacity of workers, on which it depends for production of commodities. But labor resists. The specter of subversion drives capital on a relentless 'flight to the future', expanding its territorial space and technological intensity in an attempt to destroy or circumvent an antagonist from whose value-creating power it can never, however, separate without destroying itself. In this view, the working class is not just made, but incessantly remade, as its contestation brings on successive rounds of capitalist reorganization. These in turn generate new forms of labor, and new strategies and tactics of struggle.

Historically, *operaismo* theorists discerned two major turns in this helical process of class composition, the epochs of the 'professional' and 'mass' worker. In the late nineteenth century, managerial control was stymied by the residual craft power of the artisanal labor that *operaismo* termed the 'professional worker'. Capital responds with the deskilling and automating regimes of Taylorism and Fordism. But it thereby generates the 'mass worker' of the industrial assembly line, whose organizations terrified it with prospects of revolution, wrung from it the concessions of the welfare state, and whose continuing militancy inspired Negri and his comrades.

The cycle of struggles theory was soon, however, to seem like a typically twilight flight of Minerva's owl. The 1970s wave of European and North American industrial militancy from which *operaismo* emerged brought on a devastating reply. Reaganism and Thatcherism deployed state repression, transnationalization and all the powers of the digital revolution to disassemble the industrial factory and decimate the mass worker. The counterpunch, so powerful as to break up the formations of labor parties and trade unions that had constituted the left for a century, looked like a knockout blow. The cycle of struggles appeared to have ended—and badly for those who thought it up.

Negri refused this conclusion. In Italy, his political involvements were moving from the industrial militancy of *operaismo* to the Autonomia movement. Autonomia was a percolating radical synthesis of various marginalized sectors: students, unemployed and precarious workers, feminist movements and other new social subjects.[2] As he made this shift in praxis,

Negri came up with an audacious theoretical proposition: out of capital's restructuring was emerging another cycle of struggles. And the new revolutionary subject was the 'socialized worker'.[3]

In the era of the professional worker, capital concentrated itself in the factory; in the era of the mass worker, the factory became central to society. But in the epoch of the socialized worker, Negri said, the factory disseminates out into society. Labor is deterritorialized, dispersed and decentralized in the 'factory without walls' (Negri 1989: 89). Work (production), education and training (reproduction), and leisure (consumption) all become points on an increasingly integrated circuit of capitalist activity so that 'the whole of society is placed at the disposal of profit' (Negri 1989: 79).

In a world where capital has insinuated itself everywhere, the shop floor is no longer a central locus of antagonism. Rather than dying away, however, conflict over exploitation fractally replicates, manifesting in myriad new movements that contest the logic of capital not only in workplaces, but also in homes, schools, universities, hospitals, and media. Facing this deterritorializing expansion of capital's valorization process, and the extension of its temporal measure from the working day to the life span, Negri observed that we have indeed 'gone beyond Marx'. In view of the fully socialized scope of exploitation we might, he said, choose to speak of anticapital 'not as a *worker* but as an *operator* or *agent*'. But by retaining the traditional Marxist epithet, he still chose to emphasize 'an antagonism which has never ceased to exist'—a conflict between the imperatives of hypercapital and the needs and desires of the social subjects on whose activity it depends (Negri 1989: 84).

Autonomia was defeated in the debacle of the Red Brigades and the Italian state of emergency. But Negri, imprisoned and then exiled, continued to work on the 'socialized worker' thesis. Critics would claim that he was so entranced by the a priori logic of the 'cycles of struggle' as to create a mirage of renewed resistance where none existed.[4] But as European opposition to neoliberalism began to revive in the late 1980s, Negri found fresh vindication. Looking over the French and Italian movements of students, nurses and environmentalists, he discerned a wave of struggles completely different from those of the mass worker, thematically linked to the social movements in the 1960s, but now entering a new phase characterized by a 'radically democratic form of organization . . . the rediscovery of a social perspective by the old sectors of the class struggle, the emergence of the feminist component, of workers from the tertiary sector and of "intellectual" labor' (Negri 1992a: 18). This last group, 'intellectual labor', was to become increasingly crucial to his analysis.

THE POST-FORDIST PROLETARIAT: CYBORGS
AND HACKERS

Negri was evolving these ideas at the moment when Marxian theorists were grappling with an apparent 'sea change' in capitalism, involving expanded transnationalization, new strategies of state power, and, critical to the socialized worker idea, new technologies (Harvey 1989: vii). Political economists of the Regulation School such as Michel Aglietta and Alain Lipietz were describing the shift from a 'Fordist' to a 'post-Fordist' regime of accumulation, a shift in which the move from industrial, mechanical production technologies to postindustrial digital systems was a key element (Aglietta 1979; Lipietz 1987). Regulation School theory concentrated on alterations in capital's managerial and governmental strategy—a focus which eventually laid it open to appropriation by these very forces as a sort of administrative manual for business improvement.[5] In contrast, Negri's work addressed many of the same issues as the Regulationists but, true to the *operaismo* tradition, focused on changes in subversive possibility, and on the emergent capacities of a post-Fordist proletariat.

Equally true to the *operaismo* heritage, Negri sought these possibilities in the heart of capital's new technological systems. Though *operaismo* had broken sharply with Soviet Marxism, the 'cycle of struggle' thesis showed an enduring Leninist influence. It decreed that it was precisely at capital's 'highest', most technologically and organizationally advanced point that its perennial opponent, labor, would be most dangerously reincarnated. In the case of both the 'professional' and the 'mass worker', the most striking manifestations of the autonomy of the living, variable, human element of capital emerged at the same point that its dead, fixed, machine-form was most sophisticated. So it was theoretically consistent of Negri to look for the manifestations of the next cycle of struggles amidst the new information technologies of post-Fordist capital. If the mass worker had labored on an assembly line, the socialized worker was at the end of a fiber-optic line.

Negri's orientation to the information technology issue surprised many. In his Autonomia days, he had won notoriety for his advocacy of sabotage (Negri 1979c). In the face of capital's digital revolution, many other Marxists took a similar stance, making a neo-Luddite turn.[6] But Negri's writings on the socialized worker take an opposite tack. In the post-Fordist world, he argued, capital surrounds the socialized worker with a dense web of technological devices—but this envelopment does not necessarily result in subjugation. As the system of machines becomes all-encompassing and familiar, the socialized worker enjoys an increasingly 'organic' relation to technoscience (Negri 1989: 93). Though initiated for purposes of control and command, as the system grows it becomes an 'ecology of machines'—an everyday ambience of potentials to be tapped and explored by the socialized worker, a technohabitat whose uses can no longer be exclusively dictated by capital (Negri 1989: 93).

What gave Negri such hopes that the digital environment could be a matrix of subversion? Although characteristically abstract, *The Politics of Subversion*, his most sustained statement of the socialized worker thesis, gives some sense of the concrete events fueling this optimism. It opens with a lyrical invocation of the French student strikes of 1986, a movement that not only highlighted the centrality of education to a high-technology capitalism, but was also one of the first social movements organized via computer networks, using the French predecessor to the Internet, Minitel.[7] In the context of this early experiment in 'hacktivism', Negri writes of the conflict between *communication* and *information* as central to the struggles of the 'socialized worker'. Communicative activity is 'current', distributed, transverse, dialogic; information is centralized, vertical, hierarchic and inert. Capital tries to capture the intellectual capacity of the labor force in the forms of information 'like a flat, glass screen on which is projected, fixed in black and white, the mystified cooperative potentialities of social labour—deprived of life, just like in a replay of *Metropolis*', while the direct current of communication takes transverse 'polychromatic forms' (Negri 1989: 117–18). In the era of the socialized worker, '*science, communication and the communication of knowledge*' are the raw material from which management must extract productivity—and from which subversion can blossom (Negri 1989: 116, emphasis in original).

An analysis that had started with an attempt to theorize the precarious, discarded and 'unproductive' social sectors activated in Autonomia had thus wound itself round to a position where its central protagonist was situated at the heart of post-Fordist technocapital, in the very midst of computer and telecommunication networks. Wary of charges of technocratic elitism, such as those that had surrounded Serge Mallet's earlier thesis about the revolutionary potential of technically skilled workers, Negri insisted that the intellectual powers of the socialized worker were not particular to a select cadre but the *generalized* form of labor power in a system suffused with technoscience (Mallet 1975). The new communicative and technological competencies, while most explicit among 'qualified' workers, existed in 'virtual' form even among the contingent and unemployed labor force, as the premises and prerequisites of everyday life in high-tech capitalism (Lazzarato and Negri 1991: 87). Linking hands with one of the most influential notions of postmodern theory, Donna Haraway's concept of the potentially transgressive 'cyborg' (Haraway 1985), Negri too gave a primary importance to the subversive possibilities of the prosthetic connection between flesh and technology, declaring, 'the cyborg is now the only model for theorizing subjectivity', and characterizing contemporary labor as a 'massified quality of the laboring intelligentsia, of cyborgs and hackers' (Hardt and Negri 1994: 10, 280).

FUTUR ANTÉRIEUR: GENERAL INTELLECT AND IMMATERIAL LABOR

Negri's revolutionary subject had barely completed the change from 'mass worker' to 'socialized worker' before it mutated again. The transformation took place in the pages of *Futur Antérieur*, a journal that bought together Autonomia veterans such as Negri and Paolo Virno with French, Italian and American left intellectuals such as Jean-Marie Vincent, Michael Hardt and Maurizio Lazzarato in a context of resurgent Parisian radicalism.[8] Founded in 1990, and coedited by Negri and Vincent, *Futur Antérieur* lasted for some seven years, involving hundreds of contributors and a score or more editorial committee members in a radical ferment of texts, seminars and working papers.[9] Although its collective mode of operations makes Negri's specific contributions hard to untangle from that of coauthors such as Hardt and Lazzarato, there is no doubt about his leading role in the emergence of a bold new analysis centered on 'general intellect' and 'immaterial labor'.

'General intellect' originates with Marx in a passage of *Grundrisse*, the 'Fragment on Machines', where he suggests that at a certain point in the future history of capital the creation of wealth will come to depend not on direct expenditure of labor time but on 'the general productive forces of the social brain' (Marx 1973: 699–743). This objectification of social knowledge will be crystallized in machinery—'fixed capital'—and in particular in two technologies: automated production and the networks of transport and communication integrating the world market. However, such a level of technological advance, which seems at first a capitalist utopia, contains within itself the seeds of a capitalist nightmare. Automation and communication, by reducing the need for labor power and intensifying social cooperation, between them undermine wage labor and private ownership. In the era of general intellect, 'Capital thus works towards its own dissolution as the form dominating production' (Marx 1973: 700).

For the *Futur Antérieur* group, 'The Fragment on Machines' offered a prefiguration of post-Fordist capitalism, complete with innovation milieux, robotic factories and global computer networks. But what—if anything—could now be made of the revolutionary hopes once attached to these developments? It was not, *Futur Antérieur* declared, enough to focus, as Marx had, on the accumulation of fixed capital. The critical factor was rather the variable capital—the human subjectivity—that created, supported and operated this high-technology apparatus. This subjectivity *Futur Antérieur* dubbed 'mass intellectuality'—the 'know-how'—technical, cultural, linguistic, and ethical—that supports the operation of the high-tech economy, a 'repository of knowledges indivisible from living subjects and from their linguistic co-operation' (Virno 1996b: 265).

Intimately bound up with mass intellect was what Negri, Hardt and Lazzarato now termed 'immaterial labor'.[10] In a high-technology environment, they claimed, commodities come to be 'less material', and 'more defined by cultural, informational, or knowledge components or by qualities of service and care'. The work that produces them also changes 'in a corresponding way'. Immaterial labor might thus be conceived as the labor 'that produces the informational, cultural, or affective element of the commodity' (Virno and Hardt 1996b: 261). It is the 'distinctive quality and mark' of work in 'the epoch in which information and communication play an essential role in each stage of the process of production' (Lazzarato and Negri 1991: 86).

Although there is continuity between Negri's socialized-worker writings and the *Futur Antérieur* analysis, the latter is far more theoretically ample and ambitious. 'General intellect' is a left appropriation of the utopian hopes associated with information technologies but so often identified with postindustrial neoliberalism. *Futur Antérieur* was not original in resorting to *Grundrisse* to make this recapture. Most previous Marxian speculations on the 'Fragment on Machines' had, however, focused on the crisis potential of mass unemployment as capital's drive to automation replaced living labor with the dead labor of machines. This had been a theme of both *operaismo* and Autonomia theorists, whose analysis had then been appropriated by André Gorz and turned to his own ends in his famous 'farewell to the working class', a motif echoed in the many 'end of work' forecasts appearing in the late 1980s and early 1990s in response to deindustrialization.[11] The potential for the 'reduction of obligatory labor time to a virtually negligible part of life' remained a theme of *Futur Antérieur* participants (Virno 1992: 47).

But Negri and others in the group opened up another front in the discussion by emphasizing the cooperative and creative potentials of a world where 'general intellect' manifested as networks of communication technologies. As Tiziana Terranova points out, the notion of 'general intellect' can be understood as a Marxian version of the thesis proposed by writers such as Marshall McLuhan, Kevin Kelly and Pierre Levy—that computers and telecommunications materialize a certain form of 'group mind' or 'collective intelligence'.[12] Classical Marxisms have, rightly, been contemptuous of such ideas for their technological determinism or idealism, and above all their assumption that such a collective consciousness arises as the self-reflexive awareness of global capitalism. But this rejection might be reconsidered if we position the issue within an antagonistic perspective, seeing the noosphere contested in class war—and this is the prospect the theory of 'general intellect' opens.

Where *Futur Antérieur* remained loyal to the *operaismo* heritage of some of its participants was in its optimism. The crucial question, Vincent wrote, was how far capital could contain the 'plural, multiform constantly mutating intelligence' of general intellect within its structures (Vincent 1993: 121). Negri and his coauthors found burgeoning insubordination in the strikes of a new generation of auto workers in factories where 'participative management' or 'team work'—arguably the cellular, microcosmic embodiment of 'general intellect'—had created flashpoints of resentment by requiring responsibility without yielding power; in the 'Panther' movement of Italian students against educational austerity, notable for its skillful media strategies and subversive fax-networking; and in the grievances and mobilizations of Parisian fashion and multimedia workers, an array of unrests which were eventually to detonate in the massive French general strikes of 1995–96 (Lazzarato, Negri, and Santilli 1990; Lazzarato and Negri 1993; Lazzarato 1990a, Lazzarato 1990b). As these European struggles were accumulating, exploding, and subsiding, however, 'immaterial labor' was beginning to attract attention in the transnational venues of cyberspace.

NET-THEORY: FREE LABOR AND DOT.COMMUNISM

Though Negri's writings allude to hacker culture, they contain little direct discussion of the Internet. There is, however, a manifest 'fit' between Negri's theories and cyberspace. Computer networks are, after all, the exemplary technology of the restructured, informational capital posited in his discussions of immaterial labor. The brief, fast history of the Internet can be seen as an intensively compressed and accelerated 'cycle of struggles', involving a rapid sequence of appropriations and counterappropriations that move from the military command and control system of the 1970s, to the academic research network of the 1980s, to the populist virtual community of the early 1990s, to the projects of e-commodification that rose so swiftly, and then fell so hard in the dot.com boom and bust. Today, the faltering vectors of e-capital tangle with a molecular proliferation of hacktivists, net-artists, cypherpunks and pirate autonomous zones, all of whom can be seen as manifesting the uncontrollable, self-valorizing powers of general intellect.[13]

Throughout the 1990s conventional neo-Marxism was often indifferent to these anarchic, 'techie' cybersubversions, focusing instead on gloomy forecasts of the Internet's imminent corporate subsumption.[14] In contrast, *Futur Antérieur* offered a theoretical lexicon adequate to the varied creative possibilities that political, cultural, and technological activists were exploring in cyberspace. So it was on the Net, in virtual forums such as nettime, rhizome, telepolis, and c-theory, that Negri's work found a new reception, in a world far removed from the industrial factory origins of *operaismo*.[15]

One area where his analysis struck an immediate chord was around digital struggles over intellectual property. The attempts of e-business to enclose a Net commons in commodity form has at once capitalized on the free cooperative powers of 'netizens' and also called into a being a resistant shadow-world of piracy, open-source coders and peer-to-peer networks. These digital developments uncannily corroborate Negri's assertions about the autonomy of labor. We can see how his ideas reverberate in this context by listening to their echoes in the work of two recent analyses of the net-economy, those of Tiziana Terranova and Richard Barbrook.

In her 'Free Labor: Producing Culture for the Digital Economy', Terranova focuses on the labor, 'simultaneously voluntarily given and unwaged, enjoyed and exploited', that is involved in 'building Web sites, modifying software packages, reading and participating in mailing lists and building virtual spaces in MUDs and MOOs' (Terranova 2000: 33). The transition from Fordism to post-Fordism has, she says, made obsolete the old industrial working class, but has also produced generations of workers socialized as 'active consumers' of cultural commodities. Capitalist managers need to recycle these sensibilities back into production to provide the look, style and sounds that sell music, games, film, video, and home software. But this can only be partially accomplished by the recruitment of paid workers. Media capital is obliged to harvest a field of collective cultural and affective endeavors which it 'nurtures, exploits and exhausts', selectively 'hyper-compensating some areas and ripping off others' (Terranova 2000: 53). Free web work, such as that performed by America On-Line chat room hosts or *Quake* on-line architects, represents the moment where the 'knowledgeable consumption of culture is translated into productive activities that are pleasurably embraced and at the same time often shamelessly exploited' (Terranova 2000: 37).

Terranova explicitly connects her analysis of the digital economy to 'what the Italian autonomists have called the social factory' (Terranova

2000: 33). She refers to *Futur Antérieur's* concept of general intellect, and develops its suggestion that a key feature of 'immaterial labor' is that it is 'difficult to quantify in the capitalist schema of valorization' because 'much of the value produced today thus arises from activities outside the production process proper, in the sphere of nonwork' (Virno and Hardt 1996b: 262). Picking up on this idea, Terranova proposes that 'free labor is structural to late capitalist cultural economy'. Managing this process, she says, requires a difficult channeling of collaborative flows within very 'open organizational structures' immersed in 'a culture of exchange', and in contact with the 'fast-moving world of knowledge in general' (Terranova 2000: 37). Ultimately, she is equivocal as to whether or not digital capital can pull this trick off. At one point she asserts that the 'self-organizing, collective intelligence' of networked immaterial labor 'neutralizes' the operations of capital by subverting the wage relation; later she retreats to the more modest suggestion that this 'intractable' process entails 'some crucial contradictions' (Terranova 2000: 46, 55). Although Negri would favor the first of these formulations over the second, Terranova's work is a telling instance of the Internet application of his theories.

Equally striking are the parallels between Negri's work and Barbrook's 'Cyber-Communism: How the Americans are Superseding Capitalism in Cyberspace' (Barbrook n.d.). The technoculture of the Net has, Barbrook argues, been antagonistic to the market from its start. Not only did it originate in the public sector (the Pentagon), but in its transfer to academia the Net developed a gift or potlatch economy based on the free exchange of information copied at zero cost and transmissible in zero time. To this day these capacities, embedded in digital architecture, frustrate commodification—as shown by the convulsion of copyright regimes in cyberspace. Ease of digital reproduction and the speed of network circulation are warping and blasting holes in the fabric of intellectual property, in the perpetual value-hemorrhage of 'piracy' and a plethora of open-source activity that, by producing virtual machines that can be 'continually modified, amended and improved by anyone with the appropriate programming skills', makes blatant the inadequacy of private property to the conditions of digital production (Barbrook n.d.).

'Cyber-Communism' was released before the 'download rage' of Napster, Gnutella, Free Net and other peer-to-peer networks. But Barbrook today finds in the current panic of the music industry confirmation of his view that an economy of 'interactive creativity' cannot be based on property and commodification (Barbrook 2001). While the official, explicit ideology of post-Cold War North America is a triumphal celebration of the free market, in their daily practice millions of Americans are, he says, actually involved in an on-line digital circulation of free music, films, games and information. In a pragmatic and everyday way, they are 'engaged in the slow process of superseding capitalism'. The makers of e-commerce are laying an infrastructure for the free circulation of decommodified e-goods. 'Dot.com' is dialectically generating 'dot.communism', in the ultimate Marxist instance of the contradiction between forces and relations of production (Barbrook 2001).

Barbrook, like Terranova, eventually retreats from the most radical anticapitalist implications of his own analysis. But there is a large area of agreement between his 'dot.communism' and *Futur Antérieur*'s 'general intellect'. The idea that high-tech production is destroying the law of value and deconstructing capitalism before our very eyes recurs constantly in Negri's writings, writings of which Barbrook is well aware. As Negri puts it in one of his most famous (or notorious) statements, in the cyborg world of immaterial labor,

> Cooperation, or the association of producers, is posed independently of the organizational capacity of capital; the cooperation and subjectivity of labor have found a point of contact outside of the machinations of capital. Capital becomes merely an apparatus of capture, a phantasm, and an idol. Around it move radically autonomous processes of self-valorization that not only constitute an alternative basis of potential development but also actually represent a new constituent foundation. (Hardt and Negri 1994: 282)

Negri and other *Futur Antérieur* writers often suggest that 'immaterial labor' will emancipate itself from capital not by insurrection but by 'exodus'—an oblique process of subtraction, withdrawal or defection which both refuses the existing social order and constructs another one. Barbrook's vision of a dot.communism created by the pragmatic, quotidian but massive copyright violations and collective production practices of virtual consumers and workers is arguably a concretized vision of this process. To both Negri and Barbrook, e-capital now resembles a cartoon figure that has walked off the top of a cliff into immaterial ether that cannot support it, but continues to tread air for a few moments before waking to its predicament and plummeting downward.

RENAISSANCE OF SLAVERY: NOT SO IMMATERIAL AFTER ALL?

But if 'immateriality' was corroborated and celebrated in the theoretical venues of cyberspace, it provoked skepticism and condemnation elsewhere, including from within the very autonomist tradition with which Negri is identified. One way of understanding this criticism is to note that Negri's theory of immaterial labor seems very like a Marxian mirror image of the 'knowledge work' celebrated by managerial savants from Peter Drucker through Daniel Bell to Alvin Toffler and Robert Reich. Where business futurists saw in the enhanced productivity of the technoscientific worker the salvation of capital, *Futur Antérieur* found an agent of digital subversion. Both, however, share a belief that the critical form of labor power in high-technology capital is communicational and intellectual.

Such a direct inversion of managerial orthodoxy, however, evidently risks entrapment in the arms of its bourgeois doppelgänger. The very designation 'immaterial labor'—like 'knowledge worker'—appears to occlude the obstinate embodiment of the virtual subject, and deny some very corporeal components of high-tech work such as repetitive strain injury and carpal tunnel syndrome, eyestrain and radiation hazards, ruptured circadian rhythms, terminal isolation, and workplace epidemics of hyperstress, all of which should be a critical touchstone. This problem persists despite assertions by Negri and his coauthors that 'immaterial labor' doesn't mean nonmaterial and that 'while tending towards immateriality . . . it is no less corporeal than intellectual'—protestations which, however sincere, nevertheless shut the stable door of theory after a discursive horse has bolted (Hardt and Negri 1994: 9).

Even more problematic for the 'immaterial labor' thesis, however, is the awkward persistence of all-too-grossly material work. Post-Fordism actually displays a bifurcating occupational structure, in which only one part corresponds to the ideal portrait of the technologically adept 'knowledge worker', while the other is constituted by a mass of low-end, poorly paid, insecure, service work (Henwood 1995; Golding 1996: 82). All occupations are touched by the communication revolutions (servers in coffee shops wear military style headsets; couriers carry digital signature pads; everyone uses beepers, and so on), and in this sense, the repeated observation of Negri and his coauthors that immaterial labor exists *throughout* the postindustrial proletariat is true. But the grand sweep of this argument minimizes the differences between well-skilled, well-paid symbolic analysts, and the postindustrial service sector of janitors, fast-food operatives, and data-entry clerks.

Where such criticisms of Negri's work strike most strongly, however, are in relation to gender and the international division of labor. If 'general intellect' is strongly associated with digital networked processes, then how does it take account of the traditional, and in many areas persisting, patterns, of masculine predominance and female exclusion that have characterized high-tech development? Is general intellect only half a social brain—the masculine half? And if 'immaterial labor' is made up of 'cyborgs and hackers', then how central is it to the class composition of a world where most of the population of China has never touched a computer, half the world's population has never made a phone call, and more than a third do not have electricity?

No one has made these objections more tellingly than George Caffentzis, whose arguments are especially interesting because he shares Negri's broadly 'autonomist' perspective. Caffentzis stands within a line of autonomist thought that as early as the 1980s had begun to diverge sharply from Negri's analysis. This alternative autonomism has its origins in the work of Mariarosa Dalla Costa and Selma James on the unwaged work of housewives. Anticipating themes now popular in feminist political economy, Dalla Costa and James argued that within the social factory, the reproduction of labor power occupied a crucial but unacknowledged role (Dalla Costa and James 1972). Without the—to male theorists—invisible labor process of childbearing, child raising, cooking, shopping, education, cleaning, and caring, in short, 'housework', labor power would not be ready for work each morning. Other theorists applied an analogous argument to the situation of other unwaged groups—such as students—within advanced capital. And James, drawing on her connections to Caribbean struggles, enlarged the analysis to include the unwaged work of peasant farmers and subsistence producers in the global South (Midnight Notes Collective 1992). There is a certain irony in finding the theoreticians of 'immaterial labor' discover on the Web a 'free labor' issue very similar to that which this earlier generations of analysts had pinpointed in the very material processes of the kitchen and the field, indentured servitude, sex slavery, child labor, and prison work.

If Negri's version of the cycle of struggles was implicitly Leninist in its attention to capital's 'strongest link', this other stream of autonomist thought understood Mao's insights about the possibilities of breaking its chain at the 'weak' points of maximum impoverishment. Its perspective found a North American voice in journals such as *Zerowork* and *Midnight Notes*, in which Caffentzis played a central role. While Negri and *Futur Antérieur* were gravitating towards an analysis of the 'high' end of the capitalist work hierarchy in metropolitan centers, Caffentzis and *Midnight Notes* looked more to the 'low' end of global labor power, and were far more attuned to issues of gendered and transnational superexploitation.[16] The tension between these versions of autonomist thought had been evident for some time, but it exploded when Caffentzis launched a scathing critique of the 'general intellect' thesis, accusing Negri of celebrating 'cyborgs' and 'immaterial labor' while ignoring the 'renaissance of slavery' (Caffentzis 1998).

Negri's interpretation of the *Grundrisse* was, Caffentzis said, wildly misleading. Elsewhere, Marx's analysis of capital's growing reliance on fixed capital—machinery—is counterposed against recognition of its counter-acting tendency to constantly re-recruit the living labor that provides the ultimate source of value (Caffentzis 1998). Consequently, Caffentzis argued, the rise of 'automatic processes' in industry, along with its numerically small attendant cadres of immaterial labor, must be accompanied by the creation somewhere on the planet of new masses of dispossessed labor available for a maximal intensity of exploitation: 'the computer requires the sweatshop, and the cyborg's existence is premised on the slave' (Caffentzis 1998).

These processes were empirically visible in 'new enclosures', unfolding throughout global capitalism, but most violently in the global South ('The New Enclosures' in Midnight Notes Collective 1992: 317–33). A vast new proletariat was being created as people were driven off the land by the advances of agribusiness and condemned to an existence in a desperate informal labor market revolving around industries such as the sex and drug trades, domestic labor, animal exports, smuggling of arms and humans—or to work in new industrial centers. These dispossessed popula-tions supplied the labor force for manufacturing plants whose apparent dematerialization from the high-wage North was actually only a trans-national relocation towards China, Central and Latin America, Southern Asia and Eastern Europe. This process is gendered, both because the creation of this new industrial proletariat is largely a mobilization of 'nimble-fingered', supposedly cheap and docile, women workers, and because the social costs of convulsive industrialization are relentlessly offloaded onto unpaid female housework.

Factories, agribusinesses and brothels are vital even to digital capitalism, because, Caffentzis argued, they

> . . . increase the total pool of surplus labor, help depress wages, cheapen the elements of constant capital, and tremendously expand the labor market and make possible the development of high-tech indus-tries that directly employ only a few knowledge workers or cyborgs. (Caffentzis 1998)

Negri's declaration that capital is now becoming 'merely an apparatus of capture, a phantasm, an idol' was utterly delusional. On the contrary, what was appearing on a global scale was a reinstitution of the most basic and brutal mechanisms of primitive accumulation. The new circuits of capital looked a lot less 'phantom-like', 'immaterial' and 'intellectual' to the female and Southern workers doing the grueling physical toil demanded by a capitalist 'general intellect' whose headquarters remain preponderantly male and Northern. And once one abandoned a top-down, Northern view, the exemplary figure in any new cycle of struggles is not the immaterial cyborg worker:

> Once again, as at the dawn of capitalism, the physiognomy of the world proletariat is that of the pauper, the vagabond, the criminal, the panhandler, the refugee sweatshop worker, the mercenary, the rioter. ('The New Enclosures' in Midnight Notes Collective 1992: 321)

Negri, Caffentzis remarked acidly, needed to 'expand his revolutionary geography' (Caffentzis 1998).

This was a damning critique. Negri and his coauthors from *Futur Antérieur* were not without reply. One riposte was that the centrality of immaterial labor was not so much actual as tendential. Just as textile operatives in Manchester factories of the 1820s constituted only a miniscule fraction of the global laboring population yet represented a form of work that would over the course of a century and a half become definitive of industrial capitalism, so too, the 'microserfs' of Gate's campus at Redmond are the forerunners of the future generalized forms of laboring cooperation. Nonetheless, one must ask if this classically Marxian reply, so similar in its linear model of capitalist development to the theory of inevitable march from agricultural to industrial to informational production beloved of postindustrial futurists, has *ever* really been adequate to the 'uneven and combined' aspects of accumulation.

In an era when world-cities and *maquiladora* zones are manifestly inter-dependent, the whole capitalist organization of 'general intellect' appears predicated on dividing the 'head' of the collective worker from the 'arms', 'feet', 'digestive', 'excretory', and 'reproductive' organs. Such division tends to fall along lines of gender, geography and ethnicity. To give only one example, my own research into the international division of labor of the video and computer game industry—surely a prototypical 'immaterial work' field—reveals a vast gulf between the cyborg-style software development work of predominantly male programmers and designers in Europe, Japan and North America; female workers assembling hardware in the *maquiladora* industrial zones of Central America and China; and the slave-like conditions of miners in the war zones of the Congo extracting columbine-tantalite and other rare minerals necessary to the operations of Sony PlayStations.[17] The immaterial labor theory is not well fitted to distinguish these gradations of toil, all critical to an advanced technoscientific infrastructure, and consequently risks universalizing experiences most available to labor insofar as it is both Northern and male.

EMPIRE: BIOPOLITICAL CONVOLUTIONS

With the appearance in 2000 of *Empire*, coauthored by Hardt and Negri (2000), the debate about the place of 'immaterial labor' in a transnational capitalism was raised to a new level. In contrast to the metropolitan focus of the *Futur Antérieur* discussions, *Empire*'s topic is nothing less than what is popularly known as 'globalization'. It portrays a universalizing yet decentered world-market regime, organized by no single nation or force—not even the United States—but rather through a hybrid, multilayered ensemble of political, corporate, and nongovernmental organizations, constituting itself in the very process of incessant improvised crisis control, and operating to extract profit from both the spatial and social entirety of life through a play of financial, cultural and judicial networks ultimately backed by the stupendous military force deployed in recurrent police actions. The antagonistic force uprising within and against this new world order Hardt and Negri now call 'the multitude'—the creative, pluralistic subject whose constitutive power empire simultaneously requires, requisitions and represses. The multitude is a force that in Hardt and Negri's 'Roman' metaphor can be at various moments identified with slaves, barbarians, or Christians. And the authors' inventory of its contemporary rebellions goes well beyond Eurocentric boundaries, including Los Angeles 1992, Tiananmen Square 1989, Chiapas 1994, France 1995, the Palestinian Infitada, and the struggles of refugees and 'nomadic' immigrant labor to constitute a vision of contestation on a truly world scale.

That *Empire* is a major accomplishment, which within the so-called anti- or counterglobalization movements has catalyzed an overdue debate about theoretical premises and strategic directions, needs no underlining. From its multidimensional richness of concepts I select only those that bear directly on the 'immaterial labor' debate. And here *Empire* presents a strange contradiction. On the one hand, it continues, though with modifications, Negri's emphasis on the centrality of cyborg subjects. On the other, it repudiates what Negri had previously celebrated as one of, if not the, main subversive potentials of such subjects—its communicative powers. Paradoxically, *Empire* gives us at once more and less of a 'cyber-Negri'.

In explaining this conundrum, the first thing to note is that Hardt and Negri have clearly taken note of their critics. 'General intellect' remains important in their analysis. But they now distance themselves from the *Futur Antérieur* analysis because it is too 'angelic', and treats 'new laboring practices' only in their 'incorporeal and intellectual' aspect (Hardt and Negri 2000: 30). 'General intellect' is therefore recontextualized in a new and more 'somatic' concept of 'biopolitical production', which makes a Marxian appropriation of Foucault's concept 'biopower'— so that the object of capitalist appropriation is seen not so much as 'labor power' but as 'life itself' (2000: 25–31). This is, in my view, an extremely fruitful line of thought whose significance I will discuss more fully later in this chapter.

Yet in this new constellation 'immaterial labor' still has a special priority. Hardt and Negri now identify three subcategories of such work (2000: 289–94). The first is industrial production 'informationalized' by computer and communication technologies; the second is 'symbolic analytic' work; and the third involves the 'production and manipulation of affect', the generation of a sense of ease, well-being, satisfaction, excitement or passion. This last category had appeared in Hardt and Negri's earlier formulations, but is now given more attention. In particular, they stress the importance of female labor, with its traditional burden of 'caring' work, as a component of immaterial labor, and emphasize the corporeal involvement and bodily presence integral to this kind of emotion-work. This new version of 'immaterial labor'—release 0.2—thus appears to answer or disarm accusations of high-tech vanguardism, Cartesian dualism, or masculine bias: sex workers and software developers are now both included.

This new catholicism may, however, come at a cost. Analysis that puts under one roof multimedia designers, primary school teachers, machine operatives in a computerized car plant, and strippers—all of whom fall within the definition of 'immaterial labor 0.2'—may reveal valuable commonalities. But it can also covers up chasmic differences, fault lines of segmentation, veritable continental rifts that present the most formidable barriers for the organization of counterpower. In fact, there is a certain theoretical sleight of hand at work in *Empire*. Although the concept of immateriality is enlarged to embrace 'affective', intensely corporeal and frequently female work, its defining features continue to be attributes of the 'cyborg' worker. Thus we are still told that laboring practices 'all tend toward the model of information and communication technologies', that 'the anthropology of cyberspace is really a recognition of the new human condition', that it is through the 'computerization of production [that] labor tends towards the position of abstract labor', and so forth (Hardt and Negri 2000: 291–2). Although Hardt and Negri appear to have modified some of the aspects of 'immaterial labor' that critics such as Caffentzis attacked, the cyborg, high-tech form of such labor continues to be the privileged point of reference for their theory.

In the context of this continuing defense of 'immaterial labor' a very surprising—almost bizarre—aspect of *Empire* is its treatment of communication between global struggles. In all analysis of immaterial labor to this point Negri and his collaborators had emphasized that the crucial capacity of this productive subject, the very quality that capital must expropriate, is its communicative power. And this point is emphasized again in *Empire*; communication networks, especially digital networks, are the contemporary equivalent of Roman roads, the connective lifelines of power traversing the domain of the new world order. Given this, one might predict that the insurgencies of the multitude would be rife with projects of reappropriating communication—just as Negri suggested in his earlier analysis of the socialized worker.

Yet when *Empire* considers the interrelation of global struggles, it suddenly retracts this possibility. Amazingly, Negri and Hardt assert that insurgencies from Chiapas to Paris to Seoul 'cannot communicate' with one another. Despite all the availability of networks and media, 'struggles have become all but incommunicable'. Not only do the various outbreaks lack 'a common language' and a 'common enemy'. These absences, rather than being a source of weakness are, according to Negri and Hardt, a sign of strength. So omnipresent and planetwide are the operations of imperial power that each outburst of revolt, while unable to communicate with the others and constitute a 'horizontal' cycle of struggles, can, in its own isolated singularity, 'leap vertically and touch immediately on the global level'. Thus, even though the movements of the multitude are all incommunicado one with another, they nevertheless between them constitute a 'new kind of proletarian solidarity' (Hardt and Negri 2000: 54).

This is an extraordinary declaration, not least because it repudiates what is perhaps the strongest evidence for the importance of immaterial labor to contemporary subversion. The use of communication networks of all sorts—including but not limited to the Internet—to create what Harry Cleaver terms an 'electronic fabric of struggle' has been a signal feature of recent movements against neoliberalism (Cleaver 1994: 15). The tricontinental linkages of anti-NAFTA movements; 'Zapatistas in cyberspace'; international campaigns supporting the East Timorese and Ogoni; anti-sweatshop struggles and boycotts; 'McLibel'; the networked communication of anti-bioengineering movements; the Jubilee debt abolition campaign; the transnational mobilizations against the WTO, World Bank, IMF, OECD, APEC; the multinational opposition, spun from Canada to Malaysia, against the Multilateral Agreement on Investment; the 'Battle of Seattle'—all have been movements in which cyberactivism, autonomous media and infiltration of mainstream channels have been an integral feature.[18] Internet use in particular has profoundly affected their organizational form and the convergence of their demands, not to mention catalyzing a lively discussion of countermeasures and 'net-wars' in military–industrial think tanks (Arquilla and Ronfeldt 1993). In the light of this, *Empire's* claim about the failure of multitudinous insurrections to communicate, or compose themselves into a cycle of struggle, seems far off the mark. This is all the more surprising since the 'cyber-Negri' that emerged during the 1990s seems so well positioned to comprehend these phenomena.

Empire thus presents a puzzling set of tensions. On the one hand, it makes a continuing affirmation of the 'immaterial labor' thesis, ostensibly expanding the designation to a very broad swathe of workers, yet still deriving its primary models from those in close proximity to computer and communication technologies. On the other, it offers an 'incommunicado' theory of resistances which paradoxically denies the very aspect of immaterial labor other analysts have seen as most important— the communicational circulation of struggle. Is there a key to this strange torsion?

There is, and it can be summed up in the phrase 'too smooth by half'. Too smooth, that is to say, in the sense in which Deleuze and Guattari speak of planetary capitalism creating a space that is both smooth (presenting an unimpeded global field of accumulation) and striated (in the sense of being savagely segmented by differences on which capital can play) (Deleuze and Guattari 1983, Deleuze and Guattari 1987). Repeating what is both a weakness endemic to Marxism, and perhaps a particular vulnerability in Negri's work, *Empire* emphasizes the smoothness—the homogenizing effects of global capital—at the expense of the striating divisions. By declaring the centrality of immaterial labor, it proposes a consistent underlying class composition running throughout the multitude. Because this class composition is posited as *already* existing, the successes—or failures—of communication linkages between insurgencies, which might be thought of as playing a critical role in constructing alliances, is devalued. With the very real disjunctions and frictions between different strata of labor occluded, *Empire* can celebrate the spontaneous solidarity of the multitude without descending to the awkward business of sorting out just how much commonality there really is between participants in, say, the Tiananmen Square revolt, the Intifada, and the French general strike or the Seattle Showdown, or how they might actually be tied together.

In reality, there are potentially deep differences and complex contradictions both between and within these revolts. Radical improvement in the conditions of Southern workers may entail sacrifices by their Northern counterparts; moves to global equity can collide with green agendas; Northern antiglobalization mobilizations are not immune from protectionist chauvinism; rebels against authoritarian state socialism may not necessarily and automatically be onside with revolts against global capital—and so on. To ignore these real and material tensions is simply to hand such issues over for exploitation by nationalists, fascists, and fundamentalists. Such barriers to a 'multitudinous' insurgency against capital can be overcome—and Negri and Hardt should be saluted for theorizing in a way that resonates with the spirit moving in the tear gas-shrouded streets of Seattle, Paris, and Seoul. But the project of the multitude is a task of vast articulation between diverse movements whose identity of interests is not immediately given. Because of its overexpanded category of immaterial labor, and its consequently simplified notion of planetary class composition, *Empire* masks these difficulties; but its assumption of spontaneous unanimity is one that the vicissitudes of twenty-first-century struggle will certainly reveal as all too immaterial.

UNIVERSAL LABOR, GENERAL INTELLECT AND SPECIES BEING

In raising these criticisms, it is not my intention to reject the remarkable theoretical achievements of *Empire*, but rather to propose some reconfigurations and amendments that preserve and extend Hardt and Negri's insights while avoiding their contradictions. I suggest three revisions. (1) Resituate 'immaterial labor' as one component of a broader composition of 'universal labor'. (2) Retain the concept of 'general intellect', but reject the 'incommunicado' thesis. (3) Recognize 'universal labor' and 'general intellect' as elements in the constitution of what Marx termed 'species being'.

First, recognizing the real importance of immaterial labor in today's global struggles requires decentering it from the privileged spot to which Negri assigns it. The problematic of an insurgent multitude—to use *Empire*'s term—is that of recomposing a wide variety of different types of labor, waged and unwaged. This interaction is complex, intractable, and cannot be ironed out by incrementally expanding the concept of immateriality until it includes everyone from programmers to prostitutes. Although there are any number of ways of categorizing the diversity of planetary laborers, we could, very schematically, suggest that the attention paid to 'immaterial' laborers be balanced by equal attention to at least two other groups—'material' and 'immiserated' workers. If immaterial labor is characterized according to its communicational and affective activity, then material labor is that type of work still primarily focused on shaping the physicality of products—from SUVs to running shoes to semiconductor chips—which obstinately refuse to dematerialize themselves; and immiserated labor is that part of the labor force which, through various gradations of precarious and contingent employment up to the short- and long-term reserve army of the unemployed, is treated by capital as simply surplus to requirements.

Mirroring the structure of Negri's argument, we can say that tendencies towards 'materiality' and 'immiseration', like 'immaterial' propensities, are latent—shall we say 'virtual'?—throughout the entire postindustrial workforce. All concrete work is constituted at an intersection of these three categories, which are not mutually exclusive but actualized to differing degrees along a continuum. But it is also possible to identify extremes on these continuums amongst different strata of planetary labor. The spatial concentrations of these extreme forms of labor in particular continents, regions and urban areas now constitute the 'North' and 'South' of the global order. If the paradigmatic figures of today's immaterial labor are amongst the net-workers of the World Wide Web, then those of material labor are surely in the manufacturing plants of the *maquiladoras*, export processing zones and new industrial areas; and those of immiserated labor in the vast tides of the homeless and itinerant who settle in the doorways and alleys of every rural slum and world city.

Once we differentiate these sectors of global labor, it is by no means evident that the struggles of 'immaterial labor' are the central ones on which those of other groups, as Hardt and Negri claim, 'converge' (Hardt and Negri 1994: 281). On the contrary, it may well be the insurgencies of 'immiserated/material' labor—the revolts of the Haitian maker of Disney T-shirts, or of dispossessed peasants in Chiapas or Brazil, or the East Timorese resistance fighters—that provide the critical points of focus, with which radicalized sectors of immaterial labor 'identify' and on which they 'converge' in solidarity, propelled both by a basic sense of justice and a self-protective resistance against a the global 'race to the bottom'. Negri and Guattari once observed that 'the proletariats of the most developed countries are literally terrorized by the spectacle of the extermination by hunger which Integrated World Capitalism imposes on the marginalized . . . countries' (Guattari and Negri 1990: 58). This intimidation is the turning point of capital's control over the world labor market, and it is on breaking this pivot that many world struggles now converge.

Thus while immaterial labor *is* privileged in terms of the high-technology capitalist hierarchy of work, the dynamics of struggle against that hierarchy often flow in the reverse direction, from the bottom up. Despite all the panic of music industry oligarchs, capital's anxieties about Napster users probably pale compared with its fears of specters of a cruder and more blood-drenched kind: narco-Marxo-guerrilla land wars in Latin America, labor militancy in the manufacturing zones of Southeast Asia, new cycles of unrest exploding through the Middle Eastern oil proletariat. It is, indeed, very tempting to reverse the priority Negri gives to immaterial labor by saying: in the circuits of capitalism, immiserated labor is discarded, material labor produces commodities, while immaterial labor contributes primarily to their circulation (advertising, media, e-commerce). But in the circuit of struggles, it is immiserated labor that generates spontaneous insurgencies (riots, insurrections, land wars), material labor that gives these struggles organizational form (strikes, unions) and immaterial labor that circulates these struggles (media, net-wars, etc.). In fact, such a formulation would be absurdly overschematic and hence almost as mystifying as the 'immaterial labor' thesis, but it does at least have the advantage of turning our attention to the central problem of mobilization against a world market, which is that of organizing across the 'international division of laborers' (James 1986).

I therefore propose resituating 'immaterial', 'material' and 'immiserated' work as sectors of a broader class composition of 'universal labor'. 'Universal labor' is the term Marx uses (very briefly) in Volume 3 of *Capital* to describe the 'social applications by combined labor' that support 'all scientific work, all discovery and invention'.[19] It seems an appropriate term to designate the contemporary composition of anticapitalist struggle for two reasons. First, it acknowledges the planetary dimensions of this contest, and in particular the importance of North–South linkages. Second, since 'universal' can be taken as referring not just to spatial coordinates, but rather to an enveloping, totalizing or englobing condition, the term can also be taken as affirming Negri and Hardt's insights about the multidimensional nature of the 'biopower' that capital now seeks to corral, not just in the workplace but also in homes, schools, training programs, media audiences, medical experiments and other life-spanning venues. Retaining the language of the 'cycle of struggles', but revising its terminology, we can now produce a sequence that goes 'craft worker, mass worker, universal worker'. The 'universal worker' is not a given, but an organizational creation. It is a project of political recomposition that appears to the degree that the fragmented insurgencies of 'immaterial', 'material' and 'immiserated' labor are connected.

This brings us to a second revision, addressing the relation of 'general intellect' to Hardt and Negri's 'incommunicado' thesis. The idea of networked social intelligence whose composition and control is contested between capitals and counterpower is a valuable optic for analyzing the collision between e-capital and a hydra-like array of subversions from hacktivism to peer-to-peer and open-source experiments.[20] It is in fact hard to envisage what form a twenty-first-century communism might take *other* than as a distributed but interconnected system of collective communication devoted to solving problems of a material and immaterial resource allocation.

But to do justice to the reality of this emergent 'general intellect', Negri and Hardt's 'incommunicado' thesis, declaring communication between global struggle both impossible and unnecessary, should be abandoned, or, better, reversed. Perhaps the main manifestation of oppositional collective intelligence today is the weaving of networks of communications between insurgencies. This is not just a matter of cyberactivism, but of a wide range of autonomous and alternative media—video, film, guerrilla radio, print. These are in turn elements in hybrid networks of pre- and postindustrial communication forms whose complex relays transfer news and information from e-mail exchanges to in-person meetings and back again. Partly alongside, partly separate from the creation of this 'electronic fabric of struggle' are struggles *about* the creation of the electronic fabric, contesting the capitalist architecture of the networks, and its classificatory stratifications of access. Together, these do indeed constitute a formidable accumulation of a general intellect contesting the market intelligence of e-capital.

Such a collective counterintelligence links the widely *diversified* sectors of universal labor. It creates in cyber- and media spaces a recompositional arena where the fragmentation inflicted by a deterritorialized information capital can be counteracted. One aspect of this process is the circulation of information, images and analysis from the geographical zones where the struggles of immiserated and material workers are concentrated into the more metropolitan zones where immaterial labor is congregated, to mobilize support for uprisings and to delegitimize the use of imperial force against them. Divisions between immaterial, material and immiserated labor, with all that this entails in terms of differential access to media technologies and skills, create evident problems for such a project. Reliance on the Internet can generate elitist forms of 'Cyber-Leninism' that perpetuate within anticapitalist movements the same patterns of exclusion—of the South, of the poor, and particularly of poor women and minority groups—that shape capitalism's 'information highway' strategies.[21]

This could consign struggles occurring in the 'black holes of the information economy' to yet deeper oblivion (Castells 1996). These problems should be recognized without reverting—as in Judith Hellman's recent attack on the cyberactivists supporting the Chiapas uprising—to a nostalgic mythicization of some supposed golden age of unmediated, in-person activism.[22] The paradox of insurgent organization today is not, as Hardt and Negri suggest, that struggles cannot communicate. It is a more complex and interesting one—namely that the same communication systems that constitute the general intellect of net-capital can be transformed into a revolutionary 'social brain', but only if such a project is constantly vigilant against replicating the very divisive logic against which it contends.

What is at stake in the development of 'universal labor' and 'general intellect' is nothing less than the trajectory of 'species being'. 'Species being' is the term Marx uses to refer to humanity's self-recognition as a natural species with capacity to objectify and transform the 'natural' conditions of its collective life—making 'life activity itself an object of will and consciousness' (Marx 1964). At the start of a new millennium, the issue manifests in an array of issues of almost stupefying magnitude: ecological and biospheric change; control of AIDS; xenotransplants; longevity extensions; cyborg prostheses and reproductive technologies; the fabrication of new life forms; not to mention the 'exterminist' possibilities of nuclear, chemical and biological warfare (Thompson et al. 1982).

That these issues are closely associated with the new technological powers created by 'general intellect' is, in the age of the Human Genome Project, obvious. So, too, is the continuing centrality of the problem Marx raised in relation to 'species being', namely the alienation of collective, human-transforming capacities into the hands of privatized ownership. Thus the recent revival of the concept of species being by authors such as David Harvey and Gayatri Spivak, rather than constituting a reversion to a much-reviled 'Marxist humanism', marks a crucial consideration about the collective control and direction of a technoscientific apparatus capable of operationalizing a whole series of posthuman or subhuman conditions.[23]

To suggest a renewed attention to the problematic of 'species being' is consonant with the move in *Empire* towards a theory of 'biopower'. But because of the excessive centrality given to 'immaterial labor' in *Empire*, some of the most exciting potentials of this concept remain undeveloped. In particular, the application of 'biopower' to a range of highly material ecological, life-science and genetic engineering issues remains unexplored. The struggles of contemporary communisms will, however, have as much or more to do with water and air depletion, toxic wastes and pharmaceutical rationing, the vast projects of biosphere management at stake around global warming and ozone depletion, and the biotechnological transformations of plants, animals, and humans, as with 'immaterial' digital technologies—which are, in fact, deeply imbricated in all of these matters. 'Species being', as fleetingly enunciated in *The Economic and Philosophic Manuscripts*, is a concept that invites such extensions. Unlike 'immaterial labor', it foregrounds the corporeal, sensual, sexual, gendered, and environmentally embedded condition of human existence, as well as the collective and historically changing content of this embodiment. And it does so within a Marxist, rather than a Foucauldian, language that is, I suggest, far more explicitly open to potentials of autonomy and emancipation with a networked and biotechnological world. A twenty-first century reappropriation of this category is a necessity to address the convergence now occurring between the immaterial technologies of digitization and the all-too-material processes of biotechnology that threaten the jaw-dropping prospect of recomposing 'classes' into 'clades'. Negri's own relentless determination to keep up with, or ahead of, the restructurings of capital urges us to find new concepts adequate to the scale of such transformations.

CONCLUSION: NEGRI BEYOND CYBER-NEGRI?

Negri's work on 'immaterial labor and general intellect' remains a *tour de force* of revolutionary reconception. From the first formulations of the socialized worker thesis, through the *Futur Antérieur* analysis to the pages of *Empire*, Negri's ever-transmuting theorizations about the changing composition of class have been a vital contribution to shaking Marxism out of its enthrallment with the historically specific, and fast fading, form of the European industrial proletariat, and renovating it as a vital element of twenty-first-century radicalism. In this project, his attention to the digital conditions of post-Fordist capital, and the potentials for their cyborg subversion, has been trailblazing. The reception and adaptation of his ideas by thinkers such as Terranova and Barbrook and others show how strongly those ideas have resonated amongst a generation of theorists attuned to new modalities of struggle and exodus exploding across a networked environment, and have made the construction of a 'cyber-Negri' a truly collective project—a microcosmic example, one might say, of 'general intellect' in action.[24]

It would be surprising, however, if such a bold experiment were not liable to hyperbole and overstatement. The dangers latent in Negri's focus on 'immaterial' subversions are well illustrated by other autonomist critics such as Caffentzis, who remind us that the increasingly integrated nature of planetary capital—a.k.a. 'globalization'—requires acknowledgment of differences, and connections, between digital labor and far more primeval forms of exploitation. The convolutions and contradictions around the topics of immaterial labor and communication in the pages of *Empire* mark an attempt to resolve these problems. But the attempt is, in my view, unsatisfactory, since, in qualifying and revise the hegemony of 'immaterial labor', it throws away the very element of the original theory—the importance of communicative action to contemporary struggle—that is perhaps most relevant to today's counterglobalization movements.

To preserve the undeniable value of Negri's discussions of digitized labor, and place them in a perspective that takes account of the persistence of old exploitations and newer ecological and biotechnological struggles, I have suggested a different theoretical vocabulary. This would place the idea of 'general intellect', which Negri and *Futur Antérieur* so ingeniously adapted from Marx, alongside two other terms from the margins of the Marxian archive, 'universal labor' and 'species being', both of which can also be reread and reinvented as ingredients for a twenty-first-century communist theory. 'Universal labor' is the creative force that builds contemporary technoscience; it emerges as a political force at the moments when its fragmented segments of immaterial, material and immiserated labor are networked and recomposed into a truly participative 'general intellect' that can reclaim from below the direction of 'species being' which the world market has arrogated to itself. To proceed from the 'immaterial labor' debate to investigate such new categories would be the best sort of tribute to the singular and restless theorist who inspired these reflections, a move towards the creation of a 'Negri beyond cyber-Negri'.

NOTES

1. On *operaismo* and cycle of struggles see Red Notes 1979; Cleaver 1979; Moulier 1989; Ryan 1989.
2. On Autonomia see Cleaver 1979; Moulier 1989; and also Tahon and Corten 1986 and Lotringer and Marazzi 1980.
3. The term was coined by Romano Alquati in an analysis of the student revolt. Negri first uses the term extensively in Negri 1977b, 1978, 1980b. His fullest English-language statements of the position are Negri 1988a, 1989, 1991b.
4. See Wright 2002.
5. On this point, see Levidow 1990 and Pelaez and Holloway 1990.
6. See, for example, Noble 1995.
7. For a brief account, see Marchand 1988.
8. Some of the writings of this group can be found in the collection edited by Paolo Virno and Michael Hardt, *Radical Thought in Italy: A Potential Politics* (Virno and Hardt 1996a).
9. This summary derives from Emery 1999.

10. Lazzarato and Negri 1991: 86–9. See also Virno and Hardt 1996b: 260–3 and Lazzarato 1996: 133–50 in the same volume.
11. See Gorz 1982; Aronowitz and DiFazio 1994; Aronowitz and Cutler 1998; Rifkin 1995.
12. Terranova 2000: 42. See McLuhan 1964; Kelly 1994; Levy 1999.
13. See Ludlow 2001; Critical Art Ensemble 2001.
14. See, for example, Schiller 1999 and Hermann and McChesney 1997.
15. See Bosma et al. 2000, and, for a valuable discussion of net-theory in general and nettime in particular, Lovink 2002.
16. See also the debate between Baldi 1985 and Bartleby the Scrivener 1985, both in *Midnight Notes* 8: 32–6.
17. See Dyer-Witheford, 2002b: 53–64.
18. For a thoughtful discussion on these developments from an autonomist perspective, see Cleaver 1999 and Wright 2001.
19. Marx 1981: 198–9. See also Mandel's discussion of the 'global worker' in his introduction to 'Appendix: Results of the Immediate Process of Production', in Marx 1976: 945.
20. See Dyer-Witheford 2002a: 129–64.
21. 'Cyber-Leninism' is from a call for papers for a Special Issue of *Peace Review Journal*, on 'Social Justice Movements and the Internet', ed. Bernadette Barker-Plummer and Dorothy Kidd, October 2000.
22. Hellman 1999. Cleaver's response is Cleaver 2000b. For an excellent discussion of these problems, see Kidd 2002.
23. Spivak 1999: 73–81 and Harvey 2000: 206–12, 213–32. See also, for a poignant application of this concept, Doubt 2000: 61–6. The classic critique of Marxist humanism is of course Althusser 1969.
24. For further reverberations of the 'immaterial labor' debate see discussions on 'cognitive capitalism' centered around the French journal *Multitudes*, and the series of 'free university' seminars on 'Class Composition of Cognitive Capitalism', documented at <http://www.geocities.com/CognitiveCapitalism/>.

7

Negri by Zapata: Constituent Power and the Limits of Autonomy[1]

José Rabasa

The mural *Vida y sueños de la cañada Perla*, at the community of Taniperla, Chiapas, was destroyed by the army on April 11, 1998 in an effort that sought to neutralize the constituent power that had materialized in the autonomous *municipio* Ricardo Flores Magón.[2] Next to Emiliano Zapata (the leader of the southern armies during the Mexican Revolution of 1910) stands an armed Ricardo Flores Magón, the anarcho-communist leader and theoretician of revolution, who represented the most radical wing of the insurrection of 1910. The words 'Para la lucha actividad actividad actividad es lo que demanda el momento' (For the struggle activity activity activity is what the moment demands) were extracted from Flores Magón's last essay in *Regeneración*, the organ of the radical Partido Liberal Mexicano, which advocated armed insurrection as the only way to destroy capitalism.[3] His *morral*, hung over his shoulder, bears the name of *Regeneración*, along with the name of another revolutionary publication, *El Ahuizote*; the seeds of rebellion, the letters of the word *libertad*, spin on his left hand. Flores Magón's last manifesto, directed at 'La Junta Organizadora del Partido Liberal Mexicano a los miembros del partido, a los anarquistas de todo el mundo y a los trabajadores en general' (the Organizing Junta of the Mexican Liberal Party, to the anarchists of all the world and to workers in general), was written in Los Angeles, California, and published in *Regeneración* on March 16, 1918. *Regeneración* was closed down for good on March 21, 1918. This manifesto led to the imprisonment of Flores Magón and his associate Librado Rivera, who were condemned to 20 and 15 years in prison respectively. Flores Magón died four years later, on November 20, 1922, in the federal penitentiary of Leavenworth, Kansas. Flores Magón and Zapata preside as ghosts whose ideals have prevailed beyond their death.

The Zapatista repossessions of haciendas and factories in the southern state of Morelos during the 1910 insurrection, as well as their dictum 'la tierra es de quien la trabaja' (the land belongs to those who work it), embodied the clearest example of Flores Magón's theory of Direct Action, the immediate takeover of the means of production; indeed, Zapata implemented

164

Vida y sueños de la cañada Perla, comunidad de Taniperla Chiapas. Printed with the authorization of the Junta de Buen Gobierno el Camino del Futuro. Caracol de Resistencia hacia un Nuevo Amanecer.

'Flores Magón and Zapata preside as ghosts whose ideals have prevailed beyond their death.'

the takeovers independently of Flores Magón's writings and the programs of the Partido Liberal. But it was after the Zapatista takeovers that Flores Magón came in contact with Zapata's forces, leading the Zapatistas to change their motto from the reformist 'justice, liberty, and law' to the revolutionary call for 'tierra y libertad', a position consistent with Flores Magón's anarcho-communist aphorisms on revolution: e.g., 'El verdadero revolucionario es un ilegal por excelencia' (The true revolutionary is an illegal par excellence); 'La ley conserva, la revolución renueva' (Law conserves, revolution renews); 'Los revolucionarios tenemos que ser forzosamente ilegales. Tenemos que salirnos del camino trillado de los convencionalismos y abrir nuevas vías' (As revolutionaries we must be illegals. We must divert from the beaten path of conventionalisms and open new ways) (Bartra 1972: 282). These aphorisms are reiterated today in the communiqués of Subcomandante Marcos. However, we must underscore the differences, in that Marcos and the Zapatistas in Chiapas find themselves in the predicament of advocating revolution, of inventing new paths and sensibilities, while developing political arguments for a transformation of the Mexican constitution that would recognize the right of the indigenous peoples of Chiapas and Mexico to autonomy, that is, the recognition of the right to be ruled by their normative systems, to develop their cultures and languages, and to control the natural resources within their territories.

The Acuerdos de San Andrés, signed by the Zapatistas and the federal government in February 1996, committed the federal government to a recognition of the right to self-determination and the creation of autonomous Indian communities, regions and peoples, no longer limited to individual communities. The definition of Indians as peoples is central to Convention 169 of Indigenous and Tribal Peoples (1989), of the International Labour Organization, an agreement signed by the Mexican government.[4] Autonomous indigenous regions and peoples would remain part of the Mexican nation, but would be able to determine the use of natural resources located in the regions, the commitment of the government to provide communication infrastructures, the transfer of state-run radio stations, and the promotion of the knowledge of Indian cultures and languages on a national level—all schools in the federation would include Indian languages and cultures in their curricula. This transformation of the Mexican nation in Article 4 of the constitution would paradoxically establish an autonomy from the structures of the state. I say paradoxically because, beyond the effective access to the jurisdiction of the state ('efectivo acceso a la juridicción del Estado') as specified in Article 4, the accords would recognize the noninterference of the state in the practices of their normative systems. The EZLN (Ejército Zapatista de Liberación Nacional) walked out of the dialogues on August 29, 1996, and made public the reasons for the interruption and the conditions for resuming the dialogue in a communiqué of September 3, 1996.[5] Among the conditions listed were: (1) the liberation of all the imprisoned Zapatistas; (2) a governmental interlocutor with a capacity to decide, a political willingness to negotiate and a respect for the delegation of the EZLN; (3) the installation of a commission that would follow and verify the fulfillment of Acuerdos de San Andrés; (4) serious propositions for reaching agreements in the discussions on the Mesa Dos: Democracia y Justicia (Table Two: Democracy and Justice);[6] (5) an end to the military and political harassment of Indians in Chiapas and the disbanding of paramilitary groups sponsored by the state. These have been reduced to three signals for a return to the dialogue: (1) the implementation of the accords; (2) the liberation of prisioners; (3) the withdrawal of the army. These demands were in place during the presidential campaign of President Vicente Fox, who at that time stated that he would resolve the situation in Chiapas in five minutes. The signals remain pending. The situation has only worsened since he took power.[7] Not one week goes by in which representatives from different communities from the Municipio Autónomo Ricardo Flores Magón, just to mention one entity in the state of Chiapas, do not denounce abuses by federal authorities or members of the state's Seguridad Pública (Public Security, a euphemism for the army). I must underscore that parallel denunciations are presented daily in other states.

In February and March of 2001, the EZLN held a 'Zapatour', in which Marcos and several of the Zapatista commandants visited several towns on their way to Mexico City, sharing with the people their ideals, their demands to the government, and their willingness to arrive at a peaceful solution of the conflict. Zapatour was such a success that it clouded the fame in which the recently elected Fox was basking. The peak of Zapatour was comandante Esther's address to the Congreso de la Unión, after representatives from PRI (Partido Revolucionario Institucional) and PRD (Partido de la Revolución Democrática) understood the political capital they would derive from allowing the EZLN to address Congress. Esther did not limit herself to exposing the demands of the Zapatistas, specifically of the women, rather her speech also underscored the symbolic fact of an indigenous woman addressing Congress:

> Esta tribuna es un símbolo. Por eso convocó tanta polémica. Por eso queríamos hablar en ella y por eso algunos no querían que aquí estuvieramos. Y es un símbolo también que sea yo, una mujer pobre, indígena y zapatista, quien tome la palabra y sea el mío el mensaje central de nuestra palabra como zapatistas.[8]

This tribune is a symbol. This is why it summoned up so much polemic. That is why we wanted to speak here and why some did not want us here. And it is also a symbol that it is me, a poor woman, an Indian and a Zapatista, who addresses you and that the central message of our word as Zapatistas is mine.

Once the Zapatistas returned to Chiapas, Congress approved a version of the accords that was unacceptable to them as well as to the Congreso Nacional Indígena (National Indigenous Congress), whose representatives had also addressed Congress. The approved version was even more restrictive than the one proposed by the former president Ernesto Zedillo. The law modifying Article 4 was approved by the required two-thirds of the states' legislatures. Not one day passes in which indigenous peoples do not denounce the law on regional, state, and federal levels.

Let this very brief narrative on Zapatour, the presence of the Zapatistas in Congress, and the approval of the law fulfill the function of a backdrop to my discussion of the parallelisms between Zapatismo and Negri, in particular with respect to the limits of autonomist projects. If it remains necessary to continue to indict and denounce the actions of Congress and President Fox, who could very well have vetoed the law, the objective of this paper is to create a crisis within the discourse of autonomy. My intent is not to undermine the indigenous struggles for autonomy, but to emphasize the need to think in terms of a process of autonomization and to make manifest the philosophical background that overdetermines the debates with the state—to sharpen the arms of critique for a critique of arms.

There is a tension, perhaps a paradox, an aporia, in the Zapatista revolutionary ideals and the call for a transformation of the state, a tension that according to Antonio Negri has haunted revolutionary political theory and praxis in the West since Machiavelli—a tension between constituent power, which by definition exists outside the law, and the will to control and domesticate the democratic passion of the multitude into a coherent concept of a people. The most common form of control advocates the institutionalization of a constitution and the surrender of the power of the multitude to a representative form of government: e.g., a constitutional republic, the Soviet state, a parliamentary democracy. This project of transforming the Mexican constitution as part of a revolutionary process entails an aporia between the transformation of the constitution in terms such as would enable the exercise of constituent power and the institutionalization of the constitutional changes that would demand the surrender of the multitude to a state of law. Theoreticians of constitutional law have faced a paradox, as manifest in Emile Boutmy's statement, cited by Negri: 'Constituent power is an imperative act of nation, rising from nowhere and organizing the hierarchies of law' (Boutmy 1981: 250; quoted in Negri 1999a: 2). Boutmy's phrase, 'rising from nowhere and organizing the hierarchies of law', sums up the contradiction of affirming the autonomy of the foundation of law and sovereignty. But sovereignty itself, as Negri points out, stands in opposition to constituent power: 'constitutive strength never ends up as [constituted] power, nor does the multitude tend to become a totality but, rather, a set of singularities, an open multiplicity'.[9] It is precisely constitutive strength that sets apart the 'constitutionalist paradigm [which] always refers to the "mixed constitution," the mediation of inequality, and therefore . . . is a non-democratic paradigm' from 'the paradigm of constituent power [which] is that of a force that bursts apart, breaks, interrupts, unhinges any preexisting equilibrium and possible continuity' (Negri 1999a: 10). Indeed, for Negri, 'Revolution is necessary, as necessary as the human need to be moral, to constitute oneself ethically, to free body and mind from slavery, and constituent power is the means toward this end' (Negri 1999a: 23). I am here summing up, or rather eliding, Negri's critique of a number of theoreticians ranging from Max Weber and Carl Schmitt to Hannah Arendt and Jürgen Habermas.

Negri's penchant for aphorism lends itself to citation independently of his critique of constitutionalism. *Insurgencies* consists of a series of studies of constituent power in Machiavelli's 'people in arms', Harrington's 'discovery of material determinations of the relations of power', 'the American renovation of classical constitutionalism and the French ideology of social emancipation', and 'the egalitarian impulse of communism and the enterprising spirit of the Bolsheviks' (Negri 1999a: 35). Negri notes that his is neither a genealogy nor an archaeology of constituent power, but the hermeneutic of a faculty of humankind:

> It is clear that each of these enterprises [Machiavelli, Harrington, and so on] will discover its meaning within the set of events that shapes them individually. But it is also true that the meaning of these events is inscribed in the consciousness of us all and etched in our being because it has somehow determined it. (Negri 1999a: 35)

By 'us' let us understand all subjectivities that participate in political processes that bear the imprint of these events in Euro-American history, of which history I dare to say that it affects the totality of subjects engaged in one form or another of the political discourses of the West. This generalized presence of the West makes paradoxical any distinction with a non-West grounded on a binary opposition. Indeed, we must understand this 'forced' biculturalism (West and non-West coexisting in one culture and subjectivity) as a liberatory dwelling in multiple worlds and, thereby, resist reducing the non-West to varieties of European elsewheres, however productive this category might be (see Taussig 1997). Negri's particular studies of Euro-American political theory are at once individual cases and bear universal implications. Its universality travels and incorporates other latitudes, but it never gives itself as such. In principle, the concept of constituent power would have a history only if understood in the materiality of concrete historical and social configurations. As such, its manifestations will always be specific to singular subjects and situations that cannot be exhausted by Euro-American political history.

Even if determined by the events pertaining to the history of Euro-American political theory, the multiplicity of constituent strength entails the singularity of the experience and the strength of concrete struggles. Specific histories of constituent power may very well, as in the case of indigenous struggles in Chiapas, also articulate discourses other than those of Euro-American political theory and history. This otherness—which should not be reified as the Other, but posited as an otherness, as in revolution, the impossible, and the unnameable—demands that we not only account for Indians speaking in the terms and languages of the West, but speaking about 'the West, its revolutions, and its discourses' in indigenous languages and discursive traditions.[10] In reading Negri by Zapata we will need to account for the colonial past and present of Indians, for the limits of the concept of autonomy, and for the need to think in terms of autonomization as process rather than autonomy as accomplished state.[11]

Before moving on, let me premise the discussion with a caveat: the title of this chapter, 'Negri by Zapata', inevitably invokes the rhetorical strategy of reading North by South as a subversion of the dominance European thought has had over the rest of the world—the so-called Occidentalism.[12] The reduction of Euro-American thought to a homogeneous, static Culture—the initial capital reflects that in 'Occidentalism'—not only erases all differences within the West but reduces the dynamics of cultural identity of the West to a relationship to the non-West, if this clearcut distinction still holds in geopolitical terms. This model inevitably harnesses the identity of the non-West to the subversion, transculturation, and appropriation of the West. As is well known and hardly needs repetition, but a clarification might still be in order, Hegel's dialectic of the master and the slaves has provided a language for understanding colonial dominance and its transgression. Even if this has been an enabling mode of resisting Western hegemonies, there is no reason why we should limit the identities of West and non-West alike to conceptual frames in which each defines itself in opposition to the other—as in the politics of identity and difference. Hegel conceived the dialectic of the master–slave in terms of European thought, the history of which amounts to a series of 'professorial' supersessions.[13] Its application to the history of colonialism, then, constitutes an extrapolation not originally intended, which we could further develop by imagining the dialectic in terms of an indigenous culture in which disciple overcomes master. By this, I want to suggest an indigenous subject undergoing initiation rites and gaining knowledge that has nothing to do with the West. Moreover, we can imagine this indigenous subject sitting in a seminar on Hegel's *Phenomenology of Mind*, following the unfolding of the figures without internalizing the categories as a colonized subject, rather understanding the dialectic in its European terms. She may find in the Hegelian corpus certain references to non-European cultures offensive and, perhaps, she may simply dismiss them as limitations in Hegel without having the urge to contradict him, and furthermore laugh at the superficiality of those who, having been formed in the West, reduce their philosophers to Eurocentric statements. This indigenous subject could very well love and practice Euro-American thought and find absurd the self-depreciation of those Euro-Americans who seek to invent alternative (read: nativistic) ways of thought. On the other hand, we can also imagine a Euro-American having thoughts, preoccupations, and horizons of meaning and freedom other than those in which she would be bound to differentiate herself by establishing an opposition to non-European cultures. Different horizons of meaning and revolution may meet, dialogue, and enrich each other, without establishing hierarchical relations. Even if this ideal situation would not in itself erase the hierarchies of value that we are 'all' aware exist, the articulation of its (im)possibility would counter the determinacy of current hierarchical structures.

Thus, we may be free to think Negri without having the moral obligation of subverting, appropriating, or transculturating his thought; that is, an obligation to transculturate that would go beyond the fact that making Negri travel to other latitudes and social realities already implies a transformation of his thought—a transformation that we should nevertheless see as integral to his thought. The immanence of struggles constitutes their singularity and necessary specificity. One may thus think the West with Negri, agreeing or not, without feeling bound and limited by his thought, hence, pressed to declare one's autonomy. To think Negri without applying him remains a possibility (to my mind the application of theory equals unarmed, defenseless thought), but beyond thinking within his tradition lies the possibility of thinking Negri and the West in non-Western categories. I will return to this. For now let me just point out that thinking Empire, colonial power, and the West in general has been a figure of thought in colonial situations in the Americas since the European invasion in the sixteenth century. In fact, missionaries demanded that Indians represent the colonial order and the history of their oppression in their own indigenous categories and systems of writing.[14]

In running Negri by Zapata, my aim is to outline the connections and interrelations between Euro-American thought and the project of establishing the autonomy of Indian peoples (*pueblos indígenas*). The 'by' would thus suggest a 'Zapata' reading and writing about Negri—that is, running Negri by Zapata. Ideally, neither Negri nor Zapata would be privileged. Zapata in the context of the Zapatista insurrection in Chiapas, as Marcos has repeatedly asserted in his communiqués, stands for a whole array of revolutionary practices.[15] Evocations of Zapata encompass ethico-political maxims, a folklore, a metaphysics, elements for a theory of cross-cultural communication, and an affirmation of constituent power. As I have pointed out, the concept of constituent power is one of Negri's salient signatures; Negri's *Insurgencies* is a history of a particular, but nevertheless crucial, series of Western debates and answers to the crisis posed by constituent power in political theory. Indeed, Negri equates the political with constituent power. The history of constituent power provides an instance of an exception to the commonplace that the West self-fashions itself vis-à-vis the non-West, the Other, the Orient, and what not. There is an element of truth to Occidentalism, but it bears the elements of an ideology, of a fetish that, by linking the identity of the West in a binary opposition, ends up limiting the understanding of the cultural and material fields which inform the creative imaginings of non-Western cultures. Both the West and the non-West have preoccupations, interests, and traditions that do not relate one to the other. In the history of constituent power outlined in Negri's *Insurgencies*, the Other is not the non-West, but revolution, the multitude, the democratic absolute, the impossible.

One of the findings of the Zapatistas consists precisely in defining the existence of Indian and Western forms in nonhierarchical spaces that are nevertheless linguistically, culturally, juridically, and politically distinct. In this regard, the Zapatistas should be inscribed as an instance of the 'beyond modern rationalism' that Negri calls forth in his history of constituent power (Negri 1999a: 324). The Indians participating in the debates with the government and in the drafting of the Acuerdos de San Andrés were, or at least found no inherent contradiction in desiring to be, as well versed in Euro-American traditions as in their specific Indian cultures.[16] If the critiques of indigenous fascination with First World intellectuals fulfilled a necessary ideological function parallel to the constitution of blocs of Third World countries, the paradigms of the modern nation and the national–popular underlying the political viability of these positions up to the Seventies have for all practical purposes disappeared with the weakening of the nation state and the emergence of empire, as has been defined by Michael Hardt and Antonio Negri in *Empire* (Hardt and Negri 2000). The struggle for Indian autonomy, an offshoot of the rebellion in Chiapas, aims at the heart of empire beyond the local.

In the title of this chapter, Negri *stands for* a current of thought compatible with Flores Magón's anarcho-communist revolutionary program. As it were, behind Flores Magón's image in the mural at Taniperla we may read Negri, Paolo Virno, Michael Hardt, and other representatives of recent radical Italian thought (see Virno and Hardt 1996a). Zapata, in turn, can be read as a condensation of a long line of revolutionaries which includes figures such as Rubén Jaramillo in the 1950s and 1960s, the guerrillas of Genaro Vázquez and Lucio Cabañas in the 1960s and 1970s, and obviously Marcos and the Zapatistas of today (see Bartra 1985). The images of Flores Magón and Zapata lacks the stasis of metaphor. Their position and posture in the mural suggests a metonymic flow into a historical horizon punctuated with little Zapatistas on the mountains and the rising sun.[17] Historical temporality flows from the future to the past in the mode of future anterior. To go beyond an allegorical reading of the woman in the left-hand corner as a nourishing Mother Earth, further reinforced by the two breast-like mountains next to her, is to see her placing the liberation of women as the beginning and the end of the revolution. Thus, the movement of Flores Magón and Zapata lack the fixity of ideological posts as in the typical use of portraits of Marx, Lenin, Mao, and others in socialist cults of personality: in the likeness of specters, Flores Magón and Zapata inspire the *new* movement, one that aspires to the impossible. Marcos does not figure in the mural but his 'presence', also in the manner of a ghost, presides over the armed men and women Zapatistas guarding Taniperla from the mountains. Marcos and the Zapatistas further elaborate the theoretical writings of Flores Magón and the indigenous discourse of Zapata. As such, the mural does not partake of an Apollonian impulse to fix meaning, but to communicate the strength of living labor.

Armando Bartra has pointed out apropos of Flores Magón that the most original political thought in Mexico has been written in the press, facing the need to theorize the concrete (Bartra 1972: 16). Marcos's clandestine writings and publications in Mexican newspapers, in particular in *La Jornada*, are without a doubt the most brilliant contemporary articulation of Bartra's assessment of theorizing from the concrete. In his introduction to a selection of pieces from *Regeneración,* Bartra singles out the originality of Flores Magón by underscoring the parallelism with Lenin's thought in *What Is To Be Done?* in particular, with the role of the press in a revolutionary process. Eventually Flores Magón became familiar with and wrote about Lenin and the Bolshevik revolution. We should underscore that Lenin's 'April Theses' are without doubt the most congenial to Flores Magón's anarcho-communist thought. Bartra has characterized the writings in *Regeneración* as 'textos en los que en un soplo se dice bolsheviques y zapatistas' (texts in which one says Bolshevik and Zapatista in one breath) (Bartra 1972: 488).

We also find similarities between Marcos's and Negri's thought that as far as we can ascertain were independently thought. When Hardt and Negri define communism, we can imagine Flores Magón and Marcos agreeing with their response in *Empire* to the label of anarchists:

> You are a bunch of anarchists, the new Plato on the block will finally yell at us. That is not true. We would be anarchists if we were not to speak (as did Thrasymachus and Callicles, Plato's immortal interlocutors) from the standpoint of a materiality constituted in the networks of productive cooperation, in other words, from the perspective of a humanity that is constructed productively, that is constituted through the 'common name' of freedom. No, we are not anarchists but communists who have seen how much repression and destruction of humanity have been wrought by liberal and socialist big governments. (Hardt and Negri 2000: 350)

Note that upholding the necessity of the state does not figure as a distinctive characteristic of Hardt and Negri's communism; on the contrary, they dismiss liberal and socialist big governments along with any argument for a theory in which socialism would serve as a stage in the dissolution of the state under communism. Elsewhere in *Empire,* Hardt and Negri specifically override the necessity of a transitional phase, of a purgatory: 'We are not proposing the umpteenth version of the inevitable passage through purgatory. . . . We are not repeating the schema of an ideal teleology that justifies any passage in the name of a promised land' (Hardt and Negri 2000: 47). One can also imagine the people of Taniperla as well as Marcos and the Zapatistas fully subscribing to this definition of communism without purgatory.

If Flores Magón and Lenin opened the twentieth century with an identification of revolution with armed struggle, the invention of other forms of revolutionary praxis defines both the Zapatistas' and Negri's manifestos for the twenty-first century. (I open this parenthesis to underscore that nothing is more alien to the Zapatistas and Negri than the terrorist act on the World Trade Center on September 11, 2001.) For the Zapatistas this need for new forms of revolution implies never again having the need for a January 1, 1994, the date of the initial uprising, which had a high cost in lives; for Negri and a host of radical political Italian thinkers, as expressed in 'Do You Remember Revolution?', reinventing revolution entails a demystification of violence: 'There is no "good" version of armed struggle, no alternative to the elitist practice of the Red Brigades; armed struggle is in itself incompatible with and antithetical to the new movements.'[18] For the record, let us note that the Mexican army has carried on a low-intensity war against Indian communities in violation of the suspension of hostilities on January 12, 1994, that many Zapatistas, including some from Taniperla and including Professor Valdez Ruvalcaba who coordinated the painting of the mural, were imprisoned in the penitentiary of Cerro Hueco,[19] and that Negri and other Italian intellectuals were jailed in Italian prisons on trumped-up charges of terrorism. It is not arbitrary to juxtapose the Zapatistas and radical Italian theorists. After all, Marcos has alluded to the workers' committees known as COBAS (*comitati di base*), and one of the social centers (the *centri sociali*, autonomous youth organizations for political action, which served as a model for the COBAS in lieu of forming a 'new union')[20] bore the name 'Ya Basta' in solidarity with the Chiapas uprising; the social center has evolved into the Associazione Ya Basta, which in December 2000, after assuming the initiative to collect funds in Italy, took the materials for building an electric turbine to the community of La Realidad, the headquarters of the Zapatistas in the Selva Lacandona.[21]

Even if the mural can be read as an idealization of life in an autonomous community, the *sueños* of Taniperla are not a utopia in the sense of a model of a world to be realized; they are dreams already materialized in the community's creative energy and everyday life represented in the mural. The mural was from the start a collective effort between Sergio Valdez Ruvalcaba, better known as Checo, and the people of Taniperla. Although Checo is a talented draftsman, he merely guided the community's efforts, telling them to paint whatever they wanted (cada quien dibuje lo que quiera). The community dialogued and decided on the following topics: 'el agua es vida' (water is life), 'la cooperativa por la unidad' (the cooperative for unity), 'la asamblea para decidir' (the assembly to make decisions), 'los zapatistas nos cuidan' (the Zapatistas look after us), 'Zapata por heroe y chingón' (Zapata for being a hero and a *chingón*), 'el cafetal por la ganancita' (the coffee plantation for the little earnings), 'la palabra de la mujer' (the word of women), 'la radio para comunicar' (radio for communication), 'los principales por su palabra' (the *principales* for their word).[22]

Thus, the mural itself is the result of collective dialogue, an instance of communal government represented in the mural by the woman bringing the proposals in her *morral* (which not only contains *pozol*, but also documents pertaining to the meeting's agenda, according to one of the Tzeltal painters) and the man reading a document at the entrance of the Casa Municipal. These two figures bring to the assembly the issues discussed in the separate groups of men and women. If the two circles separate the community along gender lines, the participation of men and women at the meeting will be on an equal footing. The mention that the *morral* contains *pozol* in addition to documents should not be read as merely stating that women now have proposals to make, not just food to prepare. *Pozol* is a Maya discovery, a fermented beverage made out of corn with nutritional and medicinal properties. The transnational food enterprise Quest International and the University of Minnesota obtained a patent in the United States (#5919695) for the use of a bacteria they isolated from the beverage, thereby making the medicinal properties of *pozol* private property of Quest International and the University of Minnesota (see Carson and Brooks 2000). This case is a vivid example of how transnational enterprises appropriate or rather steal the knowledge of indigenous peoples. Jacques Lacan has corrected Hegel's dialectic by arguing that the master extracts the knowledge (*savoir*) from the slaves, and that work (or rather, spoliation) produces no knowledge, contrary to what the Hegelian dialectic, or at least some of its interpreters, would lead us to believe: 'Philosophy [in this case science] in its historical function is this extraction, this treason, I would say, of the knowledge of the slave, to obtain a transmutation as knowledge of the master' (Lacan 1991: 22).

The mural is the product of living labor representing itself. Clearly, the subsequent destruction of the mural by the army represents an obstacle to the creativity of the community of Taniperla, thus exemplifying Negri's point (after Deleuze's correction of Foucault) that resistance precedes power:

> One might say in this sense that resistance is actually prior to power. When imperial government intervenes, it selects the liberatory impulses of the multitude in order to destroy them, and in return it is driven forward by resistance. . . . Each imperial action is a rebound of the resistance of the multitude that poses a new obstacle for the multitude to overcome. (Hardt and Negri 2000: 360–1)

If the mural at Taniperla was destroyed, the liberatory impulses expressed in the mural recur in other *municipios* that declared themselves autonomous self-governments. These forms of self-government do not react to the power of the army as the traditional understanding of resistance would have it, but operate under the concept of communities in resistance as a space for the construction of a new world (see Ceceña 2000). As such, the army and power in general lag behind the creative effort of rebellion—they react and devise new forms of oppression and control that seek to curtail constituent power.

In this equation, Zapata stands for the long-standing history of indigenous rebellions. Zapata also stands for the demand to recognize the *usos y costumbres*, the indigenous normative systems that can be traced back to the colonial period and perhaps in some instances to before the European invasion. The first use of the term *'usos y costumbres'* in Spanish colonial law, as far as I know, goes back to Law XIX of the New Laws of 1542 that called for a dissolution of the *encomiendas* (grants given to conquistadores in which Indians paid tribute in kind and labor) and the liberation of slaves, and prescribed love as the only acceptable treatment of Indians:

> no den lugar que en los pleitos de entre yndios o con ellos se hagan proçessos ordinarios ni aya alargas como suele aconteçer por la maliçia de algunos abogados y procuradores, sino que sumariamente sean determinados, guardando sus usos y costumbres. (Morales Padrón 1979: 434)
>
> make sure that in litigation between Indians and with them there are no ordinary processes nor continuances as they are commonly due to the evildoing of some lawyers and prosecutors, rather that cases are summarily determined, following their uses and customs.

The implementation of the *usos y costumbres* at once protects Indian communities from Spaniards, criollos, and mestizos, and alienates Indians in a separate republic, in a structure not unlike apartheid. Indians today prefer the term 'indigenous normative systems' over *usos y costumbres* (the chosen term of the Mexican government), but the colonial legacy of these separate legal apparatuses will continue to haunt them, especially if the communities choose to ignore their colonial origins.[23]

In tracing the history of colonization, we must heed the recommendation that Gayatri Chakravorty Spivak has made regarding the need to avoid the equally pernicious acts of either locating colonialism in a distant or not so distant past, or asserting a continuous colonial form of dominance to the present (Spivak 1999: 1). The first can be readily proven as false given neocolonial articulations of dominance, but more important than locating colonialism in easily identifiable practices is the mapping of forms of colonial discourse that we continue to reproduce in spite of our most honorable intentions. As for the tracing of continuous colonial forms, the danger resides in losing track of the historical nature of the different modes and categories of exercising colonial power. In this respect, we must differentiate the practices of the Enlightenment from those of the early modern period. Whereas the opposition in the context of sixteenth-century Spain is between Christians and non-Christians (pagans, Muslims, and Jews), in eighteenth-century northern Europe the opposition is between peoples with and without history, with and without writing, and/or with and without a state. I will come back to this distinction later. Even though we can trace the categories and epistemologies pertaining to both periods in Mexico and Latin America (the second in the variant of internal colonialism), the sediments of the Spanish colonization constitute historical realities very different from those in African and Asian countries whose colonial pasts date back to the late eighteenth century.

Paradoxically, Spivak's question in the title of her essay 'Can the Subaltern Speak?' (1988) builds on a binary that sets an absolute distance between Europe and its Others, a binary that has a history dating back to the eighteenth century. Spivak's question and negative answer reproduce the terms of this absolute binary in a circular argument: dominant discourses define the colonized as incapable of reasoning, hence subalterns are incapable of reasoning and need the mediation and representation of what Spivak calls First World intellectuals, a category that would include intellectuals like herself who, in spite of their colonial pasts, can fully operate in metropolitan circles. The 'subaltern cannot speak' construct would thus betrays a metalepsis, the substitution of effect for cause, a figure that Spivak knows very well as can be seen in her discussion of *hysteron proteron* in *Death of a Discipline* (2003). Indeed, my point has less to do with exposing her fallacious reasoning than with documenting the historical background in which the metalepsis makes sense. Her rhetorical sophistication and the long series of critiques and responses to the denial of speech to subalterns should warn us about the ruses imbedded in the phrasing of the question.[24] Offhand, she would seem to dismiss subalterns who learn the languages of the West while continuing to dwell in their native worlds: one is either a First World intellectual who speaks or a subaltern bound to silence. Colonizers might very well be, and most often are, incapable of understanding indigenous discourses, but there is nothing *other* than the internalization of the will of the colonizer, which pits Western discourses against indigenous life forms, that should keep subalterns from mastering the languages of the West while retaining their own. The notion that 'the subaltern can't speak' carries as its ultimate irony the corollary that if a subaltern speaks she (it is clearly a she for Spivak) would no longer be a subaltern. Under this formulation, subaltern studies assume the form of the absurd proposition, of a fetish, inasmuch as the liberatory project of recuperating subaltern histories as articulated by Ranajit Guha (who has taught us how to read the political motivations in subaltern insurrections, otherwise dismissed as irrational outbursts of violence) has transformed itself into a metaphysics of denegation and a statement of privilege.[25] Even if we were to accept that this binary between intellectuals and subalterns reflects the binaries imposed by imperial powers in the eighteenth and nineteenth centuries, we should not generalize the impossibility of subalterns speaking to other regions with different colonial histories.

Take as paradigmatic the Enlightenment's distinction between peoples with and without history, with and without a state, and the error of attributing these binaries to the form of imperialism practiced by Spain in the sixteenth and seventeenth centuries, or even before, in the so-called *reconquista* of Muslim territories in southern Spain. If there is a binary in early modern Spanish expansionism, it is between Christians and non-Christians (alternately—with their own histories, writing systems, and political states—pagans, Muslims, and Jews). These specifications have little to do with a squabble over historical facts, rather with the social, economic, and cultural sedimentations that underlie the present. In the case of those regions colonized by Spain in the early modern period we often find a second (if not a third and fourth) wave of colonization bearing the imprint of the Enlightenment. These posterior colonizations in places like Chiapas were implemented both by native elites and by foreign 'investor–settlers'.[26] Colonizations following the 'ideals' of the Enlightenment were superimposed on sociopolitical structures that were the result of 300 years of Spanish rule. It is not a matter of comparing the two models of imperialism but of tracing the effects. When at the turn of the twentieth century Zapata claims communal lands of his town of Atenecuilco that had been privatized by liberal legislation inspired in the Enlightenment, he does so on the basis of legal documents that date back to the colonial period. Spanish colonial laws included legislation that protected the communities from the kinds of expropriation that became prevalent after the wars of independence. These laws cannot be seen as merely preserving the status of Indian communities before the conquest, but also as creating traditions reflecting the influence of Christianity and the impact of the socioeconomic–technological transformation introduced by the colonial order. It is important to note that indigenous communities reinvent themselves under colonial and republican rule, wherein tradition is subject to debate.

If history played a fundamental role in defining the legitimacy of the communities, the past also bears a legacy of rebellion. The most notable figure in present-day Chiapas is the hybrid Votán Zapata, a mixture of the nonmodern embedded in Votán, the pre-Columbian numen signified as 'the guardian and heart of the people', and the modern embedded in Zapata and the Revolution of 1910. As it were, the spirit of Votán assumes an epochal instantiation in Zapata.[27] We can trace a tradition of invoking the leaders of the past spanning the very beginning of the colonial period to the present-day rebellion in Chiapas. Spanish authorities were concerned not only with learning the past to preserve the normative systems in the indigenous communities, but also with gaining knowledge regarding other uses of history in which Indians invoked the spirits of the ancient leaders in a spirit of rebellion.

Let me dwell on this last point by citing a passage from one of the *Cantares Mexicanos*, a series of songs first collected by Bernardino de Sahagún and his indigenous assistants in the 1550s:

> The ruler Atl Popoca comes to do a shield dance here in Mexico. It seems this lord lays hold of dried up egret-plume flower shields, lays hold of withered stripers, here before your eyes, Tlaxcallans. Hey! Huexotzincas, hey!
>
> It seems he's come to take a lance from the Spaniards. It seems this lord lays hold of dried-up egret-plume flower shields, lays hold of withered stripers, here before your eyes, Tlaxcallans. Hey! Huexotzincas, hey!
>
> Motelchiuh is the one who thrusts his shield, and it's the time of lords! Yes even so he sallies forth, having appeared. And when they've captured the conquistadores' guns, then Rabbit says, 'Let there be dancing!' Tlaxcallans, hey! Huexotzincas, hey![28]

The text here invokes the arrival of armed ghost warriors who are not only a threat to the Spaniards but also to their Indian allies, the Tlaxcallans and the Huexotzincas. According to Bierhorst, this song belongs to the ghost dance genre we associate with the Plains Indians; ghost dances generally invoke the warriors of old to join them in a rebellion against the colonial order. Here, the warriors of old are taking possession of the Spaniards' lances and their guns. Whatever the motivation for keeping a record of these songs, the missionaries can hardly be seen as conceiving the Nahuas as a people without history; quite the contrary, beyond writing/painting histories, the Nahuas invoked the past to bring it to life in song and dance. They are people with intense histories that haunted the Spaniards with the revival of the old, with the return of ghosts. The songs spoke a language that evaded the missionaries' comprehension. It is never a question of a lack of history but of history in a different key. And I say 'beyond writing' to underscore the performance of history in pre-Columbian and colonial Mexico, and certainly not because the Spaniards of the early modern period thought the Amerindians as a whole lacked writing; otherwise how would we explain the ubiquitous reference to writing systems and the missionary projects of reconstructing the burned codices by producing replicas of pre-Columbian writing systems? (See Rabasa 1996 and 1998.) Even when these histories were written using the Latin alphabet, their production as well as their reading must be understood in terms of an oral performance, and certainly not in the privacy of the individual world of the bourgeois writer and reader: the writing was (and continues to be) a collective practice that recorded the contribution of multiple voices and the reading a public performance that addressed the community.

There are, of course, those who denigrate and deny the status of writing to the iconic script used by Amerindians or for that matter, those who cast insults, who denigrate Indians with racist remarks, but there is, in my opinion, a much more interesting and enduring aspect to the colonial process in those texts and projects that seek to appropriate indigenous history, often a collaborative effort of Spaniards, mestizos and Indians. For instance, the ghost song and dance quoted above would be neutralized by someone like the Dominican Diego Durán, who conceived history in terms of a resurrection of the Ancient Mexican grandeur in his *Historia de la Nueva España e islas de Tierra Firme*: 'Ha sido mi deseo de darle vida y resucitarle de la muerte y olvido en que estaba, a cabo de tanto tiempo' (My desire has been to give it life and resurrect it from the death and oblivion in which it has rested for such a long time) (Durán 1984: vol. 2, 27–8). Later on in the *Historia* Durán is even more emphatic in his praise of Nahua pre-Columbian historians and his will to resurrect the dead:

> Pero los historiadores y pintores pintaban con historias vivas y matices, con el pincel de su curiosidad, con vivos colores, las vidas y hazañas de estos valerosos caballeros y señores, para que su fama volase, con la claridad del sol, por todas las naciones. Cuya fama y memoria quise yo referir en esta historia, para que, conservada aquí, dure todo el tiempo que durare, para que los amadores de la virtud se aficionen a la seguir. (Dúran 1984: vol. 2, 99)

> But the Mexican historians and painters painted with vivid histories and tints, with the brush of their curiosity, with vivid colors, the lives and feats of these courageous knights and lords, so that their fame would fly with the clarity of the sun over all nations. To their fame and glory I wish to refer in this my history, so that conserved here, it will last for the time it may last, so that the lovers of virtue may become fond of following it.

We must read this text as counterinsurgent inasmuch as it claims resurrection as a trope for writing a history that will bring to life the ancient grandeur so that the 'lovers of virtue' find a model for their actions. Durán not only alludes to Indian histories using iconic script as sources of his information, but also praises their pictorial beauty and the force of their corresponding verbal discourses. Just as he emulates the rhetorical colors of old and the inscription of history in stone, we cannot ignore the fact that Duran's history seeks to bury the past for good. In this regard we may associate Durán's *Historia* with what Michel de Certeau has said about the metaphor of resurrection in Michelet's unpublished preface to the *Histoire de France*: 'It aims at calming the dead who still haunt the present, and offering them scriptural tombs' (de Certeau 1988: 2). Nothing, however, guarantees the quieting down of the spirits of old. We can indeed imagine the pictorial component in Durán's *Historia* decorating bureaucratic buildings if not *pulquerías* (those public spaces in which the uprising of 1692 in Mexico City was gestated, chronicled by Carlos de Sigüenza y Góngora (1984)), and inspiring a whole tradition of Mexican muralists up to Diego Rivera and the *Vida y sueños de la cañada Perla*. There is, however, an ambivalence in his call for virtue inasmuch as the association of political virtue suggests Machiavelli's use of this term in *The Prince* and the historical style of his commentary on Titus Livius in *The Discourses*. Durán intends his call for virtue to the mestizos and criollos, and perhaps the indigenous elites collaborating with the Spaniards, hardly the same subjects that invoked the ghosts of old in song and dance, in an open call for rebellion!

Not unlike the ghost songs of the *Cantares Mexicanos*, the spirit of Flores Magón and especially Zapata belong to an imaginary of insurrection among the indigenous peoples of Chiapas, as evidenced in Marcos's reminiscence of Lord Ik': 'O si, como ahora se dice en las montañas, el señor Ik' no murió, sino que vive como una luz que aparece, de tanto en tanto, por entre cerros y cañadas, con el sombrero y el caballo de Zapata' [Or perhaps, as it is told today in the mountains, lord Ik' did not die, but rather lives like a light that appears off and on, between the hills and the ravines, with the hat and the horse of Zapata] (Subcomandante Marcos 1994: 79). Lord Ik' (Black Lord) was Comandante Hugo's *nom de guerre*. Hugo, an elder who according to Marcos was at the center of the uprising of January 1, 1994, died in the assault of San Cristóbal de las Casas. Ik' was also one of the founders of the EZLN and a mentor to a whole generation of Zapatistas. In the manner of a latter-day Mackandal, the famed leader of the Haitian revolution who after his death would reappear in different animal and human forms (in recuperating the oral tradition of Mackandal resides the greatness of Alejo Carpentier's novel *El Reino de este mundo* [*Kingdom of This World*]),[29] Zapata as Ik' or Ik' as Zapata testifies to the agency of the 'gods', to the power of Votán (the guardian and heart of the people), to the compatibility of the modern and the nonmodern in the Zapatista insurrection, to the hybrid figure of Votán Zapata. Note the reference to the *one* and the *multitude* in the following communiqué of 10 April 1994:

> Es y no es todo en nosotros . . . Caminado está . . . Votán Zapata, guardian y corazón del pueblo. Amo de la noche . . . Señor de la montaña . . . Nosotros . . . Votán , guardian y corazón del pueblo. Uno y muchos es. Ninguno y todos. Estando viene. Votán, guardian y corazón del pueblo. (EZLN 1994: 212, ellipses in original)

> Everything is and is not in us . . . He is walking . . . Votán Zapata, guardian and heart of the people. Lord of the night . . . Lord of the mountain . . . Us . . . Votán Zapata, guardian and heart of the people. None and all . . . As being is coming . . . Votán Zapata, guardian and heart of the people.

Votán Zapata, as one and many, attests to the singular in the multitude, to the singular subjectivity of constituent power, to the 'many' comprising the multitude that refuses to be reduced to a 'much': 'Democracy thus appears as constituent power. It is a power expressed in the multitude of singular subjects that excludes every transfer of powers. Constituent power excludes there being any type of foundation that resides outside the process of the multitude' (Hardt and Negri 1994: 311).

For in Negri the 'gods' also seem to live, but in the figure of Dionysus— or at least this is what he and Michael Hardt say in *Labor of Dionysus*: 'Our work is dedicated to the creative, Dionysian powers of the netherworld' (1994: xiv). They identify the Dionysian creator with communism: 'Communism is the only Dionysian creator' (1994: 21). Elsewhere, in his discussion of Spinoza's contributions to the theory of constituent power in *Insurgencies*, Negri speaks of '*A democratic living god*', of 'Democracy, a real democracy of right and appropriation, equal distribution of wealth, and equal participation in production [that] becomes the living god', of 'Democracy [that] is the project of the multitude, a creative force, a living god.' Negri goes on to outline the need

> to emphasize and study the relation that ties the development of constituent thought to three ideological dimensions of Western thought: the Judeo-Christian tradition of creativity, the natural right concerning the social foundation, and the transcendental theory of the foundation. Now, the development of the concept of constituent power, even in its radically critical figures, is somewhat limited by these three ideal conditions—and no matter how much it works to unhinge them, it remains partially tied to them.

Negri adopts the radical atheism of Machiavelli's, Spinoza's, and Marx's constituent theories, by which he means that 'the concept of creativity is tied essentially to man' (Negri 1999a: 305–7, emphasis in original).

All this suggests that Negri can establish at once his commitment to radical atheism while at the same time partaking of 'a metaphysics of democracy and creativity', the living god of democracy and the Dionysian spirit of communism. The secular and the atheistic have their limits, paradoxically, in the same impulse that leads Negri to critique the religious conception of creativity in Machiavelli, Spinoza, and Marx. Negri identifies this remnant of Judeo-Christian conceptions of creativity in the tendency to conceive the strength of the multitude in terms of unity: 'To claim this, however, means forgetting that the strength of the multitude is not only in the strength of the "much" but also the strength of the "many," that is, the strength of singularities and differences' (Negri 1999a: 308). This statement would make suspect any attempt to establish a unity on the principle of atheism and secularity, and even less desirable if, as Negri asserts, the crisis of constituent power, brought about by the three ideologies of the West listed above, will never be totally unhinged. It seems more pertinent to explore the ways in which the agency of the 'gods' may very well coexist with the will to a radical atheism. After all, given these ideologies haunting modern rationality, who is to deny, in the name of secularism, that it is true that 'el señor Ik' no murió, sino que vive como una luz que aparece, de tanto en tanto, por entre cerros y cañadas, con el sombrero y el caballo de Zapata' [lord Ik' did not die, rather he lives like a light that appears off and on, between the hills and the ravines, with the hat and the horse of Zapata]? Moreover, on what grounds can one invoke the autonomy of individual consciousness to denounce the heteronomy of the 'agency of the gods'? Who is to say that Votán, 'the guardian and heart of the people', does not reside within the singularities comprising the multitude?

Negri has written the following apropos of Derrida's *Specters of Marx*, a statement that could have been uttered by Flores Magón and captures well the spirit of the ghosts in the mural of Taniperla:

It seems to me that if the specter of capitalism is substantially present in Derrida's book (and with that the more recent developments of capitalist dominion), the 'specter of communism,' on the other hand, is harder to identify, if not undetectable. If Derrida sharpens the 'arms of criticism' with great zeal and intelligence, the other spectrology nevertheless goes by the wayside, the one organized through a 'criticism of arms.' Communism's ghost is not only the product of critique; it is also, and

above all, a passion, destructive of the world of capital and constructive of freedom, 'the real movement that destroys the present state of
things.' (Negri 1999b: 15; see also Derrida 1994)

After reading this passage one is left wondering, what are arms? Negri
suggests, beyond the conventional meaning of arms, i.e., *armed struggle*,
that we must invent other forms of materializing the passion of communism, the destruction of the world of capital, in the constitutive strength
of the multitude. The abandonment of armed struggle apparently poses a
contradiction in Negri's distinction between the 'arms of criticism' and the
'criticism of arms'. It seems that the solution to this aporia would reside in
the passage from the arms of criticism as critique of capital and the state to
the criticism of arms as the formation of new subjectivities; Negri takes
care to distinguish these new subjects from the 'new man', always a finished
product, of various socialist states modeled on Stalinism. In spite of the
radically different locations and socioeconomic conditions of subjects
in metropolitan centers and the Selva Lacandona, the autonomization of
subjectivities and communities carries in both locations the shared task of
a 'criticism of arms' that no longer advocates armed struggle.

In *The Politics of Subversion* Negri speaks of the socialized worker, of a
new proletariat consisting of the highly educated work force of the information age, an intellectual labor force. The student struggles in Paris in
1986 manifested for Negri the *'emergence of a new social subject*: an intellectual
subject which is nonetheless proletarian, polychrome, a collective plot of
the need for equality; a political subject that rejects the political and
immediately gives rise to an ethical determination for existence and struggle'
(Negri 1989: 47). Ethics informs the new practices and thus replaces politics, as in political parties. Here again we find great commonalities with
the Zapatistas' refusal to accommodate their struggle to the line of a particular party. The intellectual proletarian of the metropolitan centers differs
greatly from the Indian peasants comprising the insurrection in Chiapas,
but nothing keeps the multiplicity of Indian struggles from being thought
of as 'polychrome, a collective need for equality'. The task for Negri and
the Zapatistas would now consist not in establishing a new state (as in the
old model of taking over the state) but of destroying the state, 'this mon-
strous bourgeois and capitalist fetish and succeeding, as a consequence, in
devolving all its various functions to the community' (Negri 1989: 175).
The notion of devolving functions to the community presupposes a
process of autonomization in self-government. Ideally, these would be
subjects that cannot be expropriated, that is, insurgent subjects giving rise
to the power of subversion: 'Subversion is the destruction of violence that

is inherent in exploitation and runs through society, indistinctly, massively and terribly: subversion is *countervailing power*. . . . Subversion is the radical nature of the truth. It is an applied form of this radicalism. *Subversion is the calm and implacable countervailing of the masses'* (Negri 1989: 59). Negri goes on to state as one of the truths the norm against killing, whereby the task is to invent a violence to destroy the monopoly of violence by the state and exploitation that, 'because it is creative, destroys without killing' (Negri 1989: 60).

Negri defines the emergence of the new subjects within Marx's conceptual framework of a transition from 'formal subsumption' to 'real subsumption' of labor to capital. Under the real subsumption the whole society would be subjected to the capitalist mode of production (see Negri 1989: 71). Clearly, Negri is thinking of a post-Fordist proletariat that would apparently have little to do with the indigenous peoples of Chiapas, who cannot be classified as a proletariat even though they exist under the formal subsumption of capital. The 'people in arms' would consist of a mass intellectuality that now controls the entrepreneurial power of productive labor, a condition that enables Negri to envision soviets of mass intellectuality: 'The soviets of mass intellectuality can pose themselves this task by constructing, outside of the state, a mechanism within which a democracy of the everyday can organize active communication, the interactivity of citizens, and at the same time produce increasingly free and complex subjectivities' (Negri 1996a: 222). Negri's language can be transposed to the life represented in the mural at Taniperla wherein mass intellectuality would lose its First World association with new technologies and encompass any collective effort to construct a democracy of the everyday. The arms of the socialized worker (i.e., the control of the means of production) are in the hands of the post-Fordist proletariat, a condition that lends itself to political, entrepreneurial and economic autonomies. But even though the material conditions of Indians in Chiapas are at the opposite pole from a post-Fordist proletariat, we can trace similarities in the projects for the autonomization of Indian peoples. Moreover, among the demands of Zapatistas are the conditions for creating an infrastructure that would enable Indians to participate (to some extent they are already participating) in the mass intellectuality characteristic of post-Fordist societies: access to education for both men and women, communication infrastructures, control of the means of production and the natural resources within their territories. The beginnings of these are mapped out in the mural of Taniperla where we see the communal school, the introduction of electricity and the antenna emblematic of a full participation in the new communication technologies. It is important that we insist again on speaking in terms of autonomization rather than of sanctioned autonomies, for reasons not unlike the difference between *new subjectivities* of constituent power and the *new man* of constituted socialist regimes.[30]

Life in Taniperla manifests the ways in which autonomous self-government destroys capital and constructs freedom, from within an understanding of resistance that does not react but precedes power itself. The Zapatista insurrection and the political resolution of the conflict in the accords of San Andrés is perhaps the recent political event that best exemplifies the limits of constituent power laid out by Negri. The project of indigenous autonomy and its constituent power are haunted by the three limits outlined by Negri that I mentioned above. Allow me to cite them again: 'the Judeo-Christian tradition of creativity, the natural right concerning the social foundation, and the transcendental theory of the foundation' (Negri 1999a: 307). At both ends of the spectrum of 'development', of the quantitative differences of the nonmodern, the modern and the postmodern, we find in Negri and the Zapatistas a common effort to go beyond modern rationality. Both Negri's and the Zapatistas' project of autonomization, however, can never be completely free from these limits. Beyond a discussion of the extent and nature of indigenous autonomy, which has centered on geographic definitions (autonomy at the level of municipios, regions, peoples) with major implications, we must attend to the aporias the discourse of autonomy inherits from a philosophical tradition that, beginning with Kant, sought to ground moral and political thought on the individual subject.

Let me preface my remarks on Kant by stating that they limit themselves to drawing out key concepts pertaining to any project of autonomy. If Negri singles out Kant with respect to the 'transcendental theory of foundation', one can also trace the other two ideals in Kant. Because of its immediate concern with politics, peace, and human rights, I will center my discussion on Kant's *Toward a Perpetual Peace: A Philosophical Project*.

Of these three ideal conditions, the one central to the discourse of autonomy is the transcendental theory of the foundation of morals because of its immediate connection to the autonomy of individual freedom, to what Kant calls the *formal* principle, that is, the *categorical imperative*: 'So act that you can will that your maxim should become a universal law (whatever the end may be)' (Kant 1996b: 344). From this formulation of the categorical imperative in *Toward a Perpetual Peace* Kant derives the 'principle of moral politics that a people is to unite itself into a state in accordance with freedom and equality as the sole concepts of right, and this principle is not based on prudence but upon duty' (Kant 1996b: 345). These two principles bind the freedom of the individual to the natural foundation of the state.

A state organized according to the pure principles of right would in turn expect other states to organize themselves in accordance with those principles, which would also serve as a model for the union of this state with others and the lawful relationship between states. The natural right concerning the social foundation in Kant entails the discourse of human rights that grounds the demands for the recognition of rights to culture, language, and self-determination. Kant's formulation of human rights presupposes a union of politics and morals: 'The right of human beings must be held sacred, however great a sacrifice this may cost the ruling power' (Kant 1996b: 347).

If this right of human beings limits the ruling power to an ethics binding ends and means, it also creates an aporia for the principle of revolution: inasmuch as the means in revolution are by definition illegal, they cannot justify the ends. Clearly, an accomplished revolution can establish the legality of the new state on ethico-political grounds. There is as it were a period of struggle that by definition is illegal and unethical. This judgment is based on public right: 'all actions relating to the rights of others are wrong if their maxim is incompatible with publicity' (Kant 1996b: 347). Kant reminds us that by definition rebellion cannot be public. Flores Magón, Marcos, and the Zapatistas, and perhaps Negri himself, when he characterizes constituent power as existing outside the law, express this sense of illegality as a condition that paradoxically is ethical not only as to its ends, but also as to its potential critique of the present. For Flores Magón (as for Lenin and the ideology of *armed struggle* in general), the end would be synonymous with the overthrow of the state. In Negri and the Zapatistas, the critique of arms would aspire to transform existing constitutions in ways that would enable constituent strength by opening new possibilities of autonomous self-government. As such, beyond reform, the transformation of the constitution grounds the establishment of spaces for revolutionary practices aiming at the destruction of the state. One may fulfill the principle of publicity by affirming that the end of the struggle is the destruction of the state without having the obligation, in an agonistic context, of making one's strategies public. One may be public without being transparent: creativity, cunning, and surprise are unalienable rights—not because the state guarantees them, but rather because they are integral components of ethico-political practices.

As for the limits of the Judeo-Christian tradition of creativity, Kant's philosophy entails a teleological concept of nature that privileges unity as the end of all processes; for Kant, the state is the natural form of organizing society and the autonomy of the will occasions a sovereign unified subject. The moral principle and its articulation in laws and culture presuppose an evolution of reason and morality in history:

> Providence is thus justified in the course of the world; for the moral
> principle in the human being never dies out, and reason, which is capa-
> ble pragmatically of carrying out rightful ideas in accordance with that
> principle, grows steadily with advancing culture, but so too does the guilt
> for those transgressions.[31]

Kant has a moment of doubt in the possibility that humans cannot be
bettered, which he dispels by insisting that we must 'assume that the principles of right have objective reality, that is, that they can be carried out'
(1996b: 346). This amounts to an act of faith in the objectivity of the moral
maxims to avoid falling into despair. As such, the troubling thought that
humans are frail and the need to believe the contrary corrupts the autonomy of the freedom of the will and the categorical imperative. The his-
toricity itself of the evolution of morals and reasons would make suspect
the formal nature of the maxims and would bind them to particular
cultural expressions. Otherwise, what is to keep us from assuming that all
humans in all societies and moments in history have followed the principles of pure reason in the development of their governments and social
institutions, if not the belief in the superiority of the institutions that Kant
defines as more evolved, specifically a constitutional republic?

With Kant we inevitably face a tension between the multiplicity of
peoples with rights and their belonging to a single state. Kant identifies
this process of unification in constitutional terms, that is, a civil constitution or 'the act of the general will by means of which a multitude becomes
a people' (1996b: 324). Kant favors republicanism over democracy in the
taming of the multitude, what he refers to as the disorderly multitude that
has to be ruled by a representative government. In Negri's terms, constituent strength must be subordinated to constituted power. If one of the
salient characteristics of constituent power resides in its existence outside
the law, one wonders whether a dialogue is possible between the affirmation
of constituent power and the force of the multitude and the will to resolve
a conflict by the rule of law, by a constitutional resolution.

This tension between the disorderly multitude and its domestication as
a people has a parallelism, actually surfaces as a corollary to the tension
between the liberty of individual peoples and the Kantian definition of
civilization as those states in which all members would 'subject themselves
to a lawful coercion to be instituted by themselves' (Kant 1996b: 326). This
distinction entails a philosophical anthropology. We need to consider
whether there is in Kant a structural difference between what the German
philosopher calls 'European savages' and their American counterparts.

Whereas the first incorporate the defeated into the body of subjects (note the language of ingestion), the American tribes literally incorporate, that is, cannibalistically ingest the enemy. Is this a bad joke or a difference that enables him to define the superiority of Europe? We have to proceed cautiously, and perhaps go beyond a simple dismissal of Kant and look for deeper limits and unsolvable aporias not defined by a structural binary European/non-European peoples. My point is not to expose Kant's racism or imperialism but to circumscribe our own discourse from within his categories and aporias.[32]

Consider the following anticolonial statements:

> If one compares with this [the publicly lawful relation between nations] the *inhospitable* behavior of civilized, especially commercial states, the injustice they show in visiting foreign lands and peoples (which with them is tantamount to *conquering* them) goes to horrifying lengths. When America, the negro countries, the Spice islands, the Cape, and so forth were discovered, they were to them, countries belonging to no one, since they counted the inhabitants as nothing. (1996b: 329)

Further down Kant derives pleasure from the bankruptcy of the trading .companies:

> The worst of this (or, considered from the standpoint of a moral judge, the best) is that the commercial states do not even profit from this violence, that all the trading companies are on the verge of collapse; that the Sugar Islands, that place of the cruelest and most calculated slavery, yield no true profit but serve only a mediate and indeed not very laudable purpose, namely training sailors for warships and so, in turn, carrying on wars in Europe, and this for powers that make much ado of their piety. (1996b: 330)

These unintended global impacts, 'a violation of right on *one* place of the earth is felt in *all*', illustrates and justifies Kant's article: 'Cosmopolitan right shall be limited to conditions of universal *hospitality*' (1996b: 328).

Now, reconcile these statements with the following formulation of the right to impose war on societies *in a state of nature*, that is, without a state:

> But a human being (or a nation) in a mere state of nature denies me this assurance and already wrongs me just by being near me in this condition even if not actively (*facto*) yet by the lawlessness of his condition (*statu iniustu*), by which he constantly threatens me; and I can coerce him either to enter with me into a condition of being under civil laws or to leave my neighborhood. (Kant 1996b: 322)

One wonders if the condition of lawlessness will be judged on empirical principles or if this statement constitutes a mere instance of a formal distinction between civilization as societies with states and barbarism as societies without states. These statements can only be reconciled in terms of the 'good way' of coercing vis-à-vis 'bad conquest'.

Is Kant thereby inventing the very same characteristics of what Hardt and Negri have identified as the peaceful vocation of empire?[33] In Hardt and Negri's schema human-rights organizations fulfill an analogous function to the missionaries of old inasmuch as they lend moral credence to military intervention. Thus, empire surfaces as the ultimate arbiter of the right to one's culture, language, and self-determination—to one's sacrosanct autonomy as an individual and as a member of a nation.

In the case of the Acuerdos de San Andrés and the mural of Taniperla, we can distinguish at least two forms of life, defining debates over and formulations of the meaning of autonomy. In fact, the life world of Taniperla, as coded in the mural, is an instance of the right to self-determination outlined in the Acuerdos de San Andrés—the promotion of indigenous cultures and languages, the right to follow indigenous normative systems, and the definition of development from within the community. This list does not exhaust the points of the agreements, but touches on some of the most sensitive issues of the signed document. After all, indigenous languages, normative systems, and models of development affect the administration, use, and benefits to be derived from the natural resources in Chiapas. In the end, the debate comes down to a struggle between (at least) two economic models for the nation that primarily affect indigenous peoples; however, it is worthwhile remembering that the uprising of the EZLN was not for the particular rights of indigenous communities in Chiapas; rather, from the start it invoked Indian peoples as a whole and called for a transformation of the state. The call for autonomy includes not only indigenous peoples, but the right of any municipio, regardless of its ethnic composition, and moreover the right of any sector of civil society, to constitute itself as autonomous. We must also underscore that the EZLN rebellion in the main does not propose a politics for the protection of indigenous forms of life, as in an ecological model of the right of particular cultures to survive: the rebellion in itself articulates indigenous life forms.[34] As such, it exemplifies the always singular nature of constituent power and the *many* comprising the multitude. This obviously does not mean that the Mexican state has not subjected indigenous peoples to war against its life forms, but that biopower defines the terms of the struggle itself. Flores Magón stands for the languages of the West deployed in the struggle with the state over the right to self-determination and autonomy, but indigenous forms of life articulate the Zapatista communitarian ethos, its critique of modern rationality and developmentalism, and the organization of insurrection itself based on the democratic processes of consensus within the Indian communities. Under Flores Magón, we must also imagine Negri's contribution to the critique of arms (alternatives to armed struggle), and (why not?) Derrida's sharpening of the arms of critique. Deconstruction, as defined by Derrida in the *Politics of Friendship*, is inseparable from democracy—'(no deconstruction without democracy, no democracy without deconstruction)'—and as such this parenthetically expressed formula binds the two projects into an endless self-delimitation: 'Democracy is the *autos* of deconstructive self-delimitation. Delimitation not only in the name of a regulative idea and an indefinite perfectibility, but every time in the singular urgency of a *here and now*' (Derrida 1997: 105).

The debates over the meaning of democracy in the *Politics of Friendship* have *everything* and have *nothing* to do with the debates over democracy in the Acuerdos de San Andrés. They have *nothing* to do with indigenous autonomy insofar as the questions pertaining to soil and blood in Derrida's deconstruction of democracy refer to discourse inherited from Greece, as manifest in the distinction between *polemos* (as in war between nations, peoples) and *stasis* (as in civil war, internal dissent). The risk of homogenization in speaking of self-delimitation and perfectibility resides in the privilege granted to Euro-American discourses on democracy: indigenous peoples have their own history and discourses on blood and soil, which should not be reduced to nor translated into Greek categories informing Western discourses on democracy. They have *everything* to do with indigenous autonomy because deconstruction's indefinite perfectibility would promise the deliverance of the West from a discourse that can only think in terms of a single universality, whether to declare its existence, its transformative nature, or its impossibility. Nothing should keep us from imagining Indians inventing a language to discourse on these Greek terms and the meaning of deconstruction. We would thus postulate two horizons of universality that might interact with each other but at no point could one reduce the other to its categories. As such, the debates over the recognition of Indian rights to their normative systems would not entail recognition of these rights from within a singular universality, but a transformation of a hegemonic discourse. In fact, this transformation would ultimately question the desires for a new hegemonic discourse that, in this case, would validate indigenous normative systems under the principles of universality—i.e., a theory of natural rights obviously grounded in the modernity of Western discourses. This would involve a recognition, as in *re*-cognition, a knowing again of these normative systems and an accepting of them as legitimate, but also a recognition of the right to have one's own normative systems and the right to refuse others access to them. A people may choose to make them *public* to outsiders, but the demand for recognition would have nothing to do with gaining the acceptance from outsiders in a position of power and dominance, as in the dialectic of the master and the slave in Hegel's *Phenomenology*.

A tension inevitably arises in the language of the accords, which defends the right of indigenous peoples to self-determination, and the implied (often explicitly stated) assumption that indigenous people practice their languages, cultures, and normative systems regardless of the recognition of this right by the state. Again, I must underscore that my interrogation does pertain to the Indian's pursuit of autonomy, but to the discourse that haunts the arguments that, out of necessity, autonomy must be framed in legal discourse grounded in a Western philosophical tradition and the desire of the state to fix the meaning and delimit the space of autonomy. The danger here is that the language of law that seeks to promote, defend, and institutionalize indigenous life forms will subordinate the strength of the multitude and of constituent power to a constitutional resolution of the 'conflict' that will assign the proper administration of autonomy to specialists well versed in the 'correct procedures'. These specialists will range from university-trained experts in development (human or otherwise) to anthropologists who will mediate disputes on the history of the communities and the meaning of tradition. One can also expect a bureaucratic structure entrusted with the administration of funds and the capacity of judicial oversight. A whole array of human rights, presently used for the defense of indigenous peoples, could turn against the communities in the name of feminist agendas or religious tolerance. I am not saying that issues pertaining to gender or the expulsion of religious groups from communities are not already relevant in the indigenous communities—the place of women and the nondenominational temple in the mural of Taniperla prove the contrary—but that the constitutionalization of the autonomies would redefine the struggle in terms of cultural survival and particular rights. As in the ecological model, only those forms considered beautiful (read pure) would be worthy of preservation, thereby taking away the same right to self-determination the law would seek to recognize. The liberation of women and the tolerance of differences must emerge from within the indigenous life forms in order to be meaningful and creative of new possibilities of gender relations and cultural diversity not contemplated, perhaps unimaginable, by the law and its bureaucrats.[35]

Thus, the institutionalization of autonomy—the adoption of a constituted form at the expense of constituent power—would actually hinder the process of autonomization already in place. In setting out procedures for the autonomous regions, the language of the laws diminishes the role bicultural indigenous intellectuals would eventually play in the definition of the autonomous processes in their communities; 'serán los indígenas quienes dentro del marco constitucional y en el ejercicio pleno de sus derechos decidan los medios y formas en que habrán de conducir sus propios procesos de transformación' (it will be the Indians who, within the constitutional frame and the full exercise of their right, will decide the means and the forms in which they will conduct their own processes of transformation) (Hernández Navarraro and Vera Herrera 1998: 66). I limit myself to citing one instance in which language, apparently empowering to Indians, ends up subordinating them to 'a constitutional frame' that overrides the authority of their own normative systems. It calls for a new pact with the state that would assume new responsibilities with respect to Indian peoples. If it states that 'no serán ni la unilateralidad ni la subestimación sobre las capacidades indígenas para construir su futuro las que definan las políticas del Estado' (neither unilaterality nor underestimation of the Indian's capacities to construct their future will define the politics of the state), Indians lack a voice in this phrase, they remain a marginalized third person, rather than a subject exercising her constituent power. Was it unavoidable given the legal framework that the accords were articulated *in the name of* the Indians *rather than with* the Indians as interlocutors? My objective is not to undermine the importance of the accords or the necessity of creating a new juridical framework, but to isolate the elements of a crisis from within the discourse of autonomy. This crisis is nowhere better expressed than in one of the *whereas* clauses stated in a communiqué 'a los hermanos indígenas de todo México' [to all the Indian brothers in all of Mexico] by the Comité Clandestino Revolucionario Indígena (Clandestine Indigenous Revolutionary Committee) of the EZLN, signed by the comandantes Tacho, David, Zabedo and the subcomandante Marcos:

> Los problemas que existen en torno a la autonomía, justicia, representación política, mujeres, medios de comunicación y cultura, en el entendimiento de que el asunto de la libre determinación y la autonomía implica también y muy centralmente la relación de dependencia que se impone vía programas, proyectos y presupuestos, la posible remunicipalización, la forma de elección de autoridades y en general las muchas maneras de asociación y organización. (Hernández Navarraro and Vera Herrera 1998: 185)

> The problems that exist concerning autonomy, justice, political representation, women, means of communication and culture also imply

in a very central mode a relation of dependency that is imposed by means of programs, projects and budgets, the possible remunicipaliza-tion, the form of electing authorities and in general the multiple ways of association and organization.

This aporia is the consequence of an inherent disparity between the language of autonomy practiced in the communities and the language of autonomy practiced in the debates giving form to the Acuerdos de San Andrés. The language of law gives place to procedures in the administra-tion of the autonomous regions that do not give enough importance to the bicultural indigenous intellectuals who will assume the responsibility of defining the autonomization of their communities: the aporias of fem-inist discourses, of human rights, of multiple agencies ('the times of the gods and the time of history', in Dipesh Chakrabarty's terms (1997)), of coexisting pluralities of life forms, and so on, can be traced in the mural of Taniperla. The concept of autonomy in itself carries an aporia with respect to the concept of heteronomy that might very well be an integral compo-nent of an indigenous normative system. Indians would thus be demanding autonomy for the right to self-determination based on heteronomous principles. And what is to say that Votán, 'the heart of the people', is less universal than the categorical imperative?

Hegel's critique of Kant in the *Phenomenology of Mind* provides the terms for a critique of Kantian formalism, but by reading Hegel against the grain we may derive categories that enable us to speak of a plurality of coexisting universalities. Under one breath Hegel summarily dismisses Kant's formalism and any appeal to empirism: 'For universality devoid of content is formal; and an absolute content amounts to a distinction which is no distinction, i.e., means absence of content' (Hegel 1967: 445). Further down Hegel adds: 'Reason as law-giver is reduced to being reason as criterion; instead of laying down laws reason now only tests *what is* laid down' (1967: 445). Is this a mere statement of fact that we always dwell and begin in a body of law, and consequently we are limited to testing '*what is*'? Hegel suggests that the concept of autonomy, as defined by Kant, never completely sheds its heteronomous origins in a state of law that necessarily precedes or at least is coterminous with the formulation of pure rational concepts.[36]

But even if we granted Kant the formal and transcendental character of his maxims, inherent to Kant is an evolutionary model of the laws and institutions: there is nothing that can prevent that one materialization of law would entail a repudiation of a former ethos; take as an example Kant's references, more or less systematic, to race or gender. Is it that *man* out of his autonomous free will arrived at the conclusion that *women* are not inferior, or was it a transformation that came about as a result of demands placed by *women*, who in the first place did not participate in the autonomy of free will? Wouldn't definitions of who is a rational being inevitably vitiate the autonomy of the freedom of the will? Or, in accordance with the terms he uses in his essay on the question 'What is Enlightenment?' (Kant 1996a), wouldn't the answer reside in the historical moment when humanity achieves freedom to determine itself? From here the process of relativization of freedom, truth, and the law is inevitable once we trace the limits of the ever-evolving process of enlightenment as also comprising forms of de-enlightenment that would confine earlier forms of thought to particular modes of relating to the universal. As I have pointed out apropos of Derrida's view of deconstruction's indefinite perfectibility, it would include within its horizon (unless we are willing to 'impose homogenizing calculability while exalting land and blood' (Derrida 1997: 106)) the understanding that indigenous cultures and normative systems partake of a universality *defined by* and *definitive of* their form of life. Clearly, this moment in deconstruction's indefinite perfectibility would abandon its pretense to a universal applicability by opening to the possibility that deconstruction can be subject to debate and clarification in terms other than those that gave rise to it from within the discourses and categories of the West. Not all of us think in *Greek*, which does not mean that Greek does not affect us all. Furthermore, the legacy of Greek cannot be completely unhinged by a willful gesture of stepping out of Eurocentrism.

In reflecting on the mural of Taniperla and the Zapatista insurrection in general, we find that a porosity of the inside/outside of life forms entails a communication plagued by aporias, by a crisis that must not be resolved but creatively deployed in an inexhaustible affirmation of freedom. Flores Magón's seeds of freedom coexist with Zapata's maxim, 'la tierra es de quien la trabaja' (land belongs to those who work it), in two discourses that, without contradicting each other, partake of an aporia: each of the two life forms must be explained in the terms of the other. We know that Flores Magón played a part in the formulation of Zapata's maxim 'tierra y libertad' (land and freedom), and that the revolutionary insurrection from the south fed into the agrarianism of the anarcho-communism of the Partido Liberal.[37] Flores Magón and the intellectual tradition of the West, obviously including Kant's conception of autonomy and constitutionalism, Negri's concept of constituent power, and Derridean deconstruction, would have to be explained, clarified, interpreted in Tzeltal categories, and not just the other way, as in the one-way street in which the anthropological discourses of the West assume the privileged position of explaining the life forms of the rest of the world, a-concept-of-the-world-as-rest of their own creation.

The title of this chapter proposes reading Negri by Zapata, which as I have defined here would mean both 'with' Zapata, as in participating in parallel revolutionary processes that may inform each other, but also as 'by' in the sense of Negri being read by Zapata, as in the process in which Negri and the philosophical and political tradition of the West would be considered in indigenous terms. We may thus imagine Indians reading and discoursing on revolution, the impossible, and communism as formulated by Derrida, Negri, and other projects grounded in the West—under the category of the West I would include discourses that appropriate Indian (and non-Western) categories but remain within the languages and debates defined from within the West—without facing the need to have them impinge upon or pose a threat to their native discursive traditions.[38]

The many of the multitude and the strength of constituent power cannot but formulate singular projects of autonomous self-government that by definition create their own *sense* (both in meaning and direction) of universality, of revolution—beyond a will to hegemony. The danger is not the implementation of the Acuerdos de San Andrés nor that there should be laws recognizing Indian autonomies, but the reduction of the accords to a constitutional resolution of the conflict that would domesticate the constituent power of the multitude. For the crisis of constituent power to be productive, it must retain the will not to be resolved. This of course requires a multitude ready to assert its force, its practice of autonomization.

NOTES

1. I have shared this chapter with students in graduate seminars at Berkeley, the group on human development at the UN site in Bolivia, the workshop on 'Colonialismos en las Americas' at Stanford University, and the Decolonizing Religiosity, Gender, Sexuality, Globalization Reading Group at Berkeley. I have benefited greatly from these settings and would rather thank all participants than fail to mention some. Alicia Rios read an early version and provided me with invaluable commentaries. For his part, Javier Sanjinés also read the chapter and engaged me in very productive conversations on the similarities and differences between popular uprisings in Bolivia and Mexico.
2. For an account of the destruction of the mural and the attack on Taniperla and other autonomous municipios, see the monthly reports by the Centro de Derechos Humanos Fray Bartolomé de las Casas (CDHFBC), 'La disputa por la legitimidad. Aniversario de los ataques a los municipios libres' (1999), which includes a reproduction of the mural, and 'La legalidad de la injusticia' (1998). These two reports cover the events in 1997 and 1998, the years with the highest incidence of systematic violence by the Army, the so-called Seguridad Pública (Public Security, a euphemism for federal police), and Indian paramilitary groups formed by Indians associated with the Partido Revolucionario Institucional (PRI), which ruled Mexico from 1928 to 2000, when it was ousted by the current President Vicente Fox and his conservative Partido de Acción Nacional (PAN). It is important to note that the open military campaigns against autonomous municipios and sympathizers of the Zapatistas gave place to low-intensity warfare. Fox often speaks of Chiapas as a pacified territory, a fact that is contradicted by the weekly reports from the CDHFBC and other human rights

organizations, as well as by the denunciation of violence in letters from autonomous municipalities. Fox's removal of the army has simply consisted of relocating some of the military camps off the main roads.

3. This quotation slightly modifies Magón 1972: 533.

4. For the language of Convention No. 169 on Indigenous Peoples, see the website of the International Labour Organization: <www.ilo.org.htm>. You will also find relevant documents pertaining to human rights in Chiapas under 'documents' in the website of the CDHFBC: <www.laneta.apc.org/cdhbcasas> (see note 2 above).

5. This and other Zapatista communiqués have been posted on the website of the EZLN: <www.ezln.org>. Note, however, that this site is often damaged. For alternative locations for consulting the communiqués and other documents pertaining to the Zapatistas and the EZLN, see <www.fzln.org> and <www.ezlnaldf.org>.

6. In the conversations at 'Larráinzar VI', in September 1995, the government and the EZLN finally agreed on the formats for the discussion of particular issues in specific tables. Five tables were established and met in San Cristóbal and San Andrés Sacamch'en de los Pobres, as the Indian people prefer to call the town officially known as Larráinzar, until the EZLN pulled out in September 1996. The five groups began to address issues pertaining to: (1) community and autonomy: indigenous rights; (2) guarantees of justice for Indians; (3) participation and political representation of Indians; (4) situation, rights, and culture of indigenous women; (5) access to communication media. For a balance sheet of the first round of discussion, see the communiqué by the Comité Clandestino Revolucionario Indígena-Comandancia General (CCRI-CG) (1995).

7. For the text of Acuerdos de San Andrés and an analysis of the different versions, see Hernández Navarro and Vera Herrera (1998). Also see the publication by the Comisión Nacional de Intermediación (CONAI) (1999) (a commission headed by former bishop of San Cristóbal de las Casas, Samuel Ruiz García).

8. The speeches of the Zapatista given at different stops of Zapatour and those addressing Congress have been posted at <www.ezln.org>. For alternate sites see note 5.

9. Negri 1999a: 14. The passage in Italian reads: 'la potenza costitutiva non si conclude mai nel potere, né la moltitudine tende a divenire totalità ma ensieme di singularità, multiplicità aperta' (Negri 1992b: 23). I follow Boscagli's translation of *potere* as power and *potenza* as strength.

10. Although I conceive this indigenous discourse on the West from a theoretical perspective, one should consult the work on Ch'ol agrarian discourses of José Alejos García (1994 and 1999). In an essay on the relationship between missionaries and Indians in the colonial period, I examine how a *tlacuilo*, an Indian painter/writer trained in the pre-Columbian tradition, invented a pictorial vocabulary in the Codex Telleriano-Remensis to represent and reflect on the colonial order (Rabasa 1998). Telleriano-Remensis is the product of a missionary demanding an indigenous history of the power that dominated Indians; as it were, the *tlacuilo* responds to the request: 'Tell me the story of how I conquered you.' Thus, the request occasioned a situation in which the colonial observer ends up being observed. In representing colonial rule, the *tlacuilo* managed to inscribe differences in the Christianity of the Dominican and the Franciscan orders. This classification of the two orders and other semantic spaces pertaining to the culture of conquest entails a discourse that objectifies these European realities without using or getting entangled in the represented forms of thought: that is, the *tlacuilo* sees and conceptualizes the Europeans in terms of indigenous languages and systems of representation. As such, the *tlacuilo*'s history has nothing to do with an appropriation of European writing and modes of representation, which would inevitably be subject to the ambivalence of making the *proper*, but with the invention of a pictorial vocabulary to record the new realities from within indigenous systems of writing and thought. Also see Gruzinski (1999) for a reading of the translation of Ovidian motifs into an indigenous pictorial vocabulary in the murals in the church of Ixmiquilpan, Hidalgo, Mexico.

11. For a critique of the concept of autonomy as plagued with aporias and the need to think in terms of autonomization, see Hamacher 1997.
12. For a critique of the ways in which North America, i.e., scholars located in the US, reads Latin American cultural artifacts, most often under the seduction and distinction derived from metropolitan theory, see Neil Larson's brilliant essays in Larson 1995. On the construction of Latin America as an object of study in the United States, see de la Campa 1999. For a critique of Occidentalism and a definition of transculturation as a mode of subverting Western hegemony, see Coronil 1997 and Mignolo 2000.
13. Susan Buck-Morss (2000) has argued that we must trace the origin of the Hegelian dialectic of the master and the slave to articles Hegel read on the Haitian revolution. For Buck-Morss, this reading would enable us to evaluate the contributions made by the Haitian revolution to the development of European political culture and philosophy, and thereby to break from those narratives that attribute all the developments in 'universal' culture to European thinkers. The argument is interesting and to some extent convincing. Buck-Morss's denunciation of the silence kept by the philosophers of the Enlightenment regarding slavery would, paradoxically, lend credence to my argument that European thought does not constitute itself in opposition to a non-European other but with respect to its own phantoms. This does not mean that we don't find instance in which Europeans posit non-Western 'others' as inferior (colonial discourse abounds with such cases), but rather that because of their dismissal of other cultures, the non-European other hardly figured or mattered in the development of philosophical thought. Take as a symptom of this utter disregard for other cultures the fact that someone like Michel Foucault could write *The Order of Things* (1973) without mentioning imperialism once. Again, Foucault might be accused of disregarding questions pertaining to colonialism and European expansionism, but not of shaping the identity of poststructuralism in opposition to the 'rest of the world' or some other construct of the like. This observation would not deny the fact that Euro-American civilizations have been extracting and appropriating knowledge from Amerindian cultures starting with Columbus's first voyage. I have argued in *Inventing America* (1993) that the new subjectivity of modernity (the split between the subject and the object commonly associated with Descartes) emerges as a result of Columbus's need to codify unknown natural and cultural phenomena which entailed an epistemological mutation that has little or nothing to do with positing the binary, European civilization vs. Amerindian savagery. Clearly, this is part of the story but not the fundamental aspect of the epistemological mutation. In this chapter I argue that Indian struggles for autonomy and the right to govern themselves according to their normative systems do not partake of a desire to have their life forms recognized according to European models. I also have reservations on the benefit to be derived from thinking in terms of a single universality, which now according to Buck-Morss would manifest how non-Europeans have participated in shaping (Western) universality. My preference, as I will argue below, is for a concept of multiple horizons of universality.
14. See note 10.
15. Marcos's communiqués have been posted at <www.ezln.org>.
16. For documents pertaining to autonomy, forms of government in Indian communities, access to media, a plan for action, and addresses by Marcos and other members (Comandantes David, Tacho, and Zebedo) of the CCRI-CG, see Hernández Navarro and Vera Herrera (1998).
17. I owe this observation to Javier Sanjinés.
18. Virno and Hardt 1996a: 238. The collective signing of this text lays out a theory in which the alternative to violence signifies a more advanced state rather than an instance of lacking the conditions for revolution, as would be argued from a traditional Leninist position: 'Struggle and political mediation, struggle and negotiation with institutions—this perspective, in Italy as in Germany, is both possible and necessary, not because of the backwardness of the social conflict but, on the contrary,

because of the extreme maturity of its content' (ibid.). In an interview with Carlos Monsiváis, Marcos has made a similar point on political mediation and struggle from the opposite end of the geopolitical spectrum, from the Selva Lacandona, a paradoxical mixture of an area quite remote from the metropolitan centers of the Italian radicals and 'the extreme maturity of its content': 'No se plantea un asalto al Palacio de Invierno ni el derrocamiento del poder ni el fin del tirano, sino un vuelco, no sólo de los términos político-militares de la primera declaración. . . . Queremos que esta nación asuma legalmente que nos reconoce . . . que diga: "legalmente reconozco que estos que son diferentes tienen estos derecho y son parte mía"' ('We are not planning an assault on the Winter Palace nor the overthrow of power nor the end of the tyrant, but rather a turn, not only of the politico-military terms of our first declaration. . . . We want this nation to legally assume our recognition . . . to say: "I legally recognize that these people who are different have these rights and are part of me"') (Monsiváis 2001). Nevertheless, the question 'what is to be done?' remains, even if the answer differs radically from Lenin's call for a hegemonic Communist Party. The need for the vanguard party and the call to hegemonize all sectors of society is questioned by both the Zapatistas and Negri, but one wonders if this refusal does not partake of a paradox, of an aporia, inasmuch as one could speak of both calling for a hegemony of the diverse. The concept of the multitude in Negri entails a subjectivity that would overturn hegemonic programs that sought to reduce the multitude to a concept of the people held together by an encompassing ideology: 'The multitude is a multiplicity, a plane of singularities, an open set of relations, which is not homogeneous or identical with itself and bears an indistinct, inclusive relation to those outside of it. The people, in contrast, tends towards identity and homogeneity internally while posing its differences from and excluding what remains outside of it' (Hardt and Negri 2000: 103). Marcos could not be clearer in his interview with Monsiváis: 'Pienso que el fin de siglo y de milenio debiera reportar dentro de los movimientos progresistas o de izquierda . . . también un movimiento que plantea el fin de las luchas por la hegemonía' (I think that the end of the century and the millennium should also announce within progressive or leftist movements . . . a movement that proposes the end to all struggles for hegemony) (Monsiváis 2001).

19. As of June 4, 2002, President Vicente Fox has not freed the Zapatista political prisoners, a condition by the EZLN for resuming the dialogues with the government. On May 24, 2002, Enlace Civil released a communiqué by 'La Voz de Cerro Hueco', an association named after the penitentiary in which they were held in Chiapas, denouncing their liberation as an act of 'good will' from the Federal Government. They insist that they have served their sentences. They also insist that they were unjustly imprisoned in the first place and that Indians demanding their rights continue to be harassed and persecuted. They demand the liberation of political prisoners held in penitentiaries in the states of Tabasco and Queretaro. I am unsure of when Professor Valdez Ruvalcaba was freed and what his sentence was for the subversive, if not terrorist, act (in the paranoid imagination of the state) of painting a mural with the people.

20. On the COBAS and the social centers see Virno 1996c: 254. Marcos speaks of the COBAS in 'La historia de los espejos' June 9, 10, and 11, 1995 (EZLN 1995: 380).

21. See Avilés 2000. Also consult the website for the Associazione Ya Basta: <www.yabasta.it>.

22. I derive this information from the description included on the back of the reproduction prepared by the Centro de Derechos Humanos Bartolomé de las Casas (CDHFBC). See Unzueta 1999.

23. For an assessment of pre-Columbian and colonial elements in the normative systems, see Carsen 2000.

24. As an instance of this danger entailed in quick responses to Spivak, consider the following passage in *Death of a Discipline*: 'Where on this grid of reading literature as text and/or evidence of the permeability shall we put a graduate student's comment that the subaltern's remark is improbable, because only an academically educated person would know such a comprehensive list of African languages? The least sense

of the shifting demographies of Africa would correct this' (Spivak 2003: 17). Does she mean that because Africans are travelling outside their traditional spaces, they have become aware of other African languages? Would this knowledge and the possibility of its articulation be confined to those obvious manifestations of speech whose existence Spivak was not intent on denying? Or is she thinking of someone like the Nigerian doctor played by Chiwetel Ejifor in Stephen Frears's *Dirty Pretty Things* (2003), a highly educated person, but a subaltern because of his need to drive a cab and not practice medicine in London? I would also wonder about the kind of education that is imparted in the schools Spivak runs in Manbhum, India. Is the ideal that the students will learn to dwell in two or more worlds, or that they will learn the ways of the West to overcome their subalternity? Here is how she phrases the issue: 'Surely I am obliged to rewrite the aporia as a moral dilemma: How is it possible to reconcile what I touch in the field—other people—with what I teach for a living—literary criticism?' (Spivak 2003: 36). Spivak's brilliant call for a new comparative literature remains within the one-way street of translating the 'other' for metropolitan readers. Her call for learning the languages of the other (her term—I would rather use the more neutral 'non-European languages') could not be more timely, but I would push the proposal to include a reflection on the ways the other translates the projects and concepts 'we' bring into the field.

25. Ranajit Guha's oeuvre is very broad, so I will limit myself to citing his classic study *Elementary Aspects of Peasant Insurgency* (1999). My reading of 'the subaltern can't speak' as an absurdist moment is informed by White (1978). From the perspective of history as discipline, this absurd moment takes the form of the incapacity of the historian to sever her ties to the 'disenchanted world' of modernity that the discipline requires: the work of the historian and of subaltern studies would be inevitably linked to the production of subaltern pasts. I insist on the creation of subaltern pasts because these pasts do not exist in an unproblematic empirical state, rather they are the result of a particular form of thought, regardless of how much one may want to universalize disenchanted modernity as the only valid (in this case epistemologically valid) view of the world. Is the discipline of history inextricably vitiated by an epistemological elitism? Do we exercise discursive violence by the mere fact of wearing the cloak of the historian? Does this mean that we must destroy history as an institution? In this chapter I am arguing for the possibility of dwelling in a plurality of worlds and that there exists a porosity between different knowledges (as in *saberes, savoirs*) that give place to mutual critical exchanges in which neither one of these knowledges would hold an absolute epistemological privilege. Our historian of subaltern studies of India finds herself forced to generalize her own personal biography, that is, her academic elite formation (Oxford and Cambridge, and perhaps today Princeton and the rest) and her family past that would seem to lack any links (at least willingly retained or consciously assumed) to an enchanted world. It is inevitable that we reflect at this point on the parallelisms between this Indian elite and the perspective of the criollo elite that rose to power after the independence of Latin American countries in the nineteenth century. In both cases the liberation is established in terms that privilege a particular sector: the peasantry and the working class retain their status of exploited labor, but now under the tutelage of a native elite that presumes to care for its well-being (even if under a Marxist banner) and that thus displaces and domesticates the constituent power of the multitude under a definition of the people. The most visible exponent of this tendency is Chakrabarty (2000).

26. For a study of German colonization of Chiapas in the early twentieth century, see Alejos García 1999. Also see Rodolfo Stavehagen's study of transformations in the law that led to the pauperization and exclusion of Indians in Latin America after the wars of Independence, *Derechos indígenas y derechos humanos en América Latina* (1988) and the essay in which he elaborates the concept of internal colonialism, 'Clases, colonialismo y aculturación' (1963).

27. On the modern and the nonmodern in the insurrection of the EZLN, see Rabasa 1997.

28. Bierhorst 1985: 321. In addition to Bierhorst's introduction, one should consult Serge Gruzinski's reading of the *Cantares* in Gruzinski 1999. In passing, I should mention Miguel León Portilla's bitter dismissal of Bierhorst's reading and translation of the *Cantares*. I say bitter because León Portilla finds his whole work undermined by Bierhorst's assertion that the names of pre-Columbian figures, such as Netzahualcoyotl, are rhetorical and stylistic forms rather than identifications of authors. León Portilla has identified fifteen poets that he feels are authentic examples of pre-Columbian expression. Bierhorst prefers to read the colonial prints rather than identify a pure tradition. The other point that León Portilla attacks is Bierhorst's thesis of the *Cantares* as ghost songs. As can be surmised from my reading of ghostly demarcation, to borrow the title of a book on Derrida, I cannot but take Bierhorst's reading and run with it. The fear expressed by missionaries such as Sahagún and Durán regarding songs in which Indians invoked their ancient leaders—read warriors—suggests that memories of old haunted their projects; in the end, we have ghosts and songs even if there is no historical basis for Bierhorst's ghost songs, as León Portilla asserts. For León Portilla's project of recuperating an authentic pre-Columbian expressions and the identification of poets, as well as his dismissal of Bierhorst, see, for example, Léon Portilla 1992 and 1994 and his review of Bierhorst (Léon Portilla 1986).
29. Carpentier 1967. Compare the place of Mackandal in Carpentier's novelistic treatment of the Haitian revolution with the brief mention of him and the preference for the figure of Toussaint L'Overture in James 1962.
30. Since I first wrote this essay, Subcomandante Marcos (2003) wrote 'Chiapas: Treceava Estela' (Chiapas: The Thirteen Wake), an essay consisting of five parts, in which he develops the figure of the Caracol, the snail, as a new way of constructing a network of autonomous municipios and the creation of forms of self-government that create an alternative to capital. The concept and the poetics of the Caracoles merit a full essay and I will limit this note to mentioning that it materializes a political structure that furthers the process of autonomization. The formation of the Caracoles, also known as 'juntas de buen gobierno' (councils of good government) in Zapatista-controlled territories reinforces the need to conceive autonomy as a process and not as a status that would be granted by the state. In fact, Article 39 of the Mexican Constitution already grants, in the words of Marcos, the right to govern and to govern oneself. Under the Caracoles the Zapatistas no longer expect nor demand the recognition of the government, but rather they call for all Indians to act and exercise their rights as legitimate peoples and first inhabitants. For interpretative essays on the Caracoles, see the dossier in *Revista Memoria* 177 (November 2003) that includes essays by Araceli Burguete Cal y Mayor, Juan Carlos Martínez, Pablo González Casanova, and Alejandro Cerda García. In the October 2003 issue of *Revista Memoria* (176), John Holloway (2003) compares the Caracoles to holes in capitalism. For Holloway, in fact, every instance of a 'No' that negates the rule of capital and defines a new form of determining life constitutes a hole. The Zapatistas are one of the largest and most beautiful of the holes contemplated by Holloway. Holloway has systematized his ideas on new forms of revolution in Holloway 2002c.
31. Kant 1996b: 346. My reading of Kant tends to be reductive and fulfills the function of mapping out aporias in the project of autonomization. Kant has been read from within a Lacanian psychoanalytical tradition in ways that have complicated Kant's concept of the ethical subject and the possibility of ethical acts. Here I will limit myself to citing an assessment by Alenka Zupancic: 'As Kant knew very well, we are all pathological subjects, and this is what eventually led him to the conclusion that no ethical act is really possible in the world' (Zupancic 1998: 52). Even if Kant arrived at the conclusion that there are only pathological subjects and, by association, states (a Christian, indeed, a Lutheran position), his practical philosophy constitutes an effort to ground morals and politics on formal principles. I am interested in outlining the aporias inherent in the project of autonomy rather than establishing Kant's conclusion as to the impossibility of ethical acts; that is, I am assuming that the belief

in its possibility is earnest and fundamental to Kant's project. Žižek has reminded us that according to Kant we could very well 'follow the law on account of a patholog- ical reason (fear of punishment, narcissistic satisfaction, admiration of peers), while the same act can be a proper moral act if only I perform it out of the pure respect for duty, that is, duty is the sole motive for accomplishing it' (Žižek 2000: 672). Žižek goes on to present the case of an ethical act that transgresses the law, 'a transgression that, in contrast to a simple criminal violation, does not simply violate the legal norm, but redefines what is a legal norm. The moral law does not follow the good— it generates a new shape of what counts as good' (Žižek 2000: 672). Thereby, one can argue with Kant that if revolutionary acts fall outside the law, their motives and the resulting redefinition of the good could be pure ethical acts. Kant, of course, would add that if one is apprehended in the process of carrying out revolutionary illegal acts, one deserves the corresponding punishment for breaking the law. Žižek's example can be thought of in terms of the relation between constituent power and constitutional institutionalization. Kant will always adopt a position in which the constituent power of the multitude must in the last instance be subordinated to a constituted power, to a constitutional republicanism.

32. For a critique of Kant's racism and imperialism, see Spivak's reading of Kant in 'Philosophy' in Spivak 1999: 1–37.

33. The current (January 4, 2004) war against Iraq by the US-led alliance would seem- ingly contradict the peaceful vocation of empire, but the rationale for a preemptive strike as it has been articulated by the Bush administration defines the need for war in terms of preserving 'universal peace', to borrow this sixteenth-century Spanish legalistic term. The face of the United States today is that of a benevolent empire. Its disregard for the UN in going to war without its support and validation would seem to indicate that the United States is practicing nineteenth- and early twentieth- century forms of imperialism, but the opposition of major players (France and Germany, in the main) does not seemingly alter the fact that the United States sees itself—seeks to establish itself—as the military, if not the economic and political, leader of the empire. One could even argue that Empire is a historical invention of the United States. Consider that it has never, in spite of its annexations of territories that formerly belonged to Mexico, and the semicolonial status of Puerto Rico, exerted power by establishing colonial states abroad.

34. For arguments on multiculturalism that deploy an ecological perspective on the survival of indigenous cultures, see the essays collected in Taylor 1994. For a critique of the concept of multiculturalism in these essays, see Hamacher (1997).

35. Marcos has made this point in a recent interview with Carlos Monsiváis: 'No es lo mismo que llegue alguien y que diga: "Vengo a liberarlas a ustedes mujeres oprimidas" a que el propio movimiento que se genera provoque esto en las mujeres indígenas. No es lo mismo que una femenista de ciudad diga: "las mujeres indígenas tienen derechos" a que las mujeres indígenas digan, como lo acaban de hacer las de Xi' Nich y Las Abejas, en el monumento de Independencia: "Ademas, tenemos nuestras demandas como género. Nosotras queremos una paz con justicia y dignidad. No queremos la paz del pasado". Esto ya está ocurriendo y los resultados son irregulares pero creéme las soluciones no vendrán de fuera' (Monsiváis 2001). In passing I would like to mention the new film by Tunisian filmmaker Moufida Tlatli, *La Saison des hommes* (2000), where we find an insightful tension between the Tunisian law of 1956—which liberated Tunisian women to an extent beyond the most advanced Western democracies—and the law of tradition, which continues to bind women in their everyday interactions. The possibility of freedom resides within the community of women; an autistic child who learns to weave symbolizes hope for men. The men, who visit the women on the island once a year, for which event the women diligently prepare, lack any influence, and perhaps do not even exert any significant power over their lives.

36. Hegel's critique of Kantian formalism is taken as a point of departure in debates over the particularity of new social movements and their aim to transform the nature of

universality, and hence to redefine hegemony. In such a struggle for hegemony there is the risk that accomplished transformations of the universal will consolidate a constituted power that undermines the constitutive strength of the multitude, which aspires not to hegemony and the stasis achieved by the inclusion of diversity in new definitions of the universal, but to constitutional transformations that enable constituent power and further the materialization of autonomous self-governments. But then again we may understand *stásis* as internal struggle vis-à-vis *polémos* as war (see Derrida 1997: 90–93 and passim), a distinction which would amount to putting the emphasis not on instituting diversity (in subsuming constituent power in the real, as Hegel would put it) but in opening spaces for the revolutionary potential of the *many* that comprises the multitude. I am thinking here of the essays by Judith Butler, Ernesto Laclau and Slavoj Žižek in their *Contingency, Hegemony, Universality: Contemporary Dialogues on the Left* (2000). As I have pointed out in this essay, the demand for recognition of indigenous rights does not mean a recognition of the rights themselves as compatible with or as requiring a new definition of universality, but the recognition of the right to self-determination according to their normative systems. This demand does not aim at transforming the universal as defined in contemporary political discourses in the West, which inevitably partakes of a will to hegemonize; rather it aims at the right to multiple conceptions of universality. The point is not that all norms are equally valid (a flaccid relativism), but rather to propose a conception of normative systems in terms of their own horizons of universality and their own mechanisms for modifying them (a radical relativism).

37. For a development on the traffic of ideologies between Flores Magón and Zapata, see Bartra's introduction to *Regeneración* (1972).

38. This horizon of plural-world-dwelling would not involve a privileging of Western discourses, but a questioning of the pretense that all modern discourse must originate outside of and impinge upon the discourse of Indian peoples. And let us trivialize the shift I am proposing here by insisting that the anomaly, the radical gesture, would consist in imagining Derrida et al. reading and discoursing on Indian discourses: the history of Western expansionism abounds with examples of 'Derridas' intervening in and speaking for native forms of life.

8

'Now Everything Must Be Reinvented':
Negri and Revolution

Kenneth Surin

So now everything must be reinvented: the purpose of
work as well as the modalities of social life, rights as well
as freedoms.
> —Félix Guattari and Antonio Negri (1990: 9–10)

THE CURRENT PHASE OF CAPITALIST DEVELOPMENT:
REAL SUBSUMPTION

The lineaments of Antonio Negri's unswervingly rigorous reworking of the
Marxian paradigm (seen here as an ensemble of axioms or principles
governing the vast field that is capitalism, with the 'postcapitalist' and
revolutionary reconstitution of this field as this ensemble's inexpungable
regulative metaprinciple) are by now well-known.[1] Giving as much, if not
more, attention to the *Grundrisse* as to *Capital*, Negri has provided a conceptual matrix, at once faithful and deviant in regard to Marx, designed to
furnish an understanding of capital in its current manifestations, manifestations that are in turn related by Negri to an account of capital's historical
course, and grounded in a practico-epistemological context marked by
the demise of the Leninist communist parties and the evisceration of the
social democratic parties. Posing the question of the possibility of a radical
and decisive social transformation in conditions where there seem to be no
alternatives to an all-pervasive 'actually existing capitalism', Negri's reworking of the Marxian paradigm has several key components and distinctive
emphases: a periodization of the historical trajectory of capital; an insistence
on the inherently social character of capital; a stress on the crucial role
played by working classes in the composition and recomposition of capitalist relations of production; the adumbration of a new axiomatics of value
(labor is defined as inherently value-creating by Negri); a theory of the state
and the current imperial formation; a rereading of constitutional projects,
especially the American 'Jeffersonian' constitutional project; a depiction
of the *multitude* as the inherently antagonistic counterpower to capital; and
a theory, complementing the aforementioned conception of the multitude,
of the subject as a finally unconstrained self-created being. Any one of

these can serve as an entry point for the analysis of Negri's oeuvre.[2] This multifacetedness notwithstanding, the notion which perhaps provides all Negri's other principles and themes with their *modus operandi* is the one of 'real subsumption', that is, the process whereby labor power and capitalist command are extended throughout the social field, a development which in turn makes production inseparable from communication, with the outcome that (all) production is now, unavoidably, social production.[3] In 'real subsumption', moreover, the 'planner-state' of the Keynesian dispensation gives way to the 'crisis-state', in the sense that the state now has to resort to crisis (in the form of war and the preparation for war, 'low-intensity conflict', the orchestration of public alarm over 'rogue states', 'biological terrorists', 'superpredator youth', '(bogus) asylum seekers', 'Islamic fundamentalists', etc., etc.) in order to retain or reestablish its dominion.[4]

The mutation of capitalism represented by 'real subsumption' is also bound up with the emergence of a fully integrated world economy. This shift to a less regulated, more 'adaptive' and 'flexible' system of capitalist accumulation places constraints on internally regulated economic development, so that the various national regimes of accumulation come increasingly to be bypassed (but not completely superseded) by a phase of capitalist development in which transnational as well as local and regional structures of accumulation function alongside their nation-state counterparts.

In the phase in which state and society constitute a single, all-encompassing complex, the assemblages and apparatuses that comprise the capitalist system use a power of domination to secure the social co-operation that makes it possible for capital to operate: the social relations of production come therefore to constitute the core of the prevailing mode(s) of production.[5] As Negri says, in real subsumption all capital has become social capital, and this in turn generates a pervasive and 'systemic' antagonism between capital and the socialized worker (*operaio sociale*) who has replaced the mass worker of the now superseded Keynesian and Taylorist 'planner-state' dispensation.[6] The question of the constitution of the socialized worker is therefore paramount for any Marxism congruent with Negri's analysis of actually existing capitalism: the limits to capitalism in its current manifestation are set by the constitution of this worker.

Negri also maintains that the antagonisms constituting the heart of revolution pivot on the struggles of the socialized worker, and revolution is *par excellence* the autonomy made possible by the struggles of the socialized worker.[7] The ground of this revolutionary autonomy is one that encompasses the complexity of social movements in a way that is at once theoretical and practical, and its epistemic core is the conviction that revolutionary movements are motivated by a concern for the quality of life and by the constitutive desire to restructure the goals of production, especially self-production. The name for the ground of this enabling mobilization is 'constituent power', and Negri, like the Guattari of *Chaosmosis*, views revolutionary struggle very much as an exercise in autopoiesis, that is, as the self-creation of liberated subjects. The *locus classicus* for Negri's conception of constituent power as a form of autopoiesis is the section titled 'Constituent Power in Revolutionary Materialism' in the chapter 'Communist Desire and the Dialectic Restored' in *Insurgencies*, along with the section on militancy in Hardt and Negri's *Empire*, so this section therefore merits a close analysis.[8]

Negri's account of (capitalist) constituent power follows closely the narrative fashioned by Marx in *Capital* of this power's underlying logic and historical dynamic. Marx, says Negri, recognized that capitalism reconfigures constituent power by transforming its ontological properties, functions, temporal specifications, and modes of efficacy, and proceeded from here to characterize its essential logic in terms of the dialectic of freedom and necessity. The modification of constituent power accomplished by capital was also taken by Marx to involve the reconstitution of social subjects and market participants, who by virtue of this become agents and bearers of its 'substance', as they come to be constrained by capital and its appurtenances, even as they exercise command on capital's behalf. Negri points out that Marx's elaboration of the nature and scope of constituent power involved the positing of two 'vectors', viz. violence and cooperation, and that the author of *Capital* staged this power's historical movement as a progression from (primitive) accumulation to law.

Capitalism is inaugurated in the violence of a primitive accumulation ('sovereign violence'), and from this primal violence law and the state eventually ensue as the basis of cooperation, so that sovereign violence gives way in time to the violence of a state-maintained discipline. With the institution of law and the state, capitalism, having already been launched by the event of primary accumulation, can further evolve and expand. Law and the state allow the mode of production to be organized, thoroughly and comprehensively, according to the principles of capitalist accumulation, and law and right in turn function at the behest of these principles, in a mutually reinforcing symbiosis.

Once capitalism is institutionalized through the instrumentality of the law and the state, constituent power is no longer manifested as an overt 'sovereign' violence typical of the primitive accumulation that launched it, and comes instead to be expressed through the 'silent coercion of economic relations' (Negri 1999a: 254). In already existing capitalism, therefore, constituent power is modulated into an incipient violence, basically structural in character, that seeps into every social relationship. In this world of discipline, a world which 'produces the producers', says Negri,

> [t]he capital relation constitutes not only the law but also a new world. It changes humans, increases their productivity, and socializes them. It imposes itself as structure of their existence. This transformation of violence into a structure, of the juridical superstructure into a historical and institutional system, becomes more intense the more the capitalist mode of production develops. In this transformation violence does not disappear but is organized, becoming more and more a violence that orders and transforms reality. (Negri 1999a: 257)

Although capitalist accumulation has by this time moved from the primal violence that founded it to the above-mentioned successor phase defined by law and right, traces of originary violence remain within the system, except that these traces now manifest themselves as 'legitimate', 'constitutionally sanctioned' violence. At this point, another quite different process, which Negri identifies as Marx's second 'vector', opens up: capital's constituent power is not only antagonistic, predicated on violence, but is also 'systemically' conducive to cooperation. Cooperation is a directly productive and constitutive force, and, says Negri,

> [t]he productive powers of cooperation grow with its complexity. Association and contact become more and more productive the more complex the conditions of production become, with respect to the volume of the means of production, the number of cooperating subjects, and the general degree of social evolution. (Negri 1999a: 259–60)

The division of labor intensifies and expands as capitalism develops, bringing about a commensurate intensification and expansion of what Negri calls 'the force of associative productive labor', until there comes a point when this force 'begins to become indistinguishable from social activity itself' (Negri 1999a: 260). But, and this is Negri still following Marx closely, capital bifurcates these powers of cooperation into an inexorable dialectic between capitalist command and the 'solidaristic' energies that are the basis of the workers' cooperation. An inherent antagonism is therefore lodged at the core of capital's organization of the relations of production: capitalist command has willy-nilly to expropriate the capacities of the workers to generate the surplus value that is the basis of profit, while the workers are required to use these self-same capacities to form themselves into the collective enterprise necessary for the systematic organization of the productive process that will ensue in the maximization of surplus value. Capital has perforce to create the collective worker, but in constituting the collective worker it provides the very thing, the structure of cooperation, that enables workers to resist the capitalist expropriation of their productive capacities. In realizing surplus value, capital has thus unavoidably to turn the worker into an adversarial political subject, and constituent power thereby emerges as the social power of living labor, as the constitution of the liberation of the worker even in the midst of capital's expropriation of the capacities of this worker.

CONSTITUENT POWER AND LIVING LABOR

The emergence of *constituent* power from the viscera of capitalist organization and rationality to provide the structural underpinning for movements whose *raison d'être* is the overcoming of the *constituted* power that subjugates the collective worker means that Marx was correct to discern that the critique of political economy is inextricably bound up with the phenomenology of class struggle. For Negri this crucial nexus formed between constituent power and the liberation of the worker indicates that

> [t]he concept of constituent power is always the concept of a crisis, but in the opening of crisis and in the crisis of the realities that it involves—the becoming-objective of power, exploitation, and expropriation—stands also the creative element of liberation. Living labor is this same concept of crisis and constitution. Living labor is constituent power that opposes constituted power and thus constantly opens new possibilities of freedom. Constituent power determines, according to the rhythm of living labor, a space: the space of social cooperation pushed to the point of a communist redefinition of all activities and all interdependencies. It also determines a time: the open time of the destruction of exploitation and the development of liberation.[9]

Negri insists that the antagonism between the constituent power of living social labor and the constituted power of capitalist accumulation is not 'homologous', so that the struggles of the collective worker are not to be seen as attempts merely to unseat the capitalist by undertaking a kind of dialectical negation of capital's constituted power (i.e., the power of expropriation and objectification). 'The dialectic is over', declares Negri, and the liberation of living social labor, which is nothing but intense and radical 'activity', defines capital ontologically as 'residue' and not as the strict antithesis that constitutes dialectical negation (Negri 1999a: 265). The liberation of living labor takes the form of an ensemble of practices having as their object the connecting of 'freedom to desire, desire to sociality, and sociality to equality', ensuing in 'a conscious, innovative, free, and egalitarian social activity', and the theory of constituent power by virtue of this takes the form of 'the theory of a practice of liberation, desire, socialization, and equality' (1999a: 265–6). It is a specific, historically defined manifestation of constituent power that defines the capitalist, and a merely dialectical negation of the capitalist would not abolish the conceptually and practically antecedent 'space' from which this power of expropriation receives the structurally pre-given impetus that originates it.[10] The apparatus named 'capital' has a prior model of realization whose field, at once social and political, has to be invested with (a productive) desire *before* a capitalist regime of accumulation can come to possess its enabling conditions. The constituent power of the collective worker, by contrast, is an irreducible countervailing strength (*potenza*) that detaches the project of liberation from the hold of this original disempowerment designed to incapacitate living labor (a disempowerment that will allow capitalism to come into being): for Negri as for Deleuze and Guattari, capitalism arises only because the power that would prevent it from emerging, the power of what amounts to an 'ur-liberation' antecedent to liberation, has already been neutralized by the prior violent installation of the forms of cooperation that will in turn allow capital to emerge as a fully-fledged economic assemblage.

Before capital can generate anything, therefore, social labor has to be constituted and its dispositions regulated to form a world of disciplined social production and reproduction that can be submitted to the logic of capital. This enabling condition of capital, the subsumption of social labor and the socius, is not something that occurred once and for all as the 'founding event' of capitalist accumulation. On the contrary, subsumption has a continued historical dynamism. The process of subsumption has been a complex and protracted one, and, according to Negri, it only reached its culmination in the 'postindustrial' era, when yet another mutation of the subjectivity of living labor took place as the phase of 'real subsumption' was reached.[11] With the real subsumption of society, the range of the antagonistic forces that define capitalist production expands and covers society in its totality, thereby allowing these antagonisms a potentially unlimited duration and flexibility. With the generalization of capitalist command brought about by real subsumption, antagonisms and polarizations become equally omnipresent, and the areas of anticapitalist struggle can become variable and diffused.[12]

The collective worker is thus the architect of a new (political) ontology of being, and the Marxian theory of constituent power is for Negri the theory of this creative architecture of emancipated labor that Marx presented, at least in part, in the form of a phenomenology of capitalist production and accumulation.[13] The primary domain of this emancipation is the political, and the occupation of this domain by living labor, involving as it does the exercise of constituent power, is the expression of the desire of the multitude 'to become the absolute subject of the processes of strength' (Negri 1999a: 304).

Negri believes that constituent power has a metaphysico-historical trajectory which extends from Machiavelli and Spinoza to Marx, and that this materialist metaphysics of constituent power is to be differentiated from an idealist political ontology that extends from Hobbes to Hegel, since the latter could only produce a transcendental concept of sovereignty that, by being inextricably allied to *constituted* power, is unable to provide a theory of constituent power adequately harnessed to the critique of power and the critique of labor (this of course being Marx's great achievement) (Negri 1999a: 29–31). For Marx, unlike the adherents of this rival idealist tradition, constituent power finds its instrument in living labor, so that 'in the immediacy, the creative spontaneity of living labor, constituent power finds its own capacity for innovation; in the cooperative immediacy of living labor, constituent power finds its creative massification' (Negri 1999a: 33). This Marxian sociopolitical ontology also makes democracy the wholly immanent realm in which 'strength' and the multitude find the point of a creative and immensely productive convergence.[14] In this convergence, collective action and human cooperation form a new collective subject finally capable of displacing the constraints on social being imposed by capital and its constitutionalist appurtenances. It is worth quoting Negri at length on this new collective subject of living labor:

> Living labor constitutes the world, by creatively modeling, *ex novo*, the materials that it touches. It entrusts and consolidates in nature and beyond this in a second, third, and eventually umpteenth nature the constitutive power of living labor. In this process living labor transforms itself first of all. Its projection on the world is ontological, its prostheses are ontological, and its constructions are constructions of a new being. The first result of this indefinite process is the construction of the subject. The subject is a continual oscillation of strength, a continual reconfiguration of the actual possibility of strength becoming a world. The subject is the point on which the constitution of strength establishes itself. But the subject continues to take shape through the world that it itself has constructed by shaping and reshaping itself. Living labor becomes constituent power within this process. And it is within this process that the multitude is brought back to strength and discovers itself as subject. ... It is the constituent process, the

dimensions determined by the will, and the struggle and the decision on the struggle that decide the senses of being.

Far from becoming dispersive, this process is a continual determination, traversed by the concreteness of the social, by its organization, and by the continual actualization of the relation between multitude and strength. (1999a: 326–7)

Marx's achievement, according to Negri, is thus to have forged a theory of constituent power in the form of an ontology in which the social, the political, and (metaphysically denoted) being are given a new definition by living labor and by the subjectivities which emerge when the multitude finds its relation to strength.

GOING BEYOND MARX IN THE NAME OF MARX: THE POLITICAL SUBJECT IN THE TIME AFTER MODERNITY

But the historical, social, and political course taken by this new collective subject has now moved beyond the point identified by Marx in his own time (so Negri maintains).[15] Marx took the limits of this new collective subject to be instituted by 'the world of life' (Negri 1999a: 328). But the present-day embodiment of this political subject can only regard such a world as confined and confining, and prefers instead to construct and occupy virtual worlds, limited in this endeavor only by the circumscriptions, themselves virtual, of a rationality that has now mutated beyond the forms it possessed in the heyday of modernity, which was of course Marx's own time. The rationality of modernity, 'a linear logic that corrals the multitude of subjects in a unity and controls its difference through the dialectic' and which resorts to the politics of constitutionalism to impede the subject's appropriation of constituent power (1999a: 328), has been superseded by a new rationality which gives the multitude the ontological possibility of finding the strength and creativity it had been previously denied by the constitutive processes of capitalist production.

The multitude can now confer on its political project the strength bestowed by an unprecedented ontological constitution, made possible by the processes of real subsumption, whose outcome is a radically new political paradigm, 'constituent power in action' (1999a: 333), premised on a fundamental reconnection of the political with the social.[16] The changes associated with this momentous transformation include the construction of a very different rationality that will inspire the creation of new collective subjects and give history a course marked by the cessation of capitalist exploitation. This innovative rationality is taken by Negri to possess the following features: it embodies creativity against the limit imposed on it by the rationality of capitalist domination it has just superseded; it annuls the constitutional apparatus and the doctrine of right that is the basis of the 'former' rationality in favor of procedures that are generated by the multitude; it pits equality against privilege; it promotes diversity at the expense of uniformity; and it substitutes cooperation for capitalist command (1999a: 329–32).

This new rationality that comes after modernity will animate the equally novel political project associated with the multitude's possession of a dynamism based on strength (as opposed to that of a merely despotic constituted power), and it will do so by virtue of being harnessed inextricably to the rhythms of constituent power: 'living labor inheres in capital; it is closed in the very institutions where it is born, but continually it manages to destroy them' (Hardt and Negri 1994: 5). Negri therefore retains the absolutely crucial connection between constituent power and revolution that has to lie at the heart of any putatively Marxist political 'project', and consequently defines revolution as the *normality* of constituent power's 'always reopened' desire for 'the continuous, relentless, and ontologically effective transformation of time' (Negri 1999a: 334). This transformation is opposed to the 'being for death' that typifies the ramshackle but inhuman empire which must deny the ontological necessity of constituent power, and which works relentlessly to keep at bay that liberation of the multitude which is constituent power's categorical 'answer' to empire's pervasive affinity for death.[17]

THE IMPOSSIBLE POSSIBILITY OF REVOLUTION

For Marxism it is always a truism or axiom that liberation's historical and ontological trajectory is inextricably bound up with the specific character of the prevailing forces and relations of capitalist production. The critique of political economy, Marxism's kernel, is above all the critique of the thought whose function is to validate, by a pervasive 'misnaming', the regimes of exploitation that constitute the heart of capitalist production. The task of the critique of political economy is therefore to 'name' these regimes of exploitation through a critique of the operations of ideology (the primary undertaking of *The German Ideology*) and by describing the constitution and function of the instruments of capitalist exploitation (undertaken by Marx primarily in the *Grundrisse* and *Capital*).[18] For Marx and Negri the processes which subtend capitalist exploitation have as their essential basis the labor of the worker that is used by the capitalist to realize surplus value. A transformed society can emerge only when the social organization of this labor is no longer undertaken under the auspices of capitalist production and exchange and human subjectivity is freed accordingly. For Marxism this freedom or lib-eration can only be the outcome of exploitation's abolition, and not just its critique.[19] But how is exploitation to be eradicated, especially in a phase of capitalist development in which, 'after 1989', a ubiquitous and seemingly insuperable capitalism appears to have no 'exteriority' from which a feasible project of liberation can be mounted? How is revolution possible in a situa-tion that ostensibly deprives it of any enabling conditions?[20]

Negri's first move in dealing with these questions adverts to the current configuration of capitalism's relations of production, a configuration whose distinctive shape (a certain kind of 'spectrality'—here Negri is in qualified agreement with Derrida) is provided by the efforts of a new kind of productive subject engaged in immaterial and flexible labor:

> Today exploitation, or, rather, capitalist relations of production, concern a laboring subject amassed in intellectuality and cooperative force. A new paradigm: most definitely exploited, yet new, a different power, a new consistency of laboring energy, an accumulation of cooperative energy. This is a new, post-deconstructive, ontology.[21]

For Negri, this new laboring subject marks a rupture whose distinctive 'moment' is a twofold renovation, of theory and of political organization alike, which constitutes at the very least a 'new specter of liberation':

> (. . . It's natural that theory be renovated, since it renovates itself according to a mutation of the real, the old theory being one of its fun-damental agents, despite everything. . . . The person who fights or has fought for communism is certainly not nostalgic for the old organiza-tions, neither the Stalinist one, nor the folkloric one that survives on its fringes. The new communist experiment is born through the rupture with memory. And it's there that, in the present, amongst all and no specters, the only real continuity appears: that of the struggle, of the constituent spirit, of the ontological violence of transformation. The awaited event makes the past explode. 'A real coming-to-be'. In this same spirit, why should Walter Benjamin be considered a 'proto-Marxist'?)
>
> [. . .] Capitalism and communism continue to fight on a terrain made up of new spectral figures, real nonetheless, and of new movements. Attached to the new social force of mass intellectuality, a radical form of Marxism can constructively respond to renewed forms of capital's regu-lation and to the exploitation of immaterial labor. (Negri 1999b: 14–15)

The way forward, as envisioned by Negri, is experimental, involving new social movements and their attendant subjectivities and singularities (who form the insurgent anticapitalist multitude of *Empire*); and its metaphysical hinge is a resolutely materialist version of the Pascalian wager, a wager to be made in a context (in this case a capitalism with no exteriority from which the quest for liberation can ostensibly be inaugurated) whose defining features palpably echo Walter Benjamin's laicized messianism, with its decisive premise of a categorical rupture with the continuum of history.[22] The terms of this materialist wager are straightforward (and structurally homologous with the old anticapitalist refrain 'either socialism/communism or barbarism'): either the anticapitalist multitude prevails or capital does. If the first alternative is chosen, then the multitude can begin to embark on the project of constituting itself as a political subject by 'directing technologies and production toward its own joy and its own increase of power' (Hardt and Negri 2000: 396). In this way a 'symbolic' and 'imaginative' material 'mythology of reason' is created, one whose *raison d'être* is the separation of the multitude from the depredations of capital, thereby allowing 'the activity of the multitude to express itself as activity and consciousness' (Hardt and Negri 2000: 396).

The ground of this wager is not some *mysterium* or merely 'utopian' hope or fantasy ('children's fables'), however, since for Negri it is an axiom of any remotely adequate political rationality, one having as its object the proper description of capitalist production and accumulation in their diverse and pervasively irrational manifestations, that the dynamics of capitalist production and accumulation is a 'systemic' response to the prior and constituting activity of the working class. As we have seen, it is the working class that originates the nexus of social cooperation necessary for the extraction of surplus value. Capitalism is thus a response to the activity of the proletariat in the latter's actualization of social cooperation, it becomes what it is in the course of managing and containing the activity of the working class as the latter establishes the terms and bases of this originating cooperation. This activity has to be arrested and reconstituted by capital; without this arresting reconstitution, an otherwise unfettered proletarian social cooperation will proceed to organize itself as the instrument of an inexorable liberation. The upshot is that capital becomes a function of the multitude's dynamism and not vice versa.[23] The capitalist boss has to work to block the development and expression of the multitude's capacities of transformation in order to begin to exploit labor power, a task which confers on the boss's subjectivity the character of a reactive, irrational, and repetitious nonbeing: 'Empire can only isolate, divide, and segregate' (Hardt and Negri 2000: 399). In *Empire* the matter is elaborated thus:

The constitution of Empire is not the cause but the consequence of the rise of [the multitude's] new powers. It should be no surprise, then, that

Empire, despite its efforts, finds it impossible to construct a system of right adequate to the new reality of the globalization of social and economic relations. This impossibility . . . is not due to the wide extension of the field of regulation; nor is it simply the result of the difficult passage from the old system of international public law to the new imperial system. This impossibility is explained instead by the revolutionary nature of the multitude, whose struggles have produced Empire as an inversion of its own image and who now represents on this new scene an uncontainable force and an excess of value with respect to every form of right and law. (Hardt and Negri 2000: 394)

The upshot is that capital never really succeeds in depriving the proletariat/multitude of its constituent power, the power that is the sine qua non of the multitude's capacity to further its project of liberation. The multitude is always capable of a new cycle of struggle. But no model exists for the furtherance of this new phase of resistance to the forces of capitalism; 'only the multitude through its practical experimentation will offer the models and determine when and how the possible becomes real' (Hardt and Negri 2000: 411). The determining figure in this 'practical experimentation' is the militant or 'guerilla of peace', the postmodern Francis of Assisi, whose struggles, waged in the name of constituent/biopolitical power, are carried out, often in largely clandestine ways, in 'a sinuous and continuous fashion . . . across the enemy territory, preventing him from attaining the maximum concentration of the destructive force that defines his project and, in a continuous way, from attaining his force of persuasion and concentration' (Guattari and Negri 1990: 99).

MILITANCY

Negri has argued that the form of value serves as a 'material transcendental' for the constitution of the multitude, and that it can move in one or the other of two directions, that is, it can yield to the requirements of the mode of production and harmonize itself with the course of capitalist development or it can align itself with 'revolutionary practice' (Negri 1996c: 150). Militancy clearly enjoins the latter. But no matter what form value takes, its irreducible core is always a particular embodiment of labor power:

> . . . the immeasurability of the figures of value does not deny the fact that labor is the basis of any constitution of society. In fact, it is not possible to imagine (let alone describe) production, wealth, and civilization if they cannot be traced back to an accumulation of labor. That this

accumulation has no measure, nor (perhaps) rationality does not diminish the fact that its content, its foundation, its functioning is labor. The intellectual and scientific forces which have gradually become central in production are nonetheless powers of labor. The growing immateriality does not eliminate the creative function of labor, but rather exalts it in its abstraction and its productivity. The substance of value is more important than the forms which this may assume, and it is posed beyond the very division (which is now being eclipsed) between manual labor and intellectual labor. The abstract is more true than the concrete. On the other hand, only the creativity of labor (living labor in the power of its expression) is commensurate with the dimension of value. (Negri 1996c: 152)

We have seen that Negri, like Marx, believes that the organization of labor under capitalism always takes the form of a political constitution, which imposes a logic of inequality and hierarchy on the organization of labor to make it functionally available for the extraction of surplus value. Before there can be exploitation there has to be domination. But, again as we have seen, for Negri and the other thinkers of the *operaismo* movement, the field in which this domination is exercised is always one of a contestation of forces and wills, and this because the antagonistic constituent power of the proletariat has to be neutralized by capital as a necessary prolepsis to the capitalist expropriation of labor capacity. Capital only advances in response to such antagonisms.[24] It follows, therefore, that the field or terrain in which capitalist command and its proletarian antagonists engage each other is the crucial matrix for any understanding (and that includes a resolutely proletarian and indeed militant understanding) of the conditions in which anticapitalist subjects mobilize themselves for a liberation whose ultimate realization coincides with the movement to a postcapitalist society.

The field in which capitalist command is resisted and undone is characterized in *Empire* as the current postmodern or post-Fordist capitalist dispensation, in which the informatization of production is being taken to new and unprecedented levels. Following Manuel Castells and Yuko Aoyama, the authors of *Empire* distinguish between two models or paradigms of post-Fordist informatization: a *service economy model*, most typically to be found in the United States, the United Kingdom, and Canada, and the *info-industrial model*, as exemplified by the economies of Japan and Germany.[25] Service-oriented economies are marked by a significantly declining industrial sector and a correspondingly enhanced service sector, with particularly strong growth taking place in the financial domain in areas such as banking, insurance, and securitization (all of which have been revolutionized in the last couple of decades or so by the new information technologies). Info-industrial economies have experienced a relatively smaller decline in industrial manufacturing jobs than their counterpart service-oriented economies, and while they too have come to possess burgeoning service sectors that are increasingly informatized, these sectors are invariably made to subserve the requirements of manufacturing industry, usually by enabling manufacturing units to arrest productivity declines by resorting to computerized production methods. In both models informatization is promoted as a response to the crisis of the Fordist system of accumulation, a crisis brought about by the contradiction between Fordism's need to generate an abstract and relatively deskilled mass labor force while creating a high level of social cooperation, complemented at the same time by high wage levels and generally adequate welfare provision. This contradiction ensued in a more and more generalized 'refusal of work' in the advanced industrial countries in the 1960s and 1970s, manifested in industry-wide strikes and go-slows that led ultimately to the breakdown of the Fordist–Keynesian 'concordat' between labor and capital. Informatization and other technological advances, with their accompanying 'immaterialization' of labor, were a pivotal component in capital's response to the increased unruliness of mass labor that betokened Fordism's collapse.[26] This account of the causes underlying the demise of capitalism's so-called 'Golden Age' (i.e., the prolonged expansion associated with high employment, growing wages and welfare expenditures, generally high consumption, and benign business cycles that lasted in the advanced industrial countries from 1945 to around 1973–74) is generally unproblematic and is fairly widely accepted today.[27] However, the account given in *Empire* of what has transpired after the demise of Fordism, derived as it is from the two-model theory of Castells and Aoyama, is somewhat problematic. This theory, with its stress on the causal centrality of informatization, certainly lends weight to the thesis of the 'immaterialization of labor' that is central to Negri's accounts of the socialized worker and real subsumption.[28] But while the description of informatization does likewise express and capture one of the key developments that has defined capitalist accumulation since the end of the Golden Age in the 1970s, it is not evident that the architecture of this system of accumulation, especially in its latter-day manifestations, is adequately expressed by a two-model theory that, à la Castells and Aoyama, bifurcates the G7 and OECD countries into 'info-industrial' and 'info-service' economies (and this of course is not even to take the rest of the capitalist world system into consideration).

CURRENT DISPOSITION OF THE WORLD SYSTEM

There is no gainsaying that the capitalist economies underwent a fundamental reorientation after the quietus of the Keynesian planner-state in
the 1970s, as their apparatuses and governing axioms were reshaped by
the pressures of international competitiveness, supply-side adaptation,
and production-method and labor-market flexibility. This new environment compelled the economies of capitalist countries to adapt themselves
to a greatly expanded transnational economic and political domain, even
as they had to find new opportunities for accumulation in response to the
progressively insurmountable crisis of Fordism–Keynesianism. In his recent
writings Negri has acknowledged that the emergence and rapid growth of
financial markets is one of the determining features of the current regime
of accumulation. But Negri, in common with many theorists of capitalist
development, has tended to de-emphasize the role of finance-led regimes
of accumulation in contemporary capitalist expansion.[29]

The increased primacy enjoyed by financial capital over industrial capital
in the countries of the North/West in the last two decades or so is coterminous with the emergence of an equity-based growth regime in most
of the G7 and OECD countries (and the Unites States in particular). This
equity-based regime, which is perhaps still in the process of becoming
fully fledged, has made possible the reassertion of an American economic
hegemony (which admittedly could turn out to be short-lived),[30] and this
finance-led regime's growing significance will greatly affect the current
and (in all likelihood) the succeeding phases of capitalist development. It
is crucially important therefore to analyze this American-dominated equity-
based growth regime: indeed, given that this regime is preeminent among
current growth regimes, and bearing in mind also that financial markets
are the most globally integrated of all the markets, the overall plausibility
of Negri's depiction of the current phase of capitalist accumulation will
hinge on the outcome of this analysis of the mobilities of capital. Marx has
shown that the circulation of capital in the various phases it undergoes in
the expansion of value conforms to the formula

$$M—C—(LP + MP)\dots P\dots C'—M', \text{etc.}$$

where M stands for a given amount of money capital, C for a given quantity
of commodities, LP for commodity labor power, MP for the power of capital, P for a phase of production, C' for an added quantity of commodities,
and M' for an added quantity of money capital. In other words, money
yields commodities for the capitalist when a certain concentration of

commodity labor power and the power of capital ensues in a phase of production that leads to the creation of more commodities, and this in turn leads to an increase in the money capital possessed by the capitalist.[31] The passage from one phase of expansion to another therefore involves the juxtaposition of two or more forms of capital and labor power at the point of transition. The outcome, says David Harvey, is that

> Each transition constitutes . . . a mutually restraining intersection of different capacities for spatial movement. The circulation process as a whole comprises several such mutually restraining intersections, each with its own peculiar problems. As a general rule, it is far easier, for example, to go from M—C than from C—M not only because money is social power incarnate but also because it is easier to move around geographically. The mutual restraints . . . necessarily limit the over-all geographical mobility of both capital and labour power. (Harvey 1999: 405–6)

Harvey notes that financial and credit instruments provide more opportunities for dispersal in this process of the expansion of capital, thereby making possible a circumvention or relaxation of the temporal constraints that otherwise have an inhibiting effect on the circulation of capital in general, and multinational capital in particular. Some constraints do of course remain, even in a decade when international capital flows have grown exponentially: governments are invariably motivated by national self-interest when devising financial and monetary policy, and in the continued absence of a workable system of supranational regulation for credit and foreign exchange transactions, such as the Bretton Woods accord, the resultant governmental policies have a potentially stifling effect on the spatial mobility of capital. The general principle, noted by Marx in *Capital* and the *Grundrisse*, that money capital possesses an essential malleability and fluidity does however remain. Especially significant for Marx in this connection is the role of the form of capital he calls 'fictitious capital', that is, capital that is circulated without any specific relation to commodities or a productive enterprise, but which can 'valorize' itself by virtue of the fact that it can be exchanged for the surplus value manifested in commodities, that is, it can be inserted into just about any one of the numerous intersections to be found in the circuit *money→commodities→more money* (M—C—M′) that characterizes the expansion of capital.[32] With this insertion into capital's circuit of expansion, 'fictitious capital' becomes (new) money capital and is 'valorized' in the process, because this (new) money capital can now be channeled into production-based sectors, perhaps the most notable example of this being the way in which the US stock market bubble of 1998 and

1999 pulled the capitalist world out of the recession that had been threatened by the East Asian financial crisis of 1997. I shall return to the question of this 'valorization' later, since it has important implications for the formation of the constituent power of the proletariat/multitude (i.e., Negri's question par excellence).

It is difficult to do full justice here to the many facets of the epochal transformations that have taken place in extraterritorial financial markets and institutions since the early 1970s. With the abolition of restrictions on international capital movements initiated in 1973, the volume of transactions in global foreign exchange markets rose from an average of $15 billion per day in that year to $80 billion per day in 1980, to $880 billion in 1992, and to $1,260 billion in 1995. Less than 2 per cent of this sum is currently devoted to trade in goods and services (compared to 15 per cent in 1973). The proportion for foreign direct investment (FDI) is just as small, though FDI flows to developing and emerging market countries have risen significantly in the 1990s. The rest, amounting to more than a trillion dollars a day (exceeding the aggregate gold and foreign exchange holdings of all the world's central banks), is devoted to transactions, mostly short-term, by private individuals in currency and other financial markets.[33] Rates of US market capitalization have grown exponentially. In 1995 the value of US stocks reached 100 per cent of GDP, a level attained only once previously (in 1929), and in early 2000 capitalization passed 180 per cent of GDP, dropping to a level of 150 per cent by the end of the year, but still triple the 1990 level (approximately 55 per cent of GDP).[34] Several less developed countries (LDCs) have also seen a very rapid growth in stock market capitalization. Ajit Singh has made an instructive comparison between the relative times it took the United States and the LDCs to reach roughly the same capitalization ratios, and concludes that

> [t]he speed of development of Third World stock markets in the recent period may be judged from the fact that it took eighty-five years (1810–1895) for the US capitalization ratio (market capitalization as a proportion of GDP) to rise from 7 percent to 71 percent. In contrast, the corresponding Taiwanese ratio jumped from 11 percent to 74 percent in just 10 years between 1981 and 1991. Similarly, between 1983 and 1993 the Chilean ratio rose from 13.2 percent to 78 percent; the Korean from 5.4 percent to 36.2 percent and the Thai from 3.8 percent to 55.8.[35]

Liberalization and the emergence of completely new international markets for securities, futures, options, swaps, international mutual funds, international bonds (these markets were opened to developing countries in the 1990s), and American and global depository receipts have given

American companies access to the stock markets of industrialized and industrializing countries.[36] The combined assets of pension funds in the United Kingdom stand at 93 per cent of GDP, 89 per cent in the Netherlands, 87 per cent in Switzerland, and 57 per cent in the USA (in contrast to Germany, France, and Italy, where pension fund holdings only amount to around 5 per cent of GDP).[37] According to the *Guardian Weekly* (1997), the United States now has more than 2,800 mutual funds controlling over $4 trillion, with $220 billion being placed in them in 1996 alone (nearly double the 1995 total of $242 billion). At the time of the October 1987 crash there were only 812 US mutual funds managing a total of $242 billion. The World Bank estimates that the combined portfolios of US pension funds, mutual funds and insurance companies amounted to $8 trillion in 1994. In 1994 two American pension funds alone—the Teachers' Insurance and Annuity Association-College Retirement Equities Fund (TIAA-CREF) and the California Public Employees Retirement System (CALPERS)—had assets of $140 billion and $100 billion respectively, and the largest pension fund in the United Kingdom, the Post Office and British Telecom Fund, had holdings of $35 billion. The total figure for worldwide pension fund assets in 1994 was $10 trillion.[38] But in noting some of the more distinctive features of these shifts, it can be seen that in addition to the stupendous growth between 1973 and today in the overall daily volume of foreign exchange transactions, in stock market capitalization, and in the burgeoning of pension, insurance, and mutual funds, there has also been an equally marked change in the composition of the flows themselves.

THE IMPACT OF THE CURRENT FINANCE-LED/ EQUITY-BASED GROWTH REGIME

The immense proliferation of pension, insurance, and mutual funds, and the rapid growth in stock market capitalization in the volume of foreign exchange transactions, have, in conjunction with other developments that come under the rubric of 'financialization', changed radically the circuits of realization and accumulation that are currently at the disposal of the capitalist system. The revolutionary transformations brought about during the decade-long ascendancy of the finance-led/equity-based growth regime have at least two significant implications for any attempt to elucidate the nature of the antagonism between capital and the proletariat that lies at the heart of Negri's account of the constituent power of the multitude/ proletariat.

Firstly, the field of this antagonism is profoundly altered by the fact that the onset of the finance-led/equity-based growth regime has greatly multiplied capital's potential points of insertion into its circuits of realization and expansion. The vastly enhanced mobility of capital brought about by financialization affects capital in its quest for 'valorization' by enabling the capitalist to counter the crucial disadvantage (for the capitalist!) identified by Negri as one of the outcomes of real subsumption's immaterialization of labor: namely, that in real subsumption the proletariat possesses an inalienable power of social cooperation, unavoidably promoted by the capitalist in his/her quest for surplus value, that can potentially be used by the proletariat to augment its constituent power and thus to resist the depredations of the capitalist. Proletarian resistance, on this account, is always possible and, indeed, is virtually inevitable. However, while 'fictitious capital' has perforce to enter one of the extant circuits of realization as a condition of being 'valorized' (i.e., as Hilferding pointed out a long time ago, it is a condition of realizing 'fictitious capital' that it be converted into some form of industrial or productive capital), and while this conversion and its outcomes will necessarily involve it in an antagonistic relationship with the proletariat (who willy-nilly are the only source of the labor power essential to the constitution of productive capital), the flexibility afforded the possessor of 'fictitious capital' means that this particular kind of capitalist has greater control over the terms and conditions of engagement with capital's proletarian adversary. Hence, for instance, a corporation like Amazon.com, which has never made a profit throughout its existence, but which has nonetheless been hugely overvalued in the stock market for most of that time, has been able to use the capital derived from this consistently high stock-market valuation to more than offset its operating losses. The availability of these vast financial resources has also enabled Amazon.com to deal with its workforce in a less than tractable and conciliatory spirit (as typified by its resistance to unionization).[39]

Secondly, the possessor of equity-derived income is herself freed from the discipline of the wage relation that is essential to the constitution of the antagonism of the proletariat. The wealthy and superwealthy have of course never been constrained by the discipline of the wage relation in any phase of capitalist expansion, but to the extent that a greater percentage of individuals in the advanced industrialized countries are deriving a more significant share of income from equity-based sources, the greater is the leeway afforded such individuals in their efforts to obviate or neutralize (whether singly or collectively) the disciplinary force of the wage nexus.[40] The outcome of this exponential growth in equity-based wealth at the core of 'empire' has meant that the discipline of the wage relation is confined more and more to its most exploited and least-privileged denizens: more and more it is the case that to those who have much more shall be given, and to those who have less more shall be taken away. The consequences of this development for the ordering of the multitude's constituent power are potentially significant. One such consequence has been the growing use of stock options to remunerate corporate executives, giving executives an inbuilt incentive to maximize equity values while disregarding other socially more beneficial incentives. Company executives, who hitherto had been salaried managers, are now in effect manager–capitalists, and consequently find their interests aligned more with those of their shareholders (i.e., other holders of equity), and much less with those of their still-salaried employees (who of course remain stuck in the wage–labor nexus).[41]

The finance-led and equity-based regime adverted to here is variably dispersed across the advanced economies. It possesses the following distinguishing features, many of them associated with the phenomenon of 'the new economy'.[42] For the pivotal role played by the wage–labor link in Fordism it substitutes a matrix of financial institutions and innovative instruments, and the stability of the system is entrusted to the Central Bank and not to state-mediated capital–labor collective wage arrangements (as was the case in the heyday of Fordism) (Boyer 2000: 112). Firms become oriented towards capital markets and their logic of public valuation rather than meeting performance criteria based on now-outmoded principles of corporate organization and governance, and this encourages a 'short-termism' on the part of corporations, as '[s]uccessful companies capture quasi-rents downstream in fast-expanding markets for final goods and services where the goodwill resides and at the same time pass the costs of making commodities on to others'.[43] Its other characteristics have been described thus by Robert Boyer:

> Many giant mergers, capital mobility between countries, pressures on corporate governance, diffusion of equity among a larger fraction of population, all these transformations . . . lead to a totally novel regulation mode . . . [combining] labour market flexibility, price stability, developing high tech sectors, booming stock market and credit to sustain the rapid growth of consumption, and permanent optimism of expectations in firms. The capacity of each country to adapt and implement such a model would be a key factor in macroeconomic performance and would determine that country's place in a hierarchical world economy governed by the diffusion of a financialized growth régime. (Boyer 2000: 116)

At the same time, the structure of consumer demand is reconstituted as a response to unprecedented levels of product innovation and niche marketing. Since both demand and supply are generally regulated by asset price expectations (and less by the capital–wage nexus of previous regimes of accumulation), the possibility exists of a benign spiral in which heightened expectations of profits lead to an appreciation of asset prices, which in turn boosts incomes and consumer demand, and this in turn vindicates the initial heightened expectation of profits, thereby triggering off another round of self-fulfilling profit expectations. As was pointed out earlier, this new profit-propelled system enables the more privileged wage earners to rely on more than fixed wages for incomes, since they now enjoy greater access to wealth derived from equity and pension-fund holdings. Again, as has been the case with the US economy in the 1990s, the wealth originating from financial markets is able to galvanize consumption on an overall scale barely conceivable in previous regimes of accumulation. In this ostensibly benign spiral, therefore, 'the whole macroeconomic dynamic is . . . driven by the compatibility between the expectations emanating from financial markets, the reality of firms' profit growth and interest-rate dynamics, which the central bank is trying to direct' (Boyer 2000: 121).

This finance-led system, while led by the United States, is of course globalized, and so other national economies must respond to the financial rate of return available in their counterpart economies: movements of capital affect exchange rates, and a country's exchange-rate policy affects its credibility as a protagonist in global financial markets. Even the United States's perennial external trade deficits have to be financed by the savings of other countries, giving it an incentive (though there are others of course) to promote an open and 'competitive' international financial system that will give it access to the savings of Asian and European countries.[44]

The international system of financial markets has thus undergone a series of structural transformations since 1972, several of which are still taking place.[45] These include changes in the sources of international credit and the emergence of a new capital recycling mechanism, and together they began a revolutionary transformation that has continuing effects. The changes in the sources of international credit are well known, but, says Randall Germain, the more important changes have taken place in the capital recycling mechanism, that is, 'the form of credit made available to the world economy, in the networks of monetary agents which control access to this credit, and in the relationship between public monetary agents and private monetary agents within the global financial system' (Germain 1997: 136). As a result, Germain goes on to say, a new era in international finance has emerged, one that can appropriately be called 'decentralized globalization', and which is to be associated with the enfranchisement of a whole range of new and not always disciplined systemic creditors, the rise generally of unstable institutional arrangements,[46] the diminished authority and effectiveness of state and public monetary institutions (except when it came to leading the way in deregulating financial markets),[47] the complementary growth in the authority and effectiveness of private monetary institutions (towards whom the balance of power has now gravitated), and the changing of the criteria used to govern access to flows of mobile capital (these have moved in favor of the interests of private agents).[48] In 'decentralized globalization' just about anything can become the focal point of the activities of a speculative market, with no consideration being given to the question whether this market is tied to a real or projected expansion in productive capacity. A case in point here is the 1997 Kyoto Protocol on climate change, which set up a mechanism that would enable 'polluter' countries to buy emissions permits from countries with lower rates of carbon pollution, in effect securing for themselves an emissions 'credit'. Although this mechanism is not due to operate until 2008, there is now a flourishing brokerage market in these permits, worth $50 billion in 1999, and projected to reach trillions of dollars in the next few decades, as the emissions permits market links up with the speculative hedge funds and derivatives markets. One of the pivotal organizations in this emissions market is the International Emissions Trading Association, whose members include such private institutions as the Australian Stock Exchange, the International Petroleum Exchange, Shell, BP, Amoco, Statoil, and Tokyo Electric Power.[49] I shall return to the question of the disconnection of this form of capital from capitals that involve an expansion of productive capacity.

While private institutions have grown in importance, the state continues to have a role, since capital mobility is not perfect, in at least two respects. One is that the state still possesses a degree of macroeconomic policy autonomy, though this room for maneuver is nonetheless circumscribed, in varying ways and to varying degrees, by the global integration of financial markets and by the propensity of states in this situation to allow private agents use of their policy instruments in ways that effectively make these agents proxies for state and public authority. The second is the pre-eminence enjoyed by the United States (and to a lesser extent the western European nations and Japan) in determining the course and constitution of global financial markets, and allied with this is the primacy enjoyed by the financial markets in New York, Tokyo and London. A state-based hegemony is thus very much the continuing core of the international financial system. But this perduring state capability notwithstanding, today no single state or public authority has effective control of the international financial system (even if the institutions of the American hegemony and the OECD central banks have a pivotal place in this system). The result is a growing regionalization of interest rates and the declining importance of reserve requirements as financial institutions become more hybridized and their resources more interchangeable as a result (Germain 1997: 161).

There is no unitary model of how this finance-led growth regime relates to other regimes whose *raison d'être* is less the accumulation of financial assets and more the production and exchange of commodities. Boyer (2000) identifies a number of alternative post-Fordist growth regimes: Toyotism (Japan until 1990), service-led (the United States in the 1980s), information/communication technologies-led (Silicon Valley since the mid-1980s), knowledge-based (the United States since the 1990s), competition-led (most OECD countries since 1985), export-led (the East Asian 'tiger economies' before 1997), and finance-led (the United States and the United Kingdom since the 1990s) and it is evident from this typology that there can be hybrid post-Fordist formations (the US economy being knowledge-based, information/communication technologies-led, and finance-led, with the latter preponderating primarily because it is the strategic locus of the United States's resources for macroeconomic management).[50] At the same time it is scarcely deniable that the low-income LDCs have virtually no place in this system from which they can hope realistically to influence its overall direction. Fundamental asymmetries permeate the international financial system, and the divorce between 'fictitious capital' and productive capital, integral to the equity-based/ finance-led growth regime, only reinforces the worldwide economic polarization that has been a feature of capitalist accumulation since its inception.

The main source of international economic polarization in the finance-led growth regime is precisely the independence of finance capital (and 'fictitious capital') from productive capital. Finance and 'fictitious' capital, money—always money—synchronizes capitalism's production and consumption circuits, and this synchronization speeds up the processes that realize surplus value by abbreviating the linkages between production and consumption. Command over the essential instrument of synchronization, finance/money, therefore translates more or less immediately into the capacity to realize profits, and this in ways detached from the productive process itself and the direct exploitation of labor itself.[51] However, this fundamental disconnection of finance (and 'fictitious') capital from productive capital in the equity-based growth regime does not absolutely exempt 'fictitious' and finance capital from the need to find a means of 'valorization' in the production process; as Marx pointed out, if capitalists were happy simply to amass sums of money from whatever source and sit on them, that money would simply be a hoard, and would not therefore constitute *capital*. For this money to become capital it would have at some point to be inserted into the production process. This in fact is exactly what has happened in the current US-led regime of accumulation, where its stock-market driven expansion has fueled historically unprecedented levels of consumer demand that could only be satisfied by imported goods and services. The United States incurred massive trade- and current-account deficits in the process, but probably forestalled a severe world recession in the wake of the East Asian financial crisis. It would be much too optimistic to conclude from this that a systematically orchestrated international expansion is now really in prospect, with a mutually beneficial world division of labor starting to be solidified in the process. The United States's own 'bubble-based' expansion is now showing itself to be precarious and probably not as deep-rooted as previous major upswings, and in the absence of conditions likely to sustain its 1990s expansion, the suggestion that the United States's vast reservoirs of 'fictitious capital' can be 'valorized' by a subsequent and benign insertion into a globally integrated division of labor is not really credible in the longer term. This 'bubble-based' expansion is more likely than not to generate a crisis of its own.

Nonetheless, it is the case that a worldwide integrated division of labor, based on fundamental asymmetries of power between richer and poorer nations, is very much the present-day mechanism for the 'valorization' of this 'fictitious capital': the equity-market-driven expansion of the United States has generated a galloping consumption that has in turn given a powerful impetus to the export-based economies of its trading partners. These trading partners have to strive to derive benefits by performing selective functions in this equity-led regime, and while a Singapore or Hong Kong, and to a much lesser extent a China, India, or Dubai (the 'Singapore of the Arab world') may benefit in this way, a Burkina Faso or Colombia or Fiji can do little or nothing to establish even the merest toehold in such a system. The LDCs are basically confined by this system to primary commodity production (the fate of the Colombias and Fijis of this world) or to labor-intensive industrial production with a low composition of capital and still organized along Taylorist principles (e.g., the clothing, electronic, and toy industries in Vietnam, Malaysia, Guatemala, etc.). These countries are basically subcontractors for manufacturers, typically well-known companies like Nike and the Gap, in the developed (some would say 'overdeveloped') countries. So the question remains whether the more damaging effects of the fundamental asymmetries associated with the finance-led/equity-based growth regime can be surmounted by an LDC like Burkina Faso or Fiji. These asymmetries also inflect the basal antagonism between capital and the proletariat that lies at the heart of Negri's account of the constituent power of the multitude/proletariat, and it is necessary to consider whether this constituent power can be glossed in a way that takes these asymmetries sufficiently into account.

CONSTITUENT POWER AND THE PROJECT OF SURMOUNTING INTERNATIONAL ECONOMIC POLARIZATION

The emphasis being placed here on the centrality of the finance-led/equity-based growth regime in present-day capitalist accumulation should not blind us to an obvious feature of this regime, namely, that even in a regime dominated by the financialization of capital it is very much the case that the overwhelming majority of jobs, new and existing, will be in employment sectors that are not high-skill and high-wage. Negri's stress on the 'intellectual worker' and the 'immaterialization of labor' carries with it the potential pitfall that one might overlook the fact that most of the jobs created by the processes associated with post-Fordism are not in banking and financial services, or the high-skill and high-technology industrial production domains, but in the plain, old-fashioned low end of the service sector. Thus, the US Department of Labor's projections for the occupations that will provide the most jobs for the period between 1994 and 2005 indicate that the ten occupations with the greatest number of new jobs will be cashiers, janitors and cleaners, retail salespersons, waiters and waitresses, registered nurses, general managers and top executives, systems analysts, home health aides, guards, and nurses aides, orderlies, and attendants. Only 24 per cent of these can be said to constitute middle-class and owner or management occupations.[52] To be fair, Negri's point about the 'immaterialization of labor' is primarily about the impact represented by sectors that supply the current regime of capitalist accumulation with its dynamism or leading edge, and today it is banking and financial services, and the high-skill and high-technology industrial production sectors, that drive the economies of the advanced capitalist countries, just as it was heavy industry (car manufacturing, shipbuilding, etc.) that drove these economies in the heyday of Fordism (whereas today car manufacturing and shipbuilding are basically relegated to LDCs such as Malaysia, Thailand, Mexico, and Brazil). Hence, and this is one way to construe the thesis of the 'immateriality of labor', it is economic agents positioned in these high-end sectors, and not the 'material laborers' of the low-end occupations, who are best placed to capture whatever productivity gains and ensuing profits happen to be afforded by the prevailing system of accumulation, and this because the high-end sectors in this system, with their newer capitals, are more likely than not to be the loci of enhance-ments in productivity.[53] But however beguiling the notion of an 'imma-terial labor' may be, it is the 'material labor' of low-end service occupations which serves as the economic bedrock of the advanced capitalist coun-tries, and any plausible account of an anticapitalist constituent power has to be premised on this state of affairs. If this is true of the OECD countries, it is even more true of the LDCs, who are entirely at the mercy of the worldwide integrated division of labor based on fundamental asymmetries of power between richer and poorer nations, and whose basic function in the current system is to confine the LDCs to selective export-led produc-tion sectors, served by a palpably 'material' labor, while financialization and its associated 'immaterialization of labor' become the almost exclusive prerogative of the wealthier nations. That is to say, the primacy of a fun-damentally unproductive financial capital over productive capital that defines the regnant equity-based growth regime has as one of its effects the capacity of the former capital, lodged as it is in the economies of the developed nations, to organize the distribution of the constituent parts of capital in ways that militate, 'systemically', against the LDCs' prospects for economic advancement.

The proposal for a 'delinking' of the so-called peripheral economies from the global system made by Samir Amin and others has the above-described situation as its rationale: for the proponents of 'delinking', 'openness' to the world capitalist system and its increasingly deregulated markets on the part of the poorer LDCs is not likely to lead to any mean-ingful opportunities for economic advancement. In Amin's version of the delinking thesis, the economic development of the wealthy capitalist countries has always been 'autocentric', that is, determined by an internal dynamic specific to the wealthy country in question, whereas LDCs are compelled by a worldwide economic polarization, functioning principally at the level of the international division of labor, to espouse 'extraverted' policies of accumulation, so that their economic designs and aspirations are subordinated to those of the wealthy nations. Delinking aims to replace these burdensome 'extraverted' strategies of development, with their preferential option for an 'openness' to the world market, with less disabling 'autocentric' alternatives that do not take this 'openness' to be the panacea so beloved of neoliberalism.

Negri has always contended that the theory of uneven development is problematic because its proponents share a crucial premise with the very viewpoint they oppose, namely, that there is a single developmental trajectory of a hierarchical nature that encompasses all countries, with 'developmentalists' claiming that LDCs advance to the extent that they move up this hierarchy by emulating their developed counterparts, while the theorists of uneven development hold that economic marginalization is the inescapable fate of the LDCs because the hierarchical character of this developmental trajectory just about ordains that some nations remain economically backward precisely in order to furnish the advanced economies with resources to fuel their own development (see Hardt and Negri 2000: 282ff.). The corollary of this position, if one is a proponent of the theory of uneven development, is that an LDC can avoid marginalization only by uncoupling itself from the developmental hierarchy that defines the global economic system. Negri (and Hardt), however, deem this strategy of 'delinking' or isolation from the world system to be ineffective and rash since 'any attempt at isolation or separation will mean only a more brutal kind of domination by the world system, a reduction to powerlessness and poverty' (Hardt and Negri 2000: 284). This repudiation of the delinking project is not altogether unconvincing, since 'powerlessness and poverty' are already the fate of many of the countries now integrated into the capitalist world system, and inequalities between North and South have increased significantly since the end of the Golden Age: the share in global income of the poorest 20 per cent of the world's people has fallen from 2.3 per cent in 1960 and 1.4 per cent in 1991 to a 1996 level of 1.1 per cent, while the ratio of the income of the top 20 per cent to that of the poorest 20 per cent rose from 30:1 in 1960 to 61:1 in 1991, and grew still further to a figure of 78:1 in 1994.[54]

These figures point to a sober predicament for the LDCs. It is reckoned that the LDCs need to expand economically at a rate of around 6–7 per cent annually for several years if they are to provide employment opportunities for their expanding labor forces (growing at about 3.5 per cent a year in countries such as Brazil and Mexico), and if they are to hope to meet their citizens' basic needs for food, shelter, clothing, health, and education over a 20-year period.[55] Many LDCs have been subjected since the 1960s and 1970s to structural adjustment programs whose *raison d'être* is the 'openness' to the world market extolled by advocates of neoliberal capitalism. Amin's proposal for a 'delinking' of the poorer LDCs must be seen in terms of just this economic predicament, that is, one in which 'openness' to the world capitalist system on the part of the LDCs has brought the least advantaged of them catastrophic levels of poverty with little or no hope of relief. For most of the poorest LDCs the hope that citizens have an even chance of meeting their basic needs is not one that can reasonably be entertained.

Negri (and Hardt) take Amin to be championing the Albanian-type autarky he has pointedly rejected (see Amin 1990b: 158). Amin has indicated that the delinking intended to replace an 'extraverted' strategy of accumulation with its 'autocentric' counterpart can only occur as part of 'a very long transition beyond capitalism' (1994: 167). Furthermore, delinking 'does not exclude parallel action to influence the world system and make it adjust to the demands of delinking' (1994: 227), which, in conjunction with his other statements on delinking, clearly implies that Amin views delinking as a set of adaptable policies focused on the social relations of production, and definitely not as an Albanian or Pol Pot-type autarky. What is the core of this set of flexible procedures, procedures taken by Amin to involve the creation of a 'polycentric' world of interdependent economies, nation-state-based but also regionally consolidated?

In demarcating the nub of this cluster of policies, it has to be acknowledged that Amin's delinking proposal needs to be elaborated more extensively in relation to the disconnection between productive and financial (or 'fictitious') capital that is a key element in the now-hegemonic finance-led regime of growth. While Amin does retain the valuable insight that the size and composition of the reserve army of labor (i.e., unpaid and under-indemnified labor) in the LDCs is the deciding factor determining the availability of surplus value, the fact of the finance-led regime's dominance means that any proposal for a delinking has to include a broad strategy for dealing with financialization (and this Amin does not do in a really detailed way). How can the proposal for a delinking be qualified or expanded to take the financialization of the global economy adequately into account?

Lance Taylor has also advocated a partial delinking strategy on 'narrowly technical grounds' (see Taylor 1991). Taylor has analyzed extensively the data regarding the open-trade and capital-market strategies of a cross-section of 50 lower-income countries (going as far back as the economically more propitious 1960s) and discerned few gains and some losses accruing from these exogenously-oriented policies. He suggests that these LDC countries should dispense on a piecemeal basis with linkages to the markets of the North that bring 'the least benefits' or exact 'the greatest costs', concluding that a circumscribed and selective disassociation of this kind offers these LDCs a better bet for economic survival—as Taylor puts it, 'the inwardly oriented resource allocation strategy seems the least risky, especially for large countries'.[56] Without question the business of such an 'inwardly oriented resource allocation strategy' for the LDCs is going to be fraught with difficulties and obstacles. The focal point of this strategy will be the construction of an alternative growth regime for the LDCs whose justification is, ultimately, the revocation of the processes that have led to the recompradorization of these countries.[57] Financial openness along the lines specified in the so-called Washington Consensus that governs the thinking of the IMF, World Bank, WTO, and OECD is not likely to benefit the world's poorer countries. For the poorer LDCs, the reverse, tending as it does to recompradorization and economic clientalism, is a more presumptive outcome given the present-day complexion of the rulers of the world economic system. At the minimum, a raft of policy initiatives favoring 'autocentric' development will be required if this dismal outcome for the LDCs is to be obviated. These policies will be designed to ward off the depredations associated with the US-led equity-based growth regime: that is, controls on capital movements, debt forgiveness, appropriate investment strategies designed primarily to make poorer LDCs less dependent on the production of primary commodities, and the creation of regional blocs and partnerships to combine resources and consolidate LDC economic gains.[58] A key ingredient in the operation of this alternative growth regime will of course be the social and political mobilization of the appropriate classes and class fractions in the LDCs.

This mobilization supplies the basis for the composition of a constituent power germane to the economic and social needs of the LDCs, and, hopefully, if the lineaments of this mobilization can be generalized beyond the LDCs, a new counterproject to capitalism can become a more decisive reality. This counterproject is not likely to emerge, at least initially, in the developed countries, since they are, in the main, the primary beneficiaries of the global economic system that develops them at the expense of the LDCs. Those who are the beneficiaries of the profitability criteria and 'open' markets implacably enjoined by this system are not likely to align themselves with the social forces supporting this counterproject, the occasional exception notwithstanding: this counterproject, whose *raison d'être* is the imposition of decisive limits on capital, has to base itself on principles and forces which are exterior to the logic of capital. But how do we identify this exteriority and constitute a social and political order, a counterproject to capitalist logic, on the basis of it?

Samir Amin has argued that a counterproject of this kind is not likely to succeed unless the social movements that are its vehicle are able to operate at the level of the nation state; only in this way, says Amin, can the system of a globalized economic polarization be neutralized and ultimately dismantled (see Amin 1999a, 2000). Of course this counterproject has to be efficacious at other levels if it is to be successful, including the education, taxation, and bureaucratic systems, and also show itself capable of sustaining 'a more general vision of the democratization of societies and their political and economic management' (Amin 2000: 84). But this counterproject, which resembles the project of the *multitudo* of Negri and Hardt's *Empire*, is, for the LDCs at any rate, a project that involves the mobilization of a new and different kind of popular national movement. Here an important distinction between the state apparatus and the nation is to be made, and Amin has argued that the appropriation of the state apparatus is usually the object of a country's national bourgeoisie (who will reconcile themselves to recompradorization as long as it will leave the state apparatus in their hands), while the construction of the project of national liberation involves not only delinking (needed to avert recompradorization) but also the formation of a 'popular hegemonic alliance' among the people (Amin 1990a: 136).

The construction of a comprehensive national popular alliance, functioning autonomously of the state system, will furnish the stimulus for adopting a different kind of allocation strategy, one premised on a (selective) delinking subsuming the policy elements just mentioned, and embarked upon with the purpose of transmuting the state apparatus (since the state is the institutional assemblage that has final control of the regime of growth, and indeed there can be no properly constituted regime of growth without the involvement of the state). The first priority therefore is a 'destatized' collective national liberation project, the success of which will then lead to a reconstitution of the state itself. Most existing proposals for economic and political reform in the LDCs view the reform and reconstitution of the state as the principal objective whose attainment will then lead to a whole range of other benefits ('efficient' economic development, protection of human rights, the upholding of democracy, etc.). This is to put the proverbial cart before the horse, since in many LDCs the state is merely an instrument at the disposal of the ruling elite (who tend invariably to be the recipients of the substantial personal benefits to be derived from subservience to the Washington Consensus, etc.), and it will be necessary therefore to have an alternative and non-state-oriented base within the LDC in question from which the project of state reform can be initiated and sustained. There are no pregiven laws to shape or entail this outcome: only struggle—and failures always accompany successes in struggle—can do this. The only other alternative is acceptance of the current finance-led, equity-based growth regime with its concomitant American hegemony and continuing worldwide economic polarization. For the poorer peoples of the world, this is hardly a satisfactory alternative, as Negri himself has always pointed out.

This of course is only a brief sketch of a conception of constituent power adequate to the realities of globalized economic polarization. Whether or not it departs significantly from the lineaments of Negri's own account is less important than the fact of its fundamental continuity with his treatment of the ontology of transformation. In all his writings, from the early work associated with the *operaismo* tendency to *Empire*, Negri has emphasized the centrality of this ontology of transformation:

> The new communist experiment is born through the rupture with memory. A rupture distinct from any melancholy or resentment. And it's there that, in the present, amongst all and no specters, the only real continuity appears: that of the struggle, of the constituent spirit, of the ontological violence of transformation. The awaited event makes the past explode. A real coming to be. (Negri 1999b: 15)

In the model of revolutionary transformation being canvassed in this chapter, this awaited event takes the form of the struggle, involving all progressive forces but located primarily in those regions less circumscribed by the logic of capital, to create a new national liberation project that is capable of restructuring the state.[59] If Negri has underemphasized the centrality of this particular project of state restructuration for the LDCs, the assertion of its centrality is nonetheless compatible, *mutatis mutandis*, with his conception of revolutionary transformation.

NOTES

1. Negri has had fruitful collaborations with the late Félix Guattari (see opening epigraph) and with Michael Hardt that are indispensable for any understanding of his work. For his collaboration with Hardt, see *Labor of Dionysus: A Critique of the State-Form* (Hardt and Negri 1994), and *Empire* (Hardt and Negri 2000).
2. A crucial question intrudes at this point, namely, how will we know that capitalism as it is presently constituted is congruent with this Marxist theoretical armature? This congruence can only be established by resorting to a principle, a second-order principle, that is perforce not 'Marxist', and this because the applicability of Marxism to this capitalist field can only be specified metatheoretically: it is this 'transcendental' or metatheoretical proviso that indicates to us in virtue of which conditions and axioms is the field of capitalism governed by the axiomatic that is Marxism. Negri's recourse to a constitutive ontology of political practice is precisely the attempt to provide this needed metatheoretical elaboration. In formulating this ontology Negri is of course indebted as much to Spinoza as he is to Marx. There is a sense in which for Negri (and Marx!) it is Marxism that derives its saliency from class struggle rather than vice versa (though this admittedly is something of a simplification, since class struggles in capitalist dispensations in turn derive their proper 'thinkability' from Marxism). The struggles of countless human beings for a better world, and the accompanying ontology of political practice supervening upon these struggles, link the Marxist axiomatic to the capitalist field.
3. On 'real subsumption' (*sussunzione reale*), see Negri 1989: 177–90 and 1996c: 151–2. *Empire* makes it clear that the time of real subsumption is also the epoch of 'biopower', that is, 'when the entire context of reproduction is subsumed under capitalist rule, . . . when reproduction and the vital relationships that constitute it themselves become directly productive' (Hardt and Negri 2000: 364).
4. See here especially the interesting appropriation and extension of Deleuze's notion of the 'society of control' in *Empire*. On the Keynesian 'planner-state', see Negri's 1967 essay 'Keynes and the Capitalist Theory of the State', in Hardt and Negri 1994: 23–51 (another English version is to be found in Negri 1988b: 9–42). On the 'crisis-state', see Negri 1980a.

5. Strictly speaking, worldwide integrated capitalism is an amalgam of assorted modes of production, unlike at the time of Marx, when it was possible to line up modes of production in a hierarchy that lent itself to a relatively straightforward historical periodization (the succeeding dispensations of hunter–gatherer, 'Asiatic', 'feudal', 'industrial', etc.) in a way that is simply not viable today. These days, by contrast, ostensibly diverse modes of production coexist in the same space. As Negri puts it: '... capital ... now has the ability to take in completely archaic modes of organization of social work and to integrate them into production with maximum efficiency. Japan is a good example. The social mobilization of work recuperates as many levels of work as possible including the most archaic social relations of production and reproduction.... Brazil has every kind of production imaginable, from the tribal production of the Indians to computer technology so advanced that it competes with the United States. It is a country mediated to an extraordinary degree: even precapitalist forms of cooperation have been integrated into the social mechanism of production' (Negri 1988d: 82–3).

6. For more on the socialized worker, see Hardt and Negri 2000: 409ff. See also Negri 1988a.

7. Etienne Balibar has distinguished between models of social conflict that take 'agonism' and 'antagonism' as their respective fundamental operative categories. Characterizing the former as 'Machiavellian' and the latter as 'Hegelian' and 'Marxist', Balibar takes 'agonism' to involve the positing of an always changing relationship between conflicting sets of practices and powers in a way that willy-nilly relativizes the notion of class struggle. He also makes the criticism, directed at Foucault as much as anyone else, that there are forms of exploitation that are not reducible to the 'agonistic' model. See Balibar 1999. This way of distinguishing between the two models of social conflict is somewhat problematic, and not only because it misrepresents Foucault, who continued to believe in the centrality of class struggle even as he sought to take account of other forms of conflict and resistance. It is also unsatisfactory because Negri's delineation of real subsumption broadens the notion of class struggle to incorporate forms of opposition not immediately reducible to the 'workerist' view of class struggle as conflict between capital and the organized industrial proletariat, albeit while still according a decisive centrality to the various forms of contention with capitalist exploitation that continue to display themselves in the phase of real subsumption. Negri thereby merges Machiavelli and Marx, as did Althusser in his late work. The expansion and modification of the notion of class struggle remains a pivotal problematic for any attempt to reinvigorate Marxist thought, and Balibar's dichotomy fails to acknowledge our need to find concepts for a communism that exists after (and before!) Marx even as it allows that there is no way of circumventing Marx in this crucial undertaking. This stricture notwithstanding, it is possible to view Balibar's work as an important contribution to this revisionary undertaking, along with the oeuvres of Althusser, Negri, Deleuze and Guattari, Samir Amin, Bourdieu, and others.

8. According to Negri, constituent power or *pouvoir constituant* received its first significant definition from Machiavelli, who, in the absence of the conditions necessary for democracy, made constituent power into a program for securing it (Negri 1999a: 97). Negri's assessment converges with the one provided by Althusser, who regarded Machiavelli as the thinker par excellence of the untimely break in which the 'impossible' desire for revolutionary transformation can find its clandestinely powerful place. See Althusser 1999. For Negri's appraisal of Althusser's reading of Machiavelli, see Negri 1996b.

9. See Negri 1999a: 264–5. For Negri's treatment of the concept of 'crisis' in Marx's oeuvre, see Negri 1988c.

10. There seem to be two positions here that reinforce each other where Negri is concerned. One is that the dialectical negation can never in principle eliminate the space from which expropriation derives its conditions of possibility, even if it can manage to negate the figure of the capitalist: expropriation is an ensemble of *practices*, and merely negating the figure of the capitalist while leaving untouched the

conditions which enable these practices will not overcome capitalism. The other is that, in real subsumption, the logic of capital permeates even this space of practices, and this in a direct and unmediated way, so that there is now no real exteriority to capital. With no scope for mediation, there is no room for dialectical negation to operate. Or as it is put in *Empire*: 'Imperial power can no longer resolve the conflict of social forces through mediatory schemata that displace the terms of conflict. The social conflicts that constitute the political confront one another directly, without mediations of any sort' (Hardt and Negri 2000: 393).

11. See Negri 1999a: 267. See also Guattari and Negri 1990: 20ff., where it is claimed that the events of 1968 mark the point at which real subsumption reached its apogee, but at the same time also entered into a palpable phase of crisis.

12. Negri contends that constitutionalism, the political expression of capitalist command, negates the strength of the multitude through its regimentation of the political realm. The corollary of this neutralization of the strength of the multitude in the political is the multitude's decomposition in the social, so that social strength is necessarily severed from political power (Negri 1999a: 325). In real subsumption, however, the socius (which Negri places, analytically, in opposition to the merely political as grasped by constitutionalism) can be reinvested as a political field, and constituent power finally freed from its subordination to capital. Negri takes to task the Derrida of *Specters of Marx* for acknowledging, correctly, that in real subsumption Marx's law of value no longer adequately characterizes capitalism, while failing at the same time to see that the mechanisms of exploitation are just as prevalent in real subsumption as they were in previous capitalist formations, and that the theory of surplus value continues to be applicable even in the era of postindustrial capitalism with its apotheosizing of the immateriality of labor. For Negri new relations of production are of course to be associated with this current 'postindustrial' regime of accumulation, and these generate new forms of cooperation and proletarian antagonism ('the ontological violence of transformation') that Derrida simply overlooks. On this, see Negri 1999b.

13. Negri makes it clear in 'The Specter's Smile' that this phenomenology of capitalist production and accumulation is for Marx a necessary prolepsis to the production of a 'true and proper metaphysics of capital' (Negri 1999b: 7). It is also evident that the reconstruction and amplification of this Marxian metaphysics is a primary theoretical objective of Negri's.

14. Negri says that democracy for Marx is 'a real democracy of right and appropriation, equal distribution of wealth, and equal participation in production. . . .' (Negri 1999a: 306). *Insurgencies* makes it clear that by contrast the idealist political ontology to be identified with Hobbes and Hegel can only invoke a constitutionalism which uses transcendence to regulate, through the imposition of order and hierarchy, the multitude's potentiality; this idealist political metaphysics and the constitutionalism it buttresses is the negation of real democracy, in other words. See Negri 1999a: 322ff. It should be noted that the terms *potenza, potentia*, and *puissance* serve as cognates of 'strength' in Negri's scheme of things.

15. Negri takes Marx to have 'elaborated some fundamental prolegomena to future science of constituent power' (Negri 1999a: 326)—the implication being that future generations of Marxists will have to consolidate this science of general principles and historical tendencies, which, given that its object is the constantly changing creativity of living labor, will have to be modified in ways that inevitably will take it beyond the point attained in Marx's own lifetime.

16. Negri characterizes this new politics as one which appreciates '*the ontological strength of a multitude of cooperating singularities*' (Negri 1999a: 333, his emphasis), and contrasts this politics with two other outmoded conceptions of the political, one based on the notion of a constitutional command over the body politic, the other as the domain in which legitimate violence is exercised (ibid.). The latter Weberian, and ultimately neo-Kantian, conception of the state is criticized by Negri in Negri 1998, where it is also identified as the Leninist view of the state. The practico-theoretical basis for this 'new politics' is premised on the fact that '[m]aterialism should never

be confused with the development of modernity; materialism persisted throughout the development of modernity as an alternative, an alternative that was continually suppressed but always sprung up again. The Renaissance discovered the freedom of labor, the *vis viva*; materialism interpreted it and capitalist modernity subjugated it. Today the refusal of waged labor and the development of intellectual productive forces repropose intact that alternative that at the dawn of modernity was crushed and repelled' (Hardt and Negri 1994: 21). Negri's project is thus very much an attempt to present a conceptual cartography aimed at the revivification of this submerged but not totally effaced materialist project.

17. Negri advances and modifies Schumpeter's conception of capitalism as a revolutionary force which renews itself by unleashing 'waves of creative destruction' against its previous forms. Where Schumpeter conceives of a 'creative destruction' directed against itself, Negri maintains that in real subsumption the process identified by Schumpeter has mutated into a capitalist 'devalorization of the social in order to revalorize capital'. But in the course of 'devalorizing' the social, capital cannot avoid encountering its antagonist, the proletariat/multitude, and so a twofold movement ensues: on the one hand, the *constituted* power of capital is pitted against the *constituent* power of the proletariat, and on the other, the proletariat, in countering its capitalist adversary, activates an internal dynamic that enables it to enhance its own constituent power. For Negri on Schumpeter, see Negri 1989: 215–16.

18. It is significant therefore that Negri should fault Derrida's *Specters of Marx* for its failure to deal adequately with the mechanisms that have caused, and which continue to produce, exploitation. Negri grants that deconstruction is right to assert that Marx's ontological description of exploitation is no longer viable (because it was premised on a now superseded industrial model of production), but insists that the mechanisms of exploitation still exist, albeit in a new and different form. See Negri 1999b, especially p. 10. Negri's conceptual cartography is designed to furnish categories adequate to the *practicalities* of these mechanisms of exploitation in their present-day manifestations.

19. According to Negri (and Hardt), 'Communism must be conceived as a total critique in the Nietzschean sense: not only a destruction of present values, but also a creation of new values; not only a negation of what exists, but an affirmation of what springs forth. . . . Living labor is the internal force that constantly poses not only the subversion of the capitalist process of production but also the construction of an alternative' (Hardt and Negri 1994: 6).

20. On the absence of an 'exteriority' to capital, see Guattari and Negri 1990: 25. Is there a sense in which Negri 'begins' where Althusser left off? After May 1968 Althusser planned a two-volume work dealing with reproduction and revolution. However, only the first volume, dealing with reproduction, was brought to fruition (in March–April 1969). The second volume, concerned with 'class struggle in capitalist social formations', was as far as we know not even begun. This lacuna is perhaps symptomatic, coming as it did after May 1968 and its (so far) flawed aftermath. May 1968 was of course the beginning of a revolution that is still awaiting its culmination, and Negri's special achievement is to have given us the theory of class struggle that Althusser and others wanted for a time characterized by the truncation of revolutionary possibility and the deep political incertitude that accompanied this epochal 'missed opportunity'. On this aspect of Althusser's late work, see the very informative Elliot 1998.

21. Negri 1999b: 12. On the 'immateriality of labor' and the 'informatization of production', see Hardt and Negri 2000: 280–300.

22. As it is stated in *Empire*, 'The rhythm that the revolutionary movements have established is the beat of a new *aetas*, a new maturity and metamorphosis of the times' (Hardt and Negri 2000: 394). See also the invocation of Benjamin's figure of the *Angelus novus* in Negri 1996a: 222.

23. This inversion of the typically understood relation between capitalist (political) command and the social cooperation that defines proletarian activity is of course an integral feature not only of Negri's work but also of the entire *operaismo* tendency (Tronti, Asor Rosa, Cacciari et al.). On this see Yann Moulier's helpful 'Introduction' to Negri 1989, especially 19–25. In *Empire* this inversion is deemed to exist between capital and the expanded collectivity designated as the multitude (i.e., anyone whose labor is exploited by capital), and not just between capital and the industrial working class (as would have been true of a now superseded phase of capitalist development when the industrial working classes were the fulcrum of anticapitalist struggles). On this see Hardt and Negri 2000: 402.

24. Negri suggests that the sequencing of proletarian power is 'asymmetrical' in relation to capitalist power, so that the autonomy of the proletariat/multitude cannot be grasped through the categories of capital: the autonomy of the proletariat/multitude is unacceptable to capitalist command, and vice versa. See Negri 1996c: 170.

25. Hardt and Negri 2000: 286. For Castells and Aoyama, see their 'Paths Towards the Informational Society' (1994). Ronald Dore's otherwise excellent *Stock Market Capitalism: Welfare Capitalism (Japan and Germany versus the Anglo-Saxons)* (2000), is likewise marred by the simplifying contrast between the British and American capitalisms and those of Japan and Germany, with the former spearheading a 'marketization plus financialization' system of accumulation (p. 3).

26. On the demise of Fordism, see Negri 1996c: 162, and 'From the mass worker to the socialized worker, and beyond', in Negri 1989: 75–88.

27. See for example the essays collected in Marglin and Schor 1990. The major exception to this virtual consensus among academic economists regarding the collapse of Fordism is provided by Brenner and Glick 1991. Brenner and Glick observe (see p. 93) that real wages did not match productivity over the period 1958–66 (the peak of the postwar boom) and challenge the accounts of the Golden Age's benign profit loop (high wages–high consumption–high profits) which invariably lie at the heart of the consensus view. Brenner's *The Economics of Global Turbulence* (Brenner 1998) extends this critique of the consensus by invoking the notion of the inherent susceptibility of capital to long-run secular stagnation, that is, by arguing that Fordism was brought down by a declining rate of profit caused by overinvestment in fixed capitals, which led to a downward spiral of overcapacity and overproduction that brought in tow further reductions in profitability, all this leading inexorably to falls in investment and output growth, as well as in the rate of wage increase.

28. As Negri puts it: 'We are no longer in the presence of labour-power as such, or labour-time as such, but rather, we exist in a universe constituted by a circulation of information, indeed a large quantity of information.' See 'Towards new values?' in Negri 1989: 216. On immaterial labor, see also Lazzarato 1996.

29. This relative overlooking of the centrality of finance-led regimes has also been a problematic feature of the thinking of the Regulation School until very recently, when Michel Aglietta, Robert Boyer, and others, have begun to deal with the part played by deregulated financial markets in metamorphosing the structures of competition that are a central characteristic of the Regulation School's account of post-Fordism.

30. On this, see Brenner 2000.

31. Harvey 1999: 373ff. provides a useful exposition of Marx's formula. Harvey (1999: 83) quotes Marx to show that 'Capital describes its circuit normally only so long as its various phases pass uninterruptedly into one another. If capital stops short at its first phase M—C, money capital assumes the rigid form of a hoard; if it stops in the phase of production, the means of production lie without functioning on the one side, while labour power lies unemployed on the other; and if capital is stopped short in its last phase C'—M', piles of unsold commodities accumulate and clog the flow of circulation.' See Marx 1967a: 48. It should be noted however, as Marx does,

that it only takes the exchange of commodities to augment the original stock of money capital, that is, all that is needed for the realization of profit is the circuit $M—C—M'$.

32. For the notion of 'fictitious capital', see Marx 1967b: part V. See also de Brunhoff 1990: 186–7. See also Harvey 1999: 239–82, by far the most detailed analysis of 'fictitious capital'. Eighty per cent of all foreign capital transactions involve a round trip of a week or less, and most take place within a single day. For this, see Tobin 1996: xii.

33. See Bhaduri 1998: 149–58, especially p. 152. A good summary of the changes that have taken place in global financial markets in the last two decades is to be found in Helleiner 1994, Griffith-Jones 1998 and Eatwell and Taylor 2000.

34. Figures taken from Samuelson 2001.

35. See Singh (1997: 22–9, quotation from p. 23), who also makes the point that in 1992 there were 6,700 companies quoted on the Indian stock market, compared with 7,014 companies in the United States, 1,874 in the United Kingdom, and 665 in Germany. In addition, the 'average daily trading volume on the Bombay stock market has been about the same as that in London—about 45,000 trades a day' (p. 23).

36. Henwood 1997a is a readable and informative account of many of these new financial instruments and the markets in which they operate. See also Griffith-Jones and Stallings 1995: 143–73, see especially p. 153.

37. For these figures, see Clark 2000: 31.

38. For these figures, see Minns 1996: 43. Clark points out that in a time (up to the end of 1994) when US retail deposits increased by less than threefold, bonds of assorted kinds increased fivefold, corporate securities around threefold, pension/life assurance holdings by more than sixfold, and mutual fund holdings by 300-fold (2000: 28). Given the continued stock market boom of the last few years, these asset totals can be presumed to be even larger. Minns (1996) indicates that apart from the United States and the United Kingdom, the bulk of other pension-fund holdings is to be found in Japan, the Netherlands, Ireland, Argentina, Peru, Columbia, and a few other South American countries. On the 'short-termism' of pension fund managers, see Minns 1996, the detailed studies in Clark 2000, and Blackburn 2002.

39. BBC News (2001), announcing that Amazon.com was cutting 15 per cent of its workforce, said that 'Amazon's results for the period October to December 2000 . . . were slightly better than Wall Street analysts had expected. The company boosted sales by 44 per cent to $972m, slightly above the firm's own forecast. The online retailer, however, did still turn in a loss of $90.4m (£61.8m), or 25 cents a share. This compares with a loss of $184.9m or 55 cents a share one year earlier. If one-off costs are included, the losses rise to $545m.' The huge stock-market valuations of dot.com companies have another effect, namely, distorting the relation the so-called 'new economy' has to its 'old' counterpart: as Ronald Dore points out (at the time of his writing), it would take only 5 per cent of the shares of aol.com to buy the entire American steel industry. See Dore 2000: 3.

40. *Le Monde Diplomatique* (2000) reports that 'over the past two years the average wealth detained by the 400 most affluent Americans increased by $940 million per person' (p. 2). This increase is overwhelmingly equity-derived, and means that each of 400 Americans made more money in the last two years than the 1999 GNP for Sierra Leone ($700 million), Burundi and Eritrea ($800 million), and Mongolia ($900 million), and only slightly less than Mauritania and the Central African Republic ($1,000 million). For these figures, see World Bank 2001: 274–5. This surge in equity-derived wealth reflects the fact between 1980 and 1995 the index of equity prices on the New York Stock Exchange rose by a factor of 4.28 and after-tax profits by a factor of 4.68. In 1995 the S & P 500 and the NYSE jumped by 17.6 per cent and 14.6 per cent respectively, each grew by a further 23 per cent in 1996, and the S & P 500 increased by another 30 per cent and the NYSE by an additional 27 per cent in 1997. During 1998 and 1999 the NYSE increased by 20.5 per cent and 12.5 per cent respectively, and the S & P 500 by 27 per cent and 19 per cent respectively. Between 1995 and 1997 profitability in the US service sector rose by 22 per cent. The US's GDP

grew at a rate by 4.5 per cent between 1995 and 1999, and one-third of this increase can be attributed to stock-market-driven consumption. There has of course been a significant US stock exchange decline in the last three months. It should also be noted that US income inequalities have increased in the same period: between 1989 and 1997 the net worth of the top 1 per cent increased by 11.3 per cent, that of the top 5 per cent by 10 per cent, that of the top 10 per cent by 4.1 per cent, while the income of the bottom 90 per cent fell by 4.4 per cent. For these figures, see Brenner 2000.

41. In this system firms are prone to regard a satisfactory stock-market valuation as the index of corporate success, a state of affairs now generalized to the national economy, so that the national stock exchange itself becomes the crucial barometer of a country's prosperity and well-being. This point is well made in Dore 2000: 10.

42. This regime has been characterized in a number of very recent works by members of the Ecole Régulation. See for instance Aglietta 1998a, 1998b, 2000. See also Boyer 2000. Use of the writings of the Ecole Régulation in this context does not imply support of some of its other theoretical and practical positions. Negri has criticized the Ecole Régulation for the 'economic objectivism' implicit in its recourse to a 'process without a subject' when conceptualizing economic processes (Negri 1996c: 178–9). There is truth in this charge since the Ecole Régulation does emphasize overwhelmingly the role of institutional change, the development of productive systems, and the social relations of production in its accounting of economic change and development, with less emphasis being placed on the active role of the proletariat. However, Aglietta's plea (1998a) for a revived economic and social citizenship as the way to resist the excesses of economic neoliberalism can be moved in a direction which ascribes a more strategically activist role to the proletariat (not that Aglietta himself would be comfortable with Negri's 'workerist Marxism').

43. Aglietta 2000: 148 and 150. On the 'short termism' of Anglo-Saxon capitalist corporations, see Singh 2000.

44. On this, see Brenner 2000.

45. In what follows I adhere closely to the overviews presented in Germain 1997, Webb 1995, and Harmes 1998. Harmes is especially good on the shifts that have taken place in investment allocation criteria with the emergence of the new financial markets.

46. Here it is important to note that the rise of instability is not necessarily to be equated with a scaling-down of international coordination. As Webb (1995: 252ff.) points out, if anything there has been more coordination in the international economy since the 1970s, though it has not managed to provide the levels of stability previously reached.

47. There is a good account of this development in Helleiner 1994, which stresses the preeminent role of the state in fostering the integration and deregulation of markets, and in Goodman and Pauly 1993, who use a more dialectical approach which sees government policy leading to increased integration and mobility, and this new situation then leading private agents to press for even more deregulation.

48. As Webb puts it, 'governments have preferred to take their chances with unpredictable burdens imposed by private markets responding to national policy differences, rather than coordinate in order to reduce the likelihood and magnitude of future international market pressures' (1995: 259–60).

49. See Sinai 2001: 15, who takes the $50 billion figure from the *Wall Street Journal Europe*, October 17, 2000.

50. The problem with Negri's position, in my view, is that he has not placed enough emphasis on the primacy of the equity-based growth regime: if anything, as we have seen, the weight of significance in his model is on the knowledge-based, information/communication technologies, and competition-led regimes, with only a glance being directed at financialization and its impact.

51. In fact labor and the holders of fixed assets are disproportionately subject to tax burdens since they lack the mobility that is at the disposal of possessors of financial

assets. It should be noted that the ability to use credit/money to synchronize the circuits of production and consumption is precisely what allows the United States to do what no other country can do, viz. enjoy a comparatively high growth rate while having a negative savings rate and chronic external trade deficits. Basically, the United States is able to disconnect investment and savings, and to use income derived from financial-asset holdings to subsidize investment and consumption. On this disconnection, see Brenner 2000.

52. US Department of Commerce, *Statistical Abstract of the United States: 1997*, table 646, cited in Zweig 2000: 44.

53. It is precisely an outcome of the supremacy of the equity-based growth regime that struggles over the distribution of productivity gains and profits between the different elements of the regime of accumulation (labor and capital) have become more important than the production of profit itself. On this, see Weeks 1999: 62.

54. Thus, in 1994, the GNP per capita in Rwanda and Mozambique was $80 and $90 respectively, and in the US $25,800, Japan $34,630, and Switzerland $37,930. Average life expectancy at birth in Mozambique was 46 years (no figures were available for Rwanda), in the USA 77 years, Switzerland 78 years, and Japan 79 years. See World Bank 1996: 188–9.

55. These points are made in Singh 1992, from whom these figures are taken. Singh also notes that virtually throughout the 1980s, a decade of economic recession, the Latin American and African countries made net resource transfers to the developed countries, rather than vice versa: in 1984–85 alone the Latin American and African countries transferred $40 billion and $5 billion respectively to the developed nations (1992: 104ff.).

56. See Taylor 1995. Taylor has analyzed a number of results from the adoption of the prescriptions enshrined in the Washington Consensus that underpins structural adjustment programs, and judges that they have only been minimally successful as a reform package, tending to provide a combination of 'high interest rates, stagflation, deregulation and financial crashes'. This leads him to suggest that LDCs would be better off not espousing capital markets and opting instead for state-provided credit channeled through development banks or made available directly by the government. Taylor concludes that 'the Bretton Woods institutions . . . remain impervious to the fact that the invisible hand plus a minimal government (especially in its fiscal, regulatory and investment roles) do *not* necessarily act together to support sustainable economic growth' (1995: 96, emphasis in original).

57. On the avoidance of recompradorization, see Amin 1990a: 160.

58. For Amin's advocacy of these, see Amin 1999b.

59. Here I agree with Amin that the LDCs need strong states precisely in order to counter the comprador-centered alliances in these countries, which align themselves with capitalism's globalized new world order: only a strong and therefore reconstituted state is able to marshal the economic, political, cultural, and military power needed to resist this order and the comprador-centered alliances that support it in the LDCs. See Amin 1997: 150.

Bibliography

A (1977) 'Viva la confusione!', *A rivista anarchica* 7/7, October.

Acerenza, E. et al. (1977) *Operai e teoria* (Milan: Serostampa).

Aglietta, M. (1979) *A Theory of Capitalist Regulation: The US Experience* (London: New Left Books).

Aglietta, M. (1998a) 'Capitalism at the Turn of the Century: Regulation Theory and the Challenge of Social Change', *New Left Review*, First Series/232, 41–90.

Aglietta, M. (1998b) 'Le capitalisme de demain', *Notes de la Fondation Saint-Simon* 101, November.

Aglietta, M. (2000) 'Shareholder Value and Corporate Governance: Some Tricky Questions', *Economy and Society* 29, 146–59.

Alejos García, J. (1994) *Mosjäntel. Etnografía del discurso agrarista entre ch'oles de Chiapas* (Mexico City: Universidad Autónoma de México).

Alejos García, J. (1999) *Ch'ol/Kaxlan: Identidades étnicas y conflicto agrario en el norte de Chiapas, 1914–1940* (Mexico City: Universidad Nacional Autónoma de México).

Alquati, R. (1975) *Sulla FIAT e altri scritti* (Milan: Feltrinelli).

Althusser, L. (1969) 'Marxism and Humanism', in *For Marx*, trans. B. Brewster (London: Penguin).

Althusser, L. (1971) *Lenin and Philosophy*, trans. B. Brewster (New York: Monthly Review).

Althusser, L. (1999) *Machiavelli and Us*, ed. F. Matheron, trans. G. Elliot (London: Verso).

Amin, S. (1990a) *Delinking: Towards a Polycentric World*, trans. M. Wolfers (London: Zed Books).

Amin, S. (1990b) *Maldevelopment: Anatomy of a Global Failure*, trans. M. Wolfers (London: Zed Books).

Amin, S. (1994) *Re-Reading the Postwar Period: An Intellectual Itinerary*, trans. M. Wolfers (New York: Monthly Review Press).

Amin, S. (1997) *Capitalism in the Age of Globalization*, various translators (London: Zed Books).

Amin, S. (1999a) 'For a Progressive and Democratic New World Order', in F. Adams, S.D. Gupta, and K. Mengisteab (eds) *Globalization and the Dilemmas of the State in the South* (London: Macmillan), 17–32.

Amin, S. (1999b) 'Regionalization in Response to Polarizing Globalization', in B. Hettne, A. Inotai, and O. Sunkel (eds) *Globalism and the New Regionalism: Vol. 1* (New York: St. Martin's Press), 54–84.

Amin, S. (2000) 'Conditions for Re-launching Development', in K. McRobbie and K. Polanyi (eds) *Karl Polanyi: The Contemporary Significance of 'The Great Transformation'* (New York: Black Rose Books), 73–84.

Andrew, X. (1999) 'Give Up Activism', in Reclaim The Streets (eds) *Reflections on J18* <http://www.infoshop.org/octo/j18_reflections.html>, accessed December 1, 2002.

Anonymous (1978a) 'Vicenza: Il programma comunista si verifica dentro l'illegalità di massa e la crescita del contropotere proletario', *Rosso* 23–24, January.

Anonymous (1978b) 'Padova—massificare l'illegalità politica di massa', *Rosso* 23–24, January.

Antagonism (2001) 'Intervention→Communication→Participation' <http://www.geocities.com/antagonism1/misc/intervention.html>, accessed December 7, 2003.

Aronowitz, S. (1985) 'Why Work?', *Social Text* 12, 19–42.

Aronowitz, S., and J. Cutler (eds) (1998) *Post-Work: The Wages of Cybernation* (New York: Routledge).

Aronowitz, S., and W. DiFazio (1994) *The Jobless Future: Sci-Tech and the Dogma of Work* (Minneapolis: University of Minnesota Press).

Aronowitz, S., D. Esposito, W. DiFazio, and M. Yard (1998) 'The Post-Work Manifesto', in Aronowitz and Cutler 1998: 31–80.

Arquilla, J., and D. Ronfeldt (1993) 'Cyberwar Is Coming!', *Comparative Strategy* 12.2: 141–65.

Arsenale Sherwood (1997) 'Autonomia organizzazione: "Constitutio libertatis" ', January 20 <http://www.ecn.org/pad/anni70/constit.htm>, accessed June 27, 1997.

Assemblea Autonoma di Porto Marghera (1972) 'Assemblea Autonoma di Porto Marghera', now in Comitati Autonomi Operai 1976a.

Associazione Ya Basta (n.d.) Documents online at <www.yabasta.it>, accessed January 13, 2004.

A/traverso (1977a) 'Per l'autonomia', *A/traverso*, March, now in Castellano 1980a.

A/traverso (1977b) 'La rete e il nodo: dopo la militanza', *A/traverso*, February.

A/traverso (1977c) 'Assemblea di Roma: sconfiggere il minoritarismo preparare subito la rivoluzione', *Finalmente il cielo è caduto sulla terra: la rivoluzione*, March 12.

Avilés, J. (2000) 'Marcos agradece a italianos la entrega de una turbina', *La Jornada* 4, December.

Baldi, G. (1985) 'Negri Beyond Marx', *Midnight Notes* 8.

Balakrishnan, G. (ed.) (2003) *Debating Empire* (London: Verso).

Balestrini, N. (1989) *The Unseen*, trans. L. Heron (London: Verso).

Balestrini, N. (2001) *La violenza illustrata, seguita da Blackout* (Rome: DeriveApprodi).

Balestrini, N., and P. Moroni (eds) (1997) *L'Orda d'oro 1968–1977*, new edition (Milan: Fetrinelli).

Balibar, E. (1999) 'Conjectures and Conjunctures: Interview with Peter Osborne', *Radical Philosophy*, 97: 30–41.

Barbrook, R. (n.d.) 'Cyber-Communism: how the Americans are superseding capitalism in cyberspace', Hypermedia Research Centre, University of Westminster, London. Available online at <www.hrc.wmin.ac.uk/theory-cybercommunism.html>.

Barbrook, R. (2001) 'The Napsterization of Everything' presented at the conference 'Class Composition of Cognitive Capitalism', February, Paris.

Bartleby the Scrivener (1985) 'Marx Beyond Midnight', *Midnight Notes* 8.

Bartra, A. (1972) *Regeneración 1900–1918. La corriente más radical de la revolución de 1910 a través de su periódico de combate* (Mexico City: Hadise).

Bartra, A. (1985) *Los herederos de Zapata. Movimientos campesinos posrevolucionarios en México. 1920–1980* (Mexico City: Ediciones Era).

Baudrillard, J. (1975) *The Mirror of Production*, trans. M. Poster (St. Louis: Telos Press).

BBC News (2001) <http://news.bbc.co.uk/hi/english/business/newsid_1145000/1145333.stm>, accessed January 30, 2001.

Benvegnù, P. (2001) 'Intervista a Paolo Benvegnù', September 13, from the CD-ROM accompanying Borio, Pozzi, and Roggero 2002.

Berardi, F. (2000) 'Intervista a Franco "Bifo" Berardi', November 19, from the CD-ROM accompanying Borio, Pozzi, and Roggero 2002.

Bernocchi, P. (1997) *Dal '77 in poi* (Rome: Erre emme edizioni).

Bernocchi, P. et al. (1979) *Movimento settantasette: storia di una lotta* (Turin: Rosenberg & Sellier).

Bhaduri, A. (1998) 'Implications of Globalization for Macroeconomic Theory and Policy in Developing Countries', in D. Baker, G. Epstein, and R. Pollin (eds) *Globalization and Progressive Economic Policy* (Cambridge: Cambridge University Press), 149–58.

Bianchi, S. (2001) 'Intervista a Sergio Bianchi', October 21, from the CD-ROM accompanying Borio, Pozzi, and Roggero 2002.

Bierhorst, J. (trans.) (1985) *Cantares Mexicanos*, with an introduction by J. Bierhorst (Stanford: Stanford University Press [ca. 1560]).

Bifo [F. Berardi]. (1980) 'Anatomy of Autonomy', *Semiotext(e)*, special issue on 'Autonomia: Post-Political Politics,' 3/3, 148–70.

Bifo and Gomma (eds) (2002) *Alice è il diavolo. Storia di una radio sovversiva* (Milan: ShaKe).

Bihr, A. (1995) *Dall' 'assalto al cielo' all' 'alternativa'* (Pisa: BFS).

Blackburn, R. (2002) *Banking on Death, or Investing in Life: The History and Future of Pensions* (London: Verso).

Bloch, E. (1986) *The Principle of Hope*, trans. N. Plaice, S. Plaice, and P. Knight (Oxford: Basil Blackwell).

Bocca, G. (1980) *Il caso 7 aprile: Toni Negri e la grande inquisizione* (Milan: Feltrinelli).

Bocca, G. (1985) *Noi terroristi* (Milan: Garzanti).

Bologna, S. (1976a) ' "Proletari e Stato" di Antonio Negri: una recensione', *Primo Maggio* 7.

Bologna, S. (1977a) 'The Tribe of Moles', *Semiotext(e)* 3/3 (1980).

Bologna, S. (1977b) 'An Overview', now in Red Notes (eds) (1978) *Italy 1977–78: Living with an Earthquake*, second edition (London: Red Notes).

Bologna, S. (1977c) 'What is "The Movement"?', now in Red Notes (eds) (1978) *Italy 1977–78: Living with an Earthquake*, second edition (London: Red Notes).

Bologna, S. (1978a) 'Amo il rosso e il nero, odio il rosa e il viola', in S. Bologna (ed.) *La tribù delle talpe* (Milan: Feltrinelli).

Bologna, S. (1978b) 'Editoriale', *Primo Maggio* 12, Winter.

Bologna, S. (1979) ' "Primo Maggio": oltre il Movimento', *Primo Maggio* 13, Autumn.

Bologna, S. (1980) 'Composizione di classe e sistema politico', in R. Lauricella et al. (eds) (1981) *Crisi delle politiche e politiche nella crisi* (Naples: Libreria L'Ateneo di G. Pronti).

Bologna, S. (1981) 'Per una "società degli storici militanti" ', in S. Bologna et al. (eds) *Dieci interventi sulla storia sociale* (Turin: Rosenberg & Sellier).

Bologna, S. (2001) 'Intervista a Sergio Bologna', February 21, from the CD-ROM accompanying Borio, Pozzi, and Roggero 2002.

Borio, G. (2001) 'Intervista a Guido Borio', October 27, from the CD-ROM accompanying Borio, Pozzi, and Roggero 2002.

Borio, G., F. Pozzi, and G. Roggero (2002) *Futuro anteriore. Dai 'Quaderni Rossi' ai movimenti globali: ricchezze e limiti dell'operaismo italiano* (Rome: Derive Approdi). Includes a CD-ROM of interviews.

Bosma, J. et al. (eds) (2000) *Readme! Filtered By Nettime: ASCII Culture and the Revenge of Knowledge* (New York: Autonomedia).

Boutmy, E. (1981) *Studies in Constitutional Law: France, England, United States*, trans. E.M. Picey (London and New York: Macmillan).

Boyer, R. (2000) 'Is a Finance-led Growth Régime a Viable Alternative to Fordism? A Preliminary Analysis', *Economy and Society* 29, 111–45.

Brenner, R. (1998) *The Economics of Global Turbulence*, a special issue of *New Left Review*, First Series/229.

Brenner, R. (2000) 'The Boom and the Bubble', *New Left Review*, Second Series/6, 5–43.

Brenner, R., and M. Glick (1991) 'The Regulation Approach: Theory and History' in *New Left Review*, First series/188, 45–120.

Buck-Morss, S. (2000) 'Hegel and Haiti', *Critical Inquiry* 26/4, 821–65, Summer.

Butler, J., E. Laclau, and S. Žižek (2000) *Contingency, Hegemony, Universality: Contemporary Dialogues on the Left* (London, Verso).

Caffentzis, C.G. (1998) 'The End of Work or the Renaissance of Slavery? A Critique of Rifkin and Negri', presented at the 'Globalization from Below' conference, Duke University, February 6, 1998. Available online at <http://lists.village.virginia.edu/ ~spoons/global/Papers/caffentzis>.

Caminiti, L. (1997) 'L'autonomia meridionale: territorio di ombre, solarità delle lotte', in N. Balestrini and Moroni 1997.

Cantarow, E. (1972) 'Women's Liberation and Workers' Autonomy in Turin and Milan I', *Liberation*, October.

Cantarow, E. (1973) 'Women's Liberation and Workers' Autonomy in Turin and Milan II', *Liberation*, June.

Carpentier, A. (1967) *El reino de este mundo* (Barcelona: Seix Barral).

Carsen, L. (2000) 'Autonomía indígena y usos y costumbres: la innovación de la tradición', *Chiapas* 7 <http://www.ezln.org.revistachiapas/ch7carlsen.html>, accessed January 1, 2004.

Carson, J., and D. Brooks (2000) 'Pozol y biopiratería', *La Jornada*, October 7.

Castellano, L. (ed.) (1980a) *Aut. Op. La storia e i documenti: da Potere operaio all'Autonomia organizzata* (Rome: Savelli).

Castellano, L. (1980b) 'Living with Guerilla Warfare', *Semiotext(e)* 3/3.

Castellano, L. (1980c) 'Introduzione', in Castellano 1980a.

Castells, M. (1996) *The Rise of the Network Society* (Oxford: Blackwell).

Castells, M., and Y. Aoyama (1994) 'Paths towards the Informational Society: Employment Structure in G-7 Countries, 1920–90', *International Labour Review* 133, 5–33.

Cazzullo, A. (1998) *I ragazzi che volevano fare la rivoluzione. 1968–1978: storia di Lotta continua* (Milan: Mondadori).

Ceceña, A.E. (2000) 'La resistencia como espacio de construcción del nuevo mundo', *Chiapas* 7 <http://www.ezln.org/revistachiapas/ch7cecena.html>, accessed January 1, 2004.

Centro de Derechos Humanos Fray Bartolomé de las Casas (1998) 'La legalidad de la injusticia', online at <www.laneta.apc.org/cdhbcasas>, accessed January 13, 2004.

Centro de Derechos Humanos Fray Bartolomé de las Casas (1999) 'La disputa por la legitimidad. Aniversario de los ataques a los municipios libres' (includes a reproduction of the mural), at <www.laneta.apc.org/cdhbcasas>, accessed January 13, 2004.

Centro di Iniziativa Comunista Padovana (n.d.) 'L'Autonomia dopo Bologna', now in S. Acquaviva (ed.) (1979) *Terrorismo e guerriglia in Italia: la cultura della violenza* (Rome: Città Nuova Editrice).

Cevro-Vukovic, E. (1976) *Vivere a sinistra* (Rome: Arcana editore).

Chakrabarty, D. (1997) 'The Time of History and the Times of the Gods', in L. Lowe and D. Lloyd (eds) *The Politics of Culture in the Shadow of Capital* (Durham: Duke University Press), 35–60.

Chakrabarty, D. (2000) *Provincializing Europe: Postcolonial Thought and Historical Difference* (Princeton: Princeton University Press).

Ciaccio, T. (1982) 'Intervista a Teresa Ciaccio, operaia all Policlinico di Roma (3 novembre 1982)' <http://www.xs4all.nl/~welschen/Archief/ciaccio.html>, accessed September 2, 2002.

Clark, G.L. (2000) *Pension Fund Capitalism* (Oxford: Oxford University Press).

'Class Composition of Cognitive Capitalism' ('free university' seminars and related discussions), online at <http://www.geocities.com/CognitiveCapitalism/>.

Cleaver, H. (1979) *Reading Capital Politically* (Brighton: Harvester).

Cleaver, H. (1992) 'The Inversion of Class Perspective in Marxian Theory: From Valorisation to Self-Valorisation', in W. Bonefeld, R. Gunn, and K. Psychopedis (eds) *Open Marxism, Vol. II: Theory and Practice* (London: Pluto Press), 106–44.

Cleaver, H. (1994) 'The Chiapas Uprising', *Studies in Political Economy* 44.

Cleaver, H. (1999) 'Computer-Linked Social Movements and the Global Threat to Capitalism,' available at <http://www.eco.utexas.edu/faculty/Cleaver/hmchtmlpapers.html>.

Cleaver, H. (2000a) *Reading Capital Politically*, second edition (Leeds and Edinburgh: AK Press and Anti/Theses).

Cleaver, H. (2000b) 'The Virtual and Real Chiapas Support Network', available at <http://www.eco.utexas.edu/Homepages/Faculty/Cleaver/chiapas95.html>.

Collegamenti (1974) 'Organismi autonomi e "area dell'autonomia" ', *Collegamenti* 6, December, now in Martignoni and Morandini 1977.

Collegamenti (1977) 'Editoriale: l'organizzazione diretta degli operai dentro la crisi', *Collegamenti* 1, March.

Collegamenti (1978) 'Note sull'esperienza di lotta armata in Italia', *Collegamenti* 3–4, May.

Collegamenti (1979) 'Editoriale', *Collegamenti* 6–7, May.

Collettivi Politici Operai (1976a) 'Per una programma di massa', *Rosso* 3/8, April 24.

Collettivi Politici Operai (1976b) 'Compiti di fase dell'autonomia organizzata', *Rosso* 3/8, April 24.

Collettivi Politici Operai (1976c) 'Documento Politico della Segretaria dei Collettivi politici di Milano', *Rosso* 7, March 13, now in Martignoni and Morandini 1977.

Collettivi Politici Veneti (1979) 'Appunti per un discorso di fase/linea politica e prassi di un progetto comunista/sul che fare: bozza di ipotesi', *Autonomia* 14, May 1.

Collettivo editoriale 10/16 (eds) (1979) *1923 Il processo ai comunisti italiani. 1979 Il 'processo' all'autonomia operaia* (Milan: Collettivo editoriale 10/16).

Collettivo editoriale di *Autonomia* (1979) 'Per il comunismo', *Autonomia* 14, May 1.

Collettivo Politico del Berchet (1974) 'Gruppi e organismi studenteschi', *Rosso* 11, June.

Comisión Nacional de Intermediación (CONAI) (1999), *San Andrés. Marco jurídico y normativo del diálogo y negociación* (Mexico City: Serie 'Senderos de Paz', Cuaderno No. 2).

Comitati Autonomi Operai (1974) 'Autonomia operaia organizzata', *Rivolta di classe,* June 28, now in Martignoni and Morandini 1977.

Comitati Autonomi Operai (eds) (1976a) *Autonomia Operaia* (Rome: Savelli).

Comitati Autonomi Operai (1976b) 'Realismo della prassi rivoluzionaria', *Rivolta di classe* 3/1, October 15, now in Recupero 1978.

Comitati Autonomi Operai (1977) 'Una forza che vi seppellirà', *Rivolta di classe,* May, now in Castellano 1980a.

Comitati Autonomi Operai (1978a) 'BR e lotta armata', *I Volsci* 3, April.

Comitati Autonomi Operai (1978b) 'Un pò di massa, un pò violento, un pò illegale ed anche un poco armato', *I Volsci* 1, February.

Comitati Autonomi Operai (1978c) 'Per il Movimento dell'Autonomia Operaia', now at <http://www.tmcrew.org/memoria/mao/index.htm>, accessed January 26, 2001.

Comitati Autonomi Operai (1978d) 'Autonomia non è star sopra un albero', *I Volsci* 1, February.

Comitati Autonomi Operai (1978e) 'No alla clandestinità, nè per amore, nè per forza', *I Volsci* 3, April.

Comitati Autonomi Operai (1978f) 'Il '68 compie dieci anni', *I Volsci* 3, April.

Comitati Autonomi Operai (1979a) 'Parole d'ordine magnifiche, attraenti, inebrianti, che non hanno nessun fondamento', *I Volsci* 8, April.

Comitati Autonomi Operai (1979b) 'Teorema sull'Autonomia Operaia', *I Volsci* 9, July.

Comitati Autonomi Operai (1979c) 'Tra le parole e I fatti: analisi e "ceto politico" ', *I Volsci* 9, July.

Comitati Autonomi Operai (1979d) 'L'impossibile Autonomia di Metropoli', *I Volsci* 9, July.

Comitati Autonomi Operai (1980a) '930', *I Volsci* 10, March, now online at <http://www.zzz.it/~ago/autonomia/ivolsci/10/9e30.htm>, accessed May 27, 2001.

Comitati Autonomi Operai (1980b) '1530', *I Volsci* 10, March, now online at <http://www.zzz.it/~ago/autonomia/ivolsci/10/15e30.htm>, accessed May 27, 2001.

Comitati Comunisti (1976) 'Resta in vigore il decreto operaio', *Senza Tregua,* now in Castellano 1980a.

Comitati Comunisti (1977a) 'Verso un processo superiore di organizzazione comunista', *Chiamiamo comunismo* 1, March 12.

Comitati Comunisti (1977b) 'Compagni', *Chiamiamo comunismo* 1, March 12.

Comitati Comunisti (1977c) 'Compagni', *Senza Tregua,* March, now in Recupero 1978.

Comitati Comunisti Rivoluzionari (1977) *Potere Operaio per il comunismo* 1.

Comitati Comunisti Rivoluzionari (1978), 'Che fare', April 25, now in Castellano 1980a.

Comitato 7 aprile e collegio di difesa (eds) (1979) *Processo all'Autonomia* (Cosenza: Lerici).

Comitato Politico ENEL e Collettivo Policlinico (1974) 'Centralizzazione e responsabilità delle avanguardie', *Rosso* 11.

Comité Clandestino Revolucionario Indígena—Comandancia General (CCRI-CG) (1995) Communiqué of October 19, 1995, posted at <www.ezln.org>, <www.fzln. org>, and <www.ezlnaldf.org>, accessed January 1, 2004.

Convention No. 169 on Indigenous Peoples (1989), available at the web site of the International Labour Organization <www.ilo.org.htm>, consulted January 13, 2004.

Coronil, F. (1997) *The Magical State: Nature, Money, and Modernity in Venezuela* (Chicago: University of Chicago Press).

Critical Art Ensemble (2001) *Digital Resistance: Explorations in Tactical Media* (New York: Autonomedia).

Cuninghame, P. (2001) 'For an Analysis of Autonomia: An Interview with Sergio Bologna', *Left History* 7/2, Fall.

Cuninghame, P. (2002a) 'Autonomia: A Movement of Refusal. Social Movements and Social Conflict in Italy in the 1970s', doctoral dissertation, School of Health and Social Sciences, Middlesex University.

Cuninghame, P. (2002b) 'Autonomia: A Movement of Refusal: Social Movements and Social Conflict in Italy in the 1970s', paper presented at the Eighth International Conference on Alternative Futures and Popular Protest, Manchester Metropolitan University, April.

Dalla Costa, M., and S. James (1972) *The Power of Women and the Subversion of the Community* (Bristol: Falling Wall Press).

Dalmaviva, M., L. Ferrari Bravo, T. Negri, O. Scalzone, E. Vesce, and L. Zagato (1979) 'Dal carcere Rebibbia G8', *Autonomia* 15, May 19.

de Brunhoff, S. (1990) 'Fictitious Capital', in J. Eatwell, M. Milgate, and P. Newman (eds) *The New Palgrave Marxian Economics* (New York: Norton), 186–7.

de Certeau, M. (1988) *The Writing of History*, trans. T. Conley (New York: Columbia University Press).

de la Campa, R. (1999) *Latin Americanism* (Minneapolis: University of Minnesota Press).

de Sigüenza y Góngora, C. (1984) *Alboroto y motín de los indios de México. Seis obras* (Caracas: Biblioteca Ayacucho).

Del Bello, C. (ed.) (1997) *Una sparatoria tranquilla. Per una storia orale del '77* (Rome: Odradek).

Del Re, A. (1979) *Oltre il lavoro domestico: Il lavoro delle donne tra produzione e riproduzione* (Milan: Feltrinelli).

Del Re, A. (2000) 'Intervista a Alisa Del Re', July 26, from the CD-ROM accompanying Borio, Pozzi, and Roggero 2002.

Deleuze, G. (1983) *Nietzsche and Philosophy*, trans. H. Tomlinson (New York: Columbia University Press).

Deleuze, G., and F. Guattari (1983) *Anti-Oedipus: Capitalism and Schizophrenia*, trans. M. Seem et al. (New York: Viking).

Deleuze, G., and F. Guattari (1987) *A Thousand Plateaus: Capitalism and Schizophrenia*, trans. B. Massumi (London: Athlone).

Dendena, F. (2000) 'Intervista a Ferruccio Dendena', January 10, from the CD-ROM accompanying Borio, Pozzi, and Roggero 2002.

Derrida, J. (1994) *Specters of Marx: The State of the Debt, the Work of Mourning, and the new International*, trans. P. Kamuf (New York: Routledge).

Derrida, J. (1997) *Politics of Friendship*, trans. G. Collins (London: Verso).

Dore, R. (2000) *Stock Market Capitalism: Welfare Capitalism (Japan and Germany versus the Anglo-Saxons)* (Oxford: Oxford University Press).

Doubt, K. (2000) 'Feminism and Rape as a Transgression of Species Being', in *Sociology After Bosnia and Kosovo* (Oxford: Rowan and Littlefield).

Durán, D. (1984) *Historia de la Nueva España e islas de Tierra Firme*, 2 vols., ed. A.M. Garibay (Mexico City: Editorial Porrúa [ca. 1581]).

Dyer-Witheford, N. (1999) *Cyber-Marx: Cycles and Circuits of Struggle in High-Technology Capitalism* (Urbana and Chicago: University of Illinois Press).

Dyer-Witheford, N. (2002a) 'E-Capital and the Many-Headed Hydra', in G. Elmer (ed.) *Critical Perspectives on the Internet* (Lanham: Rowman and Littlefield), 129–164.

Dyer-Witheford, N. (2002b) 'Sur La Contestation du Capital Cognitif: Composition de Classes de L'Industrie des Jeux Vidéo et Sur Ordinateur', *Multitudes* 10, 53–64.

Eatwell, J., and L. Taylor (2000) *Global Finance at Risk: The Case for International Regulation* (New York: New Press).

Elliot, G. (1998) 'Ghostlier demarcations: On the posthumous edition of Althusser's writings', *Radical Philosophy* 90, 20–32.

Elson, D. 1979. 'The Value Theory of Labour', in D. Elson (ed.) *Value: The Representation of Labour in Capitalism* (Atlantic Highlands, N.J.: Humanities Press Inc.) 115–80.

Emery, E. (1999) Occasional paper No. 7, May 29 <http://www.emery.archive.mcmail. com/public_html/occas/occas7.html>.

EZLN (1994) *EZLN: Documentos y comunicados, 1 de enero/8 de agosto de 1994*, prologue by A. G. de León and 'crónica' by C. Monsiváis and E. Poniatowska (Mexico City: Editorial Era).

EZLN (1995) *EZLN. Documentos y Comunicados*, vol. 2, prologue by A.G. de León and 'crónica' by C. Monsiváis (Mexico City: Ediciones Era).

EZLN (n.d.) Documents available on websites <www.ezln.org>, <www.fzln.org>, and <www.ezlnaldf.org>.

Farnetti, P., and P. Moroni (1984) 'Collettivo Autonomo Barona: appunti per una storia impossibile', *Primo Maggio* 21, Spring.

Ferrari Bravo, L. (1984) 'Al Dott. Giovanni Palombarini giudice istruttore presso il tribunale di Padova', now in L. Ferrari Bravo (2001) *Dal fordismo alla globalizzazione. Cristalli di tempo politico* (Rome: Manifestolibri).

Fischer, L. (1964) *The Life of Lenin* (New York: Harper & Row).

Fondazione Bruno Piciacchia e Libreria Calusca di Padova (1997) 'I collettivi politici veneti', in Balestrini and Moroni 1997.

Formenti, C. (1999) 'Intervista a Carlo Formenti', December 13, from the CD-ROM accompanying Borio, Pozzi, and Roggero 2002.

Foucault, M. (1972) *The Archaeology of Knowledge*, trans. A.M. Sheridan-Smith (New York: Pantheon).

Foucault, M. (1973) *The Order of Things* (New York: Vintage Books).

Foucault, M. (1979) *Discipline and Punish: The Birth of the Prison*, trans. A. Sheridan (New York: Vintage).

Foucault, M. (1980a) *The History of Sexuality*, vol. 1, trans. R. Hurley (New York: Vintage).

Foucault, M. (1980b) *Power/Knowledge: Selected Interviews and Other Writings 1972–1977*, ed. C. Gordon (New York: Pantheon).

Foucault, M. (1980c) 'Truth and Power', in Foucault 1980b.

Frears, S. (2003) *Dirty Pretty Things* (film).

Fromm, E. (1961) *Marx's Concept of Man* (New York: Frederick Ungar Publishing).

Gaj, U. (1980) 'L'operaio "sociale", la frantumazione, il militarismo. Che prospettive ha l'autonomia milanese?', *Quotidiano dei lavoratori*, October 24.

Germain, R. (1997) *The International Organization of Credit: States and Finance in the World-Economy* (Cambridge: Cambridge University Press).

Ginsborg, P. (1990) *A History of Contemporary Italy: Society and Politics 1943–1989* (New York: Penguin).

Giovannetti, G. (1980) 'Il movimento e le leggi della guerra', *Collegamenti* 8, June.

Golding, P. (1996) 'World Wide Wedge: Division and Contradiction in the Global Information Infrastructure', *Monthly Review* 48/3.

Goodman, J., and L. Pauly (1993) 'The Obsolescence of Capital Controls? Economic Management in an Age of Global Markets', *World Politics* 46, 50–82.

Gorz, A. (1982) *Farewell to the Working Class* (London: Pluto).

Griffith-Jones, S. (1998) *Global Capital Flows: Should They be Regulated?* (New York: St. Martin's Press).

Griffith-Jones, S., and B. Stallings (1995) 'New global financial trends: implications for development', in B. Stallings (ed.) *Global Change, Regional Response: The New International Context of Development* (Cambridge: Cambridge University Press), 143–73.

Gruzinski, S. (1999) *La pensée métisse* (Paris: Fayard).

Guardian Weekly (1997), November 9.

Guattari, F., and A. Negri (1990) *Communists Like Us: New Spaces of Liberty, New Lines of Alliance*, trans. M. Ryan (New York: Semiotext(e)).

Guha, R. (1999) *Elementary Aspects of Peasant Insurgency* (Durham: Duke University Press; originally published 1983).

Hamacher, W. (1997) 'One 2 Many Multiculturalism' in H. de Vries and S. Weber (eds) *Violence, Identity, and Self-determination* (Stanford: Stanford University Press), 284–325.

Haraway, D. (1985) 'A Manifesto for Cyborgs: Science, Technology, and Socialist Feminism in the 1980s', *Socialist Review* 80: 65–107.

Hardt, M. (1993) *Gilles Deleuze: An Apprenticeship in Philosophy* (Minneapolis: University of Minnesota Press).

Hardt, M., and A. Negri (1994) *Labor of Dionysus: A Critique of the State-Form* (Minneapolis: University of Minnesota Press).

Hardt, M., and A. Negri. (2000) *Empire* (Cambridge: Harvard University Press).

Harmes, A. (1998) 'Institutional Investors and the Reproduction of Neoliberalism', *Review of International Political Economy* 5, 92–121.

Harvey, D. (1989) *The Condition of Postmodernity: An Enquiry Into the Origins of Cultural Change* (Oxford: Blackwell).

Harvey, D. (1999) *The Limits to Capital* (London: Verso).

Harvey, D. (2000) *Spaces of Hope* (Edinburgh: Edinburgh University Press).

Hegel, G.W.F. (1967) *The Phenomenology of Mind*, trans. J.B. Baillie (New York: Harper Torchbooks).

Helleiner, E. (1994) *States and the Reemergence of Global Finance: From Bretton Woods to the 1990s* (Ithaca, N.Y.: Cornell University Press).

Hellman, J. (1999) 'Real and Virtual Chiapas: Magic Realism and the Left', in L. Panitch and C. Leys (eds) *Socialist Register 2000: Necessary and Unnecessary Utopias* (London: Merlin). Also on-line at <http://www.yorku.ca/socreg>.

Henwood, D. (1995) 'Info Fetishism', in J. Brook and I. Boal (eds) *Resisting the Virtual Life: The Culture and Politics of Information* (San Francisco: City Lights) 163–72.

Henwood, D. (1997a) *Wall Street* (London: Verso).

Henwood, D. (1997b) 'Talking about Work', *Monthly Review* 49/3, 18–30.

Hermann, E., and R. McChesney (1997) *The Global Media: The New Missionaries of Corporate Capitalism* (London: Cassell).

Hernández Navarro, L., and R. Vera Herrera (eds) (1998) *Acuerdos de San Andrés* (Mexico City: Ediciones Era).

Holloway, J. (2002a) 'Time to Revolt: Reflections on Empire', *The Commoner* <http://www.commoner.org.uk/time_%20to_revolt.htm>, accessed April 19, 2003.

Holloway, J. (2002b) 'Zapatismo and the social sciences', *Capital and Class*, Autumn.

Holloway, J. (2002c) *Change the World Without Taking Power: The Meaning of Revolution Today* (London: Pluto Press).

Holloway, J. (2003) 'Los caracoles: Realismo Mágico y los agujeros en el Ozono', *Revista Memoria* 176 (October).

Insurrezione (n.d.) *Proletari, si voi sapeste . . .* (Milan).

James, C.L.R. (1962) *Black Jacobins: Toussaint L'Ouverture and the San Domingo Revolution*, second edition (New York: Vintage).

James, S. (1986) 'Marx and Feminism', *Third World Book Review* 1/6.

Kant, I. (1996a) 'An Answer to the Question: What is Enlightenment?', in *Immanuel Kant, Practical Philosophy*, trans. M. J. Gregor (Cambridge: Cambridge University Press), 11–22.

Kant, I. (1996b) 'Toward Perpetual Peace: A Philosophical Project', in *Immanuel Kant, Practical Philosophy*, trans. M. J. Gregor (Cambridge: Cambridge University Press), 317–51.

Kelly, K. (1994) *Out of Control: The Rise of Neo-Biological Civilization* (New York: Addison-Wesley).

Kidd, D. (2002) 'Which Would You Rather: Seattle or Porto Alegre?', available at <faculty.menlo.edu/~jhiggins/ourmedia/iamcr2002/papers2002/Kidd.IAMCR2002.pdf>.

Kolakowski, L. (1978) *Main Currents of Marxism: Its Rise, Growth, and Dissolution*, vol. 2, trans. P.S. Falla (Oxford: Clarendon Press).

Lacan, J. (1991) *Seminaire XVII. L'envers de la psychanalyse* (Paris: Seuil).

LaFargue, P. (1898) *The Right to Be Lazy: Being a Refutation of the 'Right to Work' of 1848*, trans. H.E. Lothrop (New York: International Publishing).

Larson, N. (1995) *North by South: On Latin American Literature, Culture and Politics* (Minneapolis: University of Minnesota Press).

Lazzarato, M. (1990a) '"Pas de sous pas de totos!": La greve des ouvriers Peugeot', *Futur Antérieur* 1, 63–76.

Lazzarato, M. (1990b) 'La "Panthère" et la communication', *Futur Antérieur* 2, 54–67.

Lazzarato, M. (1996) 'Immaterial Labor', in Virno and Hardt 1996a, 133–50.

Lazzarato, M., A. Negri, and G.C. Santilli (1990) *La Confection Dans le Quartier du Sentier. Restructuration des Formes d'Emploi et Expansion Dans un Secteur en Crise* (Paris: Rapport MIRE).

Lazzarato, M., and A. Negri (1991) 'Travail Immaterial and Subjectivité', *Futur Antérieur* 6.

Lazzarato, M., and A. Negri (1993) *Le bassin de travail immatériel dans la métropole parisienne: définition, recherches, perspectives* (Paris: Tekne-Logos).

Lebowitz, M.A. (1992) *Beyond Capital: Marx's Political Economy of the Working Class* (New York: St. Martin's Press).

Lenin, V.I. (1932) *State and Revolution* (New York: International Publishers).

Lenin, V.I. (1956) *The Development of Capitalism in Russia* (Moscow: Foreign Languages Publishing).

Lenin, V.I. (1967) *Selected Works*, 3 vols (New York: International Publishers).

Lenin, V.I. (1989) 'The Immediate Tasks of the Soviet Government', in *Lenin's Economic Writings*, ed. M. Desai (Atlantic Highlands, N.J.: Humanities Press International), 221–59.

Leonetti, F. (1976) 'Per l'orientamento del dibatitto leninista e maoista con Autonomia operaia: un altro appunto', *La voce operaia* 291, July; now in Recupero 1978.

Leonetti, F. (1979) 'Per Balestrini, nel silenzio e nella nebbia', *Il Manifesto*, June 7; now in F. Leonetti and E. Rambalidi (eds) (1983) *Il dibattito sul processo dell'autonomia (Aprile 1979–Febbraio 1983)* (Milan: Multhipla edizioni).

Leonetti, F. (2001) *La voce del corvo. Una vita (1940–2001)* (Rome: Derive Approdi).

Léon Portilla, M. (1986) Review of Bierhorst, 'Una nueva interpretación de los Cantares Mexicanos?', *Estudios de Cultura Náhuatl* 18, 385–400.

Léon Portilla, M. (1992) *Literaturas indígenas de México* (Mexico City: Fondo de Cultura Económica).

Léon Portilla, M. (1994) *Quince poetas del mundo náhuatl* (Mexico City: Editorial Diana).

Lerner, G., L. Manconi, and M. Sinibaldi (1978) *Uno strano movimento di strani studenti* (Milan: Feltrinelli).

Levidow, L. (1990) 'Foreclosing the Future', *Science and Culture* 8, 59–79.

Levy, P. (1999) *Collective Intelligence: Mankind's Emerging World in Cyberspace*, trans. R. Bononno (Cambridge, Mass.: Perseus).

Lipietz, A. (1987) *Mirages and Miracles: The Crisis of Global Fordism* (London: Verso).

Lotringer, S., and C. Marazzi (eds) (1980) *Italy: Autonomia—Post-Political Politics* (New York: Semiotext(e)).

Lovink, G. (2002) *Dark Fiber: Tracking Critical Internet Culture* (Cambridge, Mass.: MIT Press).

Ludlow, P. (ed.) (2001) *Crypto Anarchy, Cyberstates and Pirate Utopias* (Cambridge, Mass.: MIT Press).

Lumley, R. (1990) *States of Emergency: Cultures of Revolt in Italy from 1968 to 1978* (London: Verso).

M.U. (1980) 'Padova: un esiguo spazio per l'Autonomia', *Quotidiano dei lavoratori*, November 14.

Magón, R.F. (1972) 'Actividad, actividad, más actividad es lo que reclama el momento', in Bartra 1972.

Mallet, S. (1975) *Essays on the New Working Class* (St. Louis: Telos).

Mandel, E. (1977) Introduction to 'Appendix: Results of the Immediate Process of Production', in K. Marx, *Capital*, vol. 1 (New York: Vintage).

Mangano, A. et al. (1998) *Le riviste degli anni settanta. Gruppi movimenti e conflitti sociali* (Rome: Massari).

Il Manifesto (1971) 'For Communism: Theses of the Il Manifesto Group', *Politics and Society*, August.

Marchand, M. (1988) *The Minitel Saga* (Paris: Larousse).

Marglin, S., and J.B. Schor (eds) (1990) *The Golden Age of Capitalism: Reinterpreting the Postwar Experience* (Oxford: Oxford University Press).

Martignoni, G., and S. Morandini (eds) (1977) *Il diritto all'odio: dentro/fuori/ai bordi dell'area dell'autonomia* (Verona: Bertani).

Martini, L., and O. Scalzone (1997) 'Fenomeni di lotta armata ai bordi e dentro il movimento', in Balestrini and Moroni 1997.

Marx, K. (1852) *The Eighteenth Brumaire of Louis Bonaparte*, now in K. Marx and F. Engels (1979) *Collected Works*, vol. 11 (London: Lawrence & Wishart).

Marx, K. (1964) *The Economic and Philosophical Manuscripts of 1844* (New York: International Publishers).

Marx, K. (1967a) *Capital*, vol. 2 (New York: International Publishers).

Marx, K. (1967b) *Capital*, vol. 3 (New York: International Publishers).

Marx, K. (1973) *Grundrisse: Foundations of the Critique of Political Economy*, trans. M. Nicolaus (New York: Penguin).

Marx, K. (1976) *Capital*, vol. 1, trans. B. Fowkes (New York: Penguin).

Marx, K. (1981) *Capital*, vol. 3, trans. D. Fernbach (London: Penguin Books).

Marx, K. and F. Engels (1948) *The Communist Manifesto* (New York: International Publishers).

Marx, K., and F. Engels (1970) *The German Ideology*, ed. C.J. Arthur (New York: International Publishers).

Mason, T. (1979) 'The Workers' Opposition in Germany', *History Workshop Journal 9*.

McArdle, L., M. Rowlinson, S. Procter, J. Hassard, and P. Forrester (1995) 'Total Quality Management and Participation: Employee Empowerment, or the Enhancement of Exploitation?', in A. Wilkinson and H. Willmott (eds) *Making Quality Critical: New Perspectives on Organizational Change* (London: Routledge) 156–72.

McLellan, D. (1969) 'Marx's View of Unalienated Society', *Review of Politics* 31/4, 459–65.

McLuhan, M. (1964) *Understanding Media: The Extensions of Man* (New York: McGraw Hill).

Mezzarda, S. (2001) 'Intervista a Sandro Mezzarda', April 3, from the CD-ROM accompanying Borio, Pozzi, and Roggero 2002.

Midnight Notes Collective (1992) *Midnight Oil: Work, Energy, War 1973–1992* (Brooklyn N.Y.: Autonomedia).

Mignolo, W.D. (2000) *Global Designs, Local Histories* (Princeton: Princeton University Press).

Miliucci, V. (2000) 'Intervista a Vincenzo Miliucci', July 11, from the CD-ROM accompanying Borio, Pozzi, and Roggero 2002.

Minns, R. (1996) 'The Social Ownership of Capital', *New Left Review*, First Series/219.

Modugno, E. (1981) 'Mattick in Italia', *Unità proletaria* 7/3–4, December.

Le Monde Diplomatique (2000) English edition, December.

Monsiváis, C. (2001) 'Marcos, "gran interlocutor" ', *La Jornada*, January 8.

Montaldi, D. (1971) *Militanti politici di base* (Turin: Einaudi).

Morales Padrón, F. (1979) *Teoría y leyes de la conquista* (Madrid: Ediciones Cultura Hispánica del Centro Iberoamericano de Cooperación).

Moroni, G. (2001) 'Intervista a Giorgio Moroni', July 7, from the CD-ROM accompanying Borio, Pozzi, and Roggero 2002.

Moroni, P. (1994) 'Origine dei centri sociali autogestiti a Milano: Appunti per una storia possibile', in F. Adinolfi et al., *Comunità virtuali: I centri sociali in Italia* (Rome: manifestolibri).

Moss, D. (1989) *The Politics of Left-Wing Violence in Italy, 1969–85* (London: Macmillan).

Moulier, Y. (1989) Introduction to Negri, 1989, 1–46.

Moylan, T. (1986) *Demand the Impossible: Science Fiction and the Utopian Imagination* (New York: Methuen).

Neg/azione (1976) 'Autonomia operaia e autonomia dei proletari', now in Martignoni and Morandini 1977.

Negri, A. (1971) 'Crisis of the Planner-State: Communism and Revolutionary Organization', in *Revolution Retrieved: Writings on Marx, Keynes, Capitalist Crisis and New Social Subjects* (1967–83) (London: Red Notes, 1988), 91–148.

Negri, A. (1973a) 'Partito operaio contro il lavoro', in S. Bologna, P. Carpignano, and A. Negri (1974) *Crisi e organizzazione operaia* (Milan: Feltrinelli).

Negri, A. (1973b) 'Articolazioni organizzative e organizzazione complessiva: il partito di Mirafiori', in S. Bologna, P. Carpignano and A. Negri (1974) *Crisi e organizzazione operaia* (Milan: Feltrinelli).

Negri, A. (1973c) 'Rileggendo Pašukanis: note di discussion', in *La forma stato* (Milan: Feltrinelli, 1977), 161–95.

Negri, A. (1976a) 'Is there a Marxist doctrine of the state?', now in N. Bobbio (1987) *Which Socialism? Marxism, Socialism and Democracy*, trans. R. Griffin (Oxford: Polity).

Negri, A. (1976b) *Proletari e Stato: Per una discussione su autonomia operaia e compromesso storico*, second edition (Milan: Feltrinelli).

Negri, A. (1976c) *La fabbrica della strategia: 33 lezioni su Lenin* (Padua: CLEUP/LibriRossi).

Negri, A. (1977a) *La forma stato. Per la critica dell'economia politica della Costituzione* (Milan: Feltrinelli).

Negri, A. (1977b) *Il dominio e il sabotaggio. Sul metodo marxista della trasformazione sociale* (Milan: Feltrinelli).

Negri, A. (1978) *La Classe Ouvrière Contre L'Etat* (Edition Galilée: Paris).

Negri, A. (1979a) *Dall'operaio massa all'operaio sociale: Intervista sull'operaismo* (Milan: Multhipla edizioni).

Negri, A. (1979b) 'Negri's Interrogation', now in *Semiotext(e)* 3/3, 1980.

Negri, A. (1979c) *Capitalist Domination and Working Class Sabotage*, in *Working Class Autonomy and the Crisis* (London: Red Notes), 92–137.

Negri, A. (1980a) 'Crisis of the Crisis-State', in *Revolution Retrieved: Writings on Marx, Keynes, Capitalist Crisis and New Social Subjects 1967–83* (London: Red Notes), 181–97.

Negri, A. (1980b) *Del Obrero-Masa al Obrero Social* (Barcelona: Editorial Anagrama).

Negri, A. (1988a) 'Archaeology and Project: The Mass Worker and the Social Worker', in *Revolution Retrieved: Writings on Marx, Keynes, Capitalist Crisis and New Social Subjects 1967–83* (London: Red Notes), 199–228.

Negri, A. (1988b) 'Keynes and the Capitalist Theory of the State', in *Revolution Retrieved: Writings on Marx, Keynes, Capitalist Crisis and New Social Subjects 1967–83* (London: Red Notes), 9–42.

Negri, A. (1988c) 'Marx on Cycle and Crisis', in *Revolution Retrieved: Selected Writings on Marx, Keynes, Capitalist Crisis and New Social Subjects 1967–83* (London: Red Notes), 43–90.

Negri, A. (1988d) 'Interview with Toni Negri (conducted by B. Massumi and A. Jardine)', *Copyright* 1, 74–89.

Negri, A. (1989) *The Politics of Subversion: A Manifesto for the Twenty-First Century*, trans. J. Newell (Cambridge: Polity).

Negri, A. (1991a) *Marx Beyond Marx: Lessons on the Grundrisse*, trans. H. Cleaver, M. Ryan, and M. Viano (New York: Autonomedia).

Negri, A. (1991b) 'Interpretation of the Class Situation Today: Methodological Aspects', in W. Bonefeld, R. Gunn, and K. Psychopedis (eds) *Open Marxism, vol. 2: Theory and Practice* (London: Pluto), 65–105.

Negri, A. (1992a) 'Luttes Sociales et Control Systemique', *Futur Antérieur* 9/18, citations trans. N. Dyer-Witheford.

Negri, A. (1992b) *Il potere costituente* (Carnago: SugarCo, 1992).

Negri, A. (1996a) 'Constituent Republic', in Virno and Hardt 1996a, 213–22.

Negri, A. (1996b) 'Notes on the Evolution of the Thought of the Later Althusser', in A. Callari and D.F. Ruccio (eds) *Postmodern Materialism and the Future of Marxist Theory: Essays in the Althusserian Tradition* (Hanover, N.H.: Wesleyan University Press), 51–68.

Negri, A. (1996c) 'Twenty Theses on Marx: Interpretation of the Class Situation Today', trans. M. Hardt, in S. Makdisi, C. Casarino, and R.E. Karl (eds) *Marxism Beyond Marxism* (London: Routledge), 149–80.

Negri, A. (1998) 'What Can the State Still Do?', *Polygraph* 10, 9–20.

Negri, A. (1999a) *Insurgencies: Constituent Power and the Modern State*, trans. M. Boscagli (Minneapolis: University of Minnesota Press).

Negri, A. (1999b) 'The Specter's Smile' in M. Sprinker (ed.) *Ghostly Demarcations: A Symposium on Jacques Derrida's 'Specters of Marx'* (London: Verso), 5–16.

Negri, A. (2000) 'Intervista a Toni Negri', July 13, from the CD-ROM accompanying Borio, Pozzi, and Roggero 2002.

Negri, A. (2004) *Trentatre lezioni su Lenin* (Rome: ManifestoLibri).

Negri, A., et al. (1983) 'Do You Remember Revolution?', in *Revolution Retrieved* (London: Red Notes, 1988), 229–43.

Negri, A. (2005) *Books for Burning*, trans. T. Murphy et al. (London: Verso).

Nietzsche, F. (1967a) *On The Genealogy of Morals*, trans. W. Kaufmann (New York: Vintage Books).

Nietzsche, F. (1967b) *The Will to Power*, trans. W. Kaufmann (New York: Vintage).

Noble, D. (1995) *Progress Without People: New Technology, Unemployment and the Message of Resistance* (Toronto: Between the Lines).

Nordahl, R. (1987) 'Marx and Utopia: A Critique of the "Orthodox" View', *Canadian Journal of Political Science* 20/4, 755–83.

Ollman, B. (1971) *Alienation: Marx's Conception of Man in Capitalist Society* (Cambridge: Cambridge University Press).

Ollman, B. (1977) 'Marx's Vision of Communism: A Reconstruction', *Critique* 8, 4–41.

Palombarini, G. (1982) *7 Aprile: Il processo e la storia* (Venice: Arsenale Cooperativa).

Pashukanis, E. (1951) 'The General Theory of Law and Marxism', in J. Hazard (ed.) *Soviet Legal Philosophy* (Cambridge: Harvard University Press).

Passavant, P.A., and J. Dean (eds) (2004) *Empire's New Clothes: Reading Hardt and Negri* (New York: Routledge).

Pelaez, E., and J. Holloway (1990) 'Learning to Bow: Post-Fordism and Technological Determinism', *Science and Culture* 8: 15–27.

Petter, G. (1993) *I giorni dell'ombra* (Milan: Garzanti).

Pifano, D. (1995) 'Alcune riflessioni sugli anni '70', *vis-à-vis* 3.

Pifano, D. (1997) 'L'Autonomia operaia romana' in S. Bianchi and L. Caminiti (eds) *Settantasette* (Rome: Castelvecchi).

Piotte, J.-M. (1986) 'Le cheminement politique de Negri', in Tahon and Corten 1986, 17–35.

Postone, M. (1996) *Time, Labor, and Social Domination: A Reinterpretation of Marx's Critical Theory* (Cambridge: Cambridge University Press).

Potere Operaio (1973) 'Potere Operaio: Lo scioglimento', *Potere Operaio*, November; now in Martignoni and Morandini 1977.

Precari Nati (n.d.) 'Alcune considerazione sul documento delle assemblee autonome'; now at <http://www.left-dis.nl/i/autop.htm>, accessed May 29, 2001.

Progetto Memoria (1994) *La mappa perduta* (Rome: Sesibilie alle Foglie).

Puzz (1976) *Provocazione*, now in Martignoni and Morandini 1977.

Rabasa, J. (1993) *Inventing America* (Norman: University of Oklahoma Press).

Rabasa, J. (1996) 'Pre-Columbian Pasts and Indian Presents in Mexican History', in J. Rabasa, J. Sanjinés, and R. Carr (eds) *Subaltern Studies in the Americas*, special issue of *Dispositio/n* 46 (1994; published in 1996), 245–70.

Rabasa, J. (1997) 'Of Zapatismo: Reflections on the Folkloric and the Impossible in a Subaltern Insurrection', in L. Lowe and D. Lloyd (eds) *The Politics of Culture in the Shadow of Capital* (Durham: Duke University Press), 339–431.

Rabasa, J. (1998) 'Franciscans and Dominicans under the Gaze of a *Tlacuilo*: Plural-World Dwelling in an Indian Pictorial text', inaugural address, Lecture Series 14 (Berkeley: The Doe Library, University of California).

Ramirez, B. (1975) 'Self-reduction of prices in Italy', now in Midnight Notes (eds) (1990) *Midnight Oil* (New York: Autonomedia).

Recupero, N. (ed.) (1978) *1977: autonomia/organizzazione* (Catania: Pellicanolibri).

Red Notes (1979) *Working Class Autonomy and the Crisis* (London: Red Notes).

La Repubblica (1979) 'Il punto della situazione secondo il sostituto procuratore di Padova', *La Repubblica*, May 7; now in Collettivo editoriale 10/16 1979.

Rethinking Marxism (2001) 13/3–4, special issue on Hardt and Negri's *Empire*.

Revista Memoria 177 (2003) Dossier on the Caracoles, online at <http://www.memoria.com.mx/>, accessed January 1, 2004.

Revista Memoria 178 (2003), at <http://www.memoria.com.mx/>, consulted January 1, 2004.

Rifkin, J. (1995) *The End of Work: The Decline of the Global Labor Force and the Dawn of the Post-Market Era* (New York: Putnam).

Rosso (1975) 'Presupposti politici per l'organizzazione dell'autonomia operaia', *Rosso*, May–June; now in Martignoni and Morandini 1977.

Rosso (1976) 'Dopo il 20 giugno autonomia per il partito. Spariamo sui corvi', *Rosso* 3/10–11, June.

Rosso (1977a) 'Da "nuovi ribelli" a movimento politico contro lo stato', *Rosso* 19–20, June, now in Castellano 1980a.

Rosso (1977b) 'Autonomia operaia: dalla lotta della classe il processo di organizzazione proletaria sul terreno della guerra civile', *Rosso* special issue, September; now in Castellano 1980a.

Ryan, M. (1989) *Politics and Culture: Working Hypotheses for a Post-Revolutionary Society* (London: MacMillan).

Sabel, C., and M. Piore. (1984) *The Second Industrial Divide* (New York: Basic Books).

Sabrina and Chris (2002) 'Notes on Negri's *Empire*', manuscript, May 2.

Samuelson, R.J. (2001) 'Looming Storm?', at <http://www.msnbc.com/news/515993.asp>, accessed January 14, 2001.

Scalzone, O. (1978a) 'La congiuntura del movimento e i malanni della soggettività', *Pre-print* 1, December.

Scalzone, O. (1978b) 'Prefazione' to *Sulla violenza* (Rome: Savelli).

Schiller, D. (1999) *Digital Capitalism: Networking the Global Market System* (Cambridge, Mass.: MIT press).

Sinai, A. (2001) 'Lobbies derail climate accord', *Le Monde Diplomatique* (English edition), February, 15.

Singh, A. (1992) 'The Actual Crisis of the 1980s: An Alternative Policy Perspective for the Future', in A.K. Dutt and K.P. Jameson (eds) *New Directions in Development Economics* (Aldershot: Edward Elgar).

Singh, A. (1997) 'Portfolio Equity Flows and Stock Markets in Financial Liberalization', *Development* 40, 22–9.

Singh, A. (2000) 'The Anglo-Saxon Market for Corporate Control: The Financial System and International Competitiveness', in A. Singh and C. Howes (eds) *Competitiveness Matters: Industry and Economic Performance in the U.S.* (Ann Arbor: University of Michigan Press), 89–105.

Spinoza, B. (1995) *The Letters*, trans. S. Shirley (Indianapolis: Hackett).

Spinoza, B. (2000) *The Political Treatise*, trans. S. Shirley (Indianapolis: Hackett).

Spivak, G.C. (1988) 'Can the Subaltern Speak?', in C. Nelson and L. Grossberg (eds) *Marxism and the Interpretation of Culture* (Urbana: University of Illinois Press), 217–313.

Spivak, G.C. (1999) *A Critique of Postcolonial Reason: Toward a History of the Vanishing Present* (Cambridge, Mass.: Harvard University Press).

Spivak, G.C. (2003) *Death of a Discipline* (New York: Columbia University Press).

Stajano, C. (1982) *L'Italia nichilista. Il caso di Marco Donat Cattin, la rivolta, il potere* (Turin: Mondadori).

Stame, N., and F. Pisarri (1977) *I proletari e la salute. Lotte di massa al Policlinico di Roma: l'esperienza di un collettivo autonomo* (Rome: Savelli).

Stavehagen, R. (1963) 'Clases, colonialismo y aculturación', *América Latina* 6/4: 63–104.

Stavehagen, R. (1988) *Derechos indígenas y derechos humanos en América Latina* (Mexico City: El Colegio de México and Instituto Interamericano de Derechos Humanos).

Strategies: Journal of Theory, Culture and Politics (2003) 16/2, November, special issue on Antonio Negri.

Subcomandante Marcos (1994) 'La Larga travesía del dolor a la esperanza', September 22, in ELZN (1995).

Subcomandante Marcos (2003) 'Chiapas: La Treceava Estela', posted on <www.ezln.org>, <www.fzln.org>, and <www.ezlnaldf.org>, accessed January 1, 2004.

Subcomandante Marcos (n.d.) Communiqués, available online at <www.ezln.org>, <www.fzln.org>, and <www.ezlnaldf.org>, accessed January 1, 2004.

Tahon, M.-B., and A. Corten (eds) (1986) *Actes du Colloque de Montreal, L'Italie: le Philosophe et le Gendarme* (Montreal: VLB Editeur).

Taussig, M. (1997) *The Magic of the State* (New York: Routledge).

Taylor, C. (1994) *Multiculturalism: Examining the Politics of recognition*, edited and introduced by A. Gutman (Princeton: Princeton University Press).

Taylor, L. (1991) 'Economic Openness: Problems to the Century's End', in T. Banuri (ed.) *Economic Liberalization: No Panacea (The Experiences of Latin America and Asia)* (Oxford: Oxford University Press), 91–147.

Taylor, L. (1995) 'The Rocky Road to Reform: Trade, Industrial, Financial and Agricultural Strategies', in A. de Janvry, S. Radwan, E. Sadoulet, and E. Thorbecke (eds) *State, Market and Civil Organizations: New Theories, New Practices and their Implications for Rural Development* (Basingstoke: Macmillan).

Terranova, T. (2000) 'Free Labor: Producing Culture for the Digital Economy', *Social Text* 63/18, 2.

Thoburn, N. (2003) *Deleuze, Marx and Politics* (London: Routledge).

Thompson, E.P. et al. (1982) *Exterminism and Cold War* (London: Verso).

Tlatli, M. (2000) *La Saison des hommes* (film).

Tobin, J. (1996) 'Prologue', in M. ul Haq, I. Kaul, and I. Grunberg (eds) *The Tobin Tax: Coping with Financial Volatility* (Oxford: Oxford University Press).

Townley, B. (1989) 'Selection and Appraisal: Reconstituting "Social Relations"?', in J. Storey (ed.) *New Perspectives on Human Resource Management* (London: Routledge) 92–108.

Tronti, M. (1971) *Operai e capitale*, second edition (Turin: Einaudi).

Unzueta, G. (1999) 'El Mural de Taniperla: Entrevista con Sergio Ruvalcaba', *Revista Memoria*, 130.

Vecchi, B. (2001) 'Intervista a Benedetto Vecchi', April 20, from the CD-ROM accompanying Borio, Pozzi, and Roggero 2002.

Vercellone, C. (1996) 'The Anomaly and Exemplariness of the Italian Welfare State', in Virno and Hardt 1996a, 81–96.

Vignale, G. (1978) 'Autonomia esistente: pregi e miserie', *Pre-print* 1, December.

Vincent, J.-M. (1991) *Abstract Labour: A Critique*, trans. Jim Cohen (New York: St. Martin's Press).

Vincent, J.-M. (1993) 'Les automatismes sociaux et le "general intellect"', *Futur Antérieur* 16, citations trans. N. Dyer-Witheford.

Virno, P. (1992) 'Quelques notes a propos du "General Intellect"', *Futur Antérieur* 10.

Virno, P. (1996a) 'Virtuosity and Revolution: The Political Theory of Exodus', in Virno and Hardt 1996a: 189–210.

Virno, P. (1996b) 'Notes on the General Intellect', in Saree Makdisi, Cesare Casarino, and Rebecca E. Karl (eds) *Marxism Beyond Marxism* (London: Routledge).

Virno, P. (1996c) 'Do You Remember Counterrevolution?', in Virno and Hardt 1996a.

Virno, P., and M. Hardt (eds) (1996a) *Radical Thought in Italy: A Potential Politics* (Minneapolis: University of Minnesota Press).

Virno, P., and M. Hardt (1996b) 'Glossary of Concepts', in Virno and Hardt 1996a, 260–3.

La Voz de Cerro Hueco (2002), Communiqué released May 24, available at Enlace Civil <www.enlacecivil.org.mx>, accessed January 1, 2004.

Webb, M. (1995) *The Political Economy of Policy Coordination: International Adjustment Since 1945* (Ithaca: Cornell University Press).

Weeks, J. (1999) 'The Essence and Appearance of Globalization: The Rise of Financial Capital', in F. Adams, S. Dev Gupta, and K. Mengisteab (eds) *Globalization and the Dilemmas of the State in the South* (London: Macmillan).

Weeks, K. (1998) *Constituting Feminist Subjects* (Ithaca: Cornell University Press).

White, H. (1978) 'The Absurdist Moment in Contemporary Literary Theory', in *Tropics of Discourse* (Baltimore: Johns Hopkins University Press), 261–82.

Wildcat (n.d.) *Politics in the First Person: The Autonomous Workers' Movement in Italy. Wildcat Inside Story 4* (London: Wicked Messengers).

World Bank (1996) *World Development Report 1996* (Oxford: Oxford University Press).

World Bank (2001) *World Development Report 2000–2001* (Oxford: Oxford University Press).

Wright, S. (1998) 'Missed Opportunities: New Left Readings of the Italian Resistance', in A. Davidson and S. Wright (eds) *'Never Give In': The Italian Resistance and Politics* (New York: Peter Lang).

Wright, S. (2001) 'Pondering Information and Communication in Contemporary Anti-Capitalist Movements', *The Commoner: A Web Journal for Other Values*, available at <http://www.commoner.org.uk/01-7groundzero.htm>.

Wright, S. (2002) *Storming Heaven: Class Composition and Struggle in Italian Autonomist Marxism* (London: Pluto Press).

Zagato, L. (2001) 'Intervista a Lauso Zagato', November 1, from the CD-ROM accompanying Borio, Pozzi, and Roggero 2002.

Zapatistas (2001) Speeches given at different stops of Zapatour and those addressing Congress, posted in <www.ezln.org>, <www.fzln.org>, and <www.ezlnaldf.org>, accessed January 1, 2004.

Zerowork (1977) 'Introduction', *Zerowork* 2, Fall.

Žižek, S. (2000) 'Melancholy and the Act', *Critical Inquiry* 26, Summer, 657–81.

Zupancic, A. (1998) 'The Subject of the Law', in S. Žižek (ed.) *Cogito and the Unconscious* (Durham: Duke University Press).

Zweig, M. (2000) *The Working Class Majority: America's Best Kept Secret* (Ithaca: ILR/Cornell University Press).

Contributors

Sergio Bologna has been professor of history at the Universities of Trento, Milan, Padua, and Bremen, and he is presently a member of the Scientific Committee of the Micheletti Foundation for Contemporary History in Brescia. He was a leading theorist of Potere operaio and is the author of *La tribu della talpe* (1977), *Nazismo e classe operaia 1933–1993* (1997), and *Il lavoro autonomo di seconda generazione* (1997), among other works.

Arianna Bove is an independent researcher in philosophy, currently working on Michel Foucault. She is involved in the making of www.generation-online.org, where her research, articles, and translations can be found.

Alisa Del Re is professor of political science specializing in gender issues at the University of Padua. She was arrested along with Antonio Negri and other Padua faculty on April 7, 1979 and spent several years in exile, but was cleared of charges in 1981. She is the author of *Oltre il lavoro domestico* (1979), *Il genere delle politiche sociali in Europa* (1993), and *Les femmes et l'état-providence* (1994), among other works.

Nick Dyer-Witheford is an associate professor in the Faculty of Information and Media Studies at the University of Western Ontario in Canada. He is the author of *Cyber-Marx* (1999) and, with Stephen Kline and Greig de Peuter, of *Digital Play: The Interaction of Culture, Technology and Markets* (2003).

Ed Emery is a professional translator responsible for Red Notes publications throughout the Seventies and Eighties. He has also translated many works by Nobel laureate Dario Fo and Franca Rame.

Michael Hardt teaches in the Literature Program at Duke University. He is the author of *Gilles Deleuze: An Apprenticeship in Philosophy* (1993) and, in collaboration with Antonio Negri, *Labor of Dionysus: A Critique of the State Form* (1994), *Empire* (2000), and *Multitude: War and Democracy in the Age of Empire* (2004).

Timothy S. Murphy is associate professor of English at the University of Oklahoma, where he edits the journal *Genre: Forms of Discourse and Culture*. He is the author of *Wising Up the Marks: The Amodern William Burroughs* (1997) and translator of Antonio Negri's *Subversive Spinoza* (2004) and *Books for Burning* (2005).

Abdul-Karim Mustapha has edited the 'Dossier on Empire' in *Rethinking Marxism* (2003), published articles in journals such as *South Atlantic Quarterly* and *Boundary 2*, and serves on the editorial boards of *Rethinking Marxism* and *Multitudes*.

José Rabasa teaches at the University of California, Berkeley. He is the author of *Inventing America* (1994) and *Writing Violence on the Northern Frontier* (2000). His current project concerns the pictorial and verbal articulation of indigenous worlds in the early Mexican colonial period and Chiapas today.

Kenneth Surin is based in the Literature Program at Duke University, North Carolina.

Kathi Weeks is an associate professor of women's studies at Duke University. She is the author of *Constituting Feminist Subjects* (1998) and coeditor, with Michael Hardt, of *The Jameson Reader* (2000).

Steve Wright is a lecturer in the School of Information Management and Systems, Monash University. He is the author of *Storming Heaven: Class Composition and Struggle in Italian Autonomist Marxism* (2002).

Index

Note: 'n' following a page number refers to the numbered note on that page.

264   Resistance in Practice

Printed in Great Britain
by Amazon.co.uk, Ltd.,
Marston Gate.